Steck-Vaughn

GED

SOCIAL STUDIES

PROGRAM CONSULTANTS

Liz Anderson, Director of Adult Education/Skills Training
Northwest Shoals Community College
Muscle Shoals, Alabama

Mary Ann Corley, Ph.D., Director
Lindy Boggs National Center for Community Literacy
Loyola University New Orleans
New Orleans, Louisiana

Nancy Dunlap, Adult Education Coordinator
Northside Independent School District
San Antonio, Texas

Roger M. Hansard, Director of Adult Education
CCARE Learning Center
Tazewell, Tennessee

Nancy Lawrence, M.A.
Education and Curriculum Consultant
Butler, Pennsylvania

Pat L. Taylor, STARS Consultant for GEDTS
Adult Education/GED Programs
Mesa, Arizona

Harcourt Achieve

Rigby • Saxon • Steck-Vaughn

www.HarcourtAchieve.com
1.800.531.5015

Acknowledgments

Executive Editor: Ellen Northcutt

Supervising Editor: Julie Higgins

Associate Director of Design: Cynthia Ellis

Designers: Rusty Kaim
Katie Nott

Media Researcher: Sarah Fraser

Editorial Development: Learning Unlimited, Oak Park, Illinois

Production Development: LaurelTech

Cartographer: epic/QYA Design

Photography: Cover: (Constitution) ©Jack Zehrt/FPG International; (King Tut) ©VCG/FPG International; (Monument Valley) ©The Stock Market; p.32a ©Hulton-Deutsch Collection/CORBIS; p.32b ©Reagan Bradshaw; p.94 ©Reuters New Media, Inc./CORBIS; p.134a ©Reuters/Jim Bourg/Archive Photos; p.134b ©Rick Friedman/Black Star; p.176 ©Walter Hodges/Stone.

ISBN 0-7398-2834-7

Contents

What Are the GED Tests?

You have taken a big step in your life by deciding to take the GED Tests. By the time that you have opened this book, you have made a second important decision: to put in the time and effort to prepare for the tests. You may feel nervous about what is ahead, which is only natural. Relax and read the following pages to find out more about the GED Tests in general and the Social Studies Test in particular.

The GED Tests are the five tests of General Educational Development. The GED Testing Service of the American Council on Education makes them available to adults who did not graduate from high school. When you pass the GED Tests, you will receive a certificate that is regarded as equivalent to a high school diploma. Employers in private industry and government, as well as admissions officers in colleges and universities, accept the GED certificate as they would a high school diploma.

The GED Tests cover the same subjects that people study in high school. The five subject areas include: Language Arts, Writing and Language Arts, Reading (which, together, are equivalent to high school English), Social Studies, Science, and Mathematics. You will not be required to know all the information that is usually taught in high school. However, across the five tests you will be tested on your ability to read and process information, solve problems, and communicate effectively. Some of the states in the U.S. also require a test on the U.S. Constitution or on state government. Check with your local adult education center to see if your state requires such a test.

Each year more than 800,000 people take the GED Tests. Of those completing the test battery, 70 percent earn their GED certificates. The *Steck-Vaughn GED Series* will help you pass the GED Tests by providing instruction and practice in the skill areas needed to pass, practice with test items like those found on the GED Test, test-taking tips, timed-test practice, and evaluation charts to help track your progress.

There are five separate GED Tests. The chart on page 2 gives you information on the content, number of items, and time limit for each test. Because states have different requirements for how many tests you take in a day or testing period, you need to check with your local adult education center for the requirements in your state, province, or territory.

The Tests of General Educational Development

Test	Content Areas	Items	Time Limit
Language Arts, Writing, Part I	Organization 15% Sentence Structure 30% Usage 30% Mechanics 25%	50 questions	75 minutes
Language Arts, Writing, Part II	Essay		45 minutes
Social Studies	U.S. History 25% World History 15% Civics and Government 25% Geography 15% Economics 20%	50 questions	70 minutes
Science	Life Science 45% Earth and Space Science 20% Physical Science 35%	50 questions	80 minutes
Language Arts, Reading	Nonfiction Texts 25% Literary Texts 75% • Prose Fiction • Poetry • Drama	40 questions	65 minutes

Mathematics	Number Operations
	  and Number Sense 25%
	Measurement and
	  Geometry 25%
	Data Analysis, Statistics,
	  and Probability 25%
	Algebra 25%
		Part I: 25 questions with optional use of a calculator
		Part II: 25 questions without a calculator
			90 minutes

In addition to these content areas, you will be asked to answer items based on work- and consumer-related texts across all five tests. These do not require any specialized knowledge, but will ask you to draw upon your own observations and life experiences.

The Language Arts, Reading, Social Studies, and Science Tests will ask you to answer questions by interpreting reading passages, diagrams, charts and graphs, maps, cartoons, and practical and historical documents.

The Language Arts, Writing Test will ask you to detect and correct common errors in edited American English as well as decide on the most effective organization of text. The Essay portion of the Writing Test will ask you to write an essay offering your opinion or an explanation on a single topic of general knowledge.

The Mathematics Test will ask you to solve a variety of word problems, many with graphics, using basic computation, analytical, and reasoning skills.

GED Scores

After you complete each GED Test, you will receive a score for that test. Once you have completed all five GED Tests, you will receive a total score. The total score is an average of all the other scores. The highest score possible on a single test is 800. The scores needed to pass the GED vary depending on where you live. Contact your local adult education center for the minimum passing scores for your state, province, or territory.

Where Can You Go to Take the GED Tests?

The GED Tests are offered year-round throughout the United States and its possessions, on U.S. military bases worldwide, and in Canada. To find out when and where tests are held near you, contact the GED Hot Line at 1-800-62-MY-GED (1-800-626-9433) or one of these institutions in your area:

- An adult education center
- A continuing education center
- A local community college
- A public library
- A private business school or technical school
- The public board of education

In addition, the GED Hot Line and the institutions can give you information regarding necessary identification, testing fees, writing implements, and on the scientific calculator to be used on the GED Mathematics Test. Also, check on the testing schedule at each institution; some testing centers are open several days a week, and others are open only on weekends.

Other GED Resources

- www.acenet.edu This is the official site for the GED Testing Service. Just follow the GED links throughout the site for information on the test.

- www.steckvaughn.com Follow the Adult Learners link to learn more about available GED preparation materials. This site also provides other resources for adult learners.

- www.nifl.gov/nifl/ The National Institute for Literacy's site provides information on instruction, federal policies, and national initiatives that affect adult education.

- www.doleta.gov U.S. Department of Labor's Employment and Training Administration site offers information on adult training programs.

Why Should You Take the GED Tests?

A GED certificate is widely recognized as the equivalent of a high school diploma and can help you in the following ways:

Employment

People with GED certificates have proven their determination to succeed by following through with their education. They generally have less difficulty changing jobs or moving up in their present companies. In many cases, employers will not hire someone who does not have a high school diploma or the equivalent.

Education

Many technical schools, vocational schools, or other training programs may require a high school diploma or the equivalent in order to enroll in their programs. However, to enter a college or university, you must have a high school diploma or the equivalent.

Personal Development

The most important thing is how you feel about yourself. You now have the unique opportunity to accomplish an important goal. With some effort, you can attain a GED certificate that will help you in the future and make you feel proud of yourself now.

How to Prepare for the GED Tests

Classes for GED preparation are available to anyone who wants to prepare to take the GED Tests. Most GED preparation programs offer individualized instruction and tutors who can help you identify areas in which you may need help. Many adult education centers offer free day or night classes. The classes are usually informal and allow you to work at your own pace and with other adults who also are studying for the GED Tests.

If you prefer to study by yourself, the *Steck-Vaughn GED Series* has been developed to guide your study through skill instruction and practice exercises. The *Steck-Vaughn GED Exercise* books are also available to provide you with additional practice for each test. In addition to working on specific skills, you will be able to take practice GED Tests (like those in this book) in order to check your progress. For information about classes available near you, contact one of the resources in the list on page 3.

What You Need to Know to Pass the Social Studies Test

The GED Social Studies Test examines your ability to understand and use social studies information. You will be asked to think about what you read. You will not be tested on any outside knowledge about social studies. The test takes 80 minutes and has 50 items. The items are drawn from the five basic social studies content areas: United States history, world history, civics and government, economics, and geography. (The behavior sciences, psychology, sociology, and anthropology are no longer covered as a separate content area but rather are incorporated in items in the other content areas.)

Content Areas

United States History

Twenty-five percent of the test items are based on United States history and test the understanding of historical influences or the development of U.S. government, traditions, ideas, and institutions. Some items will include an excerpt from at least one of the following fundamental historical documents: Declaration of Independence, *Federalist Papers,* U.S. Constitution, and landmark Supreme Court cases.

World History

Fifteen percent of the items test the understanding of global patterns of urban and rural development over time.

Civics and Goverment

Twenty-five percent of the items test the understanding of the purposes, organization, and operation of the government of the United States, the role citizens play in how the country is run, and possible worldwide effects of decisions made by individuals, communities, and nations. At least one practical document—a source of information used by most adults in their capacities as citizens, consumers, and workers, such as voters' guide, tax forms, or surveys—will be included.

Economics

Twenty percent of the items test the understanding of the effect of economic decisions on the achievement of economic goals—what goods and services are produced and how they are produced, marketed, and used by government, business, and consumers—and the role of competition in a free-market economy. Practical documents such as statistics, budgets, and workplace documents will be used as source materials.

Geography

Fifteen percent of the items test the understanding of relationships between the location of human activities and the environment, influences of individuals and culture on and from the natural environment.

Thinking Skills

Questions on the GED Social Studies Test are based on four different types of thinking skills.

Comprehension

Comprehension questions require a basic understanding of the meaning and intent of written and graphic materials. They measure the ability to recognize a restatement, paraphrasing, or summary or to identify what is implied in the text. Twenty percent of the questions test comprehension.

Application

Application questions require the ability to use information and given or remembered ideas from one situation in a new context. They require the ability to identify an illustration of a generalization, principle, or strategy and to apply the appropriate abstraction to a new problem. Twenty percent of the questions test application skills.

Analysis

Analysis questions require the ability to break down information in order to draw a conclusion, make an inference, distinguish fact from opinion and conclusions from supporting detail, identify cause-and-effect relationships, make comparisons and contrasts, and recognize unstated assumptions. Forty percent of the questions test analysis skills.

Evaluation

Evaluation questions require the ability to assess the validity or accuracy of both written and graphic information, make judgments, draw conclusions, recognize faulty logic, and identify values and beliefs. Twenty percent of the questions test evaluation skills.

Sample Passage and Items

The following is a sample paragraph and test items. Although the paragraph is much shorter than those on the GED Test, the items that follow are similar to those on the test. Following each item is an explanation of the skill area that the item tests as well as an explanation of the correct answer.

Directions: Choose the one best answer to each item.

Items 1 to 4 refer to the following paragraph.

The Great Depression of 1929 to 1939 began with Black Tuesday, October 29, 1929. On that day New York Stock Exchange prices fell drastically as 16 million shares were sold. Later the stock market rallied, but business activity in the United States continued to decline. Too few people held too much of the country's wealth. Many ordinary people were unable to buy products that were manufactured. As manufacturer inventories mounted, plants closed and workers were laid off. As the number of unemployed rose, demand for products dropped. Banks began to fail, and individuals lost their life savings, thus losing funds that might have gone into consumer spending. The industrial depression caused an agricultural depression since the unemployed could not even buy food. In California, orange crops were dumped in the ocean because the cost of transportation would not be covered by the sale of the oranges. The poor starved while food was wasted.

1. Which is the best summary of the paragraph?

   (1) The Great Depression began with the stock market crash.
   (2) The Great Depression was a time of economic loss and personal hardship.
   (3) Many people starved during the Great Depression.
   (4) The Great Depression was a time of waste.
   (5) Wealthy people were responsible for the Great Depression.

Answer: **(2) The Great Depression was a time of economic loss and personal hardship.**

Explanation: This is an example of a comprehension item. You are asked to understand the intent of the entire paragraph. Options (1) and (3) are supporting details, while options (4) and (5) are unsupported generalizations.

2. Which statement shows a cause-and-effect relationship?

   (1) Goods were available, and people could not buy them.
   (2) Banks failed, and people lost their life savings.
   (3) The poor starved, and food was wasted.
   (4) Prices fell, and the stock market recovered.
   (5) The stock market rallied, and business activity declined.

Answer: **(2) Banks failed, and people lost their life savings.**

Explanation: This is an analysis item. When you look for the result of an event, restate the options beginning with because: Because the banks failed, people lost their life savings. If you try that with options (1), (3), (4), and (5), the sentence does not make sense in terms of what you know about the world.

3. Which of the following are modern economists probably trying to predict by keeping an eye on the stock market and unemployment figures?

   (1) destruction of the orange crop
   (2) bank failure
   (3) the future of business activity
   (4) the kind of products that should be manufactured
   (5) how people will deal with waste

Answer: (3) the future of business activity

Explanation: This is an example of an application item. You must understand the specific information in the paragraph and apply it to another situation by reasoning that economists in general might pay attention to certain economic signals. Both the stock market and unemployment figures can indicate how much consumers are spending and will be able to spend. Consumer spending influences business activity. Options (1) and (2) were results of the Depression, but would not be primary concerns of modern economists. Options (4) and (5) have nothing to do with the stock market or unemployment.

4. Which statement is supported by information in the paragraph?

   (1) Ordinary people did not know how to deal with the Great Depression.
   (2) Poverty is a serious problem in America.
   (3) Overproduction by manufacturers was partially responsible for the Great Depression.
   (4) Farming is the only safe occupation during an economic depression.
   (5) Farmers can be negatively affected by what happens in other parts of the economy.

Answer: (5) Farmers can be negatively affected by what happens in other parts of the economy.

Explanation: This is an evaluation item. You must use several skills to arrive at the answer. You must understand the main idea and the meaning of the details. Next, you have to recognize the relationship between a specific detail and the main idea. Last, you need to decide which of the options given is accurate. Option (1) has no support in the paragraph. Option (2) is true but is not discussed. Option (3) is incorrect because the problem was with purchasing power, not with overproduction. Option (4) is disproved by the paragraph.

To help you develop your reading and thinking skills, the answer for each item in this book has an explanation of why the correct answer is right and the incorrect answers are wrong. By studying these explanations, you will learn strategies for understanding and thinking about social studies.

Test-Taking Skills

The GED Social Studies Test will test your ability to apply reading and critical thinking skills to text. This book will help you prepare for this test. In addition, there are some specific ways that you can improve your performance on the test.

Answering the Test Items

- Never skim the directions. Read them carefully so that you know exactly what to do. If you are unsure, ask the test-giver if the directions can be explained.

- Read each question carefully to make sure that you know what it is asking.

- Read all of the answer options carefully, even if you think you know the right answer. Some of the answers may not seem wrong at first glance, but one answer will be the correct one.

- Before you answer a question, be sure that there is evidence in the passage to support your choice. Don't rely on what you know outside the context of the passage.

- Answer all the items. If you cannot find the correct answer, reduce the number of possible answers by eliminating all the answers you know are wrong. Then go back to the passage to figure out the correct answer. If you still cannot decide, make your best guess.

- Fill in your answer sheet carefully. To record your answers, mark one numbered space on the answer sheet beside the number that corresponds to the item. Mark only one answer space for each item; multiple answers will be scored as incorrect.

- Remember that the GED is a timed test. When the test begins, write down the time you have to finish. Then keep an eye on the time. Do not take a long time on any one item. Answer each item as best you can and go on. If you are spending a lot of time on one item, skip it, making a very light mark next to the item number on the sheet. If you finish before time is up, go back to the items you skipped or were unsure of and give them more thought. (Be sure to erase any extraneous marks you have made.)

- Don't change an answer unless you are certain your answer was wrong. Usually the first answer you choose is the correct one.

- If you feel that you are getting nervous, stop working for a moment. Take a few deep breaths and relax. Then begin working again.

Study Skills

Study Regularly

- If you can, set aside an hour to study every day. If you do not have time every day, set up a schedule of the days you can study. Be sure to pick times when you will be the most relaxed and least likely to be bothered by outside distractions.

- Let others know your study time. Ask them to leave you alone for that period. It helps if you explain to others why this is important.

- You should be relaxed when you study, so find an area that is comfortable for you. If you cannot study at home, go to the library. Most public libraries have areas for reading and studying. If there is a college or university near you, find out if you can use its library. All libraries have dictionaries, encyclopedias, and other resources you can use if you need more information while you're studying.

Organize Your Study Materials

- Be sure to have pens, sharp pencils, and paper for any notes you might want to take.

- Keep all of your books together. If you are taking an adult education class, you probably will be able to borrow some books or other study material.

- Make a notebook or folder for each subject you are studying. Folders with pockets are useful for storing loose papers.

- Keep all of your materials in one place so you do not waste time looking for them each time you study.

Read Regularly

- Read the newspaper, read magazines, read books. Read whatever appeals to you—but read! Regular, daily reading is the best way to improve your reading skills.

- Use the library to find material you like to read. Check the magazine section for publications of interest to you. Most libraries subscribe to hundreds of magazines ranging in interest from news to cars to music to sewing to sports. If you are not familiar with the library, ask a librarian for help. Get a library card so that you can check out material to use at home.

Take Notes

- Take notes on things that interest you or things that you think might be useful.

- When you take notes, do not copy the words directly from the book. Restate the information in your own words.

- Take notes any way you want. You do not have to write in full sentences as long as you can understand your notes later.

- Use outlines, charts, or diagrams to help you organize information and make it easier to learn.

- You may want to take notes in a question-and-answer form, such as: *What is the main idea? The main idea is . . .*

Improve Your Vocabulary

- As you read, do not skip a word you do not know. Instead, try to figure out what the word means. First, omit it from the sentence. Read the sentence without the word and try to put another word in its place. Is the meaning of the sentence the same?

- Make a list of unfamiliar words, look them up in the dictionary, and write down the meanings.

- Since a word may have several meanings, it is best to look up the word while you have the passage with you. Then you can try out the different meanings in the context.

- When you read the definition of a word, restate it in your own words. Use the word in a sentence or two.

- Use the Glossary at the end of this book to review the meanings of the key terms. All of the words you see in **boldface** type are defined in the Glossary. In addition, definitions of other important words are included. Use this list to review important vocabulary for the content areas you are studying.

Make a List of Subject Areas that Give You Trouble

As you go through this book, make a note whenever you do not understand something. Then ask your teacher or another person for help. Later go back and review the topic.

Taking the Test

Before the Test

- If you have never been to the test center, go there the day before you take the test. If you drive, find out where to park.

- Prepare the things you need for the test: your admission ticket (if necessary), acceptable identification, some sharpened No. 2 pencils with erasers, a watch, glasses, a jacket or sweater (in case the room is cold), and a snack to eat during breaks.

- Eat a meal and get a good night's sleep. If the test is early in the morning, set the alarm.

The Day of the Test

- Eat a good breakfast. Wear comfortable clothing. Make sure that you have all of the materials you need.

- Try to arrive at the test center about twenty minutes early. This allows time if, for example, there is a last-minute change of room.

- If you are going to be at the test center all day, you might pack a lunch. If you have to find a restaurant or if you wait a long time to be served, you may be late for the rest of the test.

Using this Book

- Start with the Pretest. It is identical to the real test in format and length. It will give you an idea of what the GED Social Studies Test is like. Then use the Pretest Performance Analysis Chart at the end of the test to figure out your areas of strength and the areas you need to review. The chart will refer you to units and page numbers to study. You also can use the Study Planner on page 31 to plan your work after you take the Pretest and again, after the Posttest.

- As you study, use the Cumulative Review and the Performance Analysis Chart at the end of each unit to find out if you need to review any lessons before continuing.

- After you complete your review, use the Posttest to decide if you are ready for the real GED Test. The Performance Analysis Chart will tell you if you need additional review. Then use the Simulated Test and its Performance Analysis Chart as a final check of your test-readiness.

SOCIAL STUDIES

Directions

This Social Studies Pretest is intended to measure your knowledge of general social studies concepts.

The questions are based on short readings or on graphs, maps, charts, cartoons, and illustrations. Study the information given and then answer the questions that follow. Refer to the information as often as necessary in answering the questions.

You should spend no more than 70 minutes in answering the 50 questions on this test. Work carefully, but do not spend too much time on any one item. Do not skip any items. Make a reasonable guess when you are not sure of an answer. You will not be penalized for incorrect answers. When time is up, mark the last item you finished. This will tell you whether you can finish the real GED Test in the time allowed. Then complete the test.

Record your answers to the questions on a copy of the answer sheet on page 361. Be sure that all required information is recorded on the answer sheet.

To record your answers, mark the numbered space on the answer sheet that corresponds to the answer you choose for each item on the test.

Example:

Early pioneers of the western frontier looked to settle on land that had adequate access to water. To ensure access to water, many early pioneers settled on land near which type of geographic feature?

(1) forests
(2) grasslands
(3) rivers
(4) glaciers
(5) oceans   ① ② ● ④ ⑤

The correct answer is <u>rivers</u>; therefore, answer space 3 should be marked on the answer sheet.

Do not rest the point of your pencil on the answer sheet while you are considering your answer. Make no stray or unnecessary marks. If you change an answer, erase your first mark completely. Mark only one answer for each question; multiple answers will be scored as incorrect. Do not fold or crease your answer sheet.

When you finish the test, use the Performance Analysis Chart on page 30 to determine whether you are ready to take the real GED Test, and, if not, which skill areas need additional review.

Adapted with permission of the American Council on Education.

Directions: Choose the <u>one best answer</u> to each question.

Questions 1 through 3 refer to the following map and information.

Earth's climate changes gradually over thousands of years. When Earth's average temperature rises, parts of the polar ice caps melt and the sea level rises everywhere. This map shows areas that might be harmed by a rise in sea level.

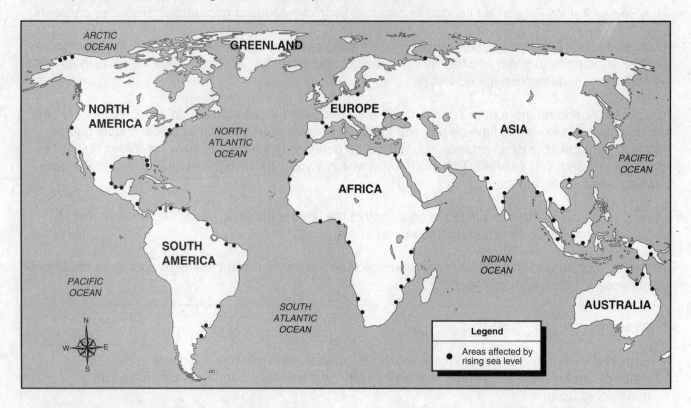

1. What is <u>most likely</u> to be the result of a slowly warming climate?

   (1) a gradual rise in the sea level
   (2) a sudden rise in the sea level
   (3) colder winters all over the world
   (4) tidal waves along the coasts
   (5) more ice trapped in the polar caps

2. On which two continents is the threat of flooding due to rising sea levels <u>most similar</u>?

   (1) North America and South America
   (2) Africa and South America
   (3) North America and Africa
   (4) Africa and Australia
   (5) Australia and North America

3. People living in which of the following places would be <u>most</u> interested in the information on this map?

   (1) Europe
   (2) coastal cities
   (3) Australia
   (4) the west coast of South America
   (5) close to the North Pole

Questions 4 through 6 refer to the following paragraph and graph.

On January 1, 1994, the North American Free Trade Agreement (NAFTA) went into effect. The agreement provided for the gradual removal of trade barriers between the United States, Mexico, and Canada. This means that goods produced in any of these nations may be sold in the other two without payment of the taxes normally placed on foreign-made goods. The graph shows the effect of NAFTA on U.S. trade with Mexico.

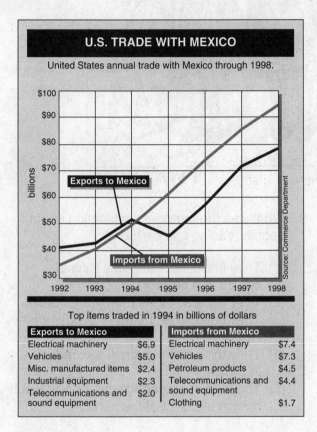

U.S. TRADE WITH MEXICO

United States annual trade with Mexico through 1998.

Exports to Mexico

Imports from Mexico

Source: Commerce Department

Top items traded in 1994 in billions of dollars

Exports to Mexico		Imports from Mexico	
Electrical machinery	$6.9	Electrical machinery	$7.4
Vehicles	$5.0	Vehicles	$7.3
Misc. manufactured items	$2.4	Petroleum products	$4.5
Industrial equipment	$2.3	Telecommunications and sound equipment	$4.4
Telecommunications and sound equipment	$2.0	Clothing	$1.7

4. Which of the following was the top item traded in 1994?

(1) electrical machinery
(2) vehicles
(3) telecommunications equipment
(4) petroleum products
(5) clothing

5. Which of the following statements about NAFTA is supported by the information?

(1) NAFTA made the United States the chief trading partner of Mexico.
(2) NAFTA reversed the trade relationship between the United States and Mexico.
(3) NAFTA made Mexico more important than Canada as a U.S. trading partner.
(4) American exports to Mexico sharply increased in the first year under NAFTA.
(5) Because of NAFTA, Mexico has become the chief supplier of clothing to the United States.

6. Based on information in the paragraph and graph, which of the following is most likely true of U.S. trade with Canada since 1994?

(1) U.S. exports to Canada have increased, but imports from Canada decreased.
(2) Imports from Canada have increased, but U.S. exports to Canada decreased.
(3) U.S. exports to Canada and imports from Canada have both increased.
(4) Imports from Canada and U.S. exports to Canada have both decreased.
(5) Imports from Canada and exports to Canada have remained about the same.

Question 7 refers to the following paragraph.

After World War II, the United States and its allies adopted a policy toward communism called "containment." This policy was based on the idea that communism be prevented from spreading beyond the countries where it already existed.

7. Which of the following world events is an example of containment?

(1) creation of the United Nations to help the nations of the world work together
(2) creation of the European Union to help improve the economy of Europe
(3) independence of India and Pakistan
(4) a limited war in Korea to drive Communist invaders of South Korea back into North Korea
(5) a revolution in Cuba that brought a Communist government to power

"WHO STOLE THE PEOPLE'S MONEY?" — DO TELL . N.Y.TIMES.   'TWAS HIM.

8. In the late 1800s, New York City's government was controlled by an organization called the Tammany Ring. Who do the men in this cartoon represent?

(1) immigrants living in New York City
(2) skilled and unskilled workers
(3) New York City voters
(4) the elected officials of New York City
(5) members of the Tammany Ring

9. What was the cartoonist assuming about the people reading this cartoon?

(1) They know the Tammany Ring is considered corrupt.
(2) They think all these men are innocent.
(3) They have never heard of the Tammany Ring.
(4) They think all the men in the cartoon are in prison.
(5) They will not recognize the well-dressed men in the front of the cartoon.

Question 10 refers to the following passage from the Declaration of Independence.

"We hold these truths to be self-evident, that all men are created equal, that they are endowed by their Creator with certain unalienable Rights, that among these are Life, Liberty and the pursuit of Happiness. That to secure these rights, Governments are instituted among Men, deriving their just powers from the consent of the governed—"

10. Which event in U.S. history best reflects the principles and values expressed by this passage?

(1) establishing the first free public schools
(2) the westward movement of pioneers
(3) amending the Constitution to abolish slavery
(4) admission of new states to the Union
(5) restricting immigration to the United States

Questions 11 through 13 refer to the following passage and graphs.

In 1995, Congress voted against a proposed constitutional amendment to set term limits for members of Congress. The Constitution does not limit the number of six-year terms a senator can serve or the number of two-year terms a House member can serve.

The idea of term limits was popular with the public. People in favor of term limits argued that Congress should be made up of ordinary citizens rather than career politicians. Opponents argued that term limits would result in a Congress with little experience.

Both Democrats and Republicans voted against the proposed amendment. A look at the length of service of the members of Congress may help explain why.

YEARS OF SERVICE OF MEMBERS OF CONGRESS, 1995

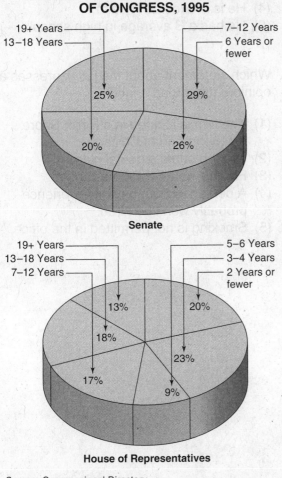

Senate

House of Representatives

Source: Congressional Directory

11. Senators with <u>more</u> than two terms in office represented what percentage of the total Senate membership in 1995?

(1) 20 percent
(2) 25 percent
(3) 26 percent
(4) 29 percent
(5) 45 percent

12. What unstated assumption does the writer make to explain why the term limits proposal was defeated?

(1) The American public opposed term limits.
(2) Term limits would create a Congress of ordinary citizens.
(3) Term limits would decrease the experience level of the legislators.
(4) Senators serve longer terms than members of the House.
(5) Members of Congress did not want term limits applied to themselves.

13. Which of the following statements is supported by the information?

(1) The House of Representatives has more members than the Senate.
(2) Senators and members of the House are elected from each state.
(3) Senators and representatives can serve a maximum of twelve years.
(4) In the 1995 Congress, the Senate had a higher proportion of members serving more than a dozen years than the House did.
(5) Most House members serve five to six years and most Senators serve thirteen to eighteen years.

Question 14 refers to the following map.

COLONIAL AMERICA, 1750

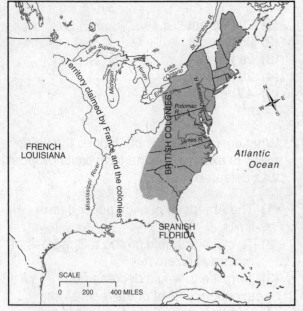

14. What development can be predicted from the information in the map?

   (1) Land disputes would erupt between the colonists and the French.
   (2) Fighting would occur between the colonists and Native Americans.
   (3) The colonists would fight the British for independence.
   (4) Slavery would become common in the Southern colonies.
   (5) France would sell Louisiana to the United States.

Questions 15 and 16 refer to the following advertisement.

15. Mike is applying for the job described in the ad. What fact should he emphasize in an interview?

   (1) He speaks two languages.
   (2) He is married and has a child.
   (3) He has worked as a bookkeeper.
   (4) He is in excellent health.
   (5) He had a B average in high school.

16. Which statement about the job expresses an opinion rather than a fact?

   (1) The firm is located in a North Shore neighborhood of Chicago.
   (2) The job offers a dental plan.
   (3) Flexible hours can be arranged.
   (4) A person without payroll experience probably won't be hired.
   (5) Smoking is not permitted in the office.

Question 17 refers to the following map.

**THE MILITARY SITUATION
IN BOSNIA-HERZEGOVINA, 1995**

Legend

- Serb forces
- Bosnian-government and Croat forces
- U.N. peacekeeping troops

SCALE

0   30 MILES

17. In the mid-1990s, the small Eastern European nation of Bosnia-Herzegovina was often in the news. Which of the following restates what the map shows about Bosnia-Herzegovina in the mid-1990s?

  (1) Bosnia-Herzegovina had declared its independence from Yugoslavia.
  (2) Bosnia-Herzegovina was occupied by various armies.
  (3) The United Nations (UN) was invading Serbia.
  (4) The United States Marines were invading Bosnia-Herzegovina.
  (5) The fighting was confined to Bosnia-Herzegovina.

Question 18 refers to the following paragraph.

  A small city has no public transportation system. Aside from walking or riding a bicycle, residents of this city who don't have cars can get around only by hiring the ABC Taxi Company. The city has no laws regulating taxi fares.

18. Which of the following is most likely to be true of the ABC Taxi Company?

  (1) The price of a taxi ride is high.
  (2) The price of a taxi ride is low.
  (3) The company's service is good.
  (4) The city will purchase the taxi company.
  (5) The company will go out of business.

Question 19 refers to the following graph.

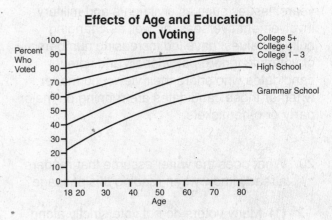

Effects of Age and Education on Voting

College 5+
College 4
College 1 – 3
High School
Grammar School

Percent Who Voted

19. According to the graph, which group of people is the most likely to vote?

  (1) younger people with some college education
  (2) older people with a grammar school education
  (3) older people with a high school education
  (4) older people with some college education
  (5) middle-aged people at all education levels

Questions 20 and 21 refer to the following passage.

Through much of the past century, most voters were loyal to a particular political party. Since the 1960s, however, this loyalty has declined. Several reasons have been offered for this change in voter attitude.

Many people think that the decline in party loyalty is caused by growing weakness in the American party system itself. Local party leaders no longer command the loyalty from party members that they once enjoyed. Fewer people register to vote, and more voters register as independents than as Democrats or Republicans. Many of those who are registered as Democrats or Republicans no longer vote strictly along party lines.

Other people believe that reasons for the decline lie in the events of the past 30 or 40 years. Issues such as civil rights and military involvement overseas, as well as changing cultural values, have led increasing numbers of voters to ignore party labels and vote for candidates who share their views, no matter whether those candidates are running on major party or other tickets.

20. What does the writer assume that readers already know when reading this passage?

(1) Many voters do not vote strictly along party lines.
(2) In the 1980s most Republicans supported the Republican President Reagan.
(3) Many voters register as independents rather than as supporters of any political party.
(4) Political and social issues cause many voters to cross party lines.
(5) The United States has a two-party political system.

21. Which of the following statements is supported by information in the passage?

(1) Divisive political and social issues likely cause voters to vote along party lines.
(2) The trend of voting on issues rather than along party lines will continue indefinitely.
(3) Third-party and independent candidates benefit from the erosion of party loyalty.
(4) President George Bush, a Republican, was defeated by Democratic challenger Bill Clinton in the 1992 election.
(5) Better people are elected when voters choose candidates on the basis of issues rather than party membership.

Question 22 refers to the following graph.

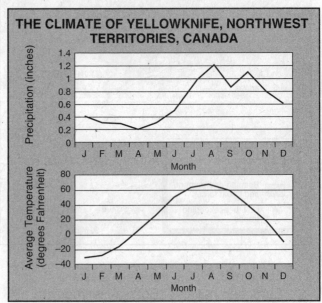

THE CLIMATE OF YELLOWKNIFE, NORTHWEST TERRITORIES, CANADA

Source: Atlas of World and Environmental Issues

22. Which of the following statements about Yellowknife, Canada, is supported by the information on the graph?

(1) Temperatures vary with the season, and there is little rain and snow.
(2) More people live there in the mild summers than during the cold winter.
(3) The temperature is constant, and precipitation varies with the season.
(4) Yellowknife enjoys warm days and cool nights with frequent rainfall year-round.
(5) Most rainfall in Yellowknife occurs in the afternoon and evening hours.

Questions 23 and 24 refer to the following map.

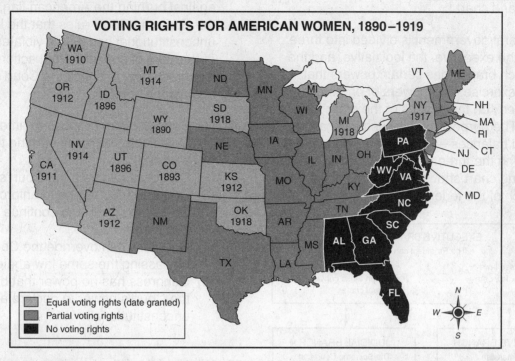

VOTING RIGHTS FOR AMERICAN WOMEN, 1890–1919

WA 1910
OR 1912
MT 1914
ND
MN
MI
VT
ME
NH
ID 1896
SD 1918
WI
NY 1917
MA
RI
NV 1914
WY 1890
NE
IA
MI 1918
PA
CT
NJ
CA 1911
UT 1896
CO 1893
IL
IN
OH
WV
VA
DE
MD
AZ 1912
NM
KS 1912
MO
KY
NC
OK 1918
AR
TN
SC
TX
MS
AL
GA
LA
FL

Equal voting rights (date granted)
Partial voting rights
No voting rights

N
W · E
S

23. According to the map, how were Oregon and Virginia different in 1918?

(1) Women could vote in all elections in Virginia but in no elections in Oregon.
(2) Women could vote in all elections in Virginia but in only some elections in Oregon.
(3) Women could vote in all elections in Oregon but in no elections in Virginia.
(4) Women could vote in all elections in Oregon but only in some elections in Virginia.
(5) Women gained the right to vote in Virginia but they already had the right to vote in Oregon.

24. Which of the following conclusions is supported by the map?

(1) Southern men were more willing than northern men to accept women as equals.
(2) Women gained full voting rights in the West before they did in the East or South.
(3) A smaller percentage of southern women worked outside the home than did women in the North.
(4) Southern women were less interested than northern women in gaining voting rights.
(5) Western states granted women partial voting rights before northern states did.

Question 25 refers to the following paragraph.

Geography and history support each other. Understanding the history of a particular region requires a knowledge of the region's geography. To understand how geography has influenced a region's development, it is necessary to study the physical features of the land, the routes available for travel, the location of population centers, and the region's economic and political characteristics.

25. Which statement best summarizes the paragraph?

(1) A geographer must also be a historian.
(2) Geography influences a region's political development.
(3) Geography affects economic development.
(4) Geography influences travel routes and the locations of a region's cities.
(5) Understanding the history of a region requires understanding the region's geography.

Questions 26 through 28 refer to the following paragraph and chart.

The federal government is divided into three branches: the executive, the legislative, and the judicial. Each branch has certain powers that only it can exercise. The powers of one branch act as a check on the actions of the other two branches. The purpose of this system—called checks and balances—is to keep a balance of power among the three branches of government. The following chart shows the specific powers of each branch of the federal government

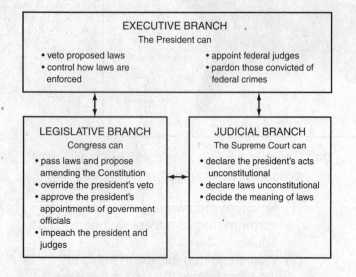

EXECUTIVE BRANCH
The President can

- veto proposed laws
- control how laws are enforced
- appoint federal judges
- pardon those convicted of federal crimes

LEGISLATIVE BRANCH
Congress can

- pass laws and propose amending the Constitution
- override the president's veto
- approve the president's appointments of government officials
- impeach the president and judges

JUDICIAL BRANCH
The Supreme Court can

- declare the president's acts unconstitutional
- declare laws unconstitutional
- decide the meaning of laws

26. Which of the following is an executive power that is a check on the power of the judicial branch?

   (1) the power to pass laws
   (2) the power to interpret the Constitution
   (3) the power to rule laws unconstitutional
   (4) the power to appoint federal judges
   (5) the power to veto new laws

27. Suppose that Congress passes a law against burning the American flag, but the Supreme Court rules that the law is unconstitutional because it violates the right of freedom of speech. What action can Congress take to check the Court's action against this law?

   (1) Congress can propose to amend the Constitution to make burning the flag a crime.
   (2) Congress can veto the Court's action.
   (3) Congress can refuse to enforce the Court's decision and continue to arrest flag burners.
   (4) Congress can override the Court's action by passing the same law again.
   (5) Congress has no power that balances the Court's power to declare a law unconstitutional.

28. Which of the following statements is a conclusion based on the paragraph and chart?

   (1) Congress must approve the president's appointment of many government officials.
   (2) The division of powers and the system of checks on those powers keep a balance of power among government's three branches.
   (3) The federal government is divided into three separate branches—the executive, legislative, and judicial branches.
   (4) The Supreme Court can decide the meaning of laws.
   (5) The president can control how laws are enforced.

Questions 29 and 30 refer to the following graphs.

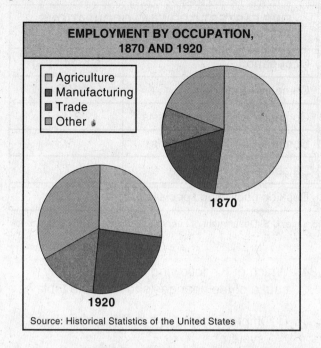

EMPLOYMENT BY OCCUPATION, 1870 AND 1920

- ☐ Agriculture
- ■ Manufacturing
- ■ Trade
- ☐ Other

1870

1920

Source: Historical Statistics of the United States

29. In which type of work were the greatest number of Americans engaged in 1870?

(1) manufacturing
(2) trade
(3) agriculture
(4) service jobs
(5) all other occupations

30. Which of the following is a conclusion that could be made from the information provided in the graphs?

(1) More than 50 percent of American workers held farming jobs in 1870.
(2) More than 50 percent of American workers held manufacturing and other jobs in 1920.
(3) In the late 1800s and early 1900s, people left cities to take up farming.
(4) The percentage of people working at trade jobs increased from 10 percent to 14 percent between 1870 and 1920.
(5) As agriculture's economic importance declined, more people took up factory work and other jobs.

Question 31 refers to the following paragraph.

Companies worldwide use various forms of advertising to make consumers aware of goods and services they have to offer. An effective advertising campaign can greatly increase sales.

31. Which of the following statements about advertising is a fact reflected in the paragraph?

(1) Consumers do not know what they want.
(2) Truly worthwhile products sell themselves without being advertised.
(3) Consumers should be informed about the products they buy.
(4) Ads can appear in print or electronic formats.
(5) Consumers will know good products when they see them.

Question 32 refers to the following graph.

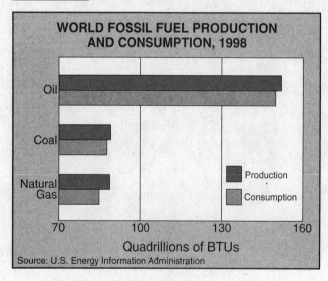

WORLD FOSSIL FUEL PRODUCTION AND CONSUMPTION, 1998

Oil

Coal

Natural Gas

■ Production
☐ Consumption

70   100   130   160

Quadrillions of BTUs

Source: U.S. Energy Information Administration

32. Which interpretation of the graph information demonstrates faulty logic?

(1) Production of coal, oil, and natural gas exceeds their consumption every year.
(2) The world produced more oil than it consumed in 1998.
(3) The largest portion of the world's fossil fuel energy in 1998 came from oil.
(4) In 1998, less energy was consumed from coal and natural gas combined than from oil.
(5) In 1998, production and consumption of natural gas was the lowest of all the fossil fuels.

Question 33 refers to the following paragraph and maps.

During the mid-1800s, the debate over slavery brought about a restructuring of the nation's two-party political system. Members of the opposing Whig and Democratic parties who were dissatisfied with their party's position on slavery joined forces to create the Republican party in 1854. The maps contrast the Republican platform regarding slavery with the legal status of slavery in the late 1850s.

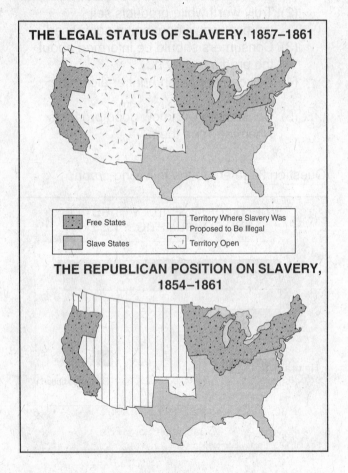

THE LEGAL STATUS OF SLAVERY, 1857–1861

Free States
Slave States
Territory Where Slavery Was Proposed to Be Illegal
Territory Open

THE REPUBLICAN POSITION ON SLAVERY, 1854–1861

33. Based on the paragraph and maps, how did the Republican position on slavery contrast with slavery's legal status in the late 1850s?

(1) Republicans agreed with most Whigs and Democrats about slavery.
(2) Republicans opposed slavery throughout the United States.
(3) Republicans were in favor of slavery throughout the United States.
(4) Republicans opposed slavery in most of the nation's western territory.
(5) Republicans did not think that slavery was an important political issue.

Question 34 is based on the following table.

FIVE FASTEST-GROWING OCCUPATIONS, 1998–2008	
Occupation	Growth (%)
Computer engineers	108
Computer support specialists	103
Computer systems analysis	93
Database administrators	77
Desktop publishing specialist	73

Source: U.S. Department of Labor *Occupational Outlook Handbook*

34. Which of the following is the most likely cause of the changes shown in the table?

(1) improvements in the U.S. educational system
(2) a workforce that lacks higher education
(3) the movement of many manufacturing jobs overseas
(4) an increasingly aging population
(5) the increasing use of computer technology

Questions 35 through 39 refer to the following passage and cartoon.

In the mid-1980s, Mikhail Gorbachev, the leader of the Soviet Union, launched a policy of reforms called "glasnost" that gave Soviet citizens more freedom over their lives. With this policy, Gorbachev hoped to transform Soviet government and establish long-lasting institutions that the people would support.

However, as the Soviets' hold on their own people and others loosened, freedom movements erupted in the USSR and in Soviet-dominated Eastern Europe. In 1989, residents of East and West Berlin tore down the wall that had divided the free and Communist sections of the city for decades. Gorbachev resigned in 1991, and the Soviet Union ceased to exist as a nation. Democracy became the new form of government in the former Communist countries.

Not all freedom movements in Communist countries were successful, however. When in 1989 thousands of students gathered in Beijing's Tiananmen Square to demand democracy in China, the government sent in the army, which killed hundreds. Communism continues, but the Cold War that split the world has ended.

"Soviet Union" © 1986 Joe Szabo. Reprinted by permission.

35. To fully understand this passage, which unstated information do you need to know?

(1) Berlin is in the Soviet Union.
(2) The Soviet Union tightly controlled the government of China.
(3) Communism did not end when the Soviet Union collapsed.
(4) The Cold War pitted the United States and its allies against the Soviet Union and its allies.
(5) China has a Communist government.

36. What effect did Gorbachev's reforms of the Soviet government have on world politics?

(1) It led to repression in the Soviet Union.
(2) It led to repression in China.
(3) It heated up the Cold War.
(4) It led to pro-democracy movements starting in many countries.
(5) It led to the rise of more powerful armies in many countries.

37. The cartoon was published in 1986. Based on the passage, what might the intravenous line going into the tombstone represent?

(1) the policy of glasnost
(2) the freedom movements that erupted in Eastern Europe
(3) the fall of the Berlin Wall
(4) Gorbachev's resignation as Soviet leader
(5) Soviet help for Chinese students at Tiananmen Square

38. Which of the following is a conclusion that the cartoonist wanted readers to draw?

(1) In the mid 1980s, the Soviet Union had a Communist government.
(2) The Soviet Union was a major force in world affairs.
(3) In the mid 1980s, the Soviet Union was on the verge of collapse.
(4) Gorbachev instituted new policies to try to prevent the fall of the Soviet Union.
(5) Gorbachev would not be able to save the Soviet Union.

39. What do the events at Tiananmen Square suggest was most important to China's leaders?

(1) world public opinion
(2) increased trade with the West
(3) freedom of speech
(4) a better education for students
(5) control by the government

Question 40 refers to the following paragraph and map.

Soon after gaining voting rights, women began working for a guarantee of legal equality. In 1972, Congress finally proposed an Equal Rights Amendment (ERA) to the Constitution. The proposed amendment guaranteed freedom from discrimination based on gender. However, in the time period allowed for adoption of the ERA, it was not ratified by enough states and it died in 1982.

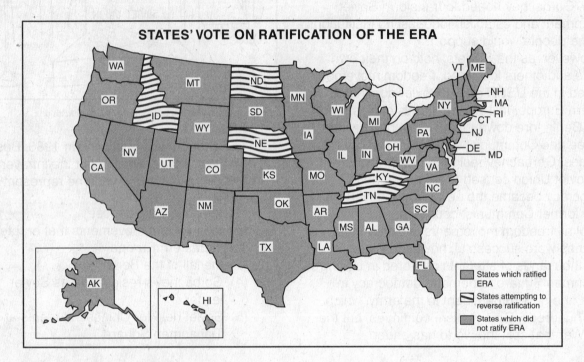

STATES' VOTE ON RATIFICATION OF THE ERA

States which ratified ERA
States attempting to reverse ratification
States which did not ratify ERA

40. Based on the ERA's history, members of Congress from which region would seem least likely to support another attempt to introduce an amendment to guarantee women's rights?

(1) New England
(2) the Great Plains
(3) the South
(4) the Northwest
(5) the Great Lakes region

Question 41 refers to the following information.

The world has experienced many instances of displacement—groups of people settling in an area and displacing other groups. One example is the settling of the American West.

41. Which of the following is another example of displacement?

(1) the United States sending manned space flights to the moon
(2) large numbers of people from Great Britain migrating to Australia
(3) private industries developing in Communist China
(4) tourism increasing in Morocco due to transportation improvements
(5) the sending of United Nations peacekeeping forces to Somalia

Questions 42 through 44 refer to the following chart.

TYPES OF POLITICAL SYSTEMS	
System	**Description**
dictatorship	one person has total power
monarchy	a member of a royal family inherits the right to rule; modern monarchs usually have little power
oligarchy	a small group, usually a wealthy or privileged class, holds power
representative democracy	all voters elect others to represent them in making laws
pure democracy	all citizens propose and make laws by voting on them directly

42. Which of the following statements is an opinion based on information in the chart?

   (1) The people have less power in an oligarchy than they have in a pure democracy.
   (2) Most monarchs today have little real power.
   (3) Oligarchies and dictatorships are similar forms of government.
   (4) In a representative democracy, the people do not directly rule themselves.
   (5) Pure democracy is a better form of government than representative democracy.

43. Letters from citizens persuade a senator to vote in favor of a law to use the national government's money to improve the state's highway system. Which type of political system is reflected in this scenario?

   (1) dictatorship
   (2) monarchy
   (3) oligarchy
   (4) representative democracy
   (5) pure democracy

44. When a government takes the form of a dictatorship, what is the main value the government leaders probably hold?

   (1) desire for control
   (2) cruelty toward the weak
   (3) freedom to elect new leaders
   (4) progress in business
   (5) wealth for only a small group

Question 45 refers to the following graph.

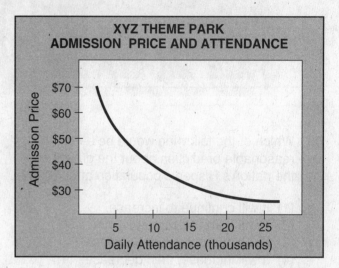

45. According to the graph, what will happen if XYZ Theme Park establishes a special, low admission price for children under age 12?

   (1) Fewer children under 12 will go to the park.
   (2) Attendance at the park will go down.
   (3) Adult attendance at the park will decline.
   (4) Park goers will spend more money on products inside the park.
   (5) Crowds at the park will get larger.

Question 46 refers to the following graph.

HISPANIC POPULATION GROWTH IN THE UNITED STATES: 1970 to 2050 (IN MILLIONS)

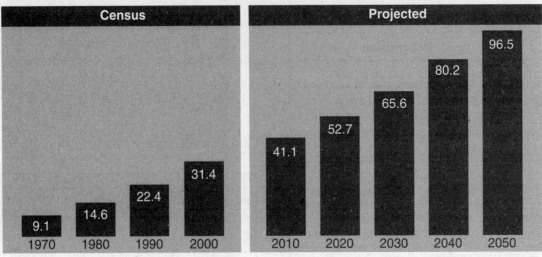

Source: U.S. Bureau of the Census

46. Which of the following would be a reasonable prediction about the growth of the nation's Hispanic population after 2050?

(1) It will continue to increase.
(2) It will start to decrease.
(3) It will decrease, then increase.
(4) It will increase, then decrease.
(5) It will level off.

Question 47 refers to the following paragraph.

The Eighteenth Amendment, which became law in 1919, banned the manufacture and sale of liquor in the United States. Support for Prohibition, as it was called, was strong in rural and small-town America, but weak in cities. Widespread refusal to obey the law led to illegal liquor sales and dishonesty among public officials. Prohibition was repealed by the Twenty-first Amendment in 1933.

47. According to the paragraph, what was one effect of Prohibition?

(1) the corruption of small-town America
(2) an increase in urban crime
(3) a more efficient court system
(4) passage of the Eighteenth Amendment
(5) the end of all liquor sales in the United States

Question 48 refers to the following paragraph and chart.

The United States Constitution created a federal system in which some governing powers are granted to the national government, some are reserved to the states, and some are shared between the national government and the states. Powers that exist at both levels of government are called "concurrent powers."

SOME POWERS OF THE NATIONAL GOVERNMENT	SOME POWERS OF THE STATE GOVERNMENTS
Borrow money	Borrow money
Collect taxes	Collect taxes
Coin money	Conduct elections
Declare war	Establish schools
Establish post offices and postal roads	Build roads
Make and enforce laws	License professions
Regulate trade between states	Make and enforce laws
	Regulate trade within the state

48. Which of the following has resulted from concurrent powers?

   (1) the system of presidential primary elections
   (2) the nation's highway system
   (3) state universities in every state in the nation
   (4) the national money system
   (5) the nation's two-party political system

Question 49 refers to the following graph.

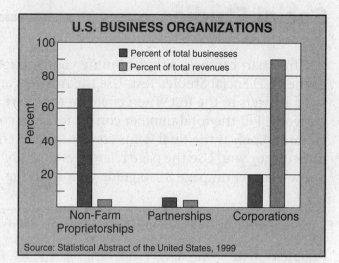

Source: Statistical Abstract of the United States, 1999

49. Which conclusion about American business is supported by information in the graph?

   (1) Partnerships are less likely to be financially successful than proprietorships.
   (2) The corporation is the least common form of business organization in the United States.
   (3) Most U.S. businesses are proprietorships, but corporations have the highest total revenues.
   (4) Most new businesses formed in the United States are proprietorships.
   (5) The highest revenues occur when the salesperson is also owner of the business.

Question 50 refers to the following paragraph.

In 1776, the Continental Congress declared the American colonies free and independent of Great Britain. In urging the delegates to the Congress to sign the Declaration of Independence, Benjamin Franklin issued the following warning: "We must indeed all hang together, or, most assuredly, we shall all hang separately."

50. Which of the following statements is an example of faulty logic?

   (1) The Declaration of Independence was addressed to Great Britain.
   (2) The American colonies united to form a Continental Congress.
   (3) Some of the delegates to the Continental Congress were against declaring independence.
   (4) Benjamin Franklin was a delegate to the Continental Congress.
   (5) Benjamin Franklin was the author of the Declaration of Independence.

Answers start on page 275.

Pretest Performance Analysis Chart
Social Studies

This chart can help you determine your strengths and weaknesses in the content and skill areas of the GED Social Studies Test. Use the Answers and Explanations starting on page 275 to check your answers to the test. Then circle on the chart the number of test items you answered correctly. Put the total number correct for each content area and skill area in each row and column. Look at the total items correct in each column and row and decide which areas are difficult for you. Use the page references to study those areas. Use a copy of the Social Studies Study Planner on page 31 to guide your studying.

Thinking Skill / Content Area	Comprehension (Lessons 1, 2, 7, 16, 18)	Analysis (Lessons 3, 4, 6, 9, 10, 11, 12, 19)	Application (Lessons 14, 15)	Evaluation (Lessons 5, 8, 13, 17, 20)	Total Correct
U.S. History (*Pages 32–93*)	**8, 29**	**9, 23, 30, 33,** 47	10, **14, 40**	**24,** 50	____/12
World History (*Pages 94–133*)	**17, 37**	35, 36, **38**	7	39	____/7
Civics and Government (*Pages 134–175*)	**11, 19, 26**	12, 20, **28, 42, 48**	**27, 43**	**13,** 21, **44**	____/13
Economics (*Pages 176–207*)	**4,** 18	**16,** 31, **34, 45**	**6, 15**	**5, 49**	____/10
Geography (*Pages 208–238*)	25	1, **2,** 46	**3,** 41	**22, 32**	____/8
Total Correct	____/10	____/20	____/10	____/10	____/50

1–40 → Use the Study Planner on page 31 to organize your work in this book.
41–50 → Use the tests in this book to practice for the GED.

Boldfaced numbers indicate questions based on charts, graphs, diagrams, and drawings.

For additional help, see the *Steck-Vaughn GED Social Studies Exercise Book.*

Social Studies Study Planner

These charts will help you to organize your study after you take the Social Studies Pretest and Posttest. After each test, use your results from the Total Correct column on the corresponding Performance Analysis Chart to complete the study planner. Place a check mark next to the areas in which you need more practice. Review your study habits by keeping track of the start and finish dates for each practice. These charts will help you to see your progress as you practice to improve your skills and prepare for the GED Test.

Pretest (pages 13–29): Use results from your **Performance Analysis Chart** (page 30).

Content	Correct/Total	✓	Page Numbers	Date Started	Date Finished
U.S. History	____/12		32–93		
World History	____/7		94–133		
Civics and Government	____/13		134–175		
Economics	____/10		176–207		
Geography	____/8		208–238		
Thinking Skills			**Lesson Numbers**	**Date Started**	**Date Finished**
Comprehension	____/10		1, 2, 7, 16, 18		
Analysis	____/20		3, 4, 6, 9, 10, 11, 12, 19		
Application	____/10		14, 15		
Evaluation	____/10		5, 8, 13, 17, 20		

Posttest (pages 239–255): Use results from your **Performance Analysis Chart** (page 256).

Content	Correct/Total	✓	Page Numbers	Date Started	Date Finished
U.S. History	____/12		32–93		
World History	____/8		94–133		
Civics and Government	____/12		134–175		
Economics	____/10		176–207		
Geography	____/8		208–238		
Thinking Skills			**Lesson Numbers**	**Date Started**	**Date Finished**
Comprehension	____/10		1, 2, 7, 16, 18		
Analysis	____/20		3, 4, 6, 9, 10, 11, 12, 19		
Application	____/10		14, 15		
Evaluation	____/10		5, 8, 13, 17, 20		

UNIT 1

United States History

In 1964, thousands of Americans marched in Washington, D.C., to rally in favor of equal civil rights for all Americans. At this rally, Dr. Martin Luther King Jr. made his famous "I Have a Dream" speech. As a result of the civil rights movement, laws were passed to ensure that all people in the United States had the same basic rights in the areas of voting, housing, and education.

The history of the United States has been a continuing search for "liberty and justice for all." Studying our history helps us understand the rights Americans value and the responsibilities of our democracy. It documents how people have struggled for these rights at home and abroad. U.S. History is an important part of the GED Social Studies Test, making up 25 percent of the test questions.

The civil rights movement changed the course of history for many Americans.

The lessons in this unit include:

Lesson 1: **European Colonization of North America**
North America was colonized first by peoples from Asia, now known as the American Indians, and later by the Europeans.

Lesson 2: **The American Revolution**
The dissatisfaction of the colonists led to the American Revolution. A new nation emerged, struggling to form a lasting government.

Lesson 3: **Westward Expansion**
After the Revolutionary War, waves of settlers from the eastern United States began to move westward across the Mississippi River toward the Pacific Ocean.

Lesson 4: **The Civil War**
The new nation was almost torn apart in the struggle over slavery. At the end of the Civil War, the union was preserved and the stage was set for a new era.

Lesson 5: **Industrialization**
The Industrial Revolution caused a shift from an agricultural to a manufacturing economy. This created both opportunities and difficult working and living conditions for workers.

Lesson 6: **The United States and the World**
In the twentieth century, the United States emerged as an international world leader. The nation focused on the struggle to expand democracy, opportunity, and prosperity.

THINKING SKILLS

○ Identifying the main idea

○ Summarizing ideas

○ Recognizing unstated assumptions

○ Analyzing cause and effect

○ Recognizing values

○ Distinguishing conclusions from supporting details

GED SKILL Identifying the Main Idea

Have you ever listened to a friend tell a story and wondered, "What is the point of this story?" The most important idea, or point, of a story or paragraph is the **main idea.** You need to look for the main idea when you read and study and when you take the GED Test.

main idea
what the paragraph or article is about; the broadest, most important idea

topic sentence
a sentence that tells the reader what the paragraph is about

How can you find the main ideas of a passage? First note how many paragraphs it has. You should find a main idea in each paragraph. Looking at these main ideas all together will point you to the main idea for the whole passage.

Each paragraph focuses on a single topic—the main idea. The main idea is presented in the **topic sentence** which often appears as the first or last sentence of the paragraph. Every other sentence in the paragraph supports this main idea. Sometimes the main idea is not stated clearly in one sentence. In that case, ask yourself, "What one thing is the writer discussing throughout the paragraph?"

Read the passage and answer the question below.

The term *Iroquois* has several meanings. It applies to a group of American Indians, their language, and their way of life. The Iroquois-speaking people lived in a region of North America called the Eastern Woodlands. Over 500 years ago, the Iroquois practiced agriculture and lived in rectangular longhouses that lodged a dozen or more families.

In the 1400s, the Iroquois formed a league or council of five tribes so that they could stand together against invasion. Village chiefs attended the council meetings. The council had complex systems for choosing leaders and making important decisions. Later, they persuaded **colonial** governments to use these systems in their joint negotiations.

Write *M* next to the sentence that best expresses the main idea of the passage.

_____ a. The term Iroquois refers to a group of North American Indian tribes who practiced agriculture and lived in longhouses.

_____ b. The people referred to as Iroquois spoke the same language and had a distinct way of life and an advanced system of self-government.

To find the main idea of a paragraph, look at the first or last sentence. One of these is often the topic sentence. If you can't find a topic sentence, look at the details. What main idea do they point to or support?

You were correct if you chose *option b.* The idea it expresses is broad enough to include the information from both paragraphs. *Option a* is a detail that is mentioned but does not include enough information to be the main idea of the passage.

Use the passage and the map to answer the questions.

American Indians, the people who first inhabited North America, adapted their way of life to the regions where they lived. Their **cultures** varied widely, depending mostly on the physical terrain and natural resources of the different regions.

The following are examples of American Indian cultures from two different regions. In the Arctic, the Inuit and Aleut fished and hunted on ice and snow. Winter houses were round, well-insulated structures covered with skins and blocks of sod. Populations were small because resources were so limited. In the dry Southwest, the Hopi and Zuni grew corn, beans, and squash. They lived in multistory structures similar to modern apartment buildings. Many families lived close together in a complex social organization.

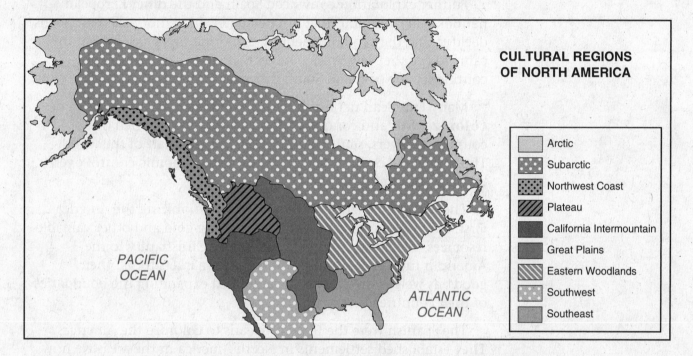

CULTURAL REGIONS
OF NORTH AMERICA

PACIFIC
OCEAN

ATLANTIC
OCEAN

Arctic
Subarctic
Northwest Coast
Plateau
California Intermountain
Great Plains
Eastern Woodlands
Southwest
Southeast

1. Write *M* next to the sentence that expresses the main idea of the first paragraph.

_____ a. A variety of factors accounted for the differences in American Indian cultures.

_____ b. The American Indians were the first people who inhabited North America.

2. Write *M* next to the sentence that expresses the main idea of the second paragraph.

_____ a. American Indians developed many different forms of housing.

_____ b. American Indian cultures differed greatly from region to region.

3. Write a sentence explaining how you determined the main idea of the second paragraph.

_____

4. Write *M* next to the sentence that expresses the main idea of the map.

_____ a. The development of American Indian culture started in the eastern regions of North America.

_____ b. There were nine American Indian cultural regions in North America.

Answers start on page 280.

Many European navigators of the 1400s sought a sea route to Asia—and its treasures of spices and gold. The first navigators sailed south, around the tip of Africa, and then east to Asia. Christopher Columbus, however, sought a shortcut. He believed that the world was round and that he could get to Asia by sailing west. He convinced Queen Isabella of Spain to finance this voyage, and he set off. When he and his crew sighted land, they assumed they had reached India and called the people they found there "Indians."

Further exploration convinced Spain and the other European nations that Columbus had reached a new land, not Asia. Europeans decided that they could benefit by exploring this place, which they came to call the New World. Today this land is known as the continents of North and South America.

Many European nations sent out explorers on voyages of **colonization** and conquest. Colonization occurs when one country discovers, settles, and exploits another part of the world. The colonizing country takes political and economic control over the new area and its people.

The Europeans had several motives for colonizing the Americas. First, they wanted to gain wealth by finding gold and other valuable resources. Next, they wanted to introduce Christianity to the American Indians. They also wanted new markets to sell their goods, as well as the glory that came with expanding the boundaries of their countries.

The Spanish were the first Europeans to colonize the Americas. They established settlements in North America in the areas we now know as Florida, Texas, New Mexico, Arizona, California, and Mexico, and in Central and South America and the islands of the Caribbean. The French colonized parts of North America in what is now eastern Canada and along the Mississippi River south to where it meets the Gulf of Mexico. They traded with American Indians for furs that sold for high prices in Europe. The Dutch settled mainly in what is now New York and New Jersey. The English settled in other parts of the eastern United States and what is now Canada. Both the Dutch and the French eventually lost their North American colonies to England.

Colonization by European countries meant tragedy for the American Indians. Colonists killed many American Indians and forced others into slavery. Colonists also took land from the American Indians. In addition, thousands of American Indians—sometimes whole villages—died from diseases the Europeans carried, such as smallpox and measles.

Directions: Choose the one best answer to each question.

Questions 1 through 3 refer to the passage on page 36.

1. What main idea do the first three paragraphs explain?

   (1) how Columbus came to the New World
   (2) why Spain sponsored trips to the New World
   (3) how Europeans became interested in the New World
   (4) the effects of colonization
   (5) why Europeans wanted to reach Asia

2. What is the main idea of the fifth paragraph?

   (1) Each European country had a different motive for colonizing the Americas.
   (2) Spanish settlements dominated the Americas.
   (3) The European countries competed with each other for land in the Americas.
   (4) The European colonizers got rich by trading with the Indians.
   (5) European countries colonized different areas of the Americas.

3. What is the main idea of the passage as a whole?

   (1) The colonization of the New World benefited many European countries, but it had a tragic effect on the land's original inhabitants.
   (2) The voyages of Christopher Columbus changed the world.
   (3) European settlers mistreated the American Indians to the point that hardly any of them survived.
   (4) Colonization occurs when one country discovers, settles, and exploits another part of the world.
   (5) European nations' motives for colonizing the New World included finding gold and other resources, spreading Christianity, and expanding their boundaries.

Questions 4 and 5 refer to the following graph.

AMERICAN INDIAN AND EUROPEAN SETTLER POPULATIONS OF THE NEW ENGLAND COLONIES, 1620–1750

Source: U.S. Bureau of the Census

4. What is the main idea of the graph?

   (1) The American Indian population of New England fell from about 80,000 to almost nothing between 1620 and 1750.
   (2) The population of European settlers in New England increased from none to 350,000 between 1620 and 1750.
   (3) The European settlers in the New England colonies drove out or killed the American Indian population.
   (4) Between 1620 and 1750, the American Indian population diminished to almost nothing while the population of European settlers grew.
   (5) The American Indians and the European settlers were unable to live together in the New England colonies.

5. What is a focus of both the graph and the last paragraph of the passage on page 36?

   (1) the decline of the American Indian population
   (2) the increase in number of colonists
   (3) life in New England
   (4) why the American Indian population declined
   (5) how the colonists treated the American Indians

Answers start on page 280.

GED Practice • Lesson 1

Directions: Choose the one best answer to each question.

Questions 1 through 3 refer to the following paragraph and excerpt.

The Pilgrims were from a religious group that was persecuted in England because their beliefs differed from the teachings of the Church of England. To escape this situation, the Pilgrims first went to Holland. Unhappy there, they then obtained permission to settle in America, near the first English colony in Virginia. In 1620, a group of colonists set sail aboard the *Mayflower* to start the second colony on England's land in the New World. However, their ship was blown off course, and they arrived far north of their intended destination. Before going ashore, the colonists wrote and signed the following agreement. It is known as the *Mayflower Compact*.

excerpt from the *Mayflower Compact*
"We whose names are underwriten, the loyall subjects of our dread soveraigne Lord King James . . . Haveing undertaken, for the glorie of God, and advancements of the Christian faith and honour of our king & countrie, a voyage to plant the first colonie in the Northerne parts of Virginia, doe . . . solemnly & mutualy . . . combine our selves togeather into a civill body politick; for our better ordering & preservation . . . to enacte, constitute, and frame shuch just & equall lawes, ordinances, Acts, constitutions, & offices, from time to time, as shall be thought . . . convenient for the generall good of the Colonie: unto which we promise all due submission and obedience."

1. What was the main idea of the *Mayflower Compact*?

   (1) to divide land among the colonists
   (2) to honor God and King James
   (3) to promise to obey all English officials
   (4) to make plans for governing the colony
   (5) to make plans to find the colonists of Virginia

2. Why do you think the Pilgrims wrote the *Mayflower Compact*?

   (1) They were lost and afraid.
   (2) Nearby American Indians refused to help them.
   (3) There was no English government where they landed.
   (4) The king had required it.
   (5) It provided for freedom of religion.

3. Which ideal in U.S. history is expressed in the *Mayflower Compact*?

   (1) the establishment of religious freedom
   (2) the growth of self-government
   (3) the end of slavery
   (4) cooperation between the colonies
   (5) independence from England

Question 4 refers to the following paragraph.

In the Massachusetts Bay Colony, the government and the church were closely related. To take part in government, men had to be members of the church. Those who disagreed with the government or the church often were banished. When Roger Williams was banished from Massachusetts, he founded Rhode Island, where religious freedom was granted to all.

4. What detail supports the paragraph's main idea that the church and government were closely related in Massachusetts?

   (1) The government of Rhode Island granted religious freedom.
   (2) People who disagreed with both the government and the church were banished.
   (3) Roger Williams founded Rhode Island after he left Massachusetts.
   (4) Massachusetts banished Roger Williams, and he had to go to Rhode Island.
   (5) Men had to belong to the church in order to take part in government.

Questions 5 through 8 refer to the following paragraph and map.

By the 1730s, there were thirteen English colonies in what is now the United States. Because of differences in geography, people in these colonies earned their living in many different ways. The New England colonies had poor soil and cold winters. However, they did have good harbors. The middle colonies had soil that was good for growing grains such as wheat. The southern colonies had warm weather and rich soil. These conditions made it possible to raise crops such as tobacco and cotton, which were grown on large farms called plantations.

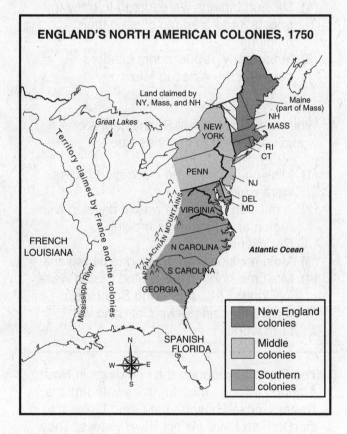

ENGLAND'S NORTH AMERICAN COLONIES, 1750

5. What is the main idea of the paragraph?

   (1) There were thirteen English colonies.
   (2) Geographic differences caused people in the colonies to make their living in different ways.
   (3) The three groups of colonies had different types of soil.
   (4) The middle and southern colonies had good soil, but New England did not.
   (5) Cotton and tobacco were important crops in the southern colonies.

6. What main idea does the information in the map show?

   (1) England's North American colonies were grouped into three categories.
   (2) France, England, and Spain all had colonies in what is now the United States.
   (3) England had thirteen colonies in what is now the United States.
   (4) The Mississippi River was located far to the west of England's colonies.
   (5) Both the English and the French claimed the land west of the Appalachian Mountains.

7. What information from the map supports the conclusion that farming in New England was more difficult than in the other colonies?

   (1) The New England colonies had territorial conflicts.
   (2) The southern colonies were the largest.
   (3) Farming was more profitable in the middle and southern colonies.
   (4) The New England colonies were the smallest.
   (5) The New England colonies were the farthest north.

8. According to the information in the map and the paragraph, in which colony were people most likely to make their living by fishing?

   (1) New Hampshire
   (2) North Carolina
   (3) Pennsylvania
   (4) Massachusetts
   (5) Virginia

TIP

Often, the title of a map and the information in its key provide clues about the map's purpose or main idea. Labels and highlighted information on the map also point to the main idea.

Answers start on page 280.

Directions: This is a ten-minute practice test. After ten minutes, mark the last question you finished. Then complete the test and check your answers. If most of your answers were correct, but you didn't finish, try to work faster next time. Choose the <u>one best answer</u> to each question.

Questions 1 through 4 refer to the following passage.

In the early 1500s, soldier-explorers called conquistadors defeated the native Aztec people in Mexico and established Spain's first colony in North America. As Spanish settlement slowly spread north, Catholic priests founded missions. Each mission consisted of a town built around a church. The Spanish founded about 150 missions in what is now the United States. Most missions were in the present-day states of Florida, Texas, New Mexico, Arizona, and California.

The purpose of a mission was to develop the surrounding region and convert its American Indians to Christianity. Gradually, large American Indian villages developed around missions. Most of the mission's work was done by these village residents. The lives of the "mission Indians" were harsh. They worked in shops, weaving cloth and making other products. In nearby fields, they tended cattle and raised a variety of crops. They were forced to obey the priests' orders and also to give up their religions. Those who resisted often were whipped.

1. What is the main idea of the first paragraph?

   (1) the duties of priests in the Spanish colonies
   (2) Spanish exploration of the United States
   (3) the conquistadors' conquest of the Aztec
   (4) the establishment of the mission system
   (5) the Spanish settlement of Mexico

2. The passage suggests that the lives of mission Indians were most like the lives of which other group?

   (1) factory workers
   (2) farmers
   (3) Catholic priests
   (4) Spanish colonists
   (5) slaves

3. Which statement supports the opinion that life for mission Indians was harsh?

   (1) Catholic priests founded the missions.
   (2) Mission Indians tended cattle and raised crops.
   (3) American Indian villages developed around the missions.
   (4) Mission Indians were forced to obey the priests' orders and to give up their religions.
   (5) In the early 1500s, conquistadors defeated the Aztec in Mexico.

4. Which sentence about Spanish missions would be easiest to verify as true?

   (1) Mission Indians who disobeyed orders were whipped.
   (2) A mission's purpose was to develop a region and convert its Indians to Christianity.
   (3) Most mission work was done by Indians.
   (4) Most missions in the United States were in Florida, Texas, and the Southwest.
   (5) Mission Indians wove cloth and did farm work.

5. The French expanded their holdings in North America through their fur trade with Indians. Traders moved beyond the Great Lakes into the Ohio and Mississippi River valleys. They spread along the tributaries of the Mississippi, traveling to the Rocky Mountains.

   From this information, what can you conclude about French colonization?

   (1) The French sold furs to American Indians.
   (2) French colonies reached the Pacific Coast.
   (3) French traders traveled mainly by water.
   (4) The French founded large cities in the Ohio River Valley.
   (5) The French sold furs to the English colonists.

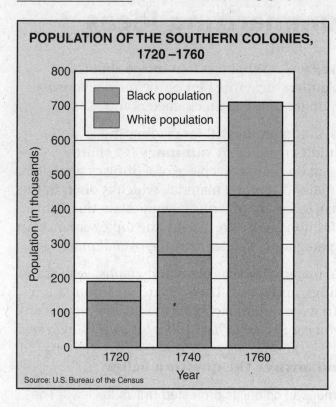

POPULATION OF THE SOUTHERN COLONIES, 1720–1760

Black population
White population

Population (in thousands)

Source: U.S. Bureau of the Census

Year

6. What was the white population of the southern colonies in 1740?

   (1) about 250
   (2) nearly 400
   (3) about 25,000
   (4) more than 250,000
   (5) nearly 400,000

7. Which of the following can be determined from this graph?

   (1) Population increased faster in the southern colonies than in any other region between 1720 and 1740.
   (2) More black people were enslaved than were free in the southern colonies in 1760.
   (3) The black population increased at a greater rate than the white population between 1720 and 1760.
   (4) More black people than white people lived in the southern colonies in 1720.
   (5) There were more white people in the northern colonies than in the southern colonies.

Democracy means that the people rule themselves. The greater the voice of the people, the more democratic the system. In a true democracy, all people have a voice in the government. However, systems of government can be democratic in different ways.

Before the outbreak of the American Revolution in 1776, the thirteen British colonies were governed in three basic ways: as royal colonies, as proprietary colonies, or as self-governing colonies. Each of these systems applied democratic principles differently.

Nine of the colonies were royal colonies. In royal colonies, the king of England appointed the governor. In proprietary colonies, the proprietor, or owner, of the colony selected the governor. Maryland and Pennsylvania were proprietary colonies. Connecticut and Rhode Island were self-governing. In self-governing colonies, the colonists themselves elected the governor and all members of the legislature.

Colonial legislatures had two sections, or houses. In most proprietary and royal colonies, the colonists elected the members of one house. The proprietor or the king appointed the other house. In Pennsylvania, however, the colonists elected both houses of the legislature.

8. Which of the following titles best expresses the main idea of this passage?

   (1) Proprietary Colonies in America
   (2) The Growth of Colonial Democracy
   (3) Systems of Colonial Government in America
   (4) The True Meaning of Democracy
   (5) Comparing Royal and Proprietary Colonies

9. According to the information in the passage, which of the following colonies was the most democratic in 1776?

   (1) Georgia
   (2) Maryland
   (3) Pennsylvania
   (4) Rhode Island
   (5) Virginia

Answers start on page 281.

GED SKILL **Summarizing Ideas**

Has anyone ever asked you, "What was that movie about?" Usually, instead of explaining the entire plot of the movie, you give a brief account or a summary of the main characters and events.

summary
a brief account of the main idea of a piece of writing or a graphic

Summarizing is also an important skill for reading and understanding social studies material. A **summary** is a short, accurate account of the main points of a piece of writing or a graphic. It always includes the main idea of the material, which is often in the title. When you summarize a piece of writing, you restate the main points in a shortened fashion. These are usually the topic sentences or main points of all the paragraphs that support the overall main idea.

To summarize visual material such as maps and graphs, look at the title and the key, headings, and labels. Then restate the information in a sentence or two. To write a summary, you should answer as many of these questions as you can: *Who? What? When? Where? Why? How?*

To summarize a passage, look for the main idea in each paragraph. Ask *who, what, when, where, why,* and *how.*

Read the passage and answer the question below.

For several years, American colonists protested British tax laws. The **colonists** did not want to pay taxes to the British, since they had no voice in making the laws. The British government sent soldiers to Boston to keep order and enforce the laws. Colonists taunted these soldiers and threw snowballs at them.

One winter day in 1770, the taunting got out of hand. The colonists didn't just throw snowballs; they also threw rocks. Then one man threw a wooden club, knocking a soldier to the ground. Suddenly, the soldiers fired into the crowd. In what later became known as the Boston Massacre, five colonists were shot to death.

Put a check mark next to the sentence that is the best summary of the entire passage.

_____ a. American colonists who felt they had been mistreated by the British government threw snowballs at British soldiers.

_____ b. The Boston Massacre occurred in 1770 when British troops, who had been sent to Boston, fired on unruly colonists.

You were correct if you chose *option b*. This sentence tells *who, what, where, when,* and *why. Option a* gives information from the first paragraph only.

Use the passage and the maps to answer the questions.

The British and French were rivals in North America. In 1754, they went to war over North American lands. This conflict became known as the French and Indian War. Americans, some led by young George Washington, joined with the British army and fought by its side. In 1763, France lost to Britain and gave up its North American colonies.

The Americans were proud of their contribution to the victory. They hoped the British would value their sacrifices. However, after the war, the British faced new problems. They had huge war debts, which they tried to pay off by taxing the American colonists. The colonists refused to pay these taxes, sometimes protesting violently. So the British victory in the French and Indian War led, step by step, to the American Revolution.

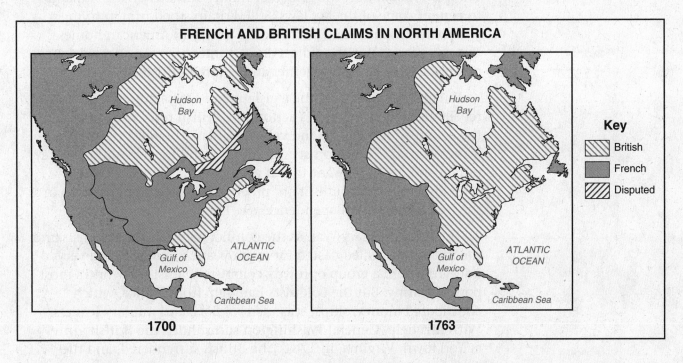

FRENCH AND BRITISH CLAIMS IN NORTH AMERICA

Key
British
French
Disputed

1700

1763

1. Write *S* next to the sentence that best summarizes the first paragraph.

   _____ a. After nine years of fighting, France lost most of its American territory.

   _____ b. In 1754, Britain and France went to war over the North American colonies.

2. Write two or three sentences summarizing the main point of the entire passage. Remember to answer the questions *Who? What? When? Where? Why?* or *How?*

   _____

   _____

3. Finish this sentence to summarize the information in the maps.

   These maps show that _____ lost most of its land in

   _____ between the years _____ and _____ .

   All _____ had left was a small territory in the _____ .

Answers start on page 281.

After the French and Indian War, the British had increasing trouble governing the American colonies. The colonists refused to pay taxes **levied** by Parliament—Britain's main governing body. Since Americans could not vote for representatives in Parliament, the colonists reasoned that Parliament had no right to tax them. "Taxation without representation is tyranny" became a rallying cry in the colonies.

Americans backed their words with action. When Parliament levied taxes, the Americans boycotted—refused to buy—British goods. These **boycotts** hurt the British economy and convinced Parliament to **repeal** some of the tax laws. Still, Britain stood firm in trying to control the colonies and sent soldiers to stay in American homes. The presence of British soldiers during times of peace angered the colonists. They banded together and ignored British law.

Britain then dissolved the legislature of Massachusetts, the most rebellious colony. With this action, the British took away one of the colonists' most basic and valued rights—the right to **self-government.** The colonists would not stand for this outrage. They united and, in 1775, went to war against Britain. In 1776, they formally broke off from Britain, proclaiming their right to do so in the Declaration of Independence. *(See box.)*

The Revolutionary War, as the conflict between the colonists and the British was called, lasted for seven years. It looked like a very uneven match: a group of rowdy colonists against the world's most powerful army. But the colonists had help from France, which contributed money, ships, seasoned soldiers, and military leaders. With this help, General Washington surrounded the British army at Yorktown, Virginia, in 1781. The British surrendered, and the Americans won the war.

KEY DOCUMENT

Excerpt from the Declaration of Independence

"We hold these truths to be self-evident: That all men are created equal; that they are endowed by their Creator with certain unalienable Rights; that among these are Life, Liberty, and the pursuit of Happiness; that, to secure these rights, Governments are instituted among Men, deriving their just powers from the consent of the governed; that whenever any Form of Government becomes destructive of these ends, it is the Right of the People to . . . institute new Government. . . . The history of the present King of Great Britain is a history of repeated injuries. . . .

He has . . . subject[ed] us to a jurisdiction foreign to our constitution, and unacknowledged by our laws: . . . quartering large bodies of armed troops among us; . . . imposing Taxes on us without our Consent; . . . depriving us, in many cases, of the benefits of Trial by Jury; . . . suspending our own Legislatures, and declaring themselves [Parliament] invested with power to legislate for us in all cases whatsoever."

Directions: Choose the one best answer to each question.

Questions 1 through 4 refer to the passage and the key document on page 44.

1. What is the main idea of the first paragraph of the passage?

   (1) Britain had trouble governing the American colonies after the French and Indian War.
   (2) American colonists were upset that they did not have a representative in Parliament.
   (3) The Americans found the British taxes far higher than they could afford.
   (4) No government can levy taxes without giving people a voice in passing the tax laws.
   (5) Americans held protests against British tax laws and boycotted British goods.

2. Which sentence best summarizes the third paragraph of the passage?

   (1) Britain stood firm in trying to enforce all its laws in colonial America.
   (2) Americans were enraged over the dissolution of the Massachusetts legislature.
   (3) Americans valued the right to govern themselves and make their own laws.
   (4) Reaction of Americans to the loss of the right to self-government led to the outbreak of the Revolutionary War.
   (5) By signing the Declaration of Independence, America broke away from British rule.

3. Which sentence best summarizes the first paragraph of the key document?

   (1) Everyone should be treated equally.
   (2) The Creator grants the right to rebel.
   (3) People would be better off without any government.
   (4) Governments are established by men.
   (5) Governments that do not protect rights of the people should be replaced.

4. Both the passage and the Declaration of Independence list injustices that the American colonists felt were done to them by the British government. Which injustice did the colonists consider the worst offense?

   (1) The British boycotted American goods.
   (2) The British imposed taxes without consent of the colonists.
   (3) The British housed large numbers of soldiers among them during peacetime.
   (4) The British refused to offer a jury trial to people accused of crimes.
   (5) The British abolished the legislature of one or more of the colonies.

Question 5 refers to the following reproduction of a painting.

The Granger Collection, New York

5. In 1783, the Treaty of Paris, signed by America and Britain, ended the Revolutionary War. The British delegation refused to pose for this painting of the writing of that treaty. What conclusion can you draw about the British from this?

   (1) They did not participate in the writing of the treaty.
   (2) They were unhappy about the treaty.
   (3) They did not sign the treaty
   (4) They did not like the Americans.
   (5) They did not like the painter.

Answers start on page 282.

Directions: Choose the one best answer to each question.

Questions 1 through 4 refer to the following passage.

During the Revolutionary War, representatives from each of the thirteen former British colonies came together to design a new national government. They wrote an agreement called the Articles of Confederation. Under the Articles, each of the thirteen colonies became an independent state. Each new state wrote its own constitution that described its form of government and the basic rights of its citizens. These rights included freedom of speech, freedom of the press, freedom of religion, and the right to trial by jury. Trade and manufacturing were also encouraged.

Under the Articles of Confederation, the states were held together only loosely. The country really did not have a national government. Soon unexpected problems led to strife among the states. Some problems arose because the states did not have uniform laws about coining, or manufacturing, money. Each state also had power to charge **tariffs,** or taxes, on goods brought in from another state. By 1787, many Americans felt that the nation needed a new plan for government.

1. Which conclusion about Americans during the Revolutionary War is supported by the passage?

   They were concerned

   (1) with specifying citizens' rights.
   (2) that all the states have the same laws.
   (3) with forming a strong central government.
   (4) about establishing a good relationship with American Indians.
   (5) about establishing a good relationship with Britain.

2. Which phrase summarizes the purpose of the Articles of Confederation?

   (1) an agreement to coin money
   (2) an agreement to form a new nation
   (3) an agreement to allow freedom of speech
   (4) a declaration of America's independence from Great Britain
   (5) a decision to charge tariffs on trade goods

3. What problems could arise if different states coined their own money?

   (1) The country might run out of precious metals needed to make the coins.
   (2) The people in different states might not be able to identify their own money.
   (3) It would be hard for states with different money systems to conduct trade.
   (4) The United States might run completely out of money.
   (5) Some states might refuse to trade with nations overseas.

4. Which current organization is most like the United States under the Articles of Confederation?

   (1) the North American Free Trade Agreement (NAFTA), which sets rules to encourage trade between the United States, Canada, and Mexico
   (2) the North Atlantic Treaty Organization (NATO), in which the United States and other nations agree to defend one another from attack
   (3) Interpol, which works to ensure cooperation among the police authorities of its member nations
   (4) the International Monetary Fund (IMF), which makes loans from a central fund to nations in financial trouble
   (5) the United Nations, where each country is represented in a General Assembly of independent nations

Questions 5 and 6 refer to the following paragraph and diagram.

   After the American Revolution, the United States gained control of the land that now forms the states of Ohio, Indiana, Michigan, Illinois, and Wisconsin. This land was called the Northwest Territory. Organizing the Northwest Territory was one of the main achievements of the U.S. government under the Articles of Confederation. The diagram shows how the land was divided into townships. The U.S. government surveyed the land to set township boundaries. Each township was further divided into 36 square sections that were sold to settlers whole or in smaller plots.

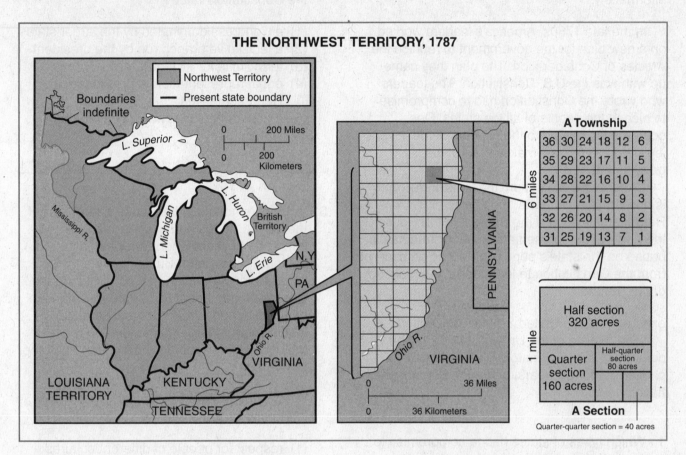

5. What is the **main** reason that the diagram focuses on section 13 of the township square?

   (1) to show how many half sections could be carved out of a whole
   (2) to show the difference in size between different sections
   (3) to present an example of how the people in each township voted to divide the land
   (4) to present an example of how all sections in a township could be divided
   (5) to show that certain sections would be the least desirable amounts of land

6. By law, one section of each township in the Northwest Territory was to be reserved to support education. What does this show about American values in the late 1700s?

   (1) Land was not valued since it was not all used for farming.
   (2) Education was valued only in the Northwest Territory since land was set aside only there.
   (3) Education was not valued since only the Northwest Territory had land for schools.
   (4) Education was valued since the government built all of the nation's schools.
   (5) Education was valued since the government set aside land for schools.

Answers start on page 282.

GED Mini-Test • Lesson 2

Directions: This is a ten-minute practice test. After ten minutes, mark the last question you finished. Then complete the test and check your answers. If most of your answers were correct, but you didn't finish, try to work faster next time. Choose the <u>one best answer</u> to each question.

<u>Questions 1 and 2</u> refer to the following information.

In the late 1780s, America's leaders worked on a new plan for the government to replace the Articles of Confederation. The plan they came up with was the U.S. Constitution. The leaders who wrote the Constitution had to compromise to please the people of all the states. One compromise related to the makeup of the legislature—the law-making part of the government.

Under the Constitution, the legislature is divided into two parts: the House of Representatives and the Senate. In the House, the number of representatives each state has is based on the state's population. Read an excerpt from the Constitution to learn about the makeup of the Senate.

excerpt from the United States Constitution
"The Senate of the United States shall be composed of two Senators from each State, chosen . . . for six Years; and each Senator shall have one Vote."

1. Which types of states had to compromise to agree on this plan for the House and the Senate?

   (1) states with large land areas and those with small land areas
   (2) states with large populations and those with small populations
   (3) states where slavery was legal and those where it was illegal
   (4) wealthy states and less wealthy states
   (5) states with high taxes and states with low taxes

2. Based on the passage, what did the writers of the Constitution value?

   (1) a Congress dominated by the larger states
   (2) a legislative branch run by the president
   (3) term limits for all legislators
   (4) equal representation in the House of Representatives
   (5) a government that would work for all states

3. American Indians in the southeastern part of the United States had been farmers for hundreds of years when Europeans started colonizing their land. But by the late 1700s, some American Indian groups, including the Cherokee, had adopted European-American patterns of agriculture. Some Cherokee leaders owned large plantations on which they used slave labor to grow cotton and other cash crops.

   What value probably motivated Cherokee leaders to become plantation owners?

   (1) respect for people of different cultures
   (2) admiration for learning
   (3) desire for wealth and prestige
   (4) a sense of justice for all peoples
   (5) loyalty toward the United States

4. Which of the following is an opinion, rather than a fact, about the Seminoles, an American Indian tribe that lived in what is now Florida?

   (1) They got food by hunting and fishing.
   (2) They took in runaway slaves.
   (3) The United States captured their leader Osceola in 1837, during truce negotiations.
   (4) They were brave, courageous warriors.
   (5) In the 1820s, they were forced to move to present-day Oklahoma.

Questions 5 through 8 are based on the following passage and chart.

After the Constitution was written, the states needed to approve it. Some states did not want to ratify the Constitution unless it was changed, or amended. They wanted the Constitution to include a list of citizens' rights. So, in 1791, a Bill of Rights was added to the Constitution as its first ten amendments.

CONSTITUTIONAL BILL OF RIGHTS	
Amendment 1	Grants freedom of religion, freedom of speech, freedom of the press, the right to assemble and to petition the government
Amendment 2	Protects the right of a citizens' militia to keep and bear arms
Amendment 3	Prohibits forced quartering of soldiers in peacetime and in wartime, except as regulated by the law
Amendment 4	Prohibits unreasonable searches and seizures and searches without warrants issued on probable cause
Amendment 5	Guarantees that people cannot: be tried twice for the same crime; be forced to speak against themselves in a trial; lose life, liberty, or property without due process of law
Amendment 6	Gives people accused of crimes rights to have a speedy, public trial by jury, to call and question witnesses, and to get legal advice
Amendment 7	Guarantees a jury trial in civil cases
Amendment 8	Protects people from unreasonable bail; prohibits cruel or unusual punishments
Amendment 9	Gives rights not mentioned in the Constitution to the people
Amendment 10	All powers not given to the national government nor denied to the states are held by either the states or the people

5. Which statement best summarizes the idea behind Amendments 4 through 8?

   (1) People accused of crimes have specific rights.
   (2) Police have the right to search people when they want to.
   (3) Police can forbid political protest meetings.
   (4) People have the right to a trial with a jury.
   (5) People cannot be tried twice for the same crime.

6. If police came to search your house without a warrant, which amendment would protect you?

   (1) the First Amendment
   (2) the Second Amendment
   (3) the Third Amendment
   (4) the Fourth Amendment
   (5) the Fifth Amendment

7. Imagine that the government forced your favorite magazine to stop publishing. Which amendment would the government be violating?

   (1) the First Amendment
   (2) the Second Amendment
   (3) the Fourth Amendment
   (4) the Ninth Amendment
   (5) the Tenth Amendment

8. You are on trial and you decide not to answer questions that the prosecutor asks you. Which amendment grants you this right?

   (1) the First Amendment
   (2) the Third Amendment
   (3) the Fifth Amendment
   (4) the Ninth Amendment
   (5) the Tenth Amendment

Answers start on page 283.

GED SKILL Recognizing Unstated Assumptions

assumption
an idea, theory, or principle that a person believes to be true

An assumption is something the writer takes for granted and does not explain. Read carefully to recognize unstated assumptions.

"I'll see you at Jenna's party tonight," a friend might say. This friend just made at least two unstated assumptions: (1) that you've been invited to the party and (2) that you plan to go. Writers make unstated **assumptions** too. You must read carefully to recognize unstated assumptions and to understand the material fully.

Writers often make assumptions about what you already know. So they do not tell you everything. For example, you read a report in the newspaper that mentions that the president is having a reception at the White House. Without being told, you know this story is about the president of the United States because the White House is the president's official residence in Washington, D.C. Sometimes writers assume that particular principles are true. For example, a writer may make the assumption that the Europeans who colonized North America had a right to move American Indians out of their way. Others may disagree strongly with this assumption.

To recognize unstated assumptions in a piece of writing, read slowly and carefully. Ask yourself, "What is this writer assuming to be true?"

Read the passage and answer the question below.

After the Revolutionary War, waves of settlers from the eastern United States began to move westward. Life in the frontier territories was difficult and dangerous. It required courage and endurance to establish farms and homes on uncleared land, deal with the Indians who inhabited the territories, and form new communities under harsh conditions.

In 1890, the director of the U.S. Census stated that the West was full of settlers. The frontier, he said, was gone, and civilization now reigned.

Put a check mark next to the sentence that is an unstated assumption made by the director of the Census.

_____ a. The West had no civilization before the settlers arrived.

_____ b. The West was full of settlers and the frontier was gone.

You were correct if you chose *option a*. The director was assuming that the American Indians who lived in the West before the settlers arrived were not civilized, an assumption many people would disagree with. *Option b* is incorrect because it is not an unstated assumption. It is a direct restatement of the Census director's statement in the second paragraph.

Use the passage and timeline to answer the questions.

At the end of the American Revolution, Great Britain gave the United States all the land it had claimed from the Appalachian Mountains west to the Mississippi River. In 1803, the United States bought the area from the Mississippi to the Rocky Mountains from France. This transaction was known as the Louisiana Purchase.

U.S. President Thomas Jefferson sponsored a group led by Meriwether Lewis and William Clark to map America's newly acquired territory west of the Mississippi River. This trip was called the Lewis and Clark expedition. The group set out in 1804 from a spot near St. Louis, sailing up the Missouri River. The expedition took more than two years. It produced scientific information, established contact with the American Indians of the area, and enabled westward expansion.

In the mid-1800s, the United States gained California and other land in the Southwest from Mexico. By the time of the Civil War, the United States held an unbroken expanse of territory from the Atlantic coast in the east to the Pacific coast in the west.

TIMELINE: 1780–1860

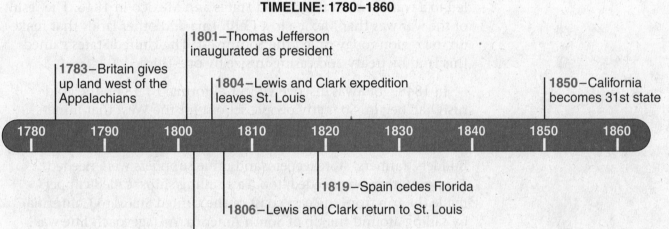

1. Put a check mark next to the statement that the writer assumes that the reader knows in the first paragraph.

    _____ a. where the Appalachian Mountains and the Mississippi River are

    _____ b. what the Louisiana Purchase is

2. Write *A* next to an unstated assumption in the first paragraph.

    _____ a. The United States expanded westward after the American Revolution.

    _____ b. European countries had the right to give away or sell lands in North America.

3. Put a check mark next to the sentence that is an assumption you can make based on the timeline.

    _____ a. California was the last state to join the Union.

    _____ b. Lewis and Clark received a hero's welcome when they returned.

    _____ c. The Louisiana Purchase opened the door to westward expansion.

Answers start on page 283.

In the 1840s, Americans moved westward, many with the sense of **manifest destiny**—meaning they believed it was their right and duty to settle the entire continent. Full of hope, people assembled long lines of wagons carrying their families and belongings. They faced the dangers of crossing rivers and hauling wagons over steep rocky ridges with ropes and chains. Other dangers included exposure to bad weather, accidents on the trail, and attack by American Indians.

In 1821, Texas, then a part of Mexico, was only sparsely settled. To attract people who would develop the area, Mexico offered land grants. The only condition was that settlers in Texas had to agree to follow Mexican laws. As the number of settlers grew, so did their objections to living under Mexican law. In 1836, Texans declared their independence from Mexico and, in 1845, joined the United States as a state. The tensions around this and other property disputes led to a war between the United States and Mexico in 1846. The result of the war was that Mexico lost California and other lands that make up the region today called the Southwest. The United States gained this land by treaty, increasing in size by one-third.

In 1848, gold was discovered in California. By 1849, the gold rush had begun. So many people set out for the West that miners compared them to an army on the march. The discovery of gold created a demand for many other goods and services. Builders, farmers, storekeepers, and mine suppliers were needed. Transportation was needed, too. Fast sailing ships, called clippers, made the trip from the east coast of the United States to California by sailing around the tip of South America. A stagecoach line was set up between Missouri and San Francisco. Finally, in 1869, the first **transcontinental** railroad opened.

Throughout the West, white settlers wanted the land that American Indians occupied so that they could dig mines, start farms, and build ranches. These settlers believed that American Indians stood in the way of progress. The settlers pressured the federal government to force American Indians to move from their homelands. In the 1850s, the United States began relocating American Indians to reservations. When tribes resisted, the U.S. army was called in to force them to move.

The government signed treaties with American Indian tribes to keep them within reservations. The treaties had few benefits for them, though, and they were pushed off their land by trickery or force. Between 1853 and 1857, American Indians lost 174 million acres of land to the federal government. In California, between 1849 and 1859, disease and attacks on American Indians took the lives of 70,000 people. By 1890, those who survived were living on reservations one-tenth the size of the land they had once called home.

Directions: Choose the one best answer to each question.

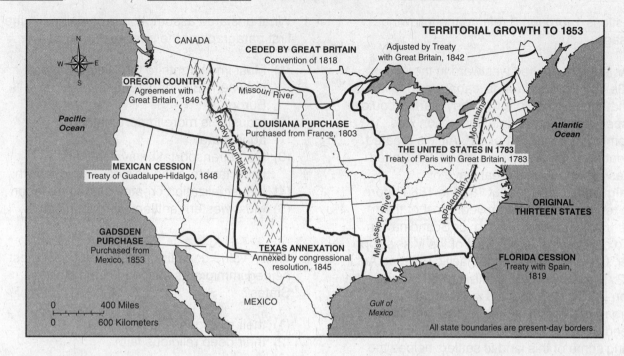

TERRITORIAL GROWTH TO 1853

CANADA

CEDED BY GREAT BRITAIN
Convention of 1818

Adjusted by Treaty
with Great Britain, 1842

OREGON COUNTRY
Agreement with
Great Britain, 1846

Missouri River

Pacific
Ocean

LOUISIANA PURCHASE
Purchased from France, 1803

Atlantic
Ocean

Rocky Mountains

MEXICAN CESSION
Treaty of Guadalupe-Hidalgo, 1848

THE UNITED STATES IN 1783
Treaty of Paris with Great Britain, 1783

ORIGINAL
THIRTEEN STATES

Appalachian

Mississippi River

GADSDEN
PURCHASE
Purchased from
Mexico, 1853

TEXAS ANNEXATION
Annexed by congressional
resolution, 1845

FLORIDA CESSION
Treaty with Spain,
1819

0   400 Miles
0   600 Kilometers

MEXICO

Gulf of
Mexico

All state boundaries are present-day borders.

Question 1 refers to the map on this page.

1. What does the map indicate about much of
    the land acquired by the United States?

    (1) It was uninhabited until 1853.
    (2) It was acquired primarily through warfare.
    (3) It had been owned by other countries.
    (4) It had been owned by American Indians.
    (5) It had been heavily settled by Europeans.

Questions 2 through 4 refer to the passage on
page 52.

2. What assumption did the Texans make when
    they declared independence from Mexico?

    (1) By treaty, the Texas land was officially part
         of the United States.
    (2) They didn't need to honor their agreement
         to live under Mexican law.
    (3) It was their manifest destiny to be
         independent of Mexico.
    (4) The Texas land belonged to the American
         Indians rather than the Mexicans.
    (5) The gold discovered in California could
         finance a war with Mexico.

3. Which sentence best summarizes the third
    paragraph of the passage?

    (1) The discovery of gold in California made
         statehood inevitable.
    (2) Good, fast, reliable transportation was
         needed to develop the West.
    (3) The gold rush spurred population growth,
         business development, and better
         transportation.
    (4) After California became a state, people
         rushed to the area, looking for gold or
         jobs.
    (5) People came to California full of hope but
         soon were discouraged because of the
         lack of goods and services.

4. Which position taken by American Indians led
    some white settlers to believe that the Indians
    stood in the way of progress?

    (1) resistance to relocation to reservations
    (2) acceptance of treaties with the
         government
    (3) fear of sickness if moved from homelands
    (4) opposition to the seizure of their lands
    (5) discontent from the loss of 70,000 lives

Answers start on page 283.

GED Practice • Lesson 3

Directions: Choose the one best answer to each question.

Questions 1 through 3 refer to the following passage.

As settlers pushed westward in the mid-1800s, they needed roads, canals, and railroads so that the farms and towns they started could prosper. At the same time, the nation was becoming more industrialized. All this created a great need for labor. As a result, the United States experienced a great wave of **immigration.** From about 1830 to 1880, more than ten million people arrived. Most of them were Irish, German, English, or Scandinavian.

To develop the region west of the Mississippi River, Congress passed the Pacific Railroad Act in 1862. The government granted **public land** to the Union Pacific Railroad and the Central Pacific Railroad companies. In return, the companies agreed to build a railroad line to the Pacific Ocean. Selling some of this land to settlers helped the companies pay for railroad construction.

Each company hired thousands of laborers for the exhausting and often hazardous work. Most of the Union Pacific's 10,000 workers were Irish immigrants. The Central Pacific's slightly larger workforce consisted mostly of Chinese laborers. Some of these Chinese had come to California during the gold rush of 1849. However, most were recruited in China and brought to the United States specifically to work on the railroad.

The Union Pacific started at Omaha, Nebraska, and began laying track westward. The Central Pacific began in Sacramento, California, and began laying track eastward. Because the government's land grants were based on the project's progress, each company wanted to be the one to lay the most track. After a seven-year effort, the two lines met at Promontory, Utah. On May 10, 1869, as a crowd of politicians, railroad officials, and workers cheered, the president of the Central Pacific drove in a golden spike to connect the tracks and complete the nation's first transcontinental railroad.

TIP An unstated assumption can be either a fact or an opinion that the writer thinks the reader shares.

1. What unstated assumption is contained in the first paragraph of the passage?

   (1) Most immigrants to the United States between 1830 and 1880 came from Europe.
   (2) Industry is more important than agriculture.
   (3) Good transportation systems are important to a region's economic growth.
   (4) Industrialization creates a need for labor.
   (5) Most western settlers were immigrants.

2. Which value does the passage suggest most helped immigrants succeed in the United States?

   (1) their willingness to work hard
   (2) their deep religious faith
   (3) their desire for personal freedom
   (4) their eagerness to participate in democratic government
   (5) their respect for the culture and traditions of their home countries

3. Which law was most similar to the Pacific Railroad Act of 1862?

   (1) the Civil Rights Act of 1866, which gave citizenship to all people born in the United States
   (2) the Chinese Exclusion Act of 1882, which outlawed the immigration of Chinese workers
   (3) the Interstate Commerce Act of 1887, which created a government agency to oversee the railroads
   (4) the Highway Act of 1956, which authorized the building of an interstate highway system
   (5) the Immigration Act of 1990, which increased the number of immigrants allowed into the United States

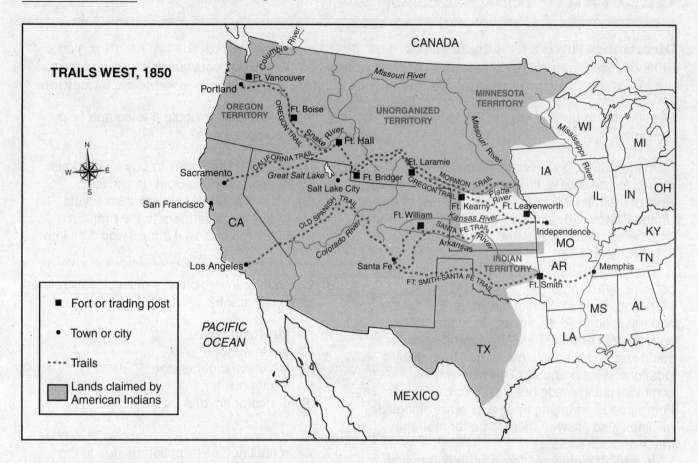

TRAILS WEST, 1850

4. On which trails would a southerner most likely have traveled to reach California?

   (1) the Oregon and California trails
   (2) the Santa Fe and Ft. Smith-Santa Fe trails
   (3) the Mormon and California trails
   (4) the Santa Fe and Old Spanish trails
   (5) the Ft. Smith-Santa Fe and Old Spanish trails

5. What assumption can be made from the information on this map?

   (1) Trails followed rivers when they could because of the water the rivers provided.
   (2) Some trails west did not cross Indian territory.
   (3) American Indian tribes fought with one another over land.
   (4) There were more forts along the Santa Fe Trail than along the Oregon Trail.
   (5) American Indians tried to sell land to passing settlers.

6. In 1851, U.S. officials and representatives of several American Indian tribes signed a treaty at Fort Laramie on the Oregon Trail. They agreed that wagon trains could cross Indian land unmolested. The treaty also allowed the government to build roads and military posts in Indian territory. In return, the United States promised the tribes $50,000 in supplies each year for fifty years. However, the U.S. Senate later changed these terms to $70,000 per year for fifteen years.

   What assumption can you make about the treaty?

   (1) The U.S. treaty negotiators lied to the American Indians.
   (2) There was conflict between American Indians and travelers on the Oregon Trail.
   (3) American Indians had no intention of obeying the treaty.
   (4) Tribes were starving and needed supplies.
   (5) This was the first treaty between the government and an American Indian tribe.

Answers start on page 284.

GED Mini-Test • Lesson 3

Directions: This is a ten-minute practice test. After ten minutes, mark the last question you finished. Then complete the test and check your answers. If most of your answers were correct, but you didn't finish, try to work faster next time. Choose the one best answer to each question.

Questions 1 through 5 refer to the following passage.

In the 1850s, government officials began to search for ways to better connect the vast region west of the Mississippi River with the rest of the United States. One solution to which they turned was the telegraph, perfected by inventor Samuel F. B. Morse in 1837.

Congress had financed the first telegraph line between Washington, D.C., and Baltimore, Maryland, in 1844. Within ten years, the device had revolutionized American life. Using Morse's code of dots and dashes, a telegraph operator could send and receive messages from distant locations in just minutes. This new way of communicating made business more efficient. For railroads, stringing telegraph wires alongside rail lines also allowed them to better manage trains and schedules.

In 1860, Congress offered $400,000 to any company willing to build a telegraph line from Missouri to California. The Western Union Telegraph Company soon began to string wire east from San Francisco and west along the Oregon Trail. The two lines met at Salt Lake City in 1861. A prominent California judge sent the first telegram. It was to President Abraham Lincoln and stated that the new telegraph line strengthened the loyalty of Californians to the United States, which was fighting the Civil War.

1. How would the telegraph have made business more efficient?

   (1) Businesses could operate with fewer employees.
   (2) Businesses could ship goods by train rather than by wagon or canal boat.
   (3) Businesses could send and receive orders more quickly than by letter.
   (4) Machines could replace production by hand.
   (5) Telegraph operators could also work making products.

2. In which situation would a telegraph help railroad operations?

   (1) to allow immigrants to buy train tickets
   (2) to prevent trains from getting lost
   (3) to help ticket agents sell train tickets
   (4) to direct passengers to the right train
   (5) to tell the station if a train would be late

3. Which later invention was most closely related to the telegraph?

   (1) the automobile
   (2) the telephone
   (3) the electric generator
   (4) the typewriter
   (5) the compact disk

4. What unstated assumption relates to the passage?

   (1) Western Union built the first telegraph line.
   (2) Congress wanted to better connect the West with the rest of the United States.
   (3) Californians did not want a telegraph line.
   (4) Before 1861, communication between California and the eastern states was very slow.
   (5) The government's $400,000 was enough to pay for constructing a western telegraph line.

5. Which statement best summarizes the main idea of this passage?

   (1) Samuel F. B. Morse was a brilliant inventor.
   (2) The telegraph helped connect the nation.
   (3) American business was inefficient in the 1850s.
   (4) Western Union was the nation's largest telegraph operator in the 1860s.
   (5) The telegraph was more important than the railroad to the nation's development.

Questions 6 through 8 refer to the map and passage.

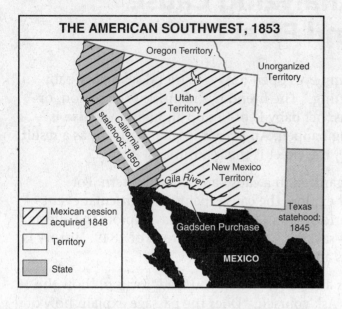

THE AMERICAN SOUTHWEST, 1853

Oregon Territory

Unorganized Territory

Utah Territory

California statehood: 1850

New Mexico Territory

Gila River

Texas statehood: 1845

Gadsden Purchase

MEXICO

Mexican cession acquired 1848

Territory

State

In 1853, U.S. President Franklin Pierce sent James Gadsden to Mexico to alter the border between the two nations. The Treaty of Guadalupe Hidalgo, which ended the war with Mexico in 1848, set the boundary at the Gila River in present-day Arizona. However, southerners wanted a transcontinental railroad from New Orleans to Los Angeles. The most suitable land for building such a line lay south of the Gila River, in Mexican territory.

Negotiations were not difficult. Mexico was in desperate financial straits after its war with the United States. President Antonio López de Santa Anna feared that he would lose power unless he obtained funds. He quickly agreed to turn over some 29 million acres to the United States in exchange for $10 million. But because of the Civil War, which preoccupied the United States from 1861 to 1865, the railroad project was postponed until the 1880s.

6. Which of the following can be concluded from information on the map and in the passage?

   (1) The Mexican people were unhappy about the loss of more territory.
   (2) Few people lived in the Gadsden Purchase.
   (3) The land that formed the Gadsden Purchase lay south of the Gila River.
   (4) Santa Anna lost power in Mexico.
   (5) The Gadsden Purchase contained no towns.

7. Which of the following statements is true of the Gadsden Purchase?

   (1) It became part of the New Mexico Territory.
   (2) It was larger in area than California.
   (3) It had railroad tracks needed to build a transcontinental railroad.
   (4) The main supporters of its purchase were northerners.
   (5) It was added to the United States shortly before California became a state.

8. What was land won by the United States in the Treaty of Guadalupe Hidalgo called?

   (1) the Mexican Cession
   (2) the New Mexico Territory
   (3) the Utah Territory
   (4) California
   (5) the Gadsden Purchase

9. When control of California and the Southwest passed from Mexico to the United States, the nearly 80,000 Spanish-speaking people in the region became U.S. citizens. However, many of them felt like "foreigners" in their own country. Settlers who flooded into the region challenged the Mexican Americans' ownership of the land. Property rights had often been based on old Spanish land grants from when Mexico had been a colony of Spain. U.S. courts usually did not recognize these titles as proof of ownership. As a result, families lost land on which they had lived for generations. Many former landowners were forced to take low-paying jobs in mines or as farm laborers to survive.

According to the passage, what was a result of U.S. acquisition of California and the Southwest?

   (1) The Mexican-American War ended.
   (2) U.S. courts changed the way they recognized titles to land.
   (3) Many foreigners moved into the Southwest.
   (4) Long-term residents suffered losses under U.S. law.
   (5) Families were broken up.

Answers start on page 284.

Lesson 4

GED SKILL Analyzing Cause and Effect

cause
what makes something happen

effect
what happens as a result of a cause

"I can barely keep my eyes open today," a friend says. "My baby was up all night coughing." The friend has identified the reason, or cause, for her tiredness: her baby kept her up all night. A **cause** is what makes something happen. An **effect** is what happens as a result of a cause. In this case, the effect is that your friend is tired.

Writing is often organized in a cause-and-effect pattern. For example, a writer may explore the causes behind a particular event— say, the Mexican-American War. Or a passage may explore the effects of a particular event—say, the California gold rush of 1849. History is concerned with causes and effects of events.

To recognize causes and effects when you read, focus on how the events are connected. Ask yourself, "Does the passage explain how or why an event occurred (the causes)? Does it focus on the results (effects) of an event?"

TIP

The words and phrases *because, since, therefore,* and *as a result* are clues that indicate a cause-and-effect relationship.

Read the passage and answer the questions below.

In 1854, Congress passed the Kansas-Nebraska Act, which allowed settlers in those states to vote on the **slavery** question. Disputes arose at once over whether Kansas would enter the Union as a free state or a slave state. As a result, Kansas and Nebraska became the sites of violent clashes between antislavery and proslavery groups.

Because of these violent incidents, the territory became known as "Bleeding Kansas." The bitterness of the struggle deepened the differences between North and South and accelerated the drift toward civil war.

1. Put a check mark next to the statement of an effect of the struggle in Kansas.

   _____ a. passage of the Kansas-Nebraska Act

   _____ b. the drift toward civil war

2. List the cause of the violent clashes in Kansas.

   _____

If you chose *option b,* for question 1, you're right. This is stated explicitly in the last sentence of the passage. *Option a* is a cause, not an effect. For question 2, the cause the passage gives for the violent clash is *the conflict over whether the territory of Kansas should enter the Union as a free state or a slave state.*

Use the passage and map to answer the questions.

In 1819, Missouri sought to enter the union as a slave state. Northerners opposed this because they wanted to preserve the balance in the Senate between slave and free states. The North was also concerned that the entire Louisiana Purchase might allow slavery. In response, Congress established a line that divided the lands of the Louisiana Purchase. Slavery would be allowed south of the line, but not north of it. This agreement is known as the Missouri Compromise.

In 1850, Congress forged a second great compromise that affected the slave question in California, Utah, New Mexico, and Washington, D.C. The compromise included a law to help slave owners capture runaway slaves. As with all compromises, each side gained something and gave up something else.

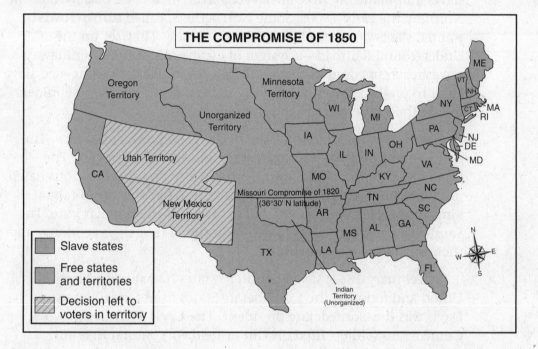

THE COMPROMISE OF 1850

1. Write *C* next to a cause that led to the Missouri Compromise.

    _____ a. The Louisiana Purchase was divided into north and south.

    _____ b. Missouri sought to enter the Union as a slave state.

2. Use the map to explain the effect of the Compromise of 1850 on the following.

   California: _____

   Utah and New Mexico: _____

3. Fill in each blank with the word *cause* or *effect*.

   Concern in the North about slavery was an important _____ of the Missouri Compromise.

   One _____ of the Compromise of 1850 was that life became more difficult for runaway slaves.

Answers start on page 285.

By the mid-1800s, the economy of the South differed dramatically from the economy of the North. Southern states relied mainly on agriculture for their financial stability. Northern states were more industrial. The North had more factories, and the South mainly imported manufactured goods from the North and from Europe. As a result, the South favored free trade with Europe, while the North wanted tariffs to be imposed on imported goods.

Slavery had also become an issue between the North and South. Black people, many of them brought from Africa, were bought and sold like property and forced to work for white people. Children of slaves automatically were enslaved. Slavery had been outlawed in the North by the early 1800s. Some Northerners, called **abolitionists,** wanted slavery outlawed in the South as well. They set up the Underground Railroad—a system of escape routes to help runaway slaves reach freedom in the North. Southern plantations needed slave labor to produce crops. Disrupting slavery would cause slaveholders to lose their investments and their way of life.

Slavery was the defining issue in the 1860 presidential race. The new Republican Party was against the expansion of slavery. The Democratic Party divided into Northern and Southern factions based on the issue. With this political splintering, Republican Abraham Lincoln was elected with much less than half the popular vote. The South saw Lincoln's election as a clear signal that their economy and their way of life were at risk.

By February 1861, seven Southern states had **seceded** from the Union and founded the Confederate States of America. Jefferson Davis was the Confederate president. The **Civil War** began when Confederate soldiers fired on Union-held Fort Sumter in South Carolina. The South wanted to take control of this fort because it symbolized the Union's power. Four more states immediately left the Union, making a total of eleven states in the Confederacy.

In the early years of the Civil War, the Confederacy performed well in battle. They had better generals than the Union had, and Confederate soldiers showed the extra zeal that comes from defending home and family. By 1863, however, the superior **resources** of the North and the Union victories at Gettysburg and Vicksburg began to wear down the Confederacy. In 1865 Confederate General Robert E. Lee surrendered to Union General Ulysses S. Grant, ending the bitter and costly Civil War. Nearly every American knew someone who had been killed or maimed in the war.

The Civil War devastated the South. Cities were in ruins; railroads had been destroyed; and thousands were hungry, homeless, and bitter about their losses. The slaves were freed, but they had neither land nor jobs; most had few skills outside farming.

Directions: Choose the one best answer to each question.

Questions 1 and 2 refer to the map.

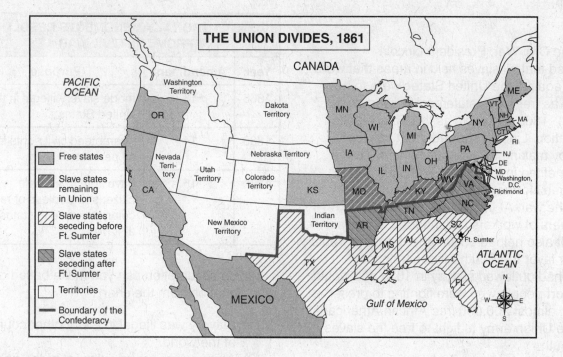

THE UNION DIVIDES, 1861

CANADA

PACIFIC OCEAN

Washington Territory

Dakota Territory

OR

Nevada Territory

Utah Territory

Colorado Territory

New Mexico Territory

CA

Nebraska Territory

KS

Indian Territory

TX

MN

WI

IA

IL

MO

AR

LA

MI

IN

KY

TN

MS

AL

OH

WV

GA

NY

PA

VA

NC

SC

FL

Washington, D.C.
Richmond

ME

VT
NH
MA
CT
RI
NJ
DE
MD

Ft. Sumter

ATLANTIC OCEAN

MEXICO

Gulf of Mexico

N
W E
S

Legend:
- Free states
- Slave states remaining in Union
- Slave states seceding before Ft. Sumter
- Slave states seceding after Ft. Sumter
- Territories
- Boundary of the Confederacy

1. How did the attack on Fort Sumter affect the states of Arkansas, Tennessee, Virginia, and North Carolina?

   (1) They seceded from the Union.
   (2) They voted to become slave states.
   (3) They voted to remain with the Union.
   (4) They voted to become free states.
   (5) They seceded from the Confederacy.

2. What does the map show about the states of Missouri, Kentucky, West Virginia, Maryland, and Delaware?

   (1) They seceded from the Union before the attack on Ft. Sumter.
   (2) They seceded from the Union during the attack on Ft. Sumter.
   (3) They seceded from the Union after the attack on Ft. Sumter.
   (4) They joined the Union after the attack on Ft. Sumter.
   (5) They remained in the Union even though they were slave states.

Questions 3 and 4 refer to the passage on page 60.

3. How did having few industries affect Southerners?

   (1) They had to start plantations and buy slaves to work on them.
   (2) They had to import most manufactured goods from the North and from Europe.
   (3) They decided to secede from the Union.
   (4) They decided to form the Confederate States of America.
   (5) They had to look to Abraham Lincoln for leadership in building industries.

4. What were the two most important causes of the Civil War?

   (1) hunger and homelessness
   (2) victories at Gettysburg and Vicksburg
   (3) abolition and the Underground Railroad
   (4) the 1860 election and Southern secession
   (5) economic tensions and land scarcity

Answers start on page 285.

Directions: Choose the one best answer to each question.

Questions 1 and 2 refer to the following paragraph.

During the Civil War, President Lincoln announced that all slaves held in areas that were rebelling against the United States were to be regarded as free. This statement, issued on January 1, 1863, is known as the Emancipation Proclamation. Lincoln showed great political wisdom by making this announcement. The North benefited in four ways. The proclamation encouraged Northerners who opposed slavery to support the war. At the same time, it deprived Southerners of workers they needed to carry on the war. It also helped ensure that England would no longer favor the South's independence; England had outlawed slavery in 1833 and would not support people who were fighting to preserve it. Finally, almost 200,000 free African Americans joined the Union army to fight to free the slaves of the South.

1. Which of the following was an effect of the Emancipation Proclamation?

   (1) Support for the war decreased in the North.
   (2) Free African Americans joined the Confederate army.
   (3) The South gained the support of England.
   (4) Southerners willingly freed their slaves.
   (5) The South's war effort was weakened.

2. According to the paragraph, why did the English refuse to aid the South in the Civil War?

   (1) They were fighting a war in Europe.
   (2) They would not help protect slavery.
   (3) They were still bitter about American independence.
   (4) They didn't want to anger President Lincoln.
   (5) They didn't have an army that could fight overseas.

Questions 3 and 4 refer to the following table.

CONSTITUTIONAL AMENDMENTS RESULTING FROM THE CIVIL WAR		
Year	Amendment	Purpose
1865	13	made slavery illegal in the United States
1868	14	guaranteed civil rights for all persons
1870	15	gave vote to all male citizens regardless of race, color, or previous status as a slave

3. Which assumption can you make based on information from the chart?

   (1) Slavery was illegal in every other country of the world.
   (2) African Americans did most of the fighting in the Civil War.
   (3) Abraham Lincoln was not reelected as president.
   (4) Only in the North did all white men and white women have the right to vote.
   (5) The Emancipation Proclamation of 1863 did not end all slavery in the United States.

4. What do the terms of the 15th Amendment suggest?

   (1) Citizens had to own land in order to vote.
   (2) Slavery still existed in some parts of the South.
   (3) Some states were not allowing former slaves to vote.
   (4) The voting age was 18.
   (5) Elections had not been held since the end of the Civil War.

Questions 5 and 6 refer to the following passage.

By the end of the Civil War, cities, farms, and transportation systems throughout the South had been almost completely destroyed. Few Southern political leaders felt any loyalty to the United States. Lincoln and other Northern leaders realized that the South's economy and government needed to be rebuilt. Former slaves also needed help finding their new roles in society. The government's actions between 1865 and 1877 to accomplish these goals and reunite the nation were known as **Reconstruction.**

Lincoln hoped to reunite the nation as painlessly as possible. He pardoned almost all Southerners for rebelling and provided that, if 10 percent of a state's voters swore allegiance to the Constitution, the state could rejoin the Union. However, **radical** members of Congress wanted to punish the South for the war. They also feared that former slaves would suffer under Lincoln's plan. After Lincoln's assassination in April 1865, the radicals quickly took control of Reconstruction. They were determined to protect black Southerners and to keep Southern "rebel" politicians from ever returning to power.

5. What does the term *Reconstruction* mean?

   (1) a plan to punish the South for Lincoln's death
   (2) a plantation system without slavery
   (3) the radical members of Congress
   (4) the effort to reunite the nation and rebuild the South
   (5) a plan to restore slavery in the South

6. Which of these details from the passage best supports the conclusion that Americans did not agree on how to treat the South after the war?

   (1) Radical Congressmen took over Reconstruction.
   (2) Former slaves needed help.
   (3) Reconstruction lasted from 1865 until 1877.
   (4) The South's economy needed to be rebuilt.
   (5) President Lincoln was assassinated.

7. Shortly before the Civil War ended, Congress created the Freedmen's Bureau to provide food, clothing, medical care, and other aid to slaves freed by the Union army. After the war, its role expanded. It supervised the wage agreements white employers made with former slaves. It also founded nearly 3,000 schools across the South.

During the Civil War, the Freedmen's Bureau functioned <u>most</u> like which modern institution?

   (1) a public school system
   (2) a public health clinic and hospital
   (3) a federal disaster relief agency
   (4) a state job placement office
   (5) a private religious charity

8. Although they finally had their freedom, most former slaves had no land and little money. Therefore, many worked on the plantations as employees of former slaveholders. At first they were paid wages. But most landowners were short of cash, too, so a new system called **sharecropping** soon developed. With this system, the landowner provided a house, tools, and seed, and the sharecropper provided the labor and skill to grow the crops. After the harvest, the landowner took one-half to two-thirds of the crops.

According to the passage, which of the following prompted the sharecropping system to develop?

   (1) Most former slaves now owned their own land.
   (2) The U.S. government failed to protect the rights of the former slaves.
   (3) White Southerners owned most of the land but had little money to pay farm workers.
   (4) Many former slaves could finally afford to leave the plantations.
   (5) Most former slaves had moved to Northern cities and needed a place to live.

 TIP A cause can have more than one effect, and an effect can itself be the cause of another effect.

Answers start on page 285.

GED Mini-Test • Lesson 4

Directions: This is a ten-minute practice test. After ten minutes, mark the last question you finished. Then complete the test and check your answers. If most of your answers were correct, but you didn't finish, try to work faster next time. Choose the <u>one best answer</u> to each question.

Questions 1 and 2 refer to the following paragraph and key document.

On November 19, 1863, President Lincoln dedicated a national cemetery at the Gettysburg battlefield. The speech he made became famous as the *Gettysburg Address*. In it, he discussed democratic ideals and the goal of reuniting the nation.

excerpt from the *Gettysburg Address*
"Four score and seven years ago, our fathers brought forth, on this continent, a new nation, conceived in Liberty, and dedicated to the proposition that all men are created equal. Now we are engaged in a great civil war, testing whether that nation, or any nation so conceived and so dedicated, can long endure."

1. The Civil War had been raging over two years when Lincoln gave the *Gettysburg Address*. What was the main purpose of his speech?

   (1) to praise the Union army for the victory
   (2) to give hope to Union prisoners of war held in Southern prison camps
   (3) to criticize Southerners for continuing to fight
   (4) to remind Northerners of the ideals for which they were fighting
   (5) to remind Northerners of the Union's lack of progress in the war

2. When Lincoln noted that the nation was founded on the principle "that all men are created equal," to what earlier document was he referring?

   (1) the Declaration of Independence
   (2) the Articles of Confederation
   (3) the U.S. Constitution
   (4) the Mayflower Compact
   (5) the Emancipation Proclamation

Questions 3 and 4 refer to the following passage.

The Union army of General Ulysses S. Grant and the Confederate army of General Robert E. Lee continued to confront each other until April 1865. On April 9, faced with being encircled and cut off from lines of supply, Lee sent a rider with a white flag of truce to arrange a meeting with General Grant. Grant suggested that Lee's battered and retreating army should surrender. Lee responded by asking his enemy for terms. Grant generously offered and Lee gratefully accepted these terms of surrender:

> ". . . officers and men paroled . . . arms and materials surrendered . . . officers to keep their side arms [pistols], and let all men who claim to own a horse or mule take the animals home with them to work their little farms."

After the surrender, Lee returned to his home in Virginia. He urged all Southerners to work for peace and harmony in a united country.

3. What effect did Grant's surrender terms <u>most likely</u> have on Lee?

   (1) They caused Lee to feel humiliated.
   (2) They generated a dislike for Grant in Lee.
   (3) They made it easier for Lee to surrender.
   (4) They encouraged Lee to keep fighting.
   (5) They turned Lee bitter toward the Union.

4. What can you conclude from the second sentence of the first paragraph of the passage?

   (1) Grant feared Lee.
   (2) Lee wanted to battle Grant's army.
   (3) Grant was willing to resupply Lee's army.
   (4) Lee knew his army was in trouble.
   (5) Lee hoped his army could escape.

Questions 5 and 6 refer to the following passage.

Even before Reconstruction ended in 1877, many white Northerners grew weary of worrying about the South. Convinced that the federal government would not stop them, some Southern whites used violence to intimidate black voters into voting for them so that they would win state elections in 1875 and 1876. These new white leaders called themselves "Redeemers" because they claimed to be taking back, or redeeming, the powers their class had lost as a result of Reconstruction. By the early 1880s, they controlled most state and local governments in the South.

Once they were back in power, these Southern whites showed little respect for black citizens and denied them their rights. The Redeemers established literacy tests and poll taxes as qualifications for voting. This worked to deny many African Americans their voting rights because they could not read or were too poor to pay the tax. Other new laws, called Jim Crow laws, established and enforced segregation of the races. By the 1890s, all Southern states had segregated public transportation and schools. Segregation soon extended to parks, theaters, cemeteries, and other public places.

Although the Redeemers turned back the clock on the South's government and society, they were forward-looking in other areas. They saw little benefit in relying on the old cotton- and tobacco-farming economy. Industrial production grew under their leadership. By 1900, the South was a major center for the manufacture of cotton textiles and tobacco products.

5. Why did Southern African Americans lose rights after Reconstruction?

(1) Northerners lobbied to improve the welfare of Southern African Americans.
(2) The federal government lost interest in the welfare of Southern African Americans.
(3) White politicians gave up power in the South.
(4) Southern states passed Jim Crow laws that prohibited segregation.
(5) Southern African Americans lost interest in voting.

6. From the information provided, what can you assume about the South's development?

(1) The Redeemers tried to prevent the South's economy from becoming strong.
(2) Southern agriculture played no part in the region's industrial growth.
(3) Southern African Americans did not share equally in the region's growing prosperity.
(4) Tobacco and cotton ceased to be important crops in the South.
(5) Northern textile mills benefited from the growth of Southern industry.

Questions 7 and 8 refer to the following graph.

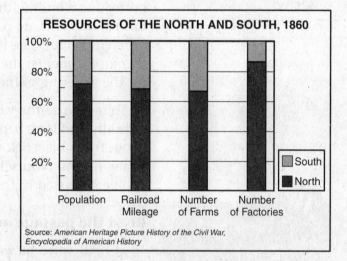

RESOURCES OF THE NORTH AND SOUTH, 1860

Source: *American Heritage Picture History of the Civil War, Encyclopedia of American History*

7. In which area did the North have the greatest advantage over the South?

(1) population
(2) railroad mileage
(3) number of farms
(4) number of factories
(5) The North had no advantage in any area.

8. Why is the information in the graph important to understanding the Civil War era?

(1) It helps explain why slavery was an issue between North and South.
(2) It shows why the war went on for so long.
(3) It helps explain why the North eventually won the war.
(4) It helps explain why Reconstruction occurred.
(5) It shows why Reconstruction took so long.

Answers start on page 286.

GED SKILL **Recognizing Values**

Society is held together by shared values. **Values** are the goals and ideals that make life meaningful. Values include what people think is important, good, beautiful, worthwhile, or sacred. Recognizing values helps us understand why people act as they do. Human beings often make decisions about what to do based on their values.

Most writing expresses some values—either those of the writer or of the people being discussed in the passage. For example, one writer may say that the building of the transcontinental railroad in the late 1800s was a magnificent accomplishment by and for the people of the United States. Another writer might say that the transcontinental railroad was built with the blood and sweat of poor workers. Both statements are based in historical fact, but they express different values. The first focuses on the values of progress and accomplishments; the second focuses on values about and concern for the suffering of individuals.

To recognize the values expressed in a piece of writing, read carefully and look behind the words. What is the writer's attitude about the subject? How are the people discussed in the passage behaving? Ask yourself, "What matters most to the writer or to the people discussed in the passage?"

values

goals and ideals; what people think is important, good, beautiful, worthwhile, or sacred

TIP

To understand the values in a piece of writing, ask yourself "What do the writer or the people depicted in the passage think is important?"

Read the passage and complete the exercise below.

In 1848, when he was 13, Scottish immigrant Andrew Carnegie got his first job working in a cotton mill 12 hours a day, 6 days a week. He had little formal education and earned about only $2 a week. Intelligent and ambitious, Carnegie advanced from job to job, determined to work his way up in life. Eventually, as a businessman, he dominated the U.S. steel industry. In 1881, the man who had been penniless as a youth sold his steel company for almost $500 million. Carnegie believed that the rich had a responsibility toward society. He donated millions of dollars for education, research, and the arts.

Put a check mark next to each statement that expresses a value in Carnegie's life.

_____ a. A person must accept whatever life they're born into.

_____ b. Hard work and ambition can lead to wealth.

_____ c. The wealthy have a responsibility to help others.

You were correct if you chose *options b* and *c*. Both were ideals, or values, in Carnegie's life. *Option a* would be incorrect because Carnegie was able to succeed even though he started out with no schooling and little money.

Use the passage and the graph to answer the questions.

The term **Industrial Revolution** describes the shift in the economy from farming to manufacturing. This shift began in Great Britain in the 1700s and reached the United States a few decades later. As a result of the Industrial Revolution, steam engines and machines replaced hand labor. People began to use products made in factories instead of making them at home.

The shift to a factory system brought many other changes. For example, the new machines required no particular skill or strength to operate. Thus, factory owners often were more interested in hiring people who would work for low wages rather than people who were highly skilled. They employed women, children, and new immigrants, who would work for the lowest wages. These employees worked long hours, always under pressure to speed up production. Neither the machines nor the work methods were designed for safety, and many workers were injured or even killed in accidents at work. People did this work out of economic necessity. Many families would not have survived unless everyone worked.

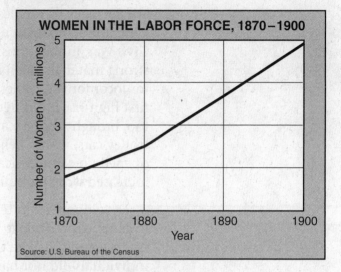

WOMEN IN THE LABOR FORCE, 1870–1900

Source: U.S. Bureau of the Census

1. Put a check mark next to the statement that describes a value of factory owners during the Industrial Revolution.

_____ a. Factory owners valued the efficient production of goods.

_____ b. Factory owners valued the skills workers brought to the job.

2. Put a check mark next to the statement that represents a value supported by both the passage and the graph.

_____ a. In the late 1800s, more and more women took jobs as a way to bring meaning to their lives.

_____ b. In the late 1800s, more and more women took jobs as a way to help their families survive.

_____ c. About 300,000 women held paying jobs by the late 1800s.

3. Write *T* if the statement is true or *F* if it is false.

_____ a. After the Industrial Revolution, society valued manufacturing more than farming.

_____ b. After the Industrial Revolution, handmade goods were valued more than factory-made products.

Answers start on page 287.

Before the Civil War, manufacturers concentrated on "light" industries, those that produced relatively small and lightweight articles, such as textiles, clothing, and leather goods. Or they processed agricultural or **natural resources** like grains or lumber. After the Civil War, innovations in technology made it possible to produce new, strong materials, such as steel. Steel was then manufactured into rails for locomotives, cables to suspend bridges, and beams for the nation's first high-rise buildings. The development of electrical power systems, too, brought about many economic developments. Electricity powered trolley cars, which helped cities grow. It powered the telegraph, which opened up communication. The installation of electric lighting increased working hours in businesses and industries.

Developments in technology could not by themselves make industry grow. Industrial growth also required people who could finance and organize the businesses and factories. Because most individuals did not have enough money to build factories on their own, they joined together to form complex organizations, such as corporations. Corporations could raise large sums of money and reduce individual financial risk. To raise money, the corporations sold stock to stockholders, who were paid dividends if the companies made a profit. With the new machinery, railroads, and power sources, these corporations could take advantage of natural resources found all over the United States.

Of course, people were also needed to work in the factories, and by 1900, 5.3 million people did so. Heavy, fast-moving machinery made the work dangerous, however, and workers received no payment if they were injured on the job. A typical worker put in twelve hours a day six days a week. For these long, risky hours, wages averaged $3 to $12 per week. Workers had no vacations or sick days and no unemployment compensation.

In the **sweatshop** system, certain products were made in people's homes. For example, a clothing manufacturer would provide the fabric, but the workers had to provide the sewing machines and other tools. Then, six to twenty people, laboring together in the one room in which they also lived, would make the clothing. They were paid according to the number of pieces they could produce.

Individuals were forced to accept these working conditions or lose their jobs. So workers started to band together against the factory owners and form **labor unions**—organizations whose purpose was to improve working conditions, wages, and benefits for members. The workers realized that, when taking demands to employers, a group would be stronger than a few individuals. Such group efforts came to be know as **collective bargaining.** Union members would agree to strike and thus shut down factory production until their demands were met.

Directions: Choose the one best answer to each question.

Questions 1 through 3 refer to the passage on page 68.

1. According to the passage, what role did corporations play in industrial growth?

   (1) They employed large numbers of people who worked at home.
   (2) They had enough money to hire inventors to develop new technology.
   (3) They had great power and so could oppose demands of labor unions.
   (4) They promoted the use of electricity to improve transportation in cities.
   (5) They raised large sums of money to develop industries and reduced individual financial risk.

2. According to the passage, which of the following were important causes of nineteenth-century economic development?

   (1) labor unions and collective bargaining efforts
   (2) growth of the textile and leather goods industries
   (3) innovations in manufacturing and the use of electricity
   (4) risky working conditions and stock dividends for investors
   (5) the Civil War and discovery of natural resources

3. According to the passage, what was an important value underlying the labor union movement?

   (1) Higher wages could make up for dangerous working conditions.
   (2) Employers should provide more education for their workers.
   (3) Sweatshop workers should receive wages rather than payment by the piece.
   (4) Workers who negotiate as a group could bargain more effectively than individual workers.
   (5) Workers should become stockholders in the corporations that employed them.

Question 4 refers to the graph below.

4. A patent is a government document that gives an inventor the exclusive right to make, use, or sell an invention.

   Which growing value underlies the trend shown in this graph?

   (1) support for big business
   (2) an interest in technological innovation
   (3) a concern for worker safety
   (4) improved worker training and education
   (5) support for government regulation

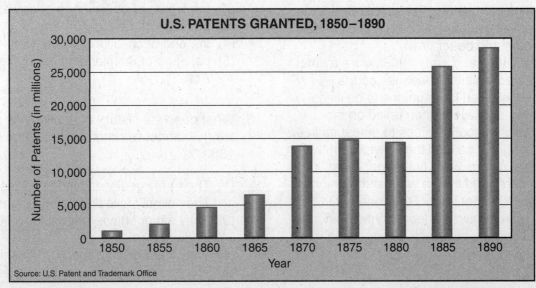

U.S. PATENTS GRANTED, 1850–1890

Source: U.S. Patent and Trademark Office

Answers start on page 287.

GED Practice • Lesson 5

Directions: Choose the one best answer to each question.

Questions 1 through 3 refer to the following passage and graph.

In the late 1800s, two labor organizations tried to improve the lives of workers. The Knights of Labor, led by Terence Powderly, was organized into separate unions for each industry. All workers in an industry were eligible to join its union, regardless of the work they performed. Skilled and unskilled workers belonged to the same union. Between 1880 and 1886, the Knights' membership grew from 10,000 to 700,000 workers.

The Knights called for higher wages, an eight-hour workday, and an end to child labor. Powderly preferred negotiation to strikes, but he had little control over the individual local unions. The Knights' reputation suffered after a series of unsuccessful **strikes** and a bombing in 1886. Membership rapidly declined, and by the 1890s, the Knights had been overshadowed by the American Federation of Labor.

The American Federation of Labor, or AFL, was organized by cigar-maker Samuel Gompers in 1886. It was successful for many of the same reasons that the Knights of Labor was not. Each member union of the AFL consisted of workers who all had the same craft or skill. Skilled workers could strike more effectively than unskilled workers, who could be easily replaced. However, rather than promote strikes, Gompers tried very hard to cooperate with employers who allowed workers to belong to a union. Under his direction, skilled workers eventually got shorter working hours and better pay.

The late 1800s and early 1900s were a time of labor-related violence. Because courts generally considered labor unions to be illegal **monopolies,** employers often relied on the police or private security forces to defeat strikes. In 1914, Congress passed the Clayton Act, which declared that unions were not monopolies; but the courts continued to rule against the unions. Not until the National Labor Relations Act in 1935 did workers gain the legal right to join unions and engage in collective bargaining with employers.

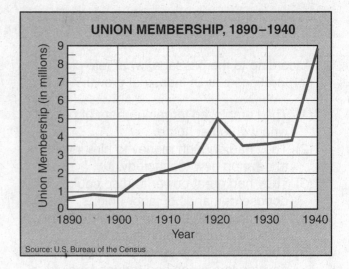

Source: U.S. Bureau of the Census

1. Using the passage, predict what would happen if the United Auto Workers lost several strikes against the nation's automakers.

   (1) Workers' wages would go up.
   (2) More unskilled workers would join the union.
   (3) The union would lose members.
   (4) Wages would become less important to union members.
   (5) Workers would worry about job safety.

2. What most likely explains the change in union membership between 1935 and 1940?

   (1) the founding of the AFL
   (2) the failure of strikes for higher wages
   (3) passage of the Clayton Act
   (4) the end of child labor in the United States
   (5) passage of the National Labor Relations Act

3. What does the history of the Knights and AFL suggest about workers' values in the late 1800s?

   (1) Their only goal was higher wages.
   (2) They blindly followed union leadership.
   (3) They did not have respect for other workers.
   (4) They were discouraged by violent strikes.
   (5) They were lazy and did not like hard work.

Questions 4 through 7 refer to the following passage and graph.

In the late 1800s, people flocked to cities to find jobs. Cities served as markets for nearby farms and as centers of new industry. Commerce, industry, immigration, and improved transportation all contributed to the development of large cities such as New York and Chicago. Cities across the North continued to grow during World War I and into the 1920s, as more than a million African Americans left the South in what became known as the Great Migration. War industries offered many job opportunities, and fewer immigrants were available to fill them because of laws passed after the war. A similar African-American migration occurred again in the 1940s, during World War II.

Rapid urban growth caused problems, such as overcrowding. People were packed into **tenements,** lacking the basic necessities for healthful living. Many of the problems that developed in poor, urban neighborhoods continue to be problems to this day.

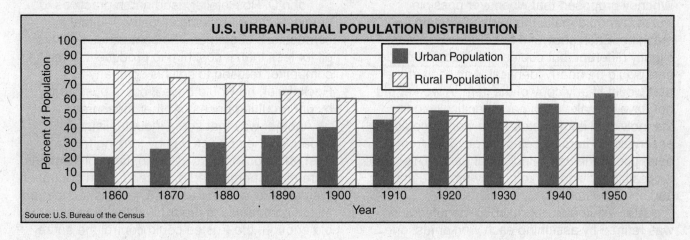

4. Which of the following was a cause of the growth of large cities?

    (1) economic recession
    (2) job opportunities
    (3) laws limiting immigration
    (4) unhealthy conditions in tenements
    (5) the invention of the automobile

5. What was the first year in which more Americans lived in cities than in rural areas?

    (1) 1860
    (2) 1900
    (3) 1920
    (4) 1930
    (5) 1950

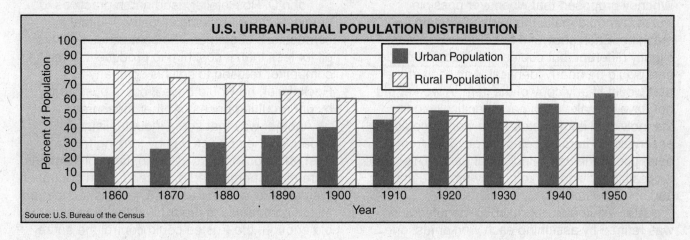
TIP To identify values, look for clues that indicate what might have influenced the actions of a person or a group.

6. According to the passage, what is one factor that likely caused the population change from 1940 to 1950 that is shown on the graph?

    (1) increased immigration
    (2) the Great Migration
    (3) the development of tenements
    (4) World War II
    (5) laws that severely limited immigration

7. Based on the passage, what values were reflected in the Great Migration?

    (1) Jobs were important to African Americans.
    (2) Healthy living was important to immigrants after World War I.
    (3) People did not want to live in crowded tenements.
    (4) Coming to America was important to immigrants after World War II.
    (5) Americans valued good transportation systems.

Answers start on page 287.

Directions: This is a ten-minute practice test. After ten minutes, mark the last question you finished. Then complete the test and check your answers. If most of your answers were correct, but you didn't finish, try to work faster next time. Choose the <u>one best answer</u> to each question.

Questions 1 and 2 refer to the following passage.

In the 1790s, a young schoolteacher named Eli Whitney introduced two important ideas for improving manufacturing—the related ideas of mass production and interchangeable parts. Whitney proposed that whenever possible workers should make the parts of an item by machine. Each copy of a handmade part was slightly different, but copies of a machine-made part would be nearly identical. Any copy of the part would fit any copy of the item. A worker did not have to make each part specifically to fit the individual item. Instead, the worker could assemble an item by selecting any part from each pile of the item's individual parts. This made it possible for workers to quickly produce many copies of the item.

Later, Whitney's approach to manufacturing was refined by assigning each worker just one step in the assembly process. Adopting this assembly line approach helped make the United States the world's leading manufacturer of goods by the end of the 1800s.

1. Which title <u>best</u> summarizes the main idea of this passage?

   (1) The Life of Eli Whitney
   (2) Making Parts to Fit
   (3) The Growth of American Industry
   (4) Improving the Lives of Workers
   (5) The Development of Mass Production

2. What values did factory owners show by adopting Whitney's methods?

   (1) Handmade products were best.
   (2) Efficiency was important.
   (3) Workers were not important.
   (4) High-quality products were not important.
   (5) The workday was too short.

Questions 3 and 4 refer to the following passage.

Most industrialists of the late 1800s were honest and public-spirited citizens. Some, however, used shady practices and mistreated others in order to enrich themselves.

John D. Rockefeller used harsh practices to dominate the oil-refining industry. To steal a competitor's customers, he sometimes sold his oil for less than it cost him to produce it. If the competitor refused to sell his company to Rockefeller, he would drive it out of business by undercutting prices or other measures.

Another way that some industrialists expanded their power was by forming trusts. First, the stockholders of competing corporations were either persuaded or forced to turn control of their stock over to a trustee. Then this trustee ran all the companies in the trust. If the trust became big enough, the trustee could control the entire industry and collect huge profits. A trust often developed a monopoly of its industry. In this way, Rockefeller controlled nearly 90 percent of the nation's oil business by the 1890s.

3. What do Rockefeller's actions, as described in the passage, suggest was most important to him?

   (1) power
   (2) wisdom
   (3) competition
   (4) friendship
   (5) honesty

4. Which conclusion is based on the passage?

   (1) Rockefeller stole oil from his competitors.
   (2) A monopoly is the only way to get rich.
   (3) All corporations were monopolies.
   (4) Rockefeller established an oil trust.
   (5) *Trust* is another name for *corporation*.

5. In the 1840s, inventor Elias Howe perfected a sewing machine that could handle heavy-duty materials. For which type of item would Howe's machine be <u>most</u> useful to increase production?

(1) blouses
(2) lace collars
(3) paper goods
(4) thread
(5) shoes

6. This 1886 political cartoon by a famous cartoonist, Thomas Nast, shows the Statue of Liberty sinking under the weight of the trusts that are covering it. What point is Nast trying to make?

(1) The Statue of Liberty is in need of repair.
(2) The power of trusts is threatening the American way of life.
(3) Forming trusts is the American way of doing business.
(4) Trusts will save the nation from economic collapse.
(5) The nation will survive despite the trusts.

Questions 7 through 9 refer to the following passage.

The rapid industrial and urban growth of the late 1800s and early 1900s led to serious problems in society. A group of writers known as "muckrakers" demanded reform. In 1904, Ida Tarbell completed *The History of the Standard Oil Company,* which reported the ruthless tactics of the oil trust. The same year, *The Shame of the Cities* by Lincoln Steffens exposed the corruption that plagued many city governments.

Probably the most widely read muckraking book was Upton Sinclair's novel *The Jungle,* published in 1906. Sinclair's graphic descriptions of the filthy conditions in the meat-packing industry prompted Congress to pass the Pure Food and Drug Act later that year. John Spargo's book *The Bitter Cry of Children,* also published in 1906, reported on the horrible lives of child workers. However, the crusade to end child labor was not successful nationwide until 1938.

7. What problem did the book *The Jungle* show?

(1) muckraker demands for reform
(2) conditions of child mine workers
(3) unhealthful meat-packing practices
(4) monopolistic practices of the beef trust
(5) ruthless tactics of the oil trust

8. Which of the following was an effect of the muckrakers' reporting?

(1) hindering reform in society
(2) making people aware of serious problems
(3) making many city officials corrupt
(4) encouraging riots over high prices
(5) showing the danger of investigative reporting

9. Which would be a modern example of muckraking?

(1) a TV news investigation of a major polluter
(2) a police investigation of suspected criminals
(3) a medical journal's report on a new disease
(4) a manufacturer's recall of a defective product
(5) a government recall of a defective product

Answers start on page 288.

GED SKILL Distinguishing Conclusions from Supporting Details

conclusion
a judgment or decision based on facts and details

supporting details
the evidence or facts that lead to a conclusion

A child listens to the teacher. He opens his book when the teacher asks him to. His homework is done. This child appears to be behaving well in school. This last statement is a **conclusion**—a judgment or decision based on facts and details. **Supporting details** (getting out his books, finishing his homework) are the evidence that leads to the conclusion. Sometimes a writer points the reader to the conclusion by using words such as *thus* or *therefore*. Other times, the reader must distinguish the conclusion from the details without such clues.

One way to identify a writer's conclusion is to draw a conclusion yourself. Add the details in the passage together, and see what larger idea you get. For example, consider these details about European immigrants to the United States in the early 1900s: They left homes and families behind. Their sea journey was difficult. U.S. customs authorities could send them back to Europe for many reasons. What conclusion can you come to? Immigrants must have had courage and determination.

Read carefully to distinguish details from the conclusion in a piece of writing. Ask yourself two questions: "What facts and details are given in the passage? What larger idea do they point to?"

Read the passage and answer the question below.

Jeannette Rankin was the first woman to serve in Congress. She represented the state of Montana for two nonconsecutive terms, 1917–1919 and 1940–1942. Rankin was one of only fifty members of Congress who opposed the U.S. declaration of war against Germany during World War I. She stood when she was called on to vote and said, "I want to stand by my country, but I cannot vote for war." She was the only member of Congress to vote against war with Japan when that country attacked Pearl Harbor, Hawaii, in 1941. In 1968, at the age of 87, she led a 5,000-woman march on Capitol Hill to protest the Vietnam War. Rankin was a courageous activist for peace.

Put a check mark next to the sentence that states the conclusion of the passage.

_____ a. Rankin opposed U.S. participation in World War I.

_____ b. Rankin was a courageous activist for peace.

Option b is a conclusion drawn in the passage. *Option a* is just one example of her activism for peace.

TIP

Sometimes a conclusion follows such words as *therefore*, *thus*, and *so*, or *what we can learn from this*. Use these words as guides to identify the conclusion.

Use the passage and the chart to answer the questions.

The United States launched its reputation as a world power in 1898 with the Spanish-American War, a war waged to liberate Cuba from Spanish rule. The United States showed its military strength at sea, defeating Spanish forces in both the Caribbean and the South China Sea and acquired land outside its borders. The war took only three months. John Hay, U.S. Secretary of State, called it a "splendid little war."

The first battle took place in May in the Philippines. There, the U.S. Navy lost only one soldier and won an overwhelming victory over the Spanish. On July 3, U.S. troops destroyed the Spanish naval force in Santiago harbor, Cuba. Again, only one U.S. soldier was killed. Santiago surrendered to U.S. forces within weeks. Another American force soon occupied Spanish-held Puerto Rico, and on July 18 the Spanish government requested a settlement with the United States.

CAUSES AND RESULTS OF THE SPANISH-AMERICAN WAR	
What caused the U.S. to go to war?	**What were the results of the war?**
• Sympathy for the Cuban fight for independence • Spanish mistreatment of Cubans • Desire to expand export markets and find new raw materials • Publication of letter from the Spanish minister that insulted the U.S. president • Sinking of the U.S. ship *Maine* in Cuba's harbor (cause still unknown)	• Cuba became independent of Spain, but it was dominated by the U.S. • U.S. took over Puerto Rico, Guam, and the Philippines • U.S. paid Spain $20 million for the Philippines • U.S. expanded its import-export markets • U.S. became known as world power

1. Put a check mark next to the sentence that states a conclusion based on the passage.

      _____ a. The United States won the Spanish-American War in 1898 and became known as a world power.

      _____ b. The United States occupied Puerto Rico three months after the Spanish-American War began.

2. Put a check mark next to the sentence that supports Hay's conclusion that the Spanish-American War was a "splendid little war."

      _____ a. The United States showed its military strength at sea and acquired land outside its borders.

      _____ b. The war lasted only three months and few U.S. soldiers died.

3. List two details from the chart that support the conclusion that the U.S. became known as a world power after the Spanish-American War.

   _____

   _____

Answers start on page 288.

Many Americans of the twentieth century wanted to follow George Washington's advice to stay out of the affairs of foreign countries. But as "the Great War" raged in Europe from 1914 to 1917, the United States found that remaining neutral was not easy. Many Americans sympathized with Great Britain and France in their fight against Germany and were horrified by the years of bloody warfare and millions of deaths. In addition, the United States had important trading relationships with European nations, so the war interfered with U.S. financial interests. Then German submarines began to sink American passenger ships, prompting U.S. entry into the war and the eventual defeat of the German army in 1918. This was the end of what was called "the war to end all wars," later called World War I.

The war left Germany in poor economic condition. Soon the unstable political situation led to the rise of dictator Adolf Hitler and the Nazi Party. Hitler wanted to make Germany the dominant power in Europe. He also adopted a racist policy aimed at killing all European Jews and other ethnic minorities. In 1936, he formed the Axis alliance with Italian dictator Benito Mussolini. In 1939, Germany attacked Poland. France and Great Britain had promised to support Poland and, thus, declared war on Germany, beginning World War II. Again the United States wanted to stay out of European affairs. But many Americans objected to the aggression of the Axis dictators.

At the same time, Japanese aggression in Asia created U.S.-Japanese tension. While Americans debated their response, Japan attacked Pearl Harbor, Hawaii, on December 7, 1941. The next day, the United States declared war on the Japanese and their allies, the European Axis powers. In 1945, the British, American, French, and Soviet allies defeated Nazi Germany. Later that year, the United States ended the war with Japan by dropping atomic bombs on Hiroshima and Nagasaki, causing massive destruction.

The peace that came in 1945 did not really settle world affairs. There was tension between the United States and the Soviet Union. **Communism** was the political and economic system of the Soviet Union, while **democracy** was the system in most of Western Europe and the United States. Under the communist system, there was only one political party; the government owned all businesses, factories, land, and resources; and people had few rights. Both the United States and the Soviet Union tried to spread their influence wherever they could. They competed in a nuclear weapons race. The tension between the two nations was referred to as the **Cold War.** A cold war involves hostility between nations but no actual fighting.

Beginning in 1988 and continuing through the early 1990s, communism collapsed in the Soviet Union and Eastern Europe, bringing a formal end to the Cold War. The economically powerful United States found itself the most influential nation in the world.

Directions: Choose the <u>one best answer</u> to each question.

<u>Questions 1 through 4</u> refer to the passage on page 76.

1. What do the details of the first paragraph explain?

   (1) how the arrival of American troops in Europe led to the defeat of Germany
   (2) why many Americans sympathized with Great Britain and France
   (3) why it was hard for the United States to remain neutral during World War I
   (4) why Great Britain and France were fighting with Germany
   (5) how millions of deaths occurred during the course of the war

2. Which of the following is a conclusion about World War II supported by details in the passage?

   (1) Germany attacked Poland in 1939.
   (2) Japan attacked Pearl Harbor, Hawaii.
   (3) The United States bombed Hiroshima and Nagasaki.
   (4) The war caused massive destruction.
   (5) Hitler and Mussolini formed the Axis alliance.

3. According to the passage, what values motivated the United States to enter into World War I?

   (1) long-standing conflicts with Germany and the need to test new weapons
   (2) business interests and concerns about human lives
   (3) concern that Germany was the aggressor against Poland and other nations
   (4) the desire to become the dominant power in Europe
   (5) tensions between communism and democracy

4. Which unstated assumption does the passage suggest lay behind Cold War tensions?

   (1) The United States wanted to remain neutral.
   (2) Unstable economic conditions in either the United States or the Soviet Union could lead to real war.
   (3) Germany might try to dominate Europe again and start a third world war.
   (4) The United States and the Soviet Union each believed its political system was the better one.
   (5) Hitler and Mussolini had been allies with the Soviet Union during part of World War II.

<u>Question 5</u> refers to the following map.

5. After World War II, Germany was split into zones occupied by the allied nations that won the war. Berlin, the former capital of Germany, was divided into East Berlin and West Berlin.

   What conclusion do the details on this map support?

   (1) Together, the allied nations controlled Berlin.
   (2) The French controlled West Germany.
   (3) The British and French controlled West Berlin.
   (4) The Americans dominated West Berlin.
   (5) The Soviets controlled all of East Germany.

Answers start on page 288.

Throughout the twentieth century, the U.S. government confronted the often-interconnected problems of poverty, **civil rights,** the environment, and urban development. The federal government made its first major attempt to deal with poverty under President Franklin Roosevelt. His task was to bring the country out of the Great Depression of 1929, which had left millions of Americans, both on farms and in cities, without food, homes, jobs, or hope. Decades later, in 1964, President Lyndon Johnson mounted a "War on Poverty." He pushed Congress to set up new antipoverty programs, allocating funds for food stamps, public housing, and Medicare—a health insurance program.

President Johnson also signed the Civil Rights Act of 1964 into law. African Americans had been working for equal rights and an end to segregation throughout the century. For example, in 1909, W.E.B. Du Bois founded the NAACP (National Association for the Advancement of Colored People), vowing to fight against "the problem of the color line." This organization sought voting rights for African Americans and equal protection under the law. Then, in 1964, the Civil Rights Act made **discrimination** based on race, color, religion, and national origin against the law. It protected the voting rights of all citizens and gave everyone the right to enter libraries, parks, restaurants, theaters, and washrooms.

The idea of environmental protection began in the late 1800s, when the nation began to realize that its natural resources were not limitless. President Theodore Roosevelt withdrew millions of acres of land from public sale and turned them into wildlife sanctuaries, national parks, and national monuments. In 1908, he called a White House conference on **conservation.** Forty-six states set up conservation agencies. By the 1960s, the public was becoming increasingly anxious about pollution of the environment. In 1970, President Nixon established the Environmental Protection Agency, or EPA, to enforce environmental protection laws.

In the late 1800s, populations in cities had swelled as people moved from small towns and farms and immigrants came from abroad. Suburban areas developed when electric streetcars were introduced, making it possible for families to live up to ten miles from the city center and ride the streetcar downtown to work or shop. In the 1950s, in response to housing shortages, land developers built millions of single-family houses on open land outside the cities. By the early 1960s, every large city in the United States was surrounded by a heavily populated ring of middle- and upper-class communities in which almost every household had at least one car. This pattern has contributed to congestion, pollution, and segregation of people by income.

Directions: Choose the <u>one best answer</u> to each question.

<u>Questions 1 through 4</u> refer to the passage on page 78 and the table on this page.

SAMPLING OF PROGRAMS OF THE ENVIRONMENTAL PROTECTION AGENCY

• Emergency Planning and Community Right-to-Know Act	• Requires industrial reporting of toxic releases and encourages planning for chemical emergencies
• Resource Conservation and Recovery Act	• Regulates solid and hazardous waste
• Pollution Prevention Act	• Seeks to prevent pollution through reduced generation of pollutants at their point of origin
• Clean Air Act	• Requires EPA to set air quality standards to focus on areas that do not attain standards
• Clean Water Act	• Establishes a program on sewage treatment construction and waste discharge
• Ocean Dumping Act	• Regulates the intentional disposal of materials into ocean waters
• Comprehensive Environmental Response, Compensation, and Liability Act (Superfund)	• Establishes a fund to clean up abandoned hazardous waste sites

---

1. Taken together, what do the details of the table suggest?

   (1) why the government is concerned about air and water pollution
   (2) why solid and hazardous waste have become such a pressing problem
   (3) what the strategy is for cleaning up hazardous waste sites
   (4) why air and water pollution are this country's biggest problems
   (5) what some of the country's biggest environmental problems are

2. Which of the following is a conclusion about suburban growth supported by the passage?

   (1) Land developers have built millions of houses on open lands outside cities.
   (2) Suburban growth contributes to congestion, pollution, and economic segregation.
   (3) Heavily populated smaller communities now surround every large city in the United States
   (4) Most residents of the suburbs belong to the middle class or the upper class.
   (5) Most suburban households have one or more cars.

3. Which values prompted the Civil Rights Act and the War on Poverty?

   (1) President Franklin Roosevelt's belief that people needed to feel hope
   (2) the belief that the environment should be preserved for future generations
   (3) the belief that all people are equal and deserve decent food, shelter, and health care
   (4) the principle that libraries, parks, and theaters should be open to all citizens
   (5) the belief that people must unite to solve "the problem of the color line"

4. According to the passage and the table, concerns about which of the following caused President Nixon to establish the EPA?

   (1) polluted air, water, and land
   (2) suburban development
   (3) national parks
   (4) overcrowding in cities
   (5) ineffective environmental laws

Answers start on page 289.

GED Practice • Lesson 6

Directions: Choose the one best answer to each question.

Questions 1 through 4 refer to the following passage.

The decade of the 1920s brought rapid industrial growth and widespread prosperity in the United States. But the economic boom came to an end with the stock market crash of 1929. Because of the crash, businesses suffered financial losses. Many had to reduce their operations or close, putting thousands out of work. These jobless workers bought fewer goods. This caused other companies to cut production and lay off workers. By 1933, the nation was in a **depression.** One out of four workers was unemployed.

Throughout most of the 1930s, millions of Americans depended on handouts to survive. Hundreds of thousands became homeless, and thousands more wandered the nation, looking for work. Many people gave up hope that they or the government could do anything to end the suffering. Some looked to radical ideas, such as communism, as a way to restore prosperity.

As the depression spread overseas, people in other nations also became desperate. In Japan, hard times made it possible for the military to gain control of the government. In parts of Europe, people were still suffering from the effects of World War I. So they were willing to support dictators like Benito Mussolini in Italy and Adolf Hitler in Germany who offered extreme solutions for their nations' problems. By the mid-1930s, the plans of these leaders to restore prosperity at the expense of other countries was moving the world toward another war. The Great Depression, as it came to be called, did not end until the United States entered World War II in 1941.

1. Which detail supports the conclusion that the United States was in a depression in the 1930s?

    (1) The 1920s was a decade of prosperity.
    (2) Europe still suffered from World War I.
    (3) Communism was a radical idea.
    (4) Some Americans became communists.
    (5) One out of four workers was unemployed.

2. Which detail in the passage supports the writer's conclusion that the solutions Hitler and Mussolini offered were "extreme"?

    (1) Europe was still suffering from the effects of World War I.
    (2) Hitler and Mussolini planned to restore prosperity at the expense of other countries.
    (3) The military gained power in Japan.
    (4) Other nations sought solutions to the depression.
    (5) The depression spread overseas from the United States.

3. According to the passage, which of the following was a major cause of the Great Depression in the United States?

    (1) the onset of World War II
    (2) the economic collapse of Germany and Italy
    (3) a major decrease in spending by Americans
    (4) the suffering of the American people
    (5) communism's growth in popularity

4. Why did U.S. entry into World War II help end the Great Depression?

    (1) The war effort required troops and manufactured goods, which created many jobs.
    (2) The fighting in Europe and Asia took Americans' minds off their problems at home.
    (3) The government's effort to defeat Italy, Germany, and Japan united Americans.
    (4) The war caused Americans to reject communism.
    (5) The war caused the stock market to crash.

When President Franklin D. Roosevelt took office in 1933, he promised a "new deal" for the American people. His goal was to pull the nation out of the worst economic crisis in its history. Like the reformers of the early 1900s, Roosevelt's aim was to conserve natural resources, regulate business, break down monopolies, and improve working conditions. By increasing the government's involvement with business and the economy, Roosevelt believed he was acting in the nation's best interests. His critics, however, saw his New Deal as a dangerous break with the American tradition of self-reliance. They feared that government handouts would weaken the character of Americans.

Many regulatory New Deal programs continue to affect the nation today. For example, the Securities and Exchange Commission (SEC), which regulates the stock market, and the Federal Deposit Insurance Corporation (FDIC), which insures depositors' savings in banks, were created during the New Deal. Many state park facilities were constructed by the Civilian Conservation Corps. The Rural Electrification Association (REA) brought electricity to areas that were without electric power until the New Deal.

MAJOR NEW DEAL PROGRAMS		
Program	Year	Purpose
Federal Emergency Relief Administration	1933	Provided money and other charity to people in need
Civilian Conservation Corps	1933	Employed young men on conservation projects
Agricultural Adjustment Administration	1933	Aided farmers and regulated farm production
National Recovery Administration	1933	Established fair-competition codes for industries
Public Works Administration	1933	Created public works projects to provide jobs
Works Progress Administration	1935	Created government projects to employ people
Social Security Administration	1935	Paid benefits to unemployed and retired workers
National Labor Relations Act	1935	Gave workers the right to join labor unions
Fair Labor Standards Act	1938	Established a 40-hour work week and minimum wage

5. Which New Deal program reflected Roosevelt's goal to break down monopolies?

   (1) the Agricultural Adjustment Administration
   (2) the Civilian Conservation Corps
   (3) the Federal Deposit Insurance Corporation
   (4) the National Labor Relations Act
   (5) the National Recovery Administration

6. Which conclusion about the New Deal is supported by the passage and the chart?

   (1) The New Deal did not address all of Roosevelt's goals.
   (2) Many New Deal programs were so effective that they were retained after the Great Depression.
   (3) All the New Deal programs worked well.
   (4) The New Deal ended the depression.
   (5) The New Deal attracted voters to the Democratic Party.

7. With which of the following programs would Roosevelt's critics have been most concerned?

   (1) the Public Works Administration
   (2) the Rural Electrification Administration
   (3) the Federal Emergency Relief Administration
   (4) the Civilian Conservation Corps
   (5) the National Labor Relations Act

8. Which is most likely to have formed the basis of government welfare programs?

   (1) the Securities and Exchange Commission
   (2) the Federal Emergency Relief Administration
   (3) the Civilian Conservation Corps
   (4) the Fair Labor Standards Act
   (5) the National Labor Relations Act

Answers start on page 289.

GED Mini-Test • Lesson 6

Directions: This is a ten-minute practice test. After ten minutes, mark the last question you finished. Then complete the test and check your answers. If most of your answers were correct, but you didn't finish, try to work faster next time. Choose the one best answer to each question.

Questions 1 through 3 refer to the following paragraph.

After World War I ended in 1918, Americans looked forward to better times. But they first had to deal with problems that resulted from the ending of the war. The war's end caused the economy to slow. Factories that had run at maximum capacity during the war, producing goods for the war, shut down to retool for peacetime production. Thousands of people who had worked in those factories were laid off. In addition, millions of veterans, home from the war, needed to find work. Competition for jobs was very strong. During the early 1920s, industrialists, farmers, immigrants, and other workers competed for their share of the prosperity they all expected peace to bring.

1. What conclusion is supported by the details in the paragraph?

   (1) The decade of the 1920s was quiet.
   (2) All wars cause economic readjustments.
   (3) Before the nation could enjoy better times, it had to deal with problems resulting from the war.
   (4) Industrialists, farmers, immigrants, and others experienced great prosperity in the 1920s.
   (5) Many Americans were concerned about the welfare of returning war veterans.

2. What can you assume from the information in the paragraph?

   (1) Unemployment was high for a few years after World War I.
   (2) Employers preferred to hire war veterans before other Americans.
   (3) The nation's industrial workers were better off than its farmers.
   (4) Many industrialists were immigrants.
   (5) Riots erupted between war veterans and immigrants.

3. The struggle among groups in the 1920s was most like what other struggle in American history?

   (1) the 1770s fight to be free from Britain
   (2) attempts to end slavery in the early 1800s
   (3) attempts to deny voting rights to African Americans in the late 1800s
   (4) demands of women for the vote in the early 1900s
   (5) demands of women and minorities for equal job opportunity in the 1970s

Question 4 refers to the following cartoon.

4. In 1917, communists seized power in Russia, adopting a red flag as a symbol of their revolution. In the United States, communists tried to gain support among workers. When more than 3,000 strikes occurred during 1919, a "Red Scare" hysteria swept the nation. The government rounded up thousands of suspected radicals.

What do these events and this 1919 cartoon suggest many Americans then believed?

   (1) All immigrants were communists.
   (2) Strikes were part of a communist plot.
   (3) All striking workers should be arrested.
   (4) The steel mill owners were communists.
   (5) Strikers should be forced back to work.

Questions 5 through 7 refer to the following passage and map.

In 1963, more than 200,000 people gathered in Washington, D.C. in what became known as the March on Washington. There civil rights leader Dr. Martin Luther King Jr. gave his now-famous "I Have a Dream" speech. He called for America to live out the ideals of the Declaration of Independence, which states that "all men are created equal."

The march was a huge success. The 24th Amendment was added to the Constitution in January 1964. It outlawed the requirement that citizens pay a poll tax in order to vote. The Civil Rights Act of 1964 banned racial discrimination in employment and public accommodations.

Some Americans, however, resisted these changes. Throughout the South, people who tried to register African Americans to vote were arrested or beaten. In early 1965, Alabama police attacked a peaceful march for civil rights. They beat the marchers and sprayed them with tear gas. In response, Congress passed the Voting Rights Act of 1965. This law established harsh penalties for interfering with voting and put voter registration under federal control. Within a few years of the passage of this law, more than half of voting-age African Americans in the South had registered to vote.

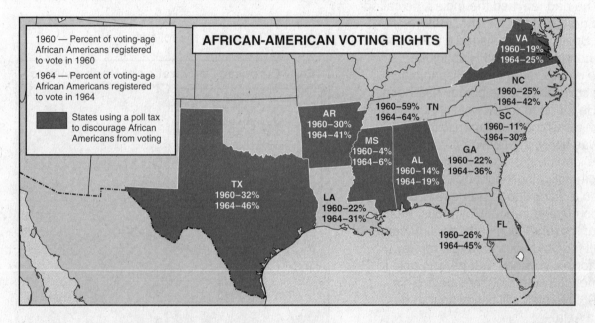

5. Which state most strongly discouraged African American voter registration?

(1) Alabama
(2) Tennessee
(3) Mississippi
(4) North Carolina
(5) South Carolina

6. Where did the 24th Amendment most likely have the greatest effect on voter registration?

(1) Tennessee
(2) Florida
(3) South Carolina
(4) Virginia
(5) Texas

7. What is the most likely reason that a higher percentage of African Americans was registered to vote in North Carolina than in Alabama?

(1) In Alabama, people were beaten for trying to secure voting rights.
(2) North Carolina had no poll tax.
(3) Alabama was farther south than North Carolina.
(4) The Voting Rights Act of 1965 was very effective.
(5) Dr. Martin Luther King Jr. lived in Alabama.

Answers start on page 290.

Unit 1 Cumulative Review United States History

Directions: Choose the one best answer to each question.

Questions 1 and 2 refer to the following passage.

Christopher Columbus believed that he could reach the Indies—the name Europeans gave to the lands and islands of East Asia—by sailing west across the Atlantic Ocean. He persuaded the king and queen of Spain to finance such a voyage.

On October 12, 1492, after several weeks at sea, Columbus reached an island in what is now called the Bahamas that he claimed for Spain and named San Salvador. Because Columbus was certain he had reached the Indies, he called natives who greeted him "Indians." Before returning to Spain, he established a colony on another island that he named Hispaniola.

When Columbus returned to Hispaniola in 1493, he discovered that the colony had been destroyed. He founded a new colony nearby and left to search for China and Japan. While Columbus was away, the natives revolted over the colonists' constant demands for gold and food. The colonists also fought over land and the American Indians' labor. Some returned to Spain and complained about Columbus. From that point on, his reputation suffered. It became more difficult for Columbus to obtain money and people for his voyages. But he was able to return to America two more times before his death in 1506. He died still believing that he had reached Asia.

Many people consider Columbus a hero because of his voyages. However, some people view his activities as the beginning of the terrible destruction of American Indian people and culture. Whatever view one holds, it is clear that Columbus's voyages were a turning point in history.

1. What title best expresses the main idea of this passage?

(1) Conflict in the Americas
(2) How Indians Got Their Name
(3) Christopher Columbus and His Work
(4) The Search for China and Japan
(5) The Spanish Exploration of America

2. Which of the following is a conclusion made by the writer of the passage?

(1) Because Columbus thought he was in Asia, he called the local people "Indians."
(2) Columbus had trouble raising money for later voyages.
(3) Columbus died in 1506.
(4) Columbus never realized that he had discovered a New World.
(5) Columbus's voyages were crucial to history.

Question 3 refers to the following map.

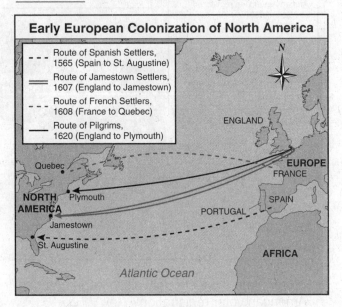

Early European Colonization of North America

- - - - Route of Spanish Settlers, 1565 (Spain to St. Augustine)
===== Route of Jamestown Settlers, 1607 (England to Jamestown)
- - - - Route of French Settlers, 1608 (France to Quebec)
——— Route of Pilgrims, 1620 (England to Plymouth)

3. Which of the following is a conclusion supported by information from the map?

(1) Spanish colonists settled in what we now call the southern United States in the late 1500s.
(2) English colonists founded Jamestown.
(3) French colonists established a settlement in what we now call Canada in the early 1600s.
(4) France, England, and Spain were major European colonizers of eastern North America.
(5) Portugal was the major European colonizer of the eastern part of South America.

Questions 4 through 6 refer to the following paragraphs and chart.

Throughout history, people from many countries have colonized and settled other areas. Such colonization and settlement are usually motivated by specific types of values. The chart below lists five of the most important categories of values that motivate colonization.

VALUES MOTIVATING COLONIZATION

economic—to gain wealth from a new area from its natural resources or through trade

religious—to practice one's religion freely or to spread one's own religion to other people

political—to make one's own country more powerful by gaining more land

scientific—to learn more about the world by exploring

social—to get away from one society's problems and to set up a better society

People from Spain, England, France, Holland, and Sweden came to North America for many different reasons. The situations described below show specific values that motivated colonization. For each situation, choose the category of values that is best illustrated.

4. Spain sent priests to the Americas to convert American Indians to the Catholic faith. Which type of value do the priests' actions illustrate?

(1) economic
(2) religious
(3) political
(4) scientific
(5) social

5. In 1607, a group of London merchants sent an expedition to Virginia to find gold and other resources. Which type of value do the merchants' actions illustrate?

(1) economic
(2) religious
(3) political
(4) scientific
(5) social

6. In the 1970s, many Americans left cities to settle in rural America, where they hoped for a more peaceful life. Which type of value do such goals illustrate?

(1) economic
(2) religious
(3) political
(4) scientific
(5) social

Questions 7 and 8 refer to the following passage.

Among the groups that settled in North America were the Quakers. Like others who disagreed with the Church of England, the Quakers in England were persecuted because of their religious beliefs. However, the Quakers had special luck. King Charles II owed money to William Penn, a prominent Quaker. The king paid Penn by giving him land in North America.

In 1682, a group of Quakers colonized Penn's land grant, which they named Pennsylvania. They treated the American Indians fairly and lived alongside them in peace. Unlike most other colonists, the Quakers tolerated people who were unlike themselves. They accepted Catholics and Jews in their colony and gave them a voice in the colony's government.

7. Which of the following was a cause of the Quakers coming to America?

(1) They founded Pennsylvania.
(2) They got along with American Indians.
(3) They wanted religious freedom.
(4) They wanted to get rich.
(5) They accepted Catholics and Jews.

8. Which detail best supports the conclusion that the Quakers were unusually lucky?

(1) They were able to move to America.
(2) Penn got land in repayment of a royal debt.
(3) They lived in peace with American Indians.
(4) Jews and Catholics lived in their colony.
(5) Most of the other colonists were intolerant.

Questions 9 through 11 refer to the following paragraph and cartoon.

After winning the French and Indian War in 1763, England decided to make its colonies pay the costs of their protection. One way it did this was by putting taxes, called excise taxes, on certain goods that the colonists purchased. Some colonists protested these taxes. In 1774, an artist drew this cartoon about the situation.

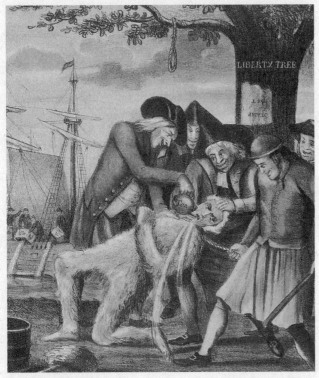

The Granger Collection, New York

9. What is the tax collector (excise man) doing in this cartoon?

   (1) collecting taxes from a group of colonists
   (2) forcing a colonist to pay his taxes
   (3) attacking a citizen of Boston
   (4) defending himself from a group of colonists
   (5) becoming intoxicated

10. Which detail best supports the conclusion that the cartoonist sympathizes with the tax collector (the excise man)?

   (1) The tax collector is frowning.
   (2) The tax collector is covered with feathers.
   (3) The Bostonians are surrounding him.
   (4) The Bostonians look like they are cruel.
   (5) The Bostonians are wearing dark hats.

11. Which value do you think the cartoonist wants to inspire?

   (1) trust in democracy
   (2) respect for the law
   (3) respect for the elderly
   (4) self-sufficiency
   (5) love of wealth

Questions 12 through 14 refer to the following paragraph.

During the Revolutionary War, the colonists were divided. Some, called patriots, were for independence. But others, called loyalists, supported the British king. It is estimated that fewer than half the colonists were patriots. The remainder either were loyalists or did not take sides during the war.

12. Which is an unstated assumption about the British that can be inferred from this information?

   (1) They were helped by some colonists.
   (2) They hired professional soldiers to fight.
   (3) They were defeated by the loyalists.
   (4) They punished loyalists they captured.
   (5) They did not take sides during the war.

13. Which statement is an unstated assumption the writer makes about the patriots?

   (1) They did not take sides during the war.
   (2) They fought against the British.
   (3) They aided the British but did not join them.
   (4) They fought on the side of the British.
   (5) They fought on the side of the loyalists.

14. What conclusion about the war is best supported by the information in the paragraph?

   (1) A majority of colonists supported the British.
   (2) A majority of colonists fought for independence.
   (3) A majority of colonists did not take sides.
   (4) The war brought a sense of unity to all the colonists.
   (5) The war caused deep divisions in America.

Unit 1: United States History

Questions 15 and 16 refer to the following paragraph.

The Articles of Confederation were replaced by the Constitution of the United States. The states' delegates who met in Philadelphia in 1787 agreed that the new nation needed a strong central government. The country faced many problems because of differences among the states. Some were larger; some were richer; and some permitted slavery, while others did not. To design a government agreeable to all the states, writers of the Constitution had to make many compromises. One difference they did not resolve, however, was slavery. If the Constitution had ended slavery, the necessary number of states probably would not have approved it.

15. Which statement gives the main idea of the paragraph?

(1) The Constitution was written by delegates from the individual states.
(2) Writers of the Constitution compromised to plan a government that all states would accept.
(3) The problem of slavery was not solved by the Constitution.
(4) The Constitution created a stronger central government than did the Articles of Confederation.
(5) The Constitution specified a better plan for government than did the Articles of Confederation.

16. Which issue did the delegates consider most threatening to national unity?

(1) taxation
(2) slavery
(3) international trade
(4) trade among the states
(5) starting a new type of government

TIP When deciding among answer choices, look at the passage to find evidence that your choice is correct.

17. Newspapers played an important role in getting the Constitution ratified, or approved. While many writers argued against the Constitution, Alexander Hamilton, James Madison, and John Jay wrote strong editorials in favor of the Constitution. These editorials convinced many people to support ratification of the Constitution. The writings became famous and were collected into a book called *The Federalist Papers*.

Which value does the publication of editorials for and against the Constitution most closely reflect?

(1) love of language
(2) desire for innovation
(3) desire for objectivity in the news
(4) respect for open debate
(5) wish for conformity

Question 18 refers to the following chart.

RATIFICATION OF THE CONSTITUTION		
State	Convention Vote	Month Ratified
Delaware	30–0	December 1787
Pennsylvania	46–23	December 1787
New Jersey	38–0	December 1787
Georgia	26–0	January 1788
Connecticut	128–40	January 1788
Massachusetts	187–168	February 1788
Maryland	63–11	April 1788
South Carolina	149–73	May 1788
New Hampshire	57–47	June 1788
Virginia	89–79	June 1788
New York	30–27	July 1788
North Carolina	194–77	November 1789
Rhode Island	34–32	May 1790

18. What can you conclude from the chart about the ratification of the Constitution?
(1) Delaware and Pennsylvania were first to ratify the Constitution.
(2) In New Jersey, all of the delegates voted in favor of the Constitution.
(3) The Constitution was approved in New York by only three votes.
(4) Ratification was difficult in the first five states but was easy in the last eight.
(5) Ratification was easy in the first five states but difficult in the last eight.

Questions 19 through 21 refer to the following paragraph and cartoon.

During the Civil War, President Abraham Lincoln was displeased with his generals. He said that General George McClellan, who built up the Union army, suffered from a case of "the slows." As a result, McClellan lost opportunities to defeat the Southern forces and win the war. Lincoln appointed McClellan overall commander twice and fired him each time. Other generals followed McClellan before Lincoln found an able leader in General Ulysses S. Grant. This cartoon appeared in a Confederate newspaper in 1863, before Grant took over the Union forces.

A CONFEDERATE POLITICAL CARTOON, 1863

MASTER ABRAHAM LINCOLN GETS A NEW TOY

19. What do the dolls on the shelves represent?

(1) the states of the Union
(2) the states of the Confederacy
(3) wounded Confederate soldiers
(4) wounded Union soldiers
(5) Union army generals

20. Who is depicted as a clown in the cartoon?

(1) the Union army commanding general
(2) the president of the Confederacy
(3) President Lincoln
(4) General McClellan
(5) General Grant

21. Based on the paragraph and the cartoon, which conclusion can you draw?

(1) The Union suffered unnecessary defeats early in the war.
(2) Union soldiers did not like McClellan.
(3) Confederate soldiers did not like their generals.
(4) McClellan was a better general than Grant.
(5) Lincoln later became unhappy with Grant.

Questions 22 and 23 refer to the following paragraph.

The end of the Civil War did not bring a quick solution to the problems of the former slaves. Although they were free, they had no place to go and few ways to make a living. Within months after the war, President Andrew Johnson and Congress started arguing over Reconstruction programs designed to combat these problems. Meanwhile, Southern state governments set up a labor system with a series of laws called Black Codes. Former slaves were required to sign one-year contracts just to get a job. If they quit during the year, they lost any wages they had earned and could be arrested for having no job. Punishment for unemployment included having their labor sold to a white employer for up to a year. Not until 1867 did the federal government gain control over Southern state governments and put an end to the Black Codes.

22. What was a purpose of the Black Codes?

(1) to help former slaves get jobs
(2) to help the rural economy of the North
(3) to bring the federal government to the South
(4) to help Reconstruction succeed
(5) to reinstate a labor system similar to slavery

23. Which value does the federal government's decision to end the Black Codes best reflect?

(1) a respect for local laws and customs
(2) a respect for religious freedom
(3) a love of learning
(4) a concern for justice
(5) a desire for compromise

Questions 24 through 26 refer to the following passage.

Lakota Sioux war chief Crazy Horse was one of the greatest American Indian leaders of the 1800s. Like the Sioux holy man Sitting Bull, he fiercely resisted white settlement in the mineral-rich Black Hills of the Dakotas, a sacred area to the Sioux. In 1876, Cheyenne and Lakota warriors led by Crazy Horse defeated Lt. Col. George Custer's troops at the Battle of Little Bighorn. After this defeat, the U.S. army stepped up its war against the Sioux. Crazy Horse and his starving band of about 1,000 were eventually forced to surrender. Crazy Horse was arrested in 1877 and a short time later was killed by a guard in a jailhouse scuffle.

Sitting Bull and his followers escaped to Canada. They held out until 1881 before starvation also forced them to surrender and live on a reservation. Sitting Bull spent the remaining years of his life resisting government attempts to force his people to live like whites. In 1890, he was killed as authorities attempted to arrest him on suspicion that he was urging American Indians to rebel.

24. In this passage, the writer assumes you know that Lakota is

    (1) a region in the Black Hills
    (2) a state in the United States
    (3) a city in western South Dakota
    (4) a part of the Sioux nation
    (5) another name for Cheyenne

25. Which sentence best states the main idea of this passage?

    (1) Crazy Horse and Sitting Bull were Sioux leaders.
    (2) Lack of food was a major problem for the Sioux in the 1870s.
    (3) Sitting Bull and Crazy Horse fought to preserve the lands and ways of their people.
    (4) Sitting Bull and Crazy Horse both died at the hands of the U.S. government.
    (5) The Sioux and Cheyenne won a major victory over the U.S. Army in 1876.

26. Based on the information in the passage, what did Sitting Bull consider most important?

    (1) education and training
    (2) reservation life
    (3) cooperation
    (4) authority
    (5) the Sioux ways of life

Questions 27 and 28 refer to the following table.

AVERAGE ANNUAL EARNINGS FOR SELECTED OCCUPATIONS—1890	
Farm laborers	$233
Public school teachers	256
Bituminous coal miners	406
Manufacturing employees	439
Street railway employees	557
Steam railroad employees	560
Gas & electricity workers	687
Ministers	794
Clerical workers in manufacturing & steam RR	848
Postal employees	878

27. What conclusion can be drawn from the table's information about street railway workers?

    (1) Some cities had mass transit by the 1890s.
    (2) Railroad employees rode on trains for free.
    (3) There were more street railway workers than teachers.
    (4) Street railway employees were the highest paid urban workers.
    (5) The street railway was replacing the steam railroad by 1890.

28. Based on the table, what was one probable cause of people moving from the rural United States to cities in 1890?

    (1) Railroads did not go into the country.
    (2) There was little need for farm laborers.
    (3) City jobs generally paid better wages.
    (4) Schoolteachers were needed in cities.
    (5) Many government jobs were available.

Questions 29 and 30 refer to the following passage.

One person who helped influence the development of industry in the South was born a slave in 1856. His name was Booker T. Washington. As a boy, Washington decided he wanted to learn to read. He taught himself the alphabet by studying the marked barrels at the salt furnace where he worked. Later, he managed to attend school. He had to take numerous jobs to support himself while he studied. He worked as a janitor at the school, as a servant for a local family, and even in a coal mine. He graduated with honors in 1875.

Washington is remembered for establishing Tuskegee Institute, a college for black students. Founded in Alabama in 1881, it was the first industrial-vocational college in the South. There, students received not only an academic education but also training in the skilled trades desired by industry. The idea worked so well that colleges for whites soon began to imitate the practice.

29. Based on the passage, what can you assume about the period when Tuskegee was founded?

(1) It was common for African Americans to attend college.
(2) African Americans were not generally admitted to colleges attended by white students.
(3) All Southern children went to school.
(4) The South had become highly industrialized.
(5) Skilled trades were commonly taught in colleges.

30. From the passage, which type of career can you conclude that graduates of Tuskegee Institute were most likely to take up?

(1) teaching in a high school
(2) training nurses
(3) running a small business
(4) skilled factory work
(5) college administration

Questions 31 and 32 refer to the following graph.

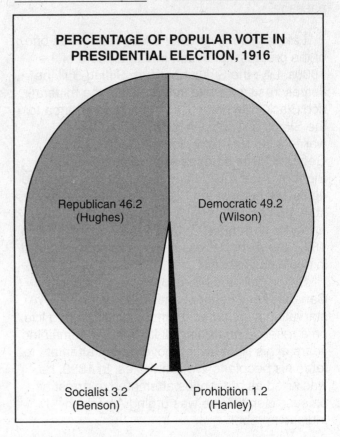

PERCENTAGE OF POPULAR VOTE IN PRESIDENTIAL ELECTION, 1916

Republican 46.2 (Hughes)

Democratic 49.2 (Wilson)

Socialist 3.2 (Benson)

Prohibition 1.2 (Hanley)

31. Which is the main idea of the graph?

(1) Hughes was the Republican Party candidate for president in 1916.
(2) Wilson was the Democratic Party candidate for president in 1916.
(3) The 1916 election was close, with Democrats winning over Republicans and two small parties.
(4) Wilson won the 1916 election by a landslide.
(5) Small political parties can greatly affect election outcomes even if they get few votes.

32. Which is a detail about the Prohibition and Socialist Parties confirmed by the graph?

(1) The Prohibition Party wanted to ban alcohol.
(2) The Socialist Party won 1.2% of the vote.
(3) The Prohibition Party won more votes.
(4) Both had supporters throughout the nation.
(5) Neither Party had very much support.

Questions 33 and 34 refer to the following information.

During the 1920s, the United States began to produce more iron, steel, cars, furniture, and other goods than the rest of the world combined. The prices of many goods fell, and millions of people were able to buy them. The incomes of businesspeople, doctors, lawyers, and salespeople rose. The average worker made about $25 or $30 a week, enough to afford home appliances such as electric vacuum cleaners, washing machines, and refrigerators. However, many New England workers lost their jobs when textile mills and shoe factories moved to the South during this period. Coal miners in Ohio and Pennsylvania also were hurt as people and industries began to switch from coal to oil and gas as sources of heat and power. Many farmers did poorly during this period as well. In 1919, a bushel of corn could buy five gallons of gasoline. By 1921, it paid for only a half gallon.

33. Which of the following details supports the conclusion that some Americans faced hard times during the 1920s?

(1) The incomes of salespeople and businesspeople rose.
(2) The production of goods increased.
(3) Workers' pay rose to $25 to $30 a week.
(4) A bushel of corn bought much less in 1921 than it did in 1919.
(5) Prices of manufactured goods decreased.

34. Which of the following conclusions is supported by the information in the passage?

(1) The 1920s was a decade of great conflict.
(2) The nation as a whole experienced poor economic times during the 1920s.
(3) Farming became an increasingly prosperous occupation in the 1920s.
(4) The average worker in the 1920s was poor.
(5) The prosperity of the 1920s was not shared by all Americans.

Questions 35 and 36 refer to the following passage.

In 1910, Japan took over the nearby Kingdom of Korea. However, at the end of World War II, Korea was freed from Japanese control and divided into two parts. North Korea became a communist nation. The government formed by South Korea opposed communism.

In 1950, North Korean forces invaded South Korea. When North Korea refused to withdraw, the United States and other members of the United Nations sent forces to South Korea. After pushing the invaders out of South Korea, the UN forces invaded and conquered much of North Korea. Then Communist China came to North Korea's aid. Chinese troops drove the UN forces back into South Korea.

After three years of fighting and negotiating, the war ended in July 1953. Korea remained divided along nearly the same border that existed before the war. In the years that followed, North Korea remained under communist control, while South Korea developed a democratic government.

35. What were the results of the Korean War?

(1) North Korea won the war and took over Korea.
(2) South Korea won the war and took over Korea.
(3) The United States won the war and took over Korea.
(4) Communist China won the war and took over Korea.
(5) The war ended in a stalemate and Korea remained divided.

36. Which of the following can you conclude from information in the passage?

(1) North and South Korea are one nation today.
(2) South Korea has a stronger economy than North Korea.
(3) South Korea was not a democracy before the Korean War.
(4) U.S. soldiers were superior to North Korean troops.
(5) The United States won the Korean War.

After World War II, Vietnam declared its independence from France. Because the independence movement was led by communists, the United States supported France in the war that followed. The United States provided supplies and equipment to the French forces fighting in Vietnam.

In 1954, the French gave up, and Vietnam was split in two. A communist government controlled North Vietnam. The United States supported the anticommunist government set up in South Vietnam. But South Vietnam's government was corrupt and oppressive. So communists and other South Vietnamese tried to overthrow it. The United States sent equipment and military advisers to help South Vietnam's army combat this rebellion. North Vietnam aided the rebels, who were called the Vietcong.

During the 1960s, the United States increased its involvement in Vietnam. The few hundred military advisers of the 1950s grew to more than 500,000 combat troops by 1968. U.S. casualties were high. For the first time, Americans were able to watch a war in progress on television. Some viewers developed doubts about the wisdom of the war. Differences of opinion about the Vietnam War sharply divided the American people, causing great tension in the society.

37. According to the passage, why did the United States support the French in Vietnam?

    (1) The French were fighting the communists.
    (2) The French were fighting the anticommunists.
    (3) The French were fighting for independence.
    (4) The French wanted to divide Vietnam.
    (5) The French needed more soldiers.

38. From the passage, what can you conclude about the Vietnam War?

    (1) The U.S. bombed North Vietnam.
    (2) Few Americans died in the war.
    (3) U.S. involvement increased gradually.
    (4) Americans at home knew little about the war.
    (5) Most Americans approved of the war.

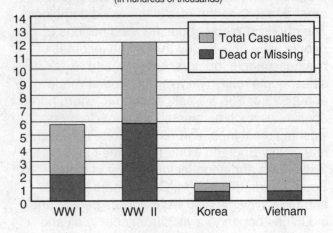

CASUALTIES IN WARS DURING THE 20TH CENTURY
(in hundreds of thousands)

39. How many more Americans were killed or missing in World War II than in World War I?

    (1) about 4,000
    (2) about 6,000
    (3) about 200,000
    (4) about 400,000
    (5) about 600,000

40. Which war had the lowest proportion of dead or missing to total casualties?

    (1) World War I
    (2) World War II
    (3) the Korean War
    (4) the Vietnam War
    (5) The information cannot be determined from the graph.

41. What conclusion can you draw based on the graph?

    (1) Few Americans lost their lives in World War I.
    (2) Few French lost their lives in World War I.
    (3) World War II was the most costly U.S. war of the twentieth century in terms of human lives.
    (4) The Korean War and Vietnam War happened recently.
    (5) The U.S. was victorious in World Wars I and II, but not in Korea or Vietnam.

Answers start on page 291.

Cumulative Review Performance Analysis
Unit 1 ● U.S. History

Use the Answers and Explanations on page 291 to check your answers to the Unit 1 Cumulative Review. Then use the chart to figure out the skill areas in which you need more practice.

On the chart, circle the questions that you answered correctly. Write the number correct for each skill area. Add the number of questions that you got correct on the Cumulative Review. If you feel that you need more practice, go back and review the lessons for the skill areas that were difficult for you.

Question	Number Correct	Skill Area	Lessons for Review
1, **9**, 15, 16 **19, 20**, 25, **31**, 35 37, **39, 40**	___/12	Comprehension	1, 2
2, **3**, 7, 8 **10**, 12, 13, 14 **18, 21**, 22, 24, **27** **28**, 29, 30, **32**, 33, 34, 36, 38, **41**	___/22	Analysis	3, 4, 6
4, 5, 6, 11 17, 23, 26	___/8	Evaluation	5
TOTAL CORRECT	___/42		

Question numbers in **boldface** are based on graphics.

UNIT 2

World History

At midnight on November 9, 1989, thousands of Germans stormed the wall that separated East and West Berlin. East Berliners tore at the Berlin Wall, venting their rage at decades of oppression. At the same time, West Berliners pounded out the tensions that had resulted from fear that they too might someday lose their freedom. By morning, the world's most notorious reminder that millions of people lacked basic human rights was coming down.

The record of world history is an ongoing struggle between some groups' efforts to control others—and of the unquenchable desire of people for freedom. Studying world history helps us understand and value the progress and remaining challenges that exist in today's world. World History is also an important part of the GED Social Studies Test, making up 15 percent of the test questions.

As TV cameras recorded the historic event, the destruction of the Berlin Wall marked the end of the Cold War and the threat of world communism.

The lessons in this unit include:

Lesson 7:   **Ancient Empires of the World**
The first civilizations developed in river valleys. Some established great empires. Others were eventually conquered by civilizations superior to their own. Internal problems caused still others to fall.

Lesson 8:   **How Nations Arose**
The desire of ethnic groups to rule themselves is as old as history. This drive is the basis for modern-day nations, as well as a cause of unrest in some regions.

Lesson 9:   **Global Expansion**
The quest for more territory, wealth, and power has been a major force in shaping world history. In the process, ideas once unique to specific regions have spread throughout the world.

Lesson 10:   **The Post-Cold War World**
The end of the Cold War raised hopes for a new world order in which people could be free of threats to their security. However, events in the 1990s demonstrated that the world still faced many challenges to peace and freedom.

> ## THINKING SKILLS
> O Identifying implications
> O Assessing the appropriateness of information
> O Analyzing cause and effect
> O Recognizing unstated assumptions (in political cartoons)

GED SKILL Identifying Implications

implication
something that is not openly stated but is hinted at or suggested

Most spoken and written information is presented to you directly. However, sometimes information is only hinted at, or implied. When an author implies something, he or she is making an **implication.** To get the most out of the information you receive, you must understand not only the stated information, but also its implications.

Identifying implications is an important skill for reading and understanding the social studies material you will encounter on the GED Test. This skill may seem difficult, but actually you identify implications every day. For example, suppose your boss tells you to be extra helpful in your dealings with a particular customer. Even though your boss does not tell you why you should be helpful, you will probably understand her implication that this is an important customer.

To identify implications in what you read, you must first identify the facts and any conclusions that the author has stated directly. Then see if any other conclusions that are not directly stated can be drawn from the material. Also, look for phrases that suggest emotions or attitudes. For example, if the author writes that someone gritted his teeth before making a decision, the author's implication is that the decision was unpleasant or difficult.

Read the passage and answer the question below.

The ancient Egyptians believed that their souls could live forever if their bodies were preserved. For this reason, they developed methods of embalming, or mummifying, the dead. Egyptians mummified animals as well as humans. Some Egyptians prayed to a cat-headed goddess named Bast and worshipped at her shrines. Merchants near the shrines raised cats and made them into mummies. Then they sold these mummies to worshipers, who made offerings of them at the shrines. A cemetery near one shrine contained thousands of cat mummies. Another site, near a shrine to a different god, contains the mummified remains of four million birds.

Put a check mark next to the sentence that states an implication the author makes in the passage.

_____ a. The ancient Egyptians kept cats as household pets.

_____ b. Mummification was an important part of ancient Egyptian religion.

You were correct if you chose *option b*. The author clearly suggests that mummification was an important religious practice. However, the facts the author presents in the passage do not support *option a*.

Read between the lines to identify implications. Remember that what is suggested but is not stated can be as important as what is stated.

Use the passage and the map to complete the exercise below.

The Nile River runs for more than 4,000 miles from the interior of Africa to the Mediterranean Sea. There are six great rapids along the Nile's length. The ancient Egyptians settled along the 750 miles of river between the sea and the first of these rapids. Each year, from June to October, rain fell near the river's source, causing it to flood the Nile Valley. Farmers harvested their crops before the flood began. When the river receded, it left a layer of silt to provide new, fertile soil. To increase production and prosperity, the Egyptians built canals to carry and store floodwater to sustain their crops.

The need to manage this network of canals led to the emergence of local rulers and eventually to a **state** under a single ruler, called a **pharaoh.** The pharaoh claimed divine descent from the gods. Egyptians counted on the pharaoh for the flood they believed to be a gift from the gods. A pharaoh could be overthrown if insufficient flooding resulted in widespread hardship and starvation.

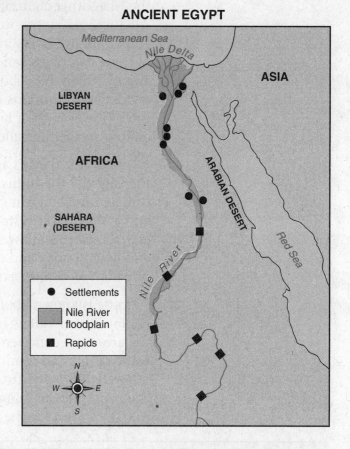

ANCIENT EGYPT

1. Write *D* next to the fact the writer states directly and *I* next to the fact that is implied by the writer.

    _____ a. The Nile Valley's floods were caused by rains falling near the Nile River's source.

    _____ b. A pharaoh's popularity and power depended on the flooding of the Nile.

2. Write an *I* next to each statement that is implied by the map.

    _____ a. Most Egyptians lived along the Nile River.

    _____ b. Most of ancient Egypt was desert.

    _____ c. The Nile floodplain extended along most of the Nile River.

3. Write an *I* next to each fact that is implied by both the map and the passage.

    _____ a. The Egyptians built canals to make better use of the floodwaters.

    _____ b. The Arabian Desert lay east of the Nile River.

    _____ c. Ancient Egyptian civilization centered along the Nile.

Answers start on page 294.

At about the same time the ancient Egyptians were farming along the Nile, other civilizations were developing near other rivers. About 7,000 years ago, the Sumerians farmed the valley between the Tigris and Euphrates rivers in present-day Iraq. Unlike the Nile, the flooding of these two rivers was unpredictable, and the Sumerians fought among themselves about rights to the water. They formed various regional governments called **city-states,** each headed by a different ruler. However, their lack of unity ultimately made their advanced culture and fertile valley attractive to invaders.

About 4,500 years ago another advanced civilization emerged in the valley of the Indus River, in what is now Pakistan. The civilization centered in two great cities, each with wide streets, a water system, and a brick sewer system for private homes. Irrigation and flood control systems allowed farmers in the nearby countryside to raise enough livestock and crops to feed each city's 40,000 residents, many of whom were merchants and craftspeople.

Little is known about early civilization in China's Huang He (Yellow River) Valley. However, about 3,500 years ago, the people of the area were conquered by invaders who swept into the region in war chariots and founded the Shang **dynasty.** As China's first ruling family, the Shang introduced flood control and irrigation systems to the people of the valley. Control of these systems allowed them to rule the region for the next 500 years.

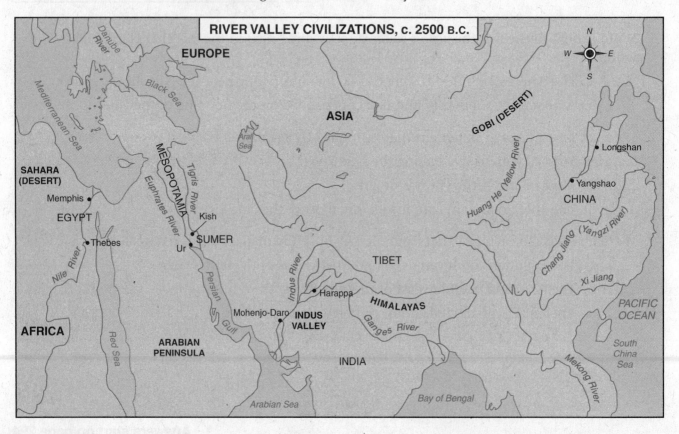

RIVER VALLEY CIVILIZATIONS, c. 2500 B.C.

Directions: Choose the one best answer to each question.

Questions 1 through 6 refer to the passage and the map on page 98.

1. What implication is suggested in the second sentence of paragraph three of the passage?

   (1) The invaders conquered the people who were living in the region.
   (2) War chariots gave the invaders an advantage over the people living in the region.
   (3) The Shang established a dynasty.
   (4) The invaders were a people called the Shang.
   (5) The Shang were a Chinese people from another region of China.

2. What conclusion is implied in the first paragraph of the passage?

   (1) The ancient Egyptians and the Sumerians began to farm at about the same time.
   (2) City-states were the Sumerians' form of government.
   (3) The Sumerians fought over water because floods were unpredictable and water was scarce.
   (4) Sumeria was attractive to invaders in part because the land was fertile.
   (5) The Sumerian city-states did not practice democracy.

3. What implication does the map suggest about ancient civilizations?

   (1) All the civilizations on the map existed at the same time.
   (2) The civilizations on the map were all farming societies.
   (3) Most of the people in ancient civilizations were farmers.
   (4) No other peoples existed in 2500 B.C. in the area shown on this map.
   (5) River valleys were critical to the development of early civilizations.

4. What can you conclude from paragraph two of the passage and the information on the map?

   (1) The people of the Indus valley migrated from the Himalayas.
   (2) Mohenjo-Daro and Harappa had water and sewer systems.
   (3) Most of the people in the Indus valley lived in Mohenjo-Daro and Harappa.
   (4) Most of the people of the Indus Valley worked in trade or industry.
   (5) Most of the people of the Indus Valley were farmers.

5. Based on the information presented on page 98, what would you expect of early advanced civilizations in the Americas?

   (1) Some of the population were city dwellers.
   (2) The rulers were hereditary kings.
   (3) Religion was important in early American cultures.
   (4) Their technology included use of the wheel.
   (5) Their dwellings were made of bricks.

6. Which of the following general conclusions about the world's earliest civilizations is suggested by the passage and the map?

   (1) A reliable source of water was not important to the development of advanced civilizations.
   (2) Establishing agriculture was an important early step in developing an advanced culture.
   (3) Early peoples made little use of science and technology to advance their civilizations.
   (4) The most advanced peoples lived under strong democratic governments.
   (5) Advanced peoples usually could not be conquered, even by enemies who were stronger or more united.

Answers start on page 294.

GED Practice • Lesson 7

Directions: Choose the one best answer to each question.

Questions 1 through 3 refer to the following passage and chart.

In about 800 B.C., organized society developed on the Greek peninsula when **clans** and **tribes** established hundreds of city-states. At first, each city-state was ruled by a tribal chief or king. By about 700 B.C., most of these rulers had been overthrown by wealthy landowners. The Greeks referred to these new governments as *aristokratika,* or **aristocracies,** meaning "rule by the best." Eventually, some aristocracies were replaced by governments in which the common people, or *demos,* had a voice in the city-state's rule. These governments were called democracies. The greatest democracy was Athens which became the centerpiece of what is called Greece's Golden Age around 400 B.C.

Although it lasted less than a hundred years, Greece's Golden Age was a time of great achievement in science, the arts, and ways of thinking about the world. Wars and the various rivalries among the city-states gradually wore down Athens' cultural leadership, but the accomplishments of that short period affected Greek civilization and the entire world for centuries to come.

Science and Thought	Art and Drama
Socrates (470 B.C.–399 B.C.): developed methods of seeking truth and knowledge that became the basis of modern education	**Aeschylus** (525 B.C.–456 B.C.): wrote the world's first dramas, or plays that contain action and dialogue
Hippocrates (460 B.C.–377 B.C.): founded medicine by teaching that diseases had natural causes and were not punishment of the gods	**Euripedes** (484 B.C.–406 B.C.): wrote the first dramas to focus on ordinary people and social issues rather than on actions of the gods
Democritus (460 B.C.–370 B.C.): developed the idea that the universe is made up of tiny particles of matter that he called atoms	**Myron** (480 B.C.–440 B.C.): sculpted *The Discus Thrower,* one of the most famous examples of ancient Greek art

1. Which of the following is implied by the passage?

   (1) Greek culture drew heavily on Egyptian civilization.
   (2) The English word *democracy* comes from the Greek term meaning "the people."
   (3) The Greek city-states were very large.
   (4) An aristocracy is a better form of government than a democracy.
   (5) Warfare encourages cultural growth.

2. What conclusion can be drawn from the chart?

   (1) The greatest playwrights came from Athens.
   (2) Myron was executed because of his art.
   (3) Socrates inspired Hippocrates' teachings.
   (4) Socrates influenced the writing of Euripedes.
   (5) The early Greeks influenced modern science.

3. What reason does the passage imply for Athens' cultural leadership in the Golden Age?

   (1) its military victory over Sparta
   (2) its desire to influence the rest of the world
   (3) its democratic form of government
   (4) the rivalries that existed among city-states
   (5) the contributions of Aeschylus and Myron

TIP To identify and understand a writer's implications, look for clues in word and sentence order that imply important ideas and connections.

As Greece was entering its Golden Age, a new power was rising on the Italian peninsula to the west. In 509 B.C., the Latin people of Rome overthrew the Etruscan kings who ruled them. They set up a **republic** in which the city's citizens elected representatives to govern them. However, an aristocracy of certain clans quickly gained control of the elected offices.

Roman laws were not written down, so it was easy for elected officials to interpret them in ways that kept their clans in power. Citizens of Rome soon demanded change. Around 450 B.C., Roman law was put in writing and became more democratic. For example, all citizens gained the right to hold public office. Citizens who owned property were also required to serve in the Roman army.

Democracy spread as Rome extended its power. By 272 B.C., Rome controlled all of Italy. The peninsula's conquered peoples all became citizens of the Roman Republic.

Moving beyond Italy, Rome invaded and defeated the powerful city of Carthage in 202 B.C. and gained control of North Africa. Next, Roman armies moved west into Spain. They also marched east, conquering Greece and its colonies in present-day Turkey. By 133 B.C., Rome's supremacy in the Mediterranean was complete.

The Romans did not grant citizenship or democratic government to peoples outside Italy. Instead, the conquered peoples were ruled by an official appointed by Rome and backed by a Roman army of occupation. These subject peoples were forced to pay high taxes to their Roman masters. Some, like the citizens of Carthage, were even enslaved by the Romans.

Government of the Roman Republic

Senate

Citizens elected upper-class Romans to a 300-member Senate, which passed laws, set foreign policy, and controlled government funds.

Popular Assemblies

Assemblies of citizens voted on laws and elected officials called tribunes. Tribunes could block acts of the Senate that were not in the public interest.

Consuls

Two elected consuls ran the government. Each consul had the power to **veto** (the Latin word meaning "I forbid") the actions of the other.

Praetors

These elected officials oversaw the legal system and interpreted questions about the law.

Censors

These officials registered citizens according to their wealth, selected candidates for the Senate, and oversaw the moral conduct of all Romans.

---

4. What implication does the passage make about Carthage?

   (1) It was located in North Africa.
   (2) It was defeated by Rome's armies.
   (3) It was more democratic than Rome.
   (4) Its conquest gave Rome supremacy in the Mediterranean region.
   (5) Its citizens became citizens of Rome.

5. Which officials of the United States government are most like the Roman praetors?

   (1) the President, who can veto acts of Congress
   (2) the senators and Congressional representatives, who pass the nation's laws
   (3) the members of the state legislatures, who pass the laws for each state
   (4) the justices of the Supreme Court, who determine if laws agree with the Constitution
   (5) the governors, who head the 50 states

6. What does the information suggest that the ancient Romans valued most?

   (1) wealth and trade
   (2) political and military power
   (3) freedom and equality for all peoples
   (4) equal rights for women
   (5) Greek art and culture

Answers start on page 295.

Directions: This is a ten-minute practice test. After ten minutes, mark the last question you finished. Then complete the test and check your answers. If most of your answers were correct, but you didn't finish, try to work faster next time. Choose the one best answer to each question.

Questions 1 through 4 refer to the following passage.

As Egypt's power began to decline after 1000 B.C., the kingdom of Kush arose to the south, in what is now Sudan. Egypt had long dominated the Nubians, black African people of Kush who lived along the southern Nile. Like the Egyptians, Nubians also built pyramids, worshipped Egypt's gods, farmed, and raised cattle.

By the early 700s B.C., Kush was powerful enough to conquer Egypt and rule it for a brief period. However, the high point in Kush history occurred between 250 B.C. and A.D. 150, when Kush became a great trade center. This brought Roman, Greek, Persian, Indian, and Chinese influences into Kush.

South of the Sahara and away from the Nile, some small-scale farming and cattle herding existed in the Sahel, a region of dry grasslands. But a lack of good forest-clearing tools slowed the development of farming in the rest of Africa's interior. In addition, the deadly tsetse fly made it difficult to raise cattle, oxen, mules, and other livestock in some areas.

One exception was the Nok society that existed between 500 B.C. and A.D. 200 in what is now northern Nigeria. This West African people raised crops and cattle and were the first known manufacturers of iron products south of the Sahara. Their civilization was also known for its clay sculptures of animals in natural poses. Ancient Nok art influenced much of the art for which West Africa later became famous.

1. What does the passage imply about the history of ancient Egypt?

   (1) Egypt's power declined after 1000 B.C.
   (2) Egypt influenced the Nok culture.
   (3) Farming and cattle herding did not take place in Egypt.
   (4) Some rulers of Egypt were black.
   (5) Egypt did not trade with Greece or Rome.

2. What does the information in the passage imply about the Nok culture?

   (1) The Nok were farmers and herders.
   (2) The Nok culture is older than Kush.
   (3) The Nok were more advanced than other peoples in West Africa.
   (4) The Nubians influenced the development of the Nok culture.
   (5) The Nok worshipped many gods.

3. What does the passage imply about the interior of Africa 2000 years ago?

   (1) It was a center of manufacturing and trade.
   (2) It was desert, and nothing grew there.
   (3) It was completely unsettled, and no people traveled there.
   (4) It was mostly grassland, and there were many farmers and herders.
   (5) It was heavily forested in most areas, but there were some farmers and herders.

4. From the 1500s to the 1800s, European nations gradually conquered the peoples of Africa and established colonies there. However, Europeans' control over some parts of Africa was slowed because they could not use animals for transportation in those regions.

Based on what you read in this and the previous passage, why do you think Europeans encountered this difficulty?

   (1) The peoples of those regions were more advanced than were other Africans.
   (2) Those regions were the home of the tsetse fly.
   (3) There were forests in those regions.
   (4) Herding and farming did not exist in those regions.
   (5) The Nok and Kush people were good fighters and had powerful armies.

Questions 5 through 7 refer to the following passage and map.

In South America, advanced civilizations first appeared along the coast of what is now Peru. The Nazca people farmed the region as early as 3000 B.C., and by 1800 B.C. they were working with metals and building large temples. A later people, the Moche, created an elaborate system of canals to irrigate their fields and raised llamas and guinea pigs for meat. By A.D. 400, the Moche kingdom extended 400 miles along the coast, linked by roads that the Inca would use about a thousand years later to rule their own empire in the same region.

Between 1800 B.C. and A.D. 900, the Maya developed a civilization across much of Central America that rivaled the ancient Mediterranean cultures. Like the early Greeks, the Maya lived in independent city-states. They cleared the forest outside each city and raised crops to feed the city's population. Some of these cities were very large. Tikal in present-day Guatemala covered 50 square miles and had a population of 75,000–100,000 in A.D. 400.

Trade was also important to the Maya. Even without pack animals or knowledge of the wheel, they carried trade goods great distances on their backs. One of Tikal's trading partners was Teotihuacán, a thousand miles away in central Mexico. With a population as high as 200,000, Teotihuacán was the largest city in ancient America.

For reasons that are still unclear, Teotihuacán, like the Mayan civilization, was gone by A.D. 900. However, around 1200, a new people, the Aztec, built a new civilization near the ruins of the great abandoned city.

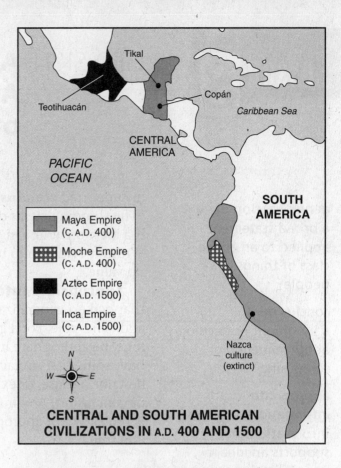

CENTRAL AND SOUTH AMERICAN CIVILIZATIONS IN A.D. 400 AND 1500

5. Based on the passage, which of the following is a similarity between the Nazca, Moche, and Mayan civilizations?

(1) They each formed city-states and lived in cities.
(2) Extensive road systems existed in each empire.
(3) Farming was important in each culture.
(4) They all arose in South America.
(5) They each declined and disappeared for reasons that are not clear.

6. Which of the following is supported by evidence presented on the map?

(1) The cities of Teotihuacán, Tikal, and Copán traded with each other.
(2) The Aztec and Inca empires existed at the same time.
(3) The Inca made use of Moche roads to conquer Copán.
(4) The Aztec built their empire on Tikal's ruins.
(5) The Aztec were active in Central America before the Maya.

7. Which of the following does Moche road-building suggest was important in the Moche culture?

(1) self-government
(2) cities
(3) learning
(4) religion
(5) trade

Answers start on page 295.

GED SKILL Assessing the Appropriateness of Information

generalization
a broad statement applied to an entire class of things or people

conclusion
a judgment or decision about someone or something

appropriate information
information that supports an idea, a generalization, or a conclusion

People often make unsupported **generalizations** and reach unsupported **conclusions.** You probably hear them all the time: "The shipping clerks don't work as hard as the sales clerks." "There is a lot more crime in this neighborhood than there used to be." Without evidence to back them up, these statements have little or no value.

Appropriate information consists of facts and other details that make a generalization or conclusion true, understandable, and believable. For a generalization or conclusion to be useful, there must be appropriate information to support it. The information must have some basis in fact. It should illustrate or provide an example, describe a cause, or explain the reasoning behind the generalization or conclusion. Any information that fails to do one of these things is probably not appropriate information, even if it is interesting and true.

Read the passage and complete the exercise below.

Today we think of a **nation** as the land where people live under the rule of a single government. For much of history, however, a nation was defined by culture rather than by boundaries or politics. All people who shared a language and **ethnic** background were a nation, even if they were governed by different rulers. The Tang emperors of China in the 700s supported Buddhism and encouraged Chinese arts. The Franks were a nation in the 500s, a thousand years before the Bourbon kings united them to form the political nation of France. Indeed, the goal of turning a cultural nation into a political nation has been a major force in world history.

TIP

To determine if information is appropriate to other material, first determine the central idea, generalization, or conclusion presented in the material.

Put a check mark next to the information that supports the conclusion that a nation is a people, not a geographic area with set boundaries.

_____ a. The Franks were a nation in the 500s, a thousand years before the Bourbon kings united them to form the political nation of France.

_____ b. The Tang emperors of China in the 700s supported Buddhism and encouraged Chinese arts.

You were correct if you chose *option a*. The passage is about the difference between the historic and modern definitions of the word *nation. Option a* illustrates this difference. The information in *option b* does not help you understand what a nation is.

Use the information to complete the exercise below.

After the collapse of the Roman Empire around 500 A.D., Europe entered a thousand-year period known as the **Middle Ages.** Western Europe gradually became a region of small **kingdoms.** Unlike the rulers of Rome, kings in Europe had no armies. Needing to protect their land, each king gave parts of it to powerful **nobles** in return for military support. These nobles then turned over part of their land to mounted warriors called **knights** for the same pledge of support and service. This system of land in exchange for support is called **feudalism.**

A king or noble granting land was called a **lord.** The noble or knight who received the land became that lord's **vassal.** A person could be both a lord and a vassal at the same time.

To ensure that a vassal could afford to carry out his duties, the lord's grant also included rights to the people who lived on the land. These peasants, called **serfs,** could not leave the land without their lord's permission. The serfs did the day-to-day work of the estate. They farmed the land, tended the livestock, and provided the food for the lord's table. Serfs also served as foot soldiers when their lord provided military aid to his lord. In Russia, the serfs were not freed until 1861.

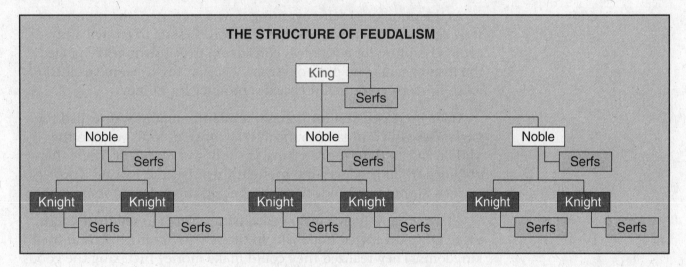

THE STRUCTURE OF FEUDALISM

Write *S* next to each statement that supports or illustrates the explanation of how feudalism works, and *N* next to each statement that is not appropriate information.

_____ 1. This system of land in exchange for support is called feudalism.

_____ 2. The serfs performed the day-to-day work of the estate.

_____ 3. Serfs farmed the land, tended the livestock, and provided the food for the lord's table.

_____ 4. In Russia, the serfs were not freed until 1861.

5. Does the diagram support the passage's generalizations about feudalism? Explain.

_____

_____

Answers start on page 296.

After the fall of the Roman Empire, trade in western Europe nearly disappeared. Feudalism encouraged self-sufficiency. Serfs grew or made nearly everything an estate needed. In addition, frequent warfare among rival kingdoms and nobles made travel, and therefore trade, dangerous. However, these conditions began to change after 1000 A.D. Political and religious leaders gained some control over the violence that plagued the early Middle Ages. Also, agricultural advances increased the food supply, causing Europe's population to increase. People began to form towns on the feudal estates.

Because towns were on a lord's property, they were under his control. Eventually, the townspeople wanted to run their towns themselves. Some towns won their independence by rebelling against the lord; others were granted political freedom to encourage development as trade centers. The lords had become interested in trade because of the Asian goods that Italian merchants began selling in Europe in the 900s.

As the number of self-governing towns increased, the number of serfs declined. A serf who escaped the lord's estate to a town and avoided capture for a year was considered free. Towns also changed the lives of serfs who did not escape. Because townspeople needed food, the serfs could sell their extra produce for money.

Trade increased still further as a result of religious wars called the **Crusades** which began around 1100. Christian lords went to the Middle East to fight the Muslims, the followers of Islam. There they obtained Asian products and brought them back to Europe. They also learned fighting methods that later helped them defend their castles.

As trade grew, merchants needed better places to sell their goods. Some kings organized trade fairs in the self-governing towns in their kingdoms. They realized they could make money by taxing the goods that were sold. In return, the kings protected the merchants from theft, assault, or arrest. Merchants gladly paid the taxes, preferring the freedom and security of the self-governing towns to doing business in villages controlled by feudal lords.

Taxes on trade benefited kings in many ways. Most importantly these taxes gave kings the money to have their own armies. A king could launch wars without having to depend on his vassals (the nobles) to help him. He also could use his army to bring his vassals under tighter control.

As kings gradually established their authority over powerful nobles, feudalism declined and nations began to be formed. For example, in 1000, what is now France was divided into provinces ruled by feudal lords. Over the next 300 years, the kings gained increasing power over the lords and the provinces they held.

Directions: Choose the one best answer to each question.

Questions 1 through 4 refer to the passage on page 106 and the maps below.

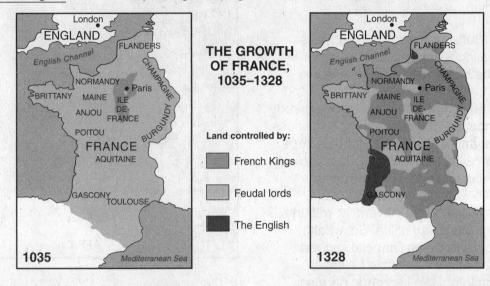

THE GROWTH OF FRANCE, 1035–1328

Land controlled by:
- French Kings
- Feudal lords
- The English

1. Which information from the passage supports the generalization that trade thrives when governments are stable and suffers when they are not?

   (1) After the fall of the Roman Empire, trade in western Europe nearly disappeared.
   (2) Townspeople wanted to run their towns themselves.
   (3) Merchants preferred doing business with kings.
   (4) As trade grew, merchants needed better places to sell their goods.
   (5) Kings used the money from taxing trade to raise armies and make war on other kings.

2. According to the passage, what reason would most likely have caused lords to encourage the development of towns as trade centers?

   (1) Feudalism encouraged self-sufficiency.
   (2) Some kings organized trade fairs in towns.
   (3) The number of serfs declined as they escaped and gained their freedom.
   (4) Lords were interested in the valuable Asian trade goods being sold throughout Europe.
   (5) Leaders helped stop some of the violence common during the early Middle Ages.

3. Does the information in the maps support the last paragraph's generalization about how nations were formed?

   (1) Yes, the maps illustrate the spread of towns in France.
   (2) Yes, the maps illustrate French kings gaining control over French nobles.
   (3) No, the maps do not identify the important early kings of France.
   (4) No, the maps show only how trade developed in France.
   (5) No, the maps show the decline of English influence in France.

4. Which generalization is supported by the details in this passage?

   (1) The fall of the Roman Empire caused trade in Europe nearly to disappear.
   (2) Feudalism encouraged the growth of nations.
   (3) Modern nations began because of trade disputes between Europe and the Middle East.
   (4) Taxes were never levied before kings began to tax the sale of trade goods.
   (5) The growth of trade helped nations form by increasing the power of kings.

Answers start on page 296.

Directions: Choose the one best answer to each question.

Questions 1 through 5 refer to the following passage and map.

During the 1300s, many Italian merchants became rich selling Asian goods in Europe. In the leisure their new wealth made possible, the merchants became interested in the art and culture of their ancestors. Their curiosity inspired the **Renaissance,** a 300-year period of advances in art, literature, and science throughout Europe. Italian scholars called humanists studied ancient Greek and Roman writings. They applied the ideas from these writings to their own world.

Humanism taught that involvement with the arts was an important part of life. So, wealthy merchants began providing financial support to artists. This help made it possible for Italian painters and sculptors like Leonardo da Vinci and Michelangelo to create masterpieces.

Literature and learning were encouraged when German printer Johann Gutenberg perfected his printing press in 1455. Because the printing press made books easier to produce, they increased in number. This development helped the ideas of the Renaissance spread across Europe.

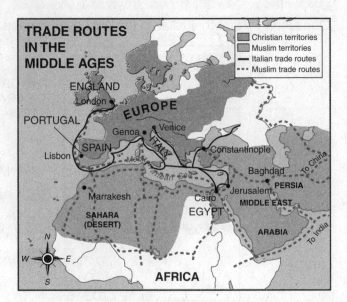

1. Which is an unstated assumption suggested by the first paragraph of the passage?

   (1) Most Italians were scholars.
   (2) Trade made merchants in Italy rich.
   (3) Ancient Romans were the Italians' ancestors.
   (4) Leonardo da Vinci and Michelangelo were Renaissance artists.
   (5) The merchants of Italy came from Asia.

2. What does the information in the first paragraph imply?

   (1) The Renaissance started in Italy.
   (2) The humanists were merchants.
   (3) The ancient Greeks and Romans produced little useful knowledge.
   (4) The Renaissance lasted about 300 years.
   (5) Trade was important to ancient Romans.

3. How does information in the last paragraph help in understanding the Renaissance?

   (1) It describes the cause of the Renaissance.
   (2) It states that the printing press was invented during the Renaissance.
   (3) It defines what the Renaissance was.
   (4) It tells why books were invented.
   (5) It explains how the Renaissance spread.

4. Which assumption can be made based on information in the passage and the map?

   (1) Italy dominated world trade.
   (2) Venice became a Renaissance center.
   (3) Muslim and Italian traders clashed.
   (4) Naples was unimportant in the Renaissance.
   (5) Florence was not a Renaissance center.

5. Which modern-day event has had an effect most like that of the printing press in the 1400s?

   (1) the popularity of cartoon art
   (2) the invention of the video tape recorder
   (3) the creation of the Internet
   (4) the growing number of shopping malls
   (5) the performance of Renaissance music

Questions 6 and 7 refer to the following passage.

In the mid-600s, Muslim traders spread their religion, Islam, beyond their homelands in the Middle East. By 750, Muslim influence had stretched across North Africa into Spain and east into India. Where Muslims gained control, science, learning, and the arts became important.

Arabs held the greatest power in the Muslim world for about 500 years. Between 1000 and 1100, however, the Turks swept out of Central Asia, conquered much of the Middle East, and converted to Islam. Eventually, leadership of the Muslim world passed to the Turks.

Around 1400, a group of Turks called Ottomans invaded Europe. By 1450, the Ottoman Empire included most of Greece and present-day Bulgaria. By 1550, the Ottomans had gained control over most of eastern Europe, the Middle East, and North Africa.

6. What is the best title for this passage?

   (1) The Influence of Religion in the Middle Ages
   (2) The Growth and Spread of Islam, 650–1550
   (3) Arab Domination in the Middle Ages
   (4) Ottoman Domination in the Middle Ages
   (5) Muslim Domination of North Africa

7. Which conclusion about the Ottoman Empire is supported by the information in the passage?

   (1) The Turks persecuted the Arabs.
   (2) The Muslims in Spain were Ottomans.
   (3) The Turks ended the Renaissance in Europe.
   (4) The arts flourished in the Ottoman Empire.
   (5) The Muslims persecuted the Christians.

TIP One way to decide if information supports a conclusion is to look for cause-and-effect relationships. Information that shows a cause of the conclusion is appropriate support for the conclusion.

Questions 8 and 9 refer to the following passage.

Beginning in the mid-800s, a series of powerful clans gained control of Japan's government. The emperor remained the symbolic ruler, but the currently dominant clan's members held all the important government jobs. The family member who headed the clan was the true head of Japan's government.

The Fujiwara family controlled the government from 857 to 1160. When two other clans challenged its power, a long civil war broke out. In 1192, the emperor named the head of the victorious clan **shogun,** or military ruler of Japan. Shogun was a hereditary title, but when a shogun died, a power struggle usually followed. Because of these rivalries, the government's authority seldom extended very far beyond the shogun's home city.

From the 1400s to the early 1600s, the real power in Japan was held by wealthy landowners called **daimyos.** Each daimyo hired professional warriors called **samurai** to protect his lands and the peasants who worked in his fields. When Tokugawa Ieyasu became shogun in 1600, the government began to re-establish control over the daimyos. Tokugawa shoguns ruled for more than 250 years. By 1868, when the last shogun was overthrown and the emperor's power restored, the modern nation of Japan emerged.

8. Samurai were most like which Europeans?

   (1) merchants
   (2) nobles
   (3) kings
   (4) knights
   (5) serfs

9. Which conclusion is best supported by the information in the passage?

   (1) Japan's emperors had great power.
   (2) The Tokugawa became emperors of Japan.
   (3) A system similar to European feudalism existed in Japan.
   (4) Japan had no emperor for about a thousand years.
   (5) The daimyos still control Japan today.

Answers start on page 297.

GED Mini-Test • Lesson 8

Directions: This is a ten-minute practice test. After ten minutes, mark the last question you finished. Then complete the test and check your answers. If most of your answers were correct, but you didn't finish, try to work faster next time. Choose the <u>one best answer</u> to each question.

Questions 1 through 3 refer to the following passage.

During the Middle Ages, Spain was very prosperous. Merchants sold Spanish glass, leatherwork and other goods as far away as India. Science and medicine flourished, and Spanish scholars studied the writings of the ancient Greeks nearly 200 years before the humanists in Italy did.

Spain's unity, prosperity, and cultural achievements were the result of its being conquered in the 700s by invading Muslims, whom the Christians called Moors. Most of these Arabs, Syrians, and North Africans settled on the rich lands of southern Spain. Only a few Christian regions survived in the mountains of the north. However, as power struggles among the Muslims divided Moorish Spain after 1031, nobles in the Christian regions gradually established kingdoms. By 1248, Christian kings had reconquered all of Spain except for Granada, a kingdom on the southern Mediterranean coast.

The size of Christian kingdoms continued to increase for hundreds of years, often through royal marriages. For example, in 1479, King Ferdinand of Aragon joined his kingdom with Castile, the kingdom of his wife Queen Isabella. In 1492, the same year their explorer Christopher Columbus sailed into the Atlantic seeking a trade route to Asia, Ferdinand and Isabella ended Muslim rule in Spain by conquering Granada. At the time of his death in 1516, Ferdinand had also conquered the remaining Christian kingdoms and established the modern nation of Spain.

1. Which is the best title for this passage?

   (1) Differences Between Muslims and Christians
   (2) Spanish Crafts and Trade
   (3) The Muslim Conquest of Spain
   (4) Muslim Contributions to Spain
   (5) How Spain Became a Nation

2. What effect did marriages among Christian royal families have on Spain's development?

   (1) They caused divisions among Muslims.
   (2) They helped Christians unite against Muslims.
   (3) They further divided Spanish Christians.
   (4) They caused Muslims to tolerate Christians.
   (5) They inspired Muslims to attack Christians.

3. Which detail is <u>least</u> important to this account of the Muslim conquest of Spain and the Christian unification of the country?

   (1) King Ferdinand of Aragon and Queen Isabella of Castile were husband and wife.
   (2) Rivalries among Muslims divided Spain.
   (3) Columbus made his voyage for Spain in the same year that the last Muslim kingdom fell.
   (4) The Muslims tolerated Spanish Christians.
   (5) Muslims in Spain included Arabs, Syrians, and North Africans.

4. The history of Portugal began in the 1100s. In 1095, the ruler of the Christian Spanish kingdoms of León and Castile gave a county in León to his daughter's husband, Henry of Burgundy, and named Henry the Count of Portugal. In 1128, however, Henry's son exiled his mother and declared himself Alfonso I, King of Portugal. Alfonso and his successors gradually extended their control south into Muslim-held territory, achieving the present-day boundaries of Portugal in 1249.

The creation of the nation of Portugal was most like the formation of what other nation?

   (1) Spain, because of the Muslims
   (2) Japan, because of the samurai
   (3) France, because of the nobility
   (4) Greece, because of the culture
   (5) China, because of trade goods

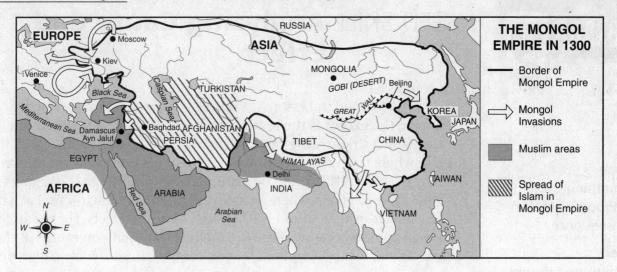

In the early 1200s, a people called the Mongols expanded west and south from a region in Central Asia now called Mongolia. In the next hundred years, led by Genghis Khan and then by his three grandsons, the Mongols established the greatest empire the world had ever seen.

Genghis Khan conquered northern China by 1215. He then turned his attention to the west. Before he died in 1227, his empire reached to the Black Sea.

Mongols led by Genghis Khan's grandson Batu swept across Russia and invaded Europe in the 1240s. Only politics saved Europe from conquest. Mongol forces had defeated Polish and Hungarian armies and were threatening Vienna in 1242 when Batu called off the attack and returned to Asia to help choose the next Mongol leader. Meanwhile, another grandson, Halagu conquered Persia by the 1250s. His invasion of the Middle East failed when he was defeated by Muslim forces in Syria in 1260.

By 1279, the third grandson, Kublai Khan, had completed his grandfather's conquest of China and extended the Mongol empire into Korea and Tibet. He also attacked Burma and Vietnam. In 1281, he attempted to add Japan to the empire.

Mongol armies struck terror wherever they went. Archers on horseback could cover 100 miles a day and, while at a full gallop, send an arrow to its target. Mongol warriors looted and destroyed places that resisted them and often put the people who lived there to death.

5. What is the topic of this passage and map?

   (1) clashes between Mongols and Muslims
   (2) Genghis Khan and his grandsons
   (3) the growth of the Mongol Empire
   (4) invasion routes of Mongol armies
   (5) the Mongol threat to Europe

6. Which assumption can be made based on the passage and the map?

   (1) The Mongol Empire extended into Africa.
   (2) The Mongols attacked Vietnam by sea.
   (3) The Mongols eventually conquered Arabia.
   (4) A Mongol invasion of Japan did not succeed.
   (5) All Mongols were Muslims.

7. What conclusion is best supported by the information in the passage and the map?

   (1) The Mongols were not good at governing their empire.
   (2) The Mongols were the fiercest warriors that the world has ever seen.
   (3) The Mongols used superior technology to overwhelm their enemies.
   (4) The Mongol Empire declined after the death of Genghis Khan.
   (5) The Mongols had a major impact on world history.

Answers start on page 298.

Lesson 9

GED SKILL Analyzing Cause and Effect

cause
something that produces a result or consequence

effect
something brought about by a cause; a result or consequence

implied cause
a cause that is not directly stated, but is only suggested or hinted at

To identify an implied cause, start with the known effect. Then look for a reason to explain why the effect happened.

As you learned in Lesson 4, a **cause** is what makes something happen; the **effect** is the result. Often an event has more than one cause, and a single cause can have many effects. Suppose that the place where you work is destroyed by fire. This one event would have many effects. Traffic would be disrupted around the site. Customers would have to go elsewhere. Employees might lose their jobs. Each of these effects in turn would be the cause of other effects. For example, losing your job because of the fire might mean that you must sell the new car you just bought because you cannot afford the car payments.

Written history, the record of real life, contains multiple causes and effects. In addition, some causes may be **implied causes**—that is, causes that are not directly stated. For example, a writer may describe a series of events and depend on the reader to understand that each event resulted from the prior event.

Another way to imply a cause is to state two or three related effects. Suppose you read in a novel that the main character's TV suddenly went blank. That could have happened for several reasons. But if you then read that the character was unable to turn on a light, the author is implying that a power failure was the cause.

Read the passage and complete the exercise below.

In the 1490s and early 1500s, Christopher Columbus made several voyages for Spain in which he explored the Caribbean islands and the coast of Central America. Meanwhile, in 1499, Spain's rival Portugal sent an expedition to explore the region farther south. On board for this voyage was an Italian-born navigator named Amerigo Vespucci. As his expedition explored the region, Vespucci decided that Columbus was wrong. This was not Asia, he concluded. Instead, he wrote, the lands were a "New World, because our ancestors had no knowledge of them." Soon mapmakers began using the name "America" on their maps to identify Amerigo Vespucci's New World.

Put a check mark next to the statement the passage indicates is the reason the Western Hemisphere is known as America.

_____ a. Spain and Portugal were competing to explore it.

_____ b. Vespucci was first to recognize it as a new world.

You were correct if you chose *option b*. The passage clearly suggests a connection between the name America and the first name of the man who realized the land was not Asia. The facts do not support *option a* as the cause.

Use the passage and the map to complete the exercise below.

Renaissance advances in science and Europe's continuing trade with Asia combined in the 1400s to launch a period called the **Age of Exploration.** The Renaissance aroused Europeans' interest in the writings of ancient geographers. Mapmaking improved, and sea captains became willing to sail longer distances.

Europeans had long known that a magnetized needle fixed to a stick and floated in water would point north. In the 1300s, they added a card marked with directions to the stick and created the compass. Another advance in Renaissance technology was the development of the astrolabe, an instrument that allowed sailors to determine their location at sea from the position of the stars. Changes in ship design made vessels faster and easier to steer. Improvements near the end of the 1400s made ships safer and more stable in open seas.

In 1418, Portuguese explorers began to explore the west coast of Africa, searching for a water route to India. At the same time, they developed a profitable trade in African slaves, ivory, and gold.

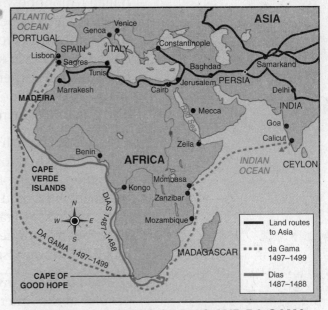

THE EXPLORATIONS OF DIAS AND DA GAMA

1. Write *C* in the blank next to each cause of the Age of Exploration.

    _____ a. creation of the compass

    _____ b. a profitable trade in African slaves, ivory, and gold

    _____ c. Europe's continuing trade with Asia

    _____ d. development of the astrolabe

2. Write *I* next to the statement that is implied as a cause of improved maps.

    _____ a. Sea captains became willing to sail longer distances.

    _____ b. Europeans became more interested in the writings of ancient geographers.

3. The map traces the efforts of Portuguese sailors Bartholomeo Dias and Vasco da Gama to sail around Africa to India. Write *I* next to the information that suggests a cause of da Gama's success.

    _____ a. Changes made to ships caused them to be safer and more stable in open seas.

    _____ b. Adding a card with directions on it to a floating needle created the compass.

    _____ c. Portuguese explorers began to explore along the west coast of Africa.

Answers start on page 298.

By the late 1400s, both Spain and Portugal were eager to break the Italians' monopoly on trade between Europe and Asia. In 1492, Spain's Queen Isabella dispatched Christopher Columbus west across the Atlantic in search of China and the islands of the Indies. Instead, although he never knew it, Columbus stumbled across an entirely new world. As others realized the significance of Columbus' finds, Spain organized more expeditions to claim, explore, conquer, and colonize immense regions in the Americas.

In 1519, Spanish conquistador Hernán Cortés and about 600 men sailed to Mexico from Spain's colony in Cuba. Equipped with horses and guns, this tiny force quickly overran the great Aztec Empire. Soon the Spanish learned of another rich empire in South America. In 1530, Spain sent Francisco Pizarro from Panama with 180 men and 37 horses to conquer the Incas in Peru. Within two years, the entire Inca Empire was also under Spanish control.

The European invasion had devastating effects on the native peoples of the Americas. They had no natural immunity to the diseases the Spanish brought with them. Epidemics killed millions of American Indians. To make up for the loss of these workers, the Spaniards imported enslaved Africans to work in the colonies. A society based on race soon developed. Africans and American Indians were at the bottom of the social ladder. At the top were colonists from Spain, followed by Spaniards born in the Americas.

As Europeans traveled back and forth from the colonies, they transported goods with them. In this way, items from the Western Hemisphere were introduced to the Eastern Hemisphere, and items from the Eastern Hemisphere came to the Americas. Because it started with Columbus, this mixing of cultures is called the Columbian Exchange.

THE COLUMBIAN EXCHANGE

THE AMERICAS

PLANTS: Corn, Potato, Tomato, Squash/ Pumpkin, Peppers (Bell, Chili), Tobacco, Pineapple, Beans (Lima, Kidney, Navy, String), Cotton, Marigold, Wild Rice, Sunflower, Peanut, Pecan, Cashew, Cocoa Bean, Cassava/Tapioca

ANIMALS: Turkey, Muskrat, Guinea Pig, Hummingbird

DISEASES: Syphilis

AFRICA, ASIA, & EUROPE

PLANTS: Wheat, Barley, Oats, Soybean, Peach, Pear, Sugar Cane, Rose, Onion, Okra, Coffee, Watermelon, Banana, Olive, Asian Rice, Lettuce

ANIMALS: Horse, Cow, Hog, Sheep, Chicken, Rabbit, House Cat

DISEASES: Smallpox, Measles, Influenza, Diphtheria, Whooping Cough, Malaria, Yellow Fever, Typhus, Cholera

Directions: Choose the one best answer to each question.

Questions 1 through 7 refer to the passage and the chart on page 114.

1. What does the passage imply was the reason Cortés was able to conquer the Aztec Empire so easily?

   (1) He commanded a huge army.
   (2) The Spanish were smarter than the Aztec.
   (3) He sailed to Mexico from Cuba.
   (4) Horses and guns were unknown to the Aztec.
   (5) The Aztec were less powerful than the Inca.

2. The passage and the chart indicate that the Spanish brought to the Americas diseases that killed millions of American Indians. This result then became a cause of what other consequence?

   (1) Enslaved Africans were brought to the Americas.
   (2) The Columbian Exchange began.
   (3) American Indians quickly developed resistance to European diseases.
   (4) Tobacco from the Americas was introduced to Europe.
   (5) Spain colonized immense regions in the Americas.

3. One cause of Columbus' first voyage was the need for a route to China. Does the passage or chart indicate another cause for the voyage?

   (1) Yes, to conquer and colonize new lands for Spain
   (2) Yes, to bring enslaved Africans to the Americas
   (3) Yes, to break the Italians' monopoly on trade between Europe and Asia
   (4) Yes, to introduce livestock to America
   (5) No, neither the passage nor the chart indicates another cause for Columbus' voyage.

4. Based on the passage, what assumption can you make about Pizzaro's expedition?

   (1) His conquest of the Inca occurred before Cortés's conquest of the Aztec.
   (2) His men died from diseases to which they had no immunity.
   (3) His force was helped by enslaved Africans.
   (4) His men had horses.
   (5) His men had guns.

5. According to the chart, one effect of the Columbian Exchange was the introduction of wheat to the Americas. What other effect of the Columbian Exchange is shown by the chart?

   (1) the introduction of corn to the Americas
   (2) the introduction of tobacco to Europe, Africa, and Asia
   (3) the introduction of coffee to Europe, Africa, and Asia
   (4) the introduction of malaria to Europe, Africa, and Asia
   (5) the introduction of syphilis to the Americas

6. What does the passage imply was the main reason for the expeditions of Cortés and Pizarro?

   (1) to kill American Indians
   (2) to spread disease to American Indians
   (3) to conquer and colonize lands for Spain
   (4) to obtain American products for Europe
   (5) to introduce European products to America

7. What unstated effect can you conclude resulted from the deaths of millions of American Indians due to European diseases?

   (1) Europeans learned how to grow corn.
   (2) It became easier to conquer the Indians.
   (3) The Columbian Exchange ended.
   (4) Europeans realized that America was a new world.
   (5) Europeans got their horses from the Indians.

Answers start on page 298.

GED Practice • Lesson 9

Directions: Choose the one best answer to each question.

<u>Questions 1 through 4</u> refer to the following passage.

The policy of one nation extending its power over weaker nations or peoples is known as **imperialism.** Imperialism has been practiced in every period of history and in all regions of the world. Ancient Greeks invaded what is now western Turkey. The Macedonians conquered the Greeks and, under the leadership of Alexander the Great, extended their control eastward to India. The Romans commanded a huge empire stretching from England to Egypt. Much later, in the 1600s and 1700s, the English colonized and controlled India and much of North America.

In the 1800s many European nations established empires. There were several reasons for this increase in imperialism. First, Europeans felt superior to other cultures. They wanted to spread their way of life and their Christian religion to other parts of the world. Second, as a result of the Industrial Revolution that started in the mid-1700s, factories could produce huge amounts of goods. With more products to sell, the industrial nations of Europe needed more places to market their goods. Third, industrial nations needed secure sources of raw materials that would allow their factories and workers to keep producing the goods.

By the early 1900s, nearly all of Africa had been colonized and divided by various European nations. France controlled most of West Africa; Britain controlled much of North and South Africa; and Belgium claimed Central Africa. Germany, Italy, Portugal and Spain also held territory in Africa. Most of Southeast Asia, large parts of China, and many islands in the South Pacific also came under European control.

1. What is the subject of this passage?

(1) the ancient Greek and Roman empires
(2) European colonization in Asia
(3) the spread of the Industrial Revolution
(4) Great Britain's world empire
(5) imperialism in world history

2. What is the reason that Europeans spread their culture and religion?

(1) The Greeks and Romans had done this.
(2) Europeans felt superior to other peoples.
(3) Imperialism required them to do it.
(4) They needed raw materials for their factories.
(5) The people the Europeans met had no culture.

3. Which is an example of imperialism?

(1) Spanish soldiers conquer the Inca Empire in the 1500s.
(2) The United States declares its independence from Great Britain in the 1770s.
(3) The world powers form the United Nations after World War II and invite other nations to join.
(4) Japan protects its industries in the 1970s by banning competing foreign goods.
(5) The United States and its allies free Kuwait in the Persian Gulf War in the 1990s.

4. Which of the following developments was a cause of European imperialism in the 1800s?

(1) the lack of armies in other nations
(2) the Industrial Revolution and the need for more markets to sell goods
(3) the need for more markets to sell goods and the desire to subjugate the people of Africa
(4) the need for more markets to sell goods and an excess of raw materials
(5) the lack of religion in other nations

TIP To decide if a cause-effect relationship exists, ask yourself whether the second event would have happened if the first event had not taken place.

Questions 5 through 8 refer to the following passage and map.

For centuries China dealt with outsiders on its own terms. The government severely limited the movement of foreign traders in China. Chinese merchants accepted only gold and silver for their tea, silks and other trade goods. In about 1800, however, British traders began offering opium from their colonies in India to pay for goods they bought in China. When China's government demanded that the drug imports be stopped, the result was a war that lasted from 1839 to 1842.

Great Britain's easy victory over China in the Opium War proved how powerful the Industrial Revolution had made European nations. To restore peace, China was forced to turn Hong Kong over to Great Britain and to give British traders special privileges in five Chinese ports.

Britain's special trade advantage with China did not last long. France and other nations soon demanded similar trade concessions. By the late 1800s, large areas of China had come under foreign control. These **spheres of influence** technically remained part of China. However, foreigners in each nation's sphere obeyed only the laws of their own nation. They were exempt from Chinese authority. Each sphere became a market for that country's products and a source of raw materials for its factories at home.

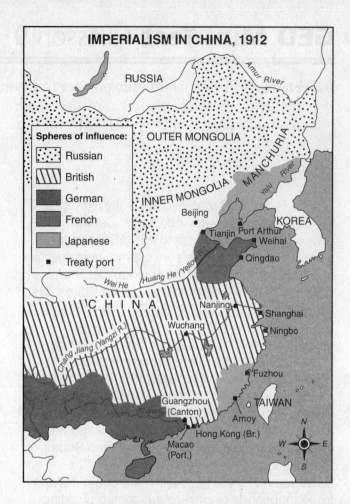

5. Which effect of the Industrial Revolution is implied in the passage?

(1) The British began to produce opium.
(2) Europe no longer desired Chinese silk.
(3) The Industrial Revolution caused the Opium War.
(4) Industrialized countries became more powerful than nonindustrial countries.
(5) The Industrial Revolution caused spheres of influence to develop in China.

6. Which nation had the smallest sphere of influence in China in 1912?

(1) France
(2) Germany
(3) Great Britain
(4) Japan
(5) Russia

7. Based on the passage, what value was most important to China when it fought the British in the Opium War?

(1) holding on to the profits of the drug trade
(2) convincing Japan that China was still strong
(3) controlling trade coming into China
(4) ending all trade with India
(5) ending the spheres of influence in China

8. What is the only appropriate conclusion about Japan that can be supported by the information on the map and in the passage?

(1) Japan was an ally of Britain and France.
(2) Japan and Russia were at war in 1912.
(3) Japan intended to conquer China and Korea.
(4) Japan wanted to expand its spheres of influence in China.
(5) Japan was an industrial nation in 1912.

Answers start on page 299.

GED Mini-Test • Lesson 9

Directions: This is a ten-minute practice test. After ten minutes, mark the last question you finished. Then complete the test and check your answers. If most of your answers were correct, but you didn't finish, try to work faster next time. Choose the <u>one best answer</u> to each question.

<u>Questions 1 through 5</u> refer to the following passage.

The Panama Canal makes Central America an important region in world trade. Central America is also important to the U.S. economy because U.S. companies have large investments in bananas, coffee, and other resources there. For both of these reasons, the United States has long supported Central American governments that were not democratic, but that brought stability to the region. Concern about stability increased after 1977, when the United States agreed to turn the canal over to Panama in 2000.

In the late 1970s, it became clear that Fidel Castro, the communist dictator of Cuba, was aiding rebels in Central America, including those in El Salvador. Supported by the United States, El Salvador's government fought back. The Salvadoran army and government death squads killed thousands of citizens suspected of siding with the rebels before peace was restored in the 1990s. American aid to Guatemala led to a similar chain of events during the same period.

In 1979, communists overthrew the U.S.-backed dictator of Nicaragua, whose family had ruled since the 1930s. The United States responded by financing, training, and arming a force known as the contras to overthrow the new government. In 1990, after a decade of war, the communists agreed to hold new elections. The U.S.-backed candidate, the daughter of a wealthy Nicaraguan family, became president.

1. What is the main purpose of this passage?

   (1) to tell about the Panama Canal
   (2) to show how imperialism affected Central America
   (3) to compare unrest in El Salvador, Guatemala, and Nicaragua
   (4) to show how U.S. investment caused imperialism in Central America
   (5) to describe the wars in Central America

2. According to the passage, what was the effect of U.S. involvement in Nicaragua?

   (1) the deaths of thousands of innocent citizens
   (2) wealthy Nicaraguans' loss of land to the poor
   (3) unhappiness in the United States over the government's policies in Nicaragua
   (4) Nicaraguans' dislike of U.S. policies
   (5) the ultimate failure of the communists in Nicaragua

3. Which cause for U.S. actions in Central America is implied in the passage?

   (1) concern for Panama Canal security
   (2) the location of Central American nations south of the United States
   (3) the importance of bananas and coffee to American consumers
   (4) the perception of Central American nations as weak
   (5) the desire of U.S. leaders to seize control of Central America

4. Which countries mentioned in the passage practiced imperialism?

   (1) the United States and Nicaragua
   (2) Nicaragua and Cuba
   (3) Cuba and the United States
   (4) the United States and El Salvador
   (5) El Salvador and Nicaragua

5. Which value was <u>least</u> important to the United States in its Central American policies?

   (1) the security of the Panama Canal
   (2) stable Central American governments
   (3) protecting American investments
   (4) strengthening democracy in Central America
   (5) preventing the spread of communism

Questions 6 through 9 refer to the following chart.

THE LANGUAGE OF IMPERIALISM

Annexation	one country adds all or part of the territory of another country to its own territory; can be accomplished by agreement or by military action
Colonialism	formal control by one nation over another with the loss of identity and independence by the nation being controlled; contrast with protectorate
Cultural imperialism	pushing a form of government, lifestyle, values, or other parts of a culture on another people; does not require conquest or political control
Dependent colony	colony in which a few officials of the controlling nation rule the population of the controlled people; contrast with settlement colony
Military intervention	one nation uses force in the territory of another, not to conquer it, but to control events there; troops are usually uninvited, but the weaker country may be pressured to "invite" intervention
Neo-imperialism	one country exploits the natural resources of another, uses its people for labor, takes unfair advantage of investment opportunities, or uses it as a market to dump surplus products, sometimes called economic imperialism
Protectorate	arrangement in which a stronger country protects a weaker one: the weaker country retains its identity as a nation, but the stronger country takes full or partial control of its affairs; contrast with colonialism
Settlement colony	colony in which large numbers of people from the controlling nation occupy the land of the controlled people; contrast with dependent colony

6. In the 1820s, Protestant missionaries from New England introduced Christianity to Hawaii. When King Kamehameha III opposed laws they wanted passed, they tried to overthrow him.

   Which type of imperialism occurred in Hawaii?

   (1) neoimperialism
   (2) cultural imperialism
   (3) annexation
   (4) creation of a dependent colony
   (5) creation of a settlement colony

7. Angola had a civil war before Portugal granted the colony independence in 1975. The United States backed a group called the FNLA, the Soviet Union favored the MPLA, and neighbor South Africa aided UNITA. When South African forces entered Angola, Soviet-backed Cuban troops arrived to support the MPLA.

   What action were the Cubans taking?

   (1) colonialism
   (2) annexation
   (3) establishing a protectorate
   (4) cultural imperialism
   (5) military intervention

8. Vietnam gained independence from China in 939 after over 1000 years of rule. Chinese Buddhism had become the guiding force in its culture. Even today, Vietnam uses the writing and government systems introduced by the Chinese.

   Which types of imperialism are illustrated here?

   (1) settlement and dependent colonies
   (2) military intervention and colonialism
   (3) colonialism and cultural imperialism
   (4) cultural imperialism and neoimperialism
   (5) neoimperialism and settlement colonies

9. In 1876 Japan forced an unwanted trade agreement on Korea; by 1910 Korea had been annexed. Thousands of people left Japan and relocated in Korea. Korea did not regain its independence until Japan's defeat in World War II.

   Which types of imperialism did Korea experience?

   (1) neoimperialism and dependent colony
   (2) protectorate formation and cultural imperialism
   (3) cultural imperialism and colonialism
   (4) neoimperialism and settlement colony
   (5) colonialism and creation of a protectorate

Answers start on page 300.

GED SKILL Recognizing Unstated Assumptions (in Political Cartoons)

assumption
something that is taken for granted and not explained

As you learned in Lesson 3, when people talk or write about a topic, they usually don't tell everything they know about it. They assume that you already know some things. Since a cartoon uses very few words to make its point, it makes many **assumptions** about what you know. To understand a political cartoon, you must recognize the cartoonist's assumptions. Look at this cartoon that was published in the early 1990s.

TIP

To identify the assumptions in a political cartoon, you must look for visual clues to the cartoonist's message, such as the appearance of the figures drawn in the cartoon.

Examine this cartoon. You see a bear, labeled *Russia* on the cap, looking at a recipe labeled *Democracy* and holding a burning pot.

Put a check mark next to the sentence that gives an unstated assumption important for understanding the cartoon.

_____ a. Russia has no tradition of democracy so it is trying to use a "recipe."

_____ b. The burning pot represents the problems Russia is having making democracy work.

You were correct if you chose *option a.* You need to know that information (the *why*) in order to understand the cartoon's message, that Russia is having difficulty changing from communism to democracy. Recognizing the meaning of the pot in *option b* (the *what* of the cartoon) does not help you understand the cartoon's significance.

Use the written information and the cartoon to complete the exercise below.

In August 1990, Iraq invaded and quickly conquered its neighbor Kuwait, a major oil producer. After Iraq failed to comply with a United Nations' demand to withdraw from Kuwait, the forces of the United States and other nations attacked Iraq and drove its army from Kuwait. The following cartoon appeared in a U.S. newspaper in August 1990.

Reprinted by permission of Bob Gorrell and Creators Syndicate, Inc.

1. Put a check mark next to the person the figure in the military uniform represents.

    _____ a. U.S. president George Bush

    _____ b. Iraq's president Saddam Hussein

2. In this cartoon, the headdress on the dead figure is a visual clue. Put a check mark next to what this figure represents.

    _____ a. The United Nations

    _____ b. Kuwait

3. Put a check mark next to an assumption the cartoonist is making about the scene pictured.

    _____ a. that you understand it is occurring in Iraq

    _____ b. that you know it is taking place in Kuwait

4. Finish this sentence to summarize the message of the cartoon.

    The cartoonist is telling the reader that Iraq is willing to destroy Kuwait in order to seize its

    _____.

Answers start on page 301.

The twentieth century was a time of great tension in the world. World War I, which lasted from 1914 to 1918, was supposed to be "the war to end all wars." It was soon followed by even greater devastation in World War II, waged from 1939 to 1945. For much of the rest of the century, people worried about nuclear annihilation as the United States and the Soviet Union faced off in the Cold War.

When World War II ended, so did the uneasy cooperation between the United States and the Soviet Union, who had been wartime allies. The world soon divided into three camps. The United States led the West, which included the major democracies—Great Britain, France, and their allies. The Soviet Union emerged as leader of the **Communist bloc,** which included its **satellite nations** in Eastern Europe as well as China and North Korea. Much of the rest of the world formed a third group of **nonaligned nations.** This group included democracies like India, as well as countries with other political systems, such as Egypt. What they shared in common was that most were **developing nations** whose economies had not reached their full potential.

The nonaligned nations bargained with both the United States and the Soviet Union for help to improve their standards of living and build their economies. The United States and Soviet Union each used aid to try to win the loyalty of these nations.

During the Cold War, the United States and the Soviet Union competed over more than the nonaligned nations. They also engaged in an **arms race** to develop weapons. When the Soviets launched the first satellite, called *Sputnik,* into space in 1957, Americans' pride was damaged. More importantly, *Sputnik* also demonstrated that the Soviets had rockets powerful enough to launch nuclear missiles against the United States. The United States speeded up both its space and rocket development programs in an attempt to close this missile gap.

Jerry Barnett, *The Indianapolis News,* 1987. Reprinted by permission.

Directions: Choose the one best answer to each question.

Questions 1 through 5 refer to the passage and the cartoon on page 122.

1. Which of the following statements best summarizes the passage?

   (1) The United States led the world's democracies in the years following World War II.
   (2) The nations of the world fought two major wars during the twentieth century—World War I and World War II.
   (3) The United States and Soviet Union competed in an arms race and for the loyalty of nonaligned nations.
   (4) The launching of *Sputnik* by the Soviet Union intensified the Cold War.
   (5) The nonaligned nations had various systems of government.

2. What is the subject of the cartoon?

   (1) the Communist bloc
   (2) the Soviet Union
   (3) the Cold War
   (4) the arms race
   (5) the nonaligned nations

3. Why are strings attached to the characters in the cartoon?

   (1) The characters are tied up.
   (2) The characters are portrayed as puppets.
   (3) The characters are about to be executed.
   (4) The characters represent warring countries.
   (5) The characters are connected to each other.

4. What do you have to know about the images in this cartoon in order to interpret it?

   (1) what the hammer and sickle symbolize
   (2) who the chairman of the PLO is
   (3) who the dictator of Cuba is
   (4) that Cuba is a communist nation
   (5) that Angola was engaged in a civil war

5. What is the message of this cartoon?

   (1) The heads of nonaligned nations do not really represent their nations at meetings.
   (2) The PLO should be recognized as a nation.
   (3) The nonaligned nations are members of an organized group that holds conferences.
   (4) There are six truly nonaligned nations.
   (5) These so-called nonaligned nations are actually controlled by the Soviet Union.

Question 6 refers to the following cartoon and the passage on page 122.

Reprinted by permission of Phil Interlandi.

"DO YOU SUPPOSE THERE'S ANY SIGNIFICANCE IN THE FACT THAT WE GOT TRANQUILIZERS JUST BEFORE THEY GOT SPUTNIKS?"

6. What is the implication of this 1957 cartoon?

   (1) People should not take tranquilizers if they are drinking alcohol.
   (2) *Sputnik* is causing increased consumption of alcohol by Americans.
   (3) Talking about the Cold War is one way to feel better about it.
   (4) The launching of *Sputnik* makes Americans worry about the arms race.
   (5) If people are worried about something, they should take tranquilizers.

Answers start on page 301.

Directions: Choose the one best answer to each question.

Questions 1 through 3 refer to the following passage and cartoon.

Since ancient times, there has been recurring yet intermittent conflict between Arabs and Jews in the biblical land called Palestine. During the centuries the region was part of the Ottoman Empire, few Jews lived in Palestine, and few conflicts arose. With the fall of the Ottoman Turks after World War I and with an influx of Jewish settlers to the region, tensions increased. They were aggravated by the British, who had made conflicting promises to both Arabs and Jews to gain their support against the Turks during the war.

Britain governed Palestine between the world wars. After World War II, the United Nations voted to divide Palestine into Arab and Jewish states. Arabs, who were the majority, felt betrayed. When Jews formed the state of Israel in 1948, surrounding Arab countries attacked. More than half of Palestine's Arabs fled. Ever since, Palestinians have sought to regain land they regard as their home. Jews, who consider their claims to the land equally valid, have resisted. Violence has often been the result. Since 1973 the United States has been trying to help settle their dispute.

Israel and the Palestinian Liberation Organization (PLO), which represents Palestinian Arabs, reached several agreements during the 1990s. However, for various reasons, each agreement collapsed before it was fully implemented. In October 1998, encouraged by President Clinton, the two sides concluded yet another agreement, which inspired the above cartoon.

NOW SHAKE HANDS...... GENTLY.

Reprinted with special permission of King Features Syndicate.

1. Why does the cartoonist depict the three figures on a platform of playing cards?

   (1) to express the view that agreements between the two sides have been shaky
   (2) to recognize the Palestinian leader's love of card-playing
   (3) to show that making treaties is like gambling
   (4) to state that the United States should stay out of Middle Eastern issues
   (5) to honor President Clinton for his role in bringing peace to the Middle East

2. According to the passage, what is the basis of the conflict between Arabs and Jews in the Middle East?

   (1) They practice different religions.
   (2) They fought on different sides in World War II.
   (3) They both lay claim to the same land.
   (4) The Ottomans set them against each other.
   (5) The British set them against each other.

3. What essential knowledge must you have in order to understand this 1998 cartoon?

   (1) The Arab is Yasir Arafat, head of the PLO.
   (2) The figure on the right is Israel's prime minister, Benjamin Netanyahu.
   (3) Israel's parliament approved the peace agreement that Netanyahu is holding.
   (4) Most agreements between Israel and the PLO have not been fully carried out.
   (5) Israel's parliament is known as the Knesset.

Questions 4 through 8 refer to the following passage and cartoon.

As World War II drew to a close, the United Nations was created in the hope of preventing future wars. UN agencies help reduce world tensions by providing loans, food, and other aid to nations in need. Most of the UN's services are generally considered worthwhile. Its role as a peacekeeper, however, is more controversial. The UN has no army. It depends on member nations to provide it with troops. Sometimes international politics makes it difficult for UN peacekeepers to accomplish their goal. Such was the case when the first Canadian and French forces were sent to Bosnia in the early 1990s. Their mission was to protect the Bosnian Muslims from the atrocities committed against them by the Christian Bosnian Serbs. This Canadian cartoon assessed the effectiveness of the UN peacekeeping mission.

ATTENTION, BOSNIAN SERBS!...THIS IS YOUR LAST CHANCE TO THROW DOWN YOUR WEAPONS!

UN

HOT AIR ▶

Malcolm Mayes/artizans.com.

4. According to the passage, why was the United Nations formed?

(1) to end World War II
(2) to provide loans to member nations
(3) to donate food to starving people
(4) to promote world peace
(5) to protect Bosnians from ethnic violence

5. What was the reason UN troops were sent to Bosnia in the early 1990s?

(1) The French and Canadians were fighting.
(2) The Muslims were experiencing atrocities.
(3) The Muslims were attacking the Christians.
(4) The UN was assembling its army.
(5) The UN was avoiding a controversy.

6. In the cartoon, what does the hair dryer with the words *hot air* represent?

(1) a new type of Bosnian hair-care process
(2) a heat wave in Bosnia
(3) weapons that the UN provided to the Muslims
(4) the last chance for peace in Bosnia
(5) empty threats by UN personnel in Bosnia

7. Which situation from daily life is most like the one pictured in the cartoon?

(1) purchasing a rifle at a gun shop
(2) getting your hair done at a new salon in town
(3) hearing a teacher threaten to suspend a bully but not following through
(4) getting mugged by a gang of hoodlums on a street corner near your home
(5) being unjustly arrested by the police for a crime you did not commit

8. The passage and the cartoon support which of the following conclusions?

(1) The UN should be disbanded.
(2) The UN should have its own army.
(3) The UN should get out of Bosnia.
(4) The UN should be able to enforce its missions.
(5) The UN should relocate Bosnian refugees to France and Canada.

TIP Editorial cartoons use images to make their point. Each major object in a cartoon symbolizes something important to its central message.

Answers start on page 302.

Directions: This is a ten-minute practice test. After ten minutes, mark the last question you finished. Then complete the test and check your answers. If most of your answers were correct, but you didn't finish, try to work faster next time. Choose <u>the one best answer</u> to each question.

Questions 1 through 5 refer to the following passage and cartoon.

In 1949, Chinese Communists led by Mao Zedong overthrew that nation's government. They converted China's economy to communism, silenced Chinese who opposed them, and ended what little democracy existed in China. After Mao died in 1976, China's leaders relaxed government control of the economy and began to let people operate their own small businesses.

This economic freedom encouraged some Chinese to push for political freedom, so in 1989, protesters gathered in the capital to demand democracy. China's leaders cracked down, sending troops to attack the protesters, killing hundreds. China's government continued its attempts to crush the pro-democracy movement in the 1990s. The movement's leaders and many other Chinese were arrested, tortured, and imprisoned. The world community condemned China for violating the human rights of its people, but China resisted demands for political reform.

Linda Boileau, *Frankfort State Journal*, Rothco Cartoon Syndicate. Reprinted by permission.

1. Which title <u>best</u> relates the content of this passage to the cartoon?

   (1) The Communist Revolution in China
   (2) Mao Zedong's Contributions to China
   (3) China Makes Political Reforms
   (4) China Moves Toward a Capitalist Economy
   (5) The Pro-democracy Movement in China

2. What was the effect of the event referred to in the cartoon?

   (1) The standard of living in China increased.
   (2) Mao Zedong was replaced as China's leader.
   (3) The world community criticized China.
   (4) Political freedom in China increased.
   (5) China's government made economic changes.

3. What does the figure on the ground in the cartoon represent?

   (1) the communist leaders of China
   (2) the United States
   (3) Mao Zedong
   (4) the protesters who demanded democracy
   (5) the overthrown 1949 government

4. Based on the cartoon and passage, what do China's leaders seem to value most?

   (1) control
   (2) truth
   (3) life
   (4) equality
   (5) human rights

5. What is the implication of this cartoon?

   (1) The desire for democracy is dead in China.
   (2) The desire for democracy is alive in China.
   (3) China's army was not in charge of the killing.
   (4) The killing of Chinese protesters is a myth.
   (5) Americans should stay out of China's affairs.

Jeff Koterba/*Omaha World-Herald*. Reprinted by permission.

In the early 1980s, it seemed as if the Cold War between the Soviet Union and the West would never end. But by 1990, Soviet political control began to break down. The next year, the Soviet Union split into independent nations. Most of the Soviet Union's satellite nations in Europe had also overthrown their communist rulers and established democratic governments. Nowhere were these events more dramatic than in Berlin, a city surrounded by communist East Germany. Since 1961 the people of East Berlin had been separated from democratic West Berlin by a wall erected by the East German government.

On November 9, 1989, thousands of Germans on both sides of the Berlin Wall began to tear it down. The collapse of the Berlin Wall signaled the end of the Cold War and doom for communism.

6. Which assumption can be made from the information in the passage?

   (1) The Soviet government opposed the Berlin Wall.
   (2) East Germany's rulers kept their people under tight control as communism was collapsing elsewhere.
   (3) Communism collapsed in the Soviet Union's satellite nations.
   (4) East Berlin was controlled by a communist government.
   (5) The countries formed from the breakup of the Soviet Union remained communist nations.

7. Which of the following has a relationship most similar to the one between East Germany and West Germany?

   (1) Canada and the United States
   (2) Great Britain and the United States
   (3) North Korea and South Korea
   (4) North Carolina and South Carolina
   (5) West Virginia and Virginia

8. Which assumption is important for you to make to understand this 1990 cartoon?

   (1) The dinosaur represents European communism, under Soviet leadership.
   (2) The dinosaur represents West Berlin.
   (3) The Soviet Union built the Berlin Wall.
   (4) The Berlin Wall was located in Germany.
   (5) The Soviet Union was responsible for the carrying out the destruction of the Berlin Wall.

9. If the cartoonist had given this cartoon a title that expresses its message, which title would he most likely have used?

   (1) Moving the Berlin Wall
   (2) The Fall of the Berlin Wall
   (3) European Communism Becomes Extinct
   (4) The Collapse of the Soviet Union
   (5) Communism Remains Big and Dangerous

Answers start on page 302.

Unit 2 Cumulative Review **World History**

Directions: Choose the <u>one best answer</u> to each question.

<u>Questions 1 through 3</u> refer to the following passage.

Some 50,000 miles of roads held Rome's empire together. The Romans wanted to be able to move soldiers from one place to another along the most direct route possible. They bridged major rivers, filled valleys, and bored tunnels through mountains in what were remarkable feats of engineering for ancient times. To create a hard surface that could be traveled in wet weather, workers tramped down the dirt base, then built the road with alternate layers of stones and concrete. The road was made slightly higher at its center to provide drainage for water on the road.

The popular saying that "all roads lead to Rome" symbolized Rome's power in the ancient world. The Romans began making road maps in about 25 B.C. when the Roman government authorized a survey of its entire road system. The project took 20 years to complete. Based on this information, a huge road map of the empire was carved in marble and displayed near the Senate building in Rome. It became a valuable source of information for Romans. Scribes made parchment copies of this master map that were rolled up and carried by Roman army personnel and travelers.

1. What was the most likely effect of Rome's road system?

   (1) Trade moved more easily in Rome's empire.
   (2) Roads to cities other than Rome were neglected.
   (3) Rome wanted greater control of its empire.
   (4) A huge stone road map was displayed in Rome.
   (5) It included more than 50,000 miles of roads.

TIP Time sequence is a clue to cause-and-effect relationships. A cause comes before an effect.

2. What quality does the passage suggest was highly valued by the Romans?

   (1) spirituality
   (2) honesty
   (3) power
   (4) compassion
   (5) humor

3. Which of the following conclusions is <u>best</u> supported by the evidence in this passage?

   (1) Roman officials took bribes from construction companies that wanted to work on road projects.
   (2) The road system weakened the empire by allowing unhappy groups to march on Rome.
   (3) Roman engineers were not highly advanced for their times.
   (4) Mapping the road system was a simple project.
   (5) A major reason for the road system was to move troops rapidly and easily within the empire.

4. The language of the ancient Romans was Latin. Although it is no longer used as a language today, five modern languages—called the Romance languages—are based on it. They are Romanian, French, Spanish, Portuguese, and Italian. The most widely spoken Romance language is Spanish, which is spoken in Spain and throughout Spain's former colonies in Latin America.

What implication is suggested by this information?

   (1) The ancient Romans were romantic.
   (2) The ancient Romans spoke all the Romance languages.
   (3) The ancient Romans spoke both Latin and Italian.
   (4) Spain was once part of the Roman Empire.
   (5) Latin America was once part of the Roman Empire.

Marco Polo became a world explorer at age 17. In 1271, he set out for China with his father and uncle who were Venetian merchants. After three years of travel across central Asia by ship and camels, the Polos arrived in Shang-tu at the summer palace of Kublai Khan, the Mongol emperor of China. Marco quickly became a favorite of the khan and for 17 years traveled throughout China as the khan's representative.

Near the end of this time, the Polos were ready to return home. At first, the khan was unwilling to let them leave. But in 1292 he agreed and allowed them to sail to Persia. From there they were finally able to reach Venice in 1295—24 years later.

Shortly after Marco Polo's return to Italy, he gave a detailed account of his experiences to a writer. The book that resulted is known today as *The Travels of Marco Polo.* For more than 300 years, it remained the only published description of East Asia available in Europe.

THE TRAVELS OF MARCO POLO, 1271–1295

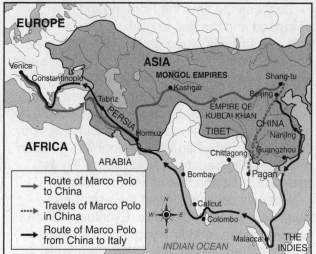

5. What does the passage imply was the reason for Marco Polo's journey to China?

   (1) to become a world explorer
   (2) as part of a trade mission
   (3) to write a book about his experiences
   (4) a desire to travel around the region
   (5) to please his father

6. Which city did Marco Polo most likely visit as the khan's representative?

   (1) Venice
   (2) Nanjing
   (3) Malacca
   (4) Chittagong
   (5) Pagan

7. Which unstated assumption is suggested about Marco Polo and Kublai Khan?

   (1) Kublai Khan feared Marco Polo.
   (2) They enjoyed traveling together.
   (3) Kublai Khan admired and trusted Marco Polo.
   (4) Marco Polo feared Kublai Khan.
   (5) The khan helped Marco Polo write his book.

8. The Polos' trips to China and back each took three years. What map information supports the idea that they took less time on their return trip?

   (1) On the trip to China they traveled through Persia.
   (2) The trip home was along a more direct route than was the trip to China.
   (3) The trip to China covered a much greater distance than did the trip home.
   (4) The trip home required the Polos to cross Tibet.
   (5) The trip home was mainly over water, while the trip to China was mainly over land.

9. Great Zimbabwe was a major city and fort in southern Africa in the 1200s and 1300s. The fort and the market inside it covered 60 acres. The ruins of Great Zimbabwe have yielded copper and gold items and pieces of Chinese porcelain.

What conclusion is best supported by this information?

   (1) Marco Polo knew about Great Zimbabwe.
   (2) Africans made many trips to China.
   (3) Kublai Khan knew about Great Zimbabwe.
   (4) Gold at Great Zimbabwe came from China.
   (5) Trade was important to Great Zimbabwe.

Questions 10 through 12 are based on the following passage.

Between the time the Roman Empire collapsed and the first English settlers arrived in North America, three great civilizations rose and fell in West Africa. The earliest of these was Ghana, which developed in the 300s along a caravan route between North Africa and West Africa. By 1000 A.D., Ghanaians had become rich in the salt, gold, and slave trades. But religious conflict erupted when the kingdom was invaded by Muslim Berbers from North Africa. By the mid-1200s, Ghana had ceased to exist.

Ghana's decline allowed the rise of a neighboring kingdom—Mali. Eventually Ghana became a part of Mali's empire that stretched from the West African interior to the Atlantic Coast. At the height of Mali's culture and power in the early 1300s, Timbuktu, its capital city, was an important center of learning. Its Islamic university attracted scholars from Egypt and Arabia. Then a series of weak rulers caused Mali to decline. However, Mali managed to keep control of the trade routes to North Africa until the mid-1400s. Then it was conquered by Songhay, a kingdom that it had once ruled.

Under Songhay control, West African culture thrived. Trade in gold, ivory, and slaves flourished. Timbuktu grew to include 180 Islamic schools and three Islamic universities that taught astronomy, poetry, medicine, and religion. Their libraries held large collections of ancient Greek and Roman writings. By the mid-1500s, education rivaled trade as Timbuktu's major activity.

10. What implication about Ghana is suggested by the information in the passage?

    (1) Ghana's power declined when it was conquered by Mali.
    (2) Ghanaians valued education and financed schools from the profits of their trade.
    (3) Ghana became a source of slaves for the Mali and Songhay empires.
    (4) Islam was not very important in Ghana before the Muslim Berber invasion.
    (5) Ghana was the northernmost black-African kingdom in Africa.

11. Which generalization about Ghana, Mali, and Songhay is supported by the passage?

    (1) Education held an important place in all three cultures.
    (2) Each of them was conquered by one of the others.
    (3) Weak rulers caused the decline of all three kingdoms.
    (4) The economy of each was based on trade.
    (5) Each kingdom had a great university.

12. According to the passage, which value seems to have been least important in Songhay culture?

    (1) human rights
    (2) education
    (3) wealth
    (4) literature
    (5) religion

13. Widespread poverty and political unrest plagued Russia in the early 1900s. When Russia became involved in World War I in 1914, the war strained the nation to the breaking point. In 1917, Russia's ruler, Czar Nicholas II, resigned. A temporary government was set up until elections could be held. But before they occurred, Russian Communists called Bolsheviks, led by V. I. Lenin, overthrew the government and pulled Russia out of the war. A bloody civil war began, which ended in a Communist victory in 1922. The Communists maintained their control of Russia until the collapse of the Soviet Union in 1991.

Which of the following is a conclusion that can be drawn from this information?

    (1) A civil war in Russia caused the czar to resign.
    (2) The Bolsheviks immediately brought an end to poverty in Russia.
    (3) Many Russians did not want to have a Communist government.
    (4) The civil war in Russia was long and bloody.
    (5) The Bolsheviks brought the czar back to power.

Questions 14 through 17 refer to the following passage and chart.

Inspired by the American and French revolutions, Spanish colonists in Latin America rose in revolt in the early 1800s. The movement began in southern South America in 1810, when Spanish rebels led by José de San Martín seized control of the colonial government. Six years later, the rebels declared independence and named their country the United Provinces of the Rio de la Plata. Meanwhile, another group of colonists had broken away and had already formed the independent nation of Paraguay.

In northern South America, the struggle was much more difficult. The revolt there also began in 1810. But a long and bloody war followed. Rebel leader Simón Bolívar was not able to liberate northern South America until 1819.

Meanwhile, San Martín moved his army west, in a difficult crossing of the Andes Mountains, into the region known as Chile. There he joined with Chilean patriot Bernardo O'Higgins to overcome Spanish resistance in 1818. Next, San Martín marched his forces north along South America's Pacific coast to capture Lima, Peru. The Spanish government fled, and San Martín declared Peru independent in 1821.

Preoccupied and weakened by wars in Europe that followed the French Revolution, Spain was unable to effectively resist these independence movements. By 1825, its Latin American empire was completely gone. In 1822, Brazil, Portugal's only colony in South America, also became independent.

INDEPENDENCE IN SOUTH AMERICA	
Country	Date of Independence
Argentina	1816
Bolivia	1825
Chile	1818
Colombia	1819
Ecuador	1830
Panama	1903
Paraguay	1811
Peru	1821
Uruguay	1828
Venezuela	1830

14. What title best summarizes the content of the passage?

(1) How European Wars Affected Spain and South America
(2) How Spain Lost Its South American Empire
(3) How Spain and Portugal Divided Latin America
(4) Comparing the American, French, and Latin American Revolutions
(5) Comparing and Contrasting Bolívar and San Martín

15. What assumption can you make about Argentina, based on the information in the chart and the passage?

(1) It was originally part of Chile.
(2) It is located south of Brazil.
(3) It was the first South American nation to become independent.
(4) It was a colony of Portugal.
(5) It was originally called the United Provinces of the Rio de la Plata.

16. Based on the passage, what caused Spain's defeat in Latin America?

(1) Spain's Latin American colonists were inspired by the American Revolution.
(2) The Latin American rebels had better generals than the Spanish.
(3) Spain's Latin American colonies became independent.
(4) Wars in Europe consumed too many of Spain's military resources.
(5) U.S. citizens aided the Latin American rebels.

17. Which of the following is a summary of the information in the chart?

(1) Peru became independent before Paraguay.
(2) Most of South America was free by 1830.
(3) No country became independent after the late 1800s.
(4) Chile became independent before Colombia.
(5) Most Spanish colonists joined the rebellion.

Questions 18 through 21 refer to the following passage and cartoon.

For nearly a century after the Union of South Africa was created in 1910, the nation was controlled by its white minority. Black South Africans, who made up the vast majority of the population, were denied the right to vote.

After World War II, the government introduced a policy of apartheid, meaning "apartness," that regulated nearly every aspect of black South Africans' lives. When the African National Congress (ANC), a black-rights organization, protested the government's policies, it was banned. Its leader, Nelson Mandela, was sentenced to life in prison in 1962.

Despite these actions, opposition to apartheid grew during the following decades. The South African government responded with increased violence. In the 1980s, people around the world, as well as growing numbers of white South Africans, called for an end to apartheid.

By 1990, many apartheid laws had been relaxed or repealed. The ban on the ANC was lifted, and Mandela was freed. However black South Africans continued to press for full and equal rights. The government finally agreed to South Africa's first all-race elections.

In April 1994, millions of black South Africans waited patiently in long lines to take part in their first national election. Nelson Mandela was elected South Africa's first black president, winning an overwhelming majority of the votes.

18. Which of the following sentences best summarizes the content of the second paragraph?

(1) The policy of apartheid in South Africa was similar to the policy of racial segregation in the United States.
(2) The tactics used to protest apartheid were later copied by American civil rights leaders.
(3) The introduction of apartheid caused protests, which brought government crackdowns against black South Africans.
(4) Apartheid meant that black South Africans had to carry identity cards, live in separate areas, and work for less pay than whites.
(5) Apartheid helped South Africa's white minority hold on to political control.

Jack Higgins, courtesy of the *Chicago Sun-Times*.

19. What is the main idea of paragraph three?

(1) South Africa's government responded violently to protests
(2) Many people around the world opposed apartheid.
(3) Some white South Africans opposed apartheid.
(4) Opposition to apartheid grew.
(5) World opinion ended apartheid.

20. What does the wrist iron and chain symbolize in the cartoon?

(1) black South Africans
(2) low wages
(3) violent change
(4) the ANC
(5) apartheid

21. What does the cartoonist assume you know when he expects you to understand this 1994 cartoon?

(1) The white population of South Africa far outnumbers its black population.
(2) Black South Africans had to travel long distances to vote in 1994.
(3) The 1994 election was the first in which black South Africans had the right to vote.
(4) The white South African government had freed Nelson Mandela from prison in 1990.
(5) Nelson Mandela was the leader of the ANC.

Answers start on page 304.

Cumulative Review Performance Analysis
Unit 2 • World History

Use the Answers and Explanations starting on page 304 to check your answers to the Unit 2 Cumulative Review. Then use the chart to figure out the skill areas in which you need more practice.

On the chart, circle the questions that you answered correctly. Write the number correct for each skill area. Add the number of questions that you got correct on the Cumulative Review. If you feel that you need more practice, go back and review the lessons for the skill areas that were difficult for you.

Questions	Number Correct	Skill Area	Lessons for Review
4, 5, **6**, 10, 14, **17**, 18, 19, **20**	____/9	Comprehension	1, 2, 7
1, 7, 13, **15**, 16, **21**	____/6	Analysis	3, 4, 6, 9, 10
2, 3, **8**, 9, 11, 12	____/6	Evaluation	5, 8
TOTAL CORRECT	____/21		

Question numbers in **boldface** are based on graphics.

Civics and Government

"We, the people of the United States . . ." These words are from the Preamble, or introduction, to the U.S. Constitution. The Constitution spells out the basic laws of the government of the United States. It defines the powers of the national government, establishes and limits federal power over the states, and spells out the freedoms of U.S. citizens. Since the early years of our nation, the Constitution has described both the nature of our government and the civic responsibility of the people.

Understanding how our government and political system work is key to preserving our position as a free people. That is why civics and government is an important part of the GED Social Studies Test, making up 25 percent of the test questions.

The ability to vote for our elected officials is our most fundamental right and responsibility.

The lessons in this unit include:

Lesson 11: **Modern Government**
There are several basic types of government in the modern world. Many are democracies like the U.S. system and others are not. Other types include monarchies, oligarchies, and dictatorships.

Lesson 12: **Structure of the U.S. Government**
At the national level, there is a balance of power between the three branches of government. There are also important similarities and differences between the political processes at the federal, state, and local levels.

Lesson 13: **U.S. Politics in Action**
Political parties developed in the early days of the American republic and have existed ever since. The two-party system and third parties have had an important effect on the development of our system of government. Voting and other forms of citizen participation are key to making our system work.

Lesson 14: **U.S. Government and Its Citizens**
The Constitution states that one goal of American government is promoting the general welfare of the nation. The government provides many benefits and services to its citizens and raises the money for these expenditures through taxation.

THINKING SKILLS

○ Distinguishing fact from opinion

○ Comparing and contrasting

○ Identifying faulty logic

○ Applying information to new contexts

GED SKILL Distinguishing Fact from Opinion

fact
a real occurrence or event

opinion
someone's beliefs or feelings about something

A **fact** is information about something that actually happened or actually exists. For example, when a news reporter covers a political demonstration and writes about what demonstrators are doing and saying, the reporter is reporting on things that exist and events that are taking place. These things and events are facts.

An **opinion** is an interpretation of the facts. Opinions are influenced by people's interests, by what they know about a subject, and by their experience with related facts. Opinions can lead people to act on the facts they know. Demonstrators express their opinions in the slogans on their signs ("Unfair to workers!") and in their speeches ("Vote no!"). They support one view of a political issue and reject contrary views that other people may hold.

Political arguments are full of opinions. Although opinions are always *about* facts, they are not always *based on* facts or on sound reasoning. However, political opinions usually are presented as if they are facts. It is up to you to decide whether the statements are logical and based on valid information.

Read the following passage and complete the exercise below.

Some people think that the U.S. government has been successful in dealing with the nation's social and economic problems. The 1960s and 1970s saw the passage of laws to outlaw racial discrimination. These laws are believed by some to have reduced injustice, inequality, and poverty in America. However, other people think that government has not significantly improved the lives of the poor and of racial and ethnic minorities. In their view, the government represents the interests of the wealthy. Racial injustice and inequality continue to be major problems.

Put a check mark next to the statement that is a fact.

_____ a. The 1960s and 1970s saw the passage of laws to outlaw racial discrimination.

_____ b. Racial injustice and inequality continue to be major problems.

You were correct if you chose *option a.* The passage of these laws is a fact that can be verified. Whether poverty, racial injustice, and inequality are still major problems is an opinion with which some people agree and others disagree.

TIP

Remember that a fact can be proven to be true; an opinion is a judgment that may or may not be true. Certain words provide a clue that a statement is an opinion. These words include *should, ought to, better,* and *worse.*

Use the passage and the newspaper ad to complete the exercise below.

Governments have five basic functions in a social system. First, a government represents the people of a society in dealing with other governments. Second, a government takes responsibility for making laws and enforcing them. The laws of a society reflect the general way people are expected to behave. For example, a law against theft means that stealing is regarded as unacceptable behavior in that society. Third, government protects the society against dangers and threats that come from both within and outside the nation. Fourth, a government settles disputes between conflicting interests within a society. It sets up systems, such as courts, and processes, such as elections, that help resolve differences and promote systematic methods of decision-making. Finally, government coordinates and develops goals for society and carries them out. In a democracy, many of these goals come from groups in the society. Sometimes it is not possible for people to achieve these goals alone, so they ask for government help. The following ad is an example of this process.

1. The following statements are based on information from the passage. Write *F* next to the statements that are facts and *O* next to the statements that are opinions.

    _____ a. Governments have five basic functions in a social system.

    _____ b. Theft is acceptable in some situations.

    _____ c. If two groups have a dispute, the government can be called in to help resolve the issue.

    _____ d. The government should help all people and groups achieve their goals.

2. Put a check mark next to the statement that is an opinion held by the sponsor of the ad.

    _____ a. Teenage drivers have a large number of accidents.

    _____ b. Teenage drivers are unsafe and a menace on the highways.

Answers start on page 306.

The United States and most other countries operate according to political principles that are relatively new in the world's history. The first principle is **centralized government.** In times past, the functions of government were usually exercised by military leaders, church officials, and people of noble birth. Eventually, a central government took over many of these functions. Government now oversees public safety, national security, education, trade, and transportation.

The second principle of modern government is **legal authority.** In traditional systems, a leader had power because of family wealth and power. Today, a leader's power comes from the authority of the office that he or she holds. Citizens in modern states expect leaders to follow legal guidelines.

The third principle is **mass participation.** Throughout history, decisions about governing have been made by one person or by a small group of powerful people. Over time, people from other levels of society have gained a voice in how government is run. Today, leaders are chosen by large numbers of people, and they are expected to govern in the best interests of the nation.

In conclusion, **authoritarian governments** are centralized and are not supported by mass participation or legal authority. A single leader or a small group is the only real authority. **Democratic governments** are also centralized, but their power lies in the hands of the people. The following chart describes types of government in each category.

Forms of Authoritarian Government		
System	**Description**	**Examples**
autocracy	All authority is held by one person. In an **absolute monarchy,** the ruler is a king or queen. All other autocracies are **dictatorships.**	Saudi Arabia is one of only a few absolute monarchies. Cuba is ruled by the dictator, Fidel Castro.
oligarchy	A small group holds power because of its wealth, military power, or social position.	In China, all political power is held by the leaders of the Communist Party.
Forms of Democratic Government		
System	**Description**	**Examples**
direct democracy	The people govern themselves by voting on issues and passing laws in mass meetings.	New England town meetings and some districts in Switzerland are direct democracies.
republic	The people elect representatives and give them the power to make laws and govern.	The United States is one of many republics in the modern world.
constitutional monarchy	The monarch shares power with a legislature or is only the ceremonial head of government.	Great Britain is ruled by Parliament, and the monarch's role is ceremonial.

Directions: Choose the one best answer to each question.

Questions 1 through 8 refer to the passage and the chart on page 138.

1. In a government built on modern principles, what is the basis of a leader's authority?

   (1) power
   (2) wealth
   (3) military force
   (4) law
   (5) personal whim

2. What is the main purpose of the chart on page 138?

   (1) to list the principles of modern government
   (2) to compare authoritarian and democratic governments
   (3) to compare autocracy and oligarchy
   (4) to compare direct democracy and constitutional monarchy
   (5) to define absolute monarchy and dictatorship

3. After the former Soviet Union broke up, Russia elected a legislature and a president. Which type of government did this establish?

   (1) a dictatorship
   (2) a constitutional monarchy
   (3) an autocracy
   (4) an oligarchy
   (5) a republic

4. Although the official head of Denmark's government is Queen Margrethe II, an elected parliament makes the nation's laws. Of what system of government is Denmark an example?

   (1) an oligarchy
   (2) a republic
   (3) a constitutional monarchy
   (4) a direct democracy
   (5) an absolute monarchy

5. Which of the following is an opinion related to the information in the passage and the chart?

   (1) Modern leaders hold power by the authority of their office.
   (2) Most modern governments are centralized.
   (3) Mass participation is the most important principle of modern government.
   (4) A New England town meeting is an example of direct democracy.
   (5) Cuba is a dictatorship.

6. When a dictator dies, how will the nation's government most likely be affected?

   (1) The government will continue as usual.
   (2) The government will be in chaos.
   (3) The nation will become a democracy.
   (4) The dictator's oldest child will automatically come to power.
   (5) The people will elect a new leader.

7. Which details in the chart support its definitions of the forms of modern government?

   (1) opinions about how well each form of government works
   (2) facts about each government's basic principles
   (3) opinions about the role of citizens
   (4) names of political offices and leaders
   (5) facts about the history of government

8. Which conclusion is supported by the information on page 138?

   (1) The nature of government has changed over time.
   (2) The basic principles of government have not changed throughout history.
   (3) All governments have the same basic structure.
   (4) Military rulers no longer have any power.
   (5) Absolute monarchs and dictators are evil.

Answers start on page 306.

GED Practice • Lesson 11

Directions: Choose the one best answer to each question.

Questions 1 through 4 refer to the following passage.

Power is the ability to control people's behavior. There are three basic ways to get power over people: through force, through authority, and through influence.

Force is based on making people do things against their will. Because physical force makes people afraid, they will do things they do not want to do.

Authority is the power of leaders to get the people to obey the laws. It is based on the belief that those leaders have a right to rule.

Influence is a form of persuasion. An individual who has a strong personality, who is important or wealthy, or who has the support of many other people can persuade people to do things. However, the power to govern usually requires more than influence.

A stable government is based on what is called **legitimate power.** Such power is considered proper and acceptable by the people who obey it. It comes from having a leader who has the authority to make decisions that people will follow, even if they do not always agree with the decisions. Force is considered illegitimate power because it does not have the support or consent of the people governed. Legitimate power generally results in better and more effective government than does illegitimate power.

1. Which of the following statements is an opinion of the writer of this passage?

   (1) Legitimate power is power that is considered to be proper and acceptable.
   (2) Force is illegitimate power.
   (3) Legitimate power results in better government than does illegitimate power.
   (4) Force makes people do things that they do not want to.
   (5) Some people can be persuaded to do things by a person who is important or wealthy.

2. After the death of King Baudouin in 1993, his son Albert became king of Belgium. Which type of power is illustrated by the rule of King Albert?

   (1) influence
   (2) force
   (3) persuasion
   (4) authority
   (5) elective office

3. According to the passage, how are people's opinions important to the exercise of power?

   (1) People's opinions are not at all important to the exercise of power.
   (2) People's support is necessary for power to be legitimate.
   (3) People's opinions can be easily changed.
   (4) People's opinions can be influenced by force.
   (5) Public opinion is the basis for all types of power.

4. What effect does force have in the exercise of power?

   (1) It has little, if any, effect.
   (2) It turns illegitimate power into legitimate power.
   (3) It allows wealthy people to have power.
   (4) It causes people to believe what the government tells them.
   (5) It makes people behave in ways that government leaders desire.

TIP

The words *believe, think, feel, best,* and *worst* often signal that an opinion is being stated.

Questions 5 through 8 refer to the following passage and diagram.

The **presidential system** in the United States is one of the forms that democratic government may take. Another democratic form of government is the **parliamentary system.** In this system, an elected **legislature,** or parliament, directs both the legislative and the **executive** functions of government.

In a presidential system, the chief executive, or president, is chosen by the voters. In a parliamentary system, the chief executive is the **prime minister.** He or she must be a member of the parliament. With the parliament's approval, the prime minister selects other members from its ranks to form a ruling **cabinet.** These ruling officials are not only part of the legislature, they are also subject to its direct control. They stay in office only as long as their policies have the support of the legislature.

The parliamentary system is the most common form of democratic government in the world today. Great Britain, Japan, and India are among the nations using this system.

TWO BASIC FORMS OF DEMOCRATIC GOVERNMENT

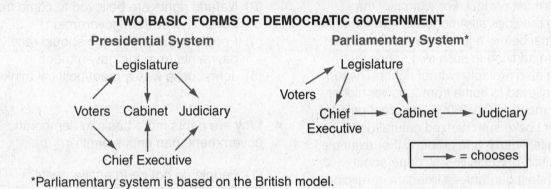

*Parliamentary system is based on the British model.

5. Who chooses the prime minister in a parliamentary system of government?

   (1) the president
   (2) the voters
   (3) the cabinet
   (4) the legislature
   (5) the judiciary

6. Which of the following statements is an opinion?

   (1) In a parliamentary system, the legislature has more power than in a presidential system.
   (2) The parliamentary system is a more common form of government than the presidential system.
   (3) The parliamentary system is a better form of government than the presidential system.
   (4) The prime minister in a parliamentary system is similar to the president in a presidential system.
   (5) Both the presidential and the parliamentary systems include a cabinet.

7. Who chooses the judges for the court system in a parliamentary form of government?

   (1) the cabinet
   (2) the parliament
   (3) the prime minister
   (4) the voters
   (5) the prime minister and the legislature

8. What evidence best supports the conclusion that the prime minister of Great Britain is a less independent leader than the U.S. president?

   (1) The prime minister must be a member of the legislature.
   (2) The prime minister must resign if he or she loses an important vote in the legislature.
   (3) The prime minister must appoint a cabinet.
   (4) The prime minister is directly responsible to the voters.
   (5) The parliamentary system is the most common form of democratic government.

Answers start on page 307.

GED Mini-Test • Lesson 11

Directions: This is a ten-minute practice test. After ten minutes, mark the last question you finished. Then complete the test and check your answers. If most of your answers were correct, but you didn't finish, try to work faster next time. Choose the one best answer to each question.

Questions 1 through 4 refer to the following passage.

Americans are used to hearing that they have certain rights and privileges. But what are rights and how do they differ from privileges? In legal terms, rights are powers and freedoms that government must protect. For example, the Constitution provides all Americans with the right to a public trial before a jury if they are accused of a crime. In addition to such civil rights, the Constitution also protects natural rights. These are rights believed to come from a power higher than government. In the 1600s, the great political thinker John Locke summarized natural rights as the right to life, liberty, and property. For example, the Constitution protects liberty, or personal freedom, when it guarantees freedom of religion.

In contrast to rights are entitlements. These can best be thought of as privileges or benefits that government provides by law to people who meet certain requirements. Examples include a Social Security pension, payments to farmers who grow certain crops, and government payments to people who are unemployed. Unlike rights, entitlements can be limited in time and can be legally taken away.

1. Which is an example of a natural right?

   (1) freedom of speech
   (2) a public trial
   (3) a license to practice medicine
   (4) paying taxes
   (5) government payments to the unemployed

2. What is an example of an entitlement?

   (1) freedom of the press
   (2) trial by a jury
   (3) a government-guaranteed student loan
   (4) the ability to quit your job
   (5) the ability to put your house up for sale

3. Which of the following is an opinion expressed in or implied by the passage?

   (1) Privileges are more important to Americans than are rights.
   (2) Civil rights are more important than natural rights.
   (3) Natural rights are believed to come from a power higher than government.
   (4) People who have no job should receive payments from the government.
   (5) John Locke was a great political thinker.

4. Why are rights more basic to democratic government than entitlements?

   (1) People do not need entitlements.
   (2) Government can lawfully take away entitlements, but not rights.
   (3) Entitlements are protected by the Constitution but rights are not.
   (4) Rights apply only to U.S. citizens but entitlements apply to all U.S. residents.
   (5) Natural rights aren't protected in the Constitution since they come from a higher power.

5. Democracies and totalitarian governments have different goals as well as different structures. An important goal in a democracy is to ensure freedom and dignity for all individuals. The major goal of a totalitarian government is to maintain control over all aspects of people's lives.

Based on the information above, if you lived under a totalitarian government, which of the following could you expect?

   (1) to be able to choose your nation's leader
   (2) to send your children to a private school
   (3) to be able to choose where you live
   (4) to be limited in where you could travel
   (5) to always have a job

Democracy will not continue to exist merely because Americans consider it to be the best system of government. It is made possible only by a strong belief in and strict practice of the following five principles.

The Five Pillars of Democracy
The Importance of the Individual Each person's worth and dignity must be recognized and respected by all others at all times. At the same time, however, each person's individual interests must be secondary to the interests of all the individuals who make up the society.
The Equality of All Persons Each person is entitled to equal opportunity and equal treatment by the law. The principle does not mean that all people are born with the same abilities or that they have a right to an equal share of the nation's wealth.
Majority Rule and Minority Rights Majority rule is the basis of democracy. However, majority rule without minority rights destroys democracy. The majority must be willing to listen to the minority and recognize its right by lawful means to become the majority.
The Need for Compromise In a society that emphasizes individualism and equality, few public questions will have only two points of view. The blending of competing interests through compromise is needed to find the position most acceptable to the largest number.
Individual Freedom Democracy cannot exist in an atmosphere of absolute freedom. That would eventually lead to rule by the strongest members of society. However, in democracy, each person has as much freedom as possible without interfering with the rights of others.

For Americans, these principles do more than guide a system of government. They have become part of our way of life. We expect to be able to choose our own way of doing things in our day-to-day living. However, because personal freedom is taken for granted, there is a danger of imposing our own ways and values on someone else. We must recognize that one person's choice may not be right for another person. We must also keep in mind that our rights and freedom are not without limits. Supreme Court Justice Oliver Wendell Holmes once said, "My right to swing my fist ends where the other fellow's nose begins." For democracy to work, each of us must give up some personal freedom to maintain the freedom of society as a whole.

6. What opinion about freedom is expressed in the passage?

   (1) that it has accompanying responsibilities
   (2) that it is an important entitlement
   (3) that exercising it is not really possible
   (4) that it is leading the nation into danger
   (5) that it should have no limits

7. Which of the following is true of a democracy?

   (1) The majority must always have its way.
   (2) People should share equally in the nation's resources.
   (3) Equality is its most important principle.
   (4) It is built on respect for individual differences.
   (5) It will always exist in the United States.

8. What democratic value was Justice Holmes expressing when he said that his right to swing his fist ended where the other fellow's nose began?

   (1) that personal freedom is not important in a democratic society
   (2) that in a democracy no person's rights can be allowed to interfere with the rights of others
   (3) that all people in a democracy should be allowed to have an equal opportunity to succeed
   (4) that fighting and violence are not rights in a democratic society
   (5) that democratic government cannot succeed in an atmosphere where differences of opinion exist

Answers start on page 307.

GED SKILL **Comparing and Contrasting**

comparing
looking for similarities in things

contrasting
looking for differences in things

When comparing and contrasting things, look for similarities among them first. When you know how things are the same, it will be easier to see how they are different.

Suppose you want to buy a used car. You find some cars with features you desire, but they have been driven many miles. Others have low mileage and the right features, but they are not the model you want or a color you like. The prices also differ, so choosing a car is even more confusing. The only way to make a good decision is to compare and contrast the characteristics of each car.

Comparing and **contrasting** involve examining two or more things to understand how they are the same and how they are different. Looking for similarities and differences in things often helps you evaluate them. Whether you realize it or not, when you evaluate something, you are comparing it to and contrasting it with something with which you are familiar.

The most important step in using this skill is to establish the categories of things to be compared and contrasted. The categories you use must be parallel. For example, it would not be helpful to compare the sound system in one car to the color of another. Creating broad categories also increases the chances of finding similarities and differences. Sound systems would be a better category than CD players, since some cars may have only radios and others may have radios with CD players.

Read the following passage and answer the question below.

In 1973, in a reaction to the Vietnam War, Congress passed the War Powers Act. This law prohibits the president from involving American troops in combat for longer than 60 days unless Congress declares war or authorizes a longer period. If neither action occurs, Congress can require the president to bring the troops home at the end of 60 days.

The War Powers Act is one example of the way Congress translates the will of the American people into law. In a democratic system of government, the people rule—either directly or through officials they elect to represent them. In many states, if the people do not like a law passed by state or local elected officials, they can demand an election called a **referendum** and vote to repeal the law.

Put a check mark next to the statement that explains how referendums and the War Powers Act are similar.

_____ a. Both limit the power of elected government leaders.

_____ b. Both are intended to keep the national government from becoming too powerful.

You were correct if you chose *option a.* Both are checks on what elected leaders can do. *Option b* is incorrect because the passage says that referendums apply only to state and local governments.

Use the passage and the diagrams to complete the exercise below.

Americans have a strong tradition of local self-government. There are about 86,000 local governments in the United States. They are of three basic types: counties, municipalities, and special districts. County and municipal governments generally are responsible for roads, police and fire protection, sewage and sanitation, and services to people with special needs. Special districts generally provide the most costly public services, such as drinkable water and public transportation. The local school district is the most common type of special district. Special districts often cross city and even county boundaries.

Municipal governments are formed when a group of people ask the state legislature for permission to **incorporate,** or set up a legal community. The state responds by issuing a **charter** to the group, which allows them to form a government and specifies the type of government. The two most common forms of municipal government are shown below.

FORMS OF CITY GOVERNMENT

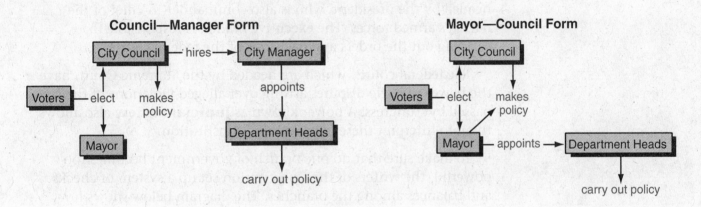

1. Put a check mark next to the way counties, municipalities, and special districts are similar.

   _____ a. They require incorporation and a charter from the state.

   _____ b. They provide services to the people of an area.

2. Write *S* next to the characteristics that are similarities of the mayor-council and the council-manager forms of municipal government; write *D* next to the characteristics that are differences.

   _____ a. who chooses the mayor

   _____ b. who chooses the council

   _____ c. who appoints the department heads

   _____ d. who makes city policy

Answers start on page 308.

GED CONTENT Structure of the U.S. Government

The U.S. **federal** government divides governing power among three branches: a legislative, or law-making branch, an executive, or law-enforcing branch, and a judicial, or law-interpreting branch. Each branch is separate from and largely independent of the others.

The power to make laws is held by Congress, which consists of two houses or parts. Each state is represented by two people in the **Senate.** In the **House of Representatives,** the number of legislators is determined by the population of each state. The **Constitution** gives Congress many powers, including the power to declare war, to regulate trade between states, and to raise money and authorize how it will be spent. All bills to raise money must originate in the House of Representatives.

The responsibility to execute, or carry out and enforce, the laws passed by Congress is held by the executive branch. This branch is headed by the president, who is also commander-in-chief of the nation's armed forces. The executive branch is responsible for carrying out the orders and decisions of the federal courts.

The federal courts, which are headed by the Supreme Court, have the power to settle disputes arising over alleged violations of the laws passed by Congress. A power known as **judicial review** also allows them to interpret these laws and the Constitution.

To make sure that no one branch of government becomes too powerful, the writers of the Constitution set up a system of checks and balances among the branches. The diagram below shows how some of these checks and balances work.

MAJOR CHECKS AND BALANCES IN THE U.S. GOVERNMENT

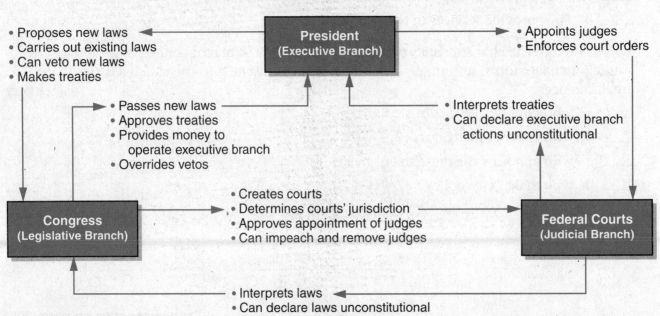

- Proposes new laws
- Carries out existing laws
- Can veto new laws
- Makes treaties

President (Executive Branch)

- Appoints judges
- Enforces court orders

- Passes new laws
- Approves treaties
- Provides money to operate executive branch
- Overrides vetos

- Interprets treaties
- Can declare executive branch actions unconstitutional

Congress (Legislative Branch)

- Creates courts
- Determines courts' jurisdiction
- Approves appointment of judges
- Can impeach and remove judges

Federal Courts (Judicial Branch)

- Interprets laws
- Can declare laws unconstitutional

Directions: Choose the one best answer to each question.

Questions 1 through 6 refer to the passage and the diagram on page 146.

1. Which statement contrasts the Senate and the House of Representatives?

   (1) The Congress consists of the Senate and the House of Representatives.
   (2) All tax laws must originate in the House of Representatives.
   (3) States are represented equally in the Senate and according to their population in the House.
   (4) The Supreme Court can declare acts of Congress to be unconstitutional.
   (5) The Senate and House each consist of members from every state in the United States.

2. Which power is shared by the president and Congress?

   (1) levying taxes
   (2) enforcing laws
   (3) making trade agreements with other nations
   (4) waging war against other nations
   (5) enforcing court orders

3. How is the judicial branch's power to check the legislative branch similar to its check on the executive branch?

   (1) The Supreme Court carries out the laws of Congress and the president's executive orders.
   (2) The Supreme Court appoints the president's cabinet as well as the committees of Congress.
   (3) The Supreme Court can declare laws and executive branch actions to be unconstitutional.
   (4) The Supreme Court must approve treaties that the president makes with foreign countries.
   (5) The Supreme Court can force the president and Congress to obey its orders.

4. What basic difference exists between the legislative function and the executive function as they apply to the nation's laws?

   (1) Congress makes laws and treaties, and the president decides what they mean.
   (2) Congress passes laws, and the executive branch carries them out.
   (3) Both the president and members of Congress can propose laws.
   (4) Congress interprets laws, and the president interprets treaties.
   (5) The money to operate the executive branch comes from Congress.

5. Which of the following statements about the structure of the U.S. government is a fact, not an opinion?

   (1) The national government has too much power.
   (2) The major powers of government have been divided among its three branches.
   (3) Congress has more power than the president.
   (4) The judicial branch is the most powerful branch of government.
   (5) The president should not have the power to veto laws passed by Congress.

6. Which statement about checks on government is supported by the diagram?

   (1) The executive branch alone is responsible for checking the power of the legislative branch.
   (2) The legislative branch alone is responsible for checking the power of the judicial branch.
   (3) The judicial branch alone is responsible for checking the power of the executive branch.
   (4) Each of the three branches of government checks the power of the other two branches.
   (5) Each of the three branches of government checks the power of the president.

Answers start on page 308.

GED Practice • Lesson 12

Directions: Choose the one best answer to each question.

Questions 1 through 5 refer to the following passage.

Like the United States, the fifty states also divide power among legislative, executive, and judicial branches. The executive branch in each state is headed by a governor. Every state has a **bicameral** or two-house legislature except Nebraska, which has a **unicameral** or one-house legislature. State court systems vary widely. In some states, the voters elect the judges. In others, they are elected by the legislature. In still others, they are appointed by the governor.

For most of the nation's history, state constitutions have severely limited the powers of governors. Most terms lasted only two years, and some states limited the governor to one term. Although the office has gradually gained power, most governors have limited authority to appoint executive-branch officials. Unlike members of the president's cabinet, major state executives, such as the secretary of state and attorney general, are usually elected by the people.

In Congress, states are represented in the House of Representatives according to their populations. State legislatures are similarly set up: each district in a state legislature's lower house (often called the general assembly) contains roughly the same number of people. A set number of lower house districts form one district in the state senate. In most states, senators serve four-year terms and members of the general assembly serve for two years. Unlike members of Congress, state legislators generally are not well paid and they work only part time.

1. What is the main purpose of this passage?

   (1) to compare state governors and the president
   (2) to explain the structure of state court systems
   (3) to compare state and national governments
   (4) to trace the growing power of state governors
   (5) to compare and contrast state legislatures

2. Which characteristic of state government varies the most from state to state?

   (1) how executive branch officials are selected
   (2) the length of state legislators' terms
   (3) the structure and representation scheme of state legislatures
   (4) how judges are selected
   (5) the powers of state governors

3. Which of the following is the most similar to the majority of state legislatures?

   (1) the legislature of Nebraska
   (2) the Congress of the United States
   (3) the U.S. Supreme Court
   (4) state executive officials
   (5) a president's cabinet

4. Which form of government does the structure of state government best illustrate?

   (1) a dictatorship
   (2) a monarchy
   (3) a direct democracy
   (4) a representative democracy
   (5) a bicameral legislature

5. How are state and local governments similar?

   (1) All the officials in both are elected.
   (2) Both have bicameral legislatures.
   (3) Power in both is divided among branches.
   (4) Judges at both levels are appointed.
   (5) Both are funded primarily by an income tax.

TIP In comparing and contrasting, consider only information that fits the category being compared and contrasted.

Questions 6 through 8 refer to the following passage and diagram.

The framers of the Constitution in 1787 realized that as time passed and society changed, people's requirements of government would also change. So the Constitution provides ways that it can be amended, or changed. Twenty-seven **amendments** have been added to the Constitution in the more than two centuries it has been the law of the land. The first ten amendments, the **Bill of Rights,** were added in 1791. Since then, 17 amendments have been added, including amendments that ended slavery, defined the rights of citizenship, and provided for the direct election of U.S. senators by the people. Other amendments have limited the president to two terms and authorized the government to tax people's incomes.

Article V of the Constitution establishes a two-step amendment process. First an amendment must be formally proposed. Then it must be **ratified,** or approved, by the states. Many ideas exist for amendments, but very few of these are actually proposed. Even fewer are ratified. In 1972, for example, Congress proposed an amendment to make it illegal to discriminate against people because of their gender. The proposal died in 1982 because it had not been ratified by the required number of states. On the other hand, the Twenty-Seventh Amendment on the timing of pay raises for Congress was proposed by Congress in 1789, but was not ratified until 1992, more than two centuries later!

METHODS OF AMENDING THE CONSTITUTION

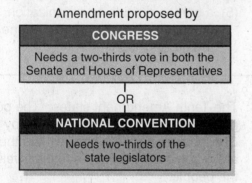

Amendment proposed by

CONGRESS
Needs a two-thirds vote in both the Senate and House of Representatives

OR

NATIONAL CONVENTION
Needs two-thirds of the state legislators

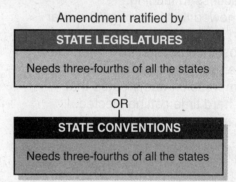

Amendment ratified by

STATE LEGISLATURES
Needs three-fourths of all the states

OR

STATE CONVENTIONS
Needs three-fourths of all the states

6. Which amendment has increased the people's power and voice in government?

   (1) the amendment limiting the president's terms
   (2) the amendment authorizing an income tax
   (3) the amendment changing the selection of senators
   (4) the amendment making it illegal to discriminate on the basis of gender
   (5) the Twenty-Seventh Amendment

7. What does the amendment process suggest the framers valued most?

   (1) direct democracy
   (2) increasing government power
   (3) rule by working people
   (4) rule by the rich and powerful
   (5) adaptability and orderly change

8. When you compare the processes for proposing and ratifying amendments, what can you conclude about the motivations or beliefs of the framers?

   (1) They believed that no amendments to the Constitution would ever be proposed.
   (2) They were confident that no amendments would ever be added to the Constitution.
   (3) They wanted it to be more difficult to add amendments than to propose them.
   (4) They thought that state legislatures would propose most of the amendments that Congress would ratify.
   (5) They expected more amendment proposals to come from national conventions than from state conventions.

Answers start on page 309.

GED Mini-Test • Lesson 12

Directions: This is a ten-minute practice test. After ten minutes, mark the last question you finished. Then complete the test and check your answers. If most of your answers were correct, but you didn't finish, try to work faster next time. Choose the <u>one best answer</u> to each question.

Questions 1 through 3 refer to the following passage.

The National Political Women's Caucus once did a study of the success rates of male and female candidates for election to state and federal offices. The study determined that a candidate's gender made no difference in whether he or she would be elected. Instead, it found that the critical factor in election contests was whether a candidate was an incumbent, that is, someone running for reelection to an office he or she already held. Incumbents' advantages include better access to funding.

The study showed that incumbents win far more often than the candidates who challenge them. Since most incumbents have been men, and most women who have run against them have lost, the impression was created that women have a hard time getting elected. However, most men who run against incumbents also lose.

1. According to the passage, who is most likely to win an election?

    (1) a male challenger
    (2) a female challenger
    (3) the challenger, regardless of gender
    (4) the incumbent, regardless of gender
    (5) someone who has held another office

2. What is the basis for the belief that women have a difficult time getting elected to office because of their gender?

    (1) Women are elected only to minor offices.
    (2) Female challengers lose more elections than male challengers do.
    (3) Women frequently lose against incumbents.
    (4) Women do not campaign enough.
    (5) Men campaign more aggressively than women do.

3. To which of the following do the findings of the National Political Women's Caucus <u>best</u> apply?

    (1) a sports team trying to win the championship against the team that won last year
    (2) a student trying to get an A in a math class when he's gotten no better than a C before
    (3) a poet hoping to win a poetry competition when she has never entered one before
    (4) an actor trying to get the lead in a play when he's had only small parts before
    (5) a person outside an organization competing for a job with someone inside the organization

4. The Tenth Amendment states: "The powers not delegated to the United States by the Constitution, nor prohibited by it to the States, are reserved to the States respectively, or to the people."

    What is the <u>main</u> concern of the amendment?

    (1) to divide and delegate powers
    (2) to expand federal powers
    (3) to limit the power of the Constitution
    (4) to expand the power of the Senate
    (5) to ensure the power of the House of Representatives

5. Many cities have neighborhood groups that meet regularly so that the residents can deal with issues that affect the neighborhood. Which kind of political activity do these neighborhood group meetings <u>most closely</u> resemble?

    (1) writing political party platforms
    (2) speaking at a meeting of a city council
    (3) electing government representatives
    (4) ratifying an amendment
    (5) making decisions in a direct democracy

Questions 6 through 9 refer to the following paragraph and chart.

The original Constitution left it to each state to determine which Americans could vote. In 1789, when the Constitution took effect, all states limited the right to vote to white males who owned property. States gradually loosened their restrictions on voting. However, not all did so at the same rate or in the same way. As a result, people who could vote in some states could not vote in others. As time passed, Congress took control of voting through constitutional amendments to extend voting rights and to make them uniform in every state. These amendments are summarized below.

Although the Constitution now clearly defines who has the right to vote, the states still retain some power in this area. For example, many states still deny the right to vote to persons who are mentally ill or who have been convicted of serious crimes. At the moment, Congress seems content to let these state restrictions continue to exist.

The Voting Rights Amendments		
Amendment	Year Ratified	Provisions
Fifteenth Amendment	1870	Prohibited denial of voting rights based on race.
Nineteenth Amendment	1920	Extended voting rights to women.
Twenty-Third Amendment	1961	Allowed Washington, D.C., residents to vote for president.
Twenty-Fourth Amendment	1964	Abolished poll taxes—fees people had to pay in order to vote.
Twenty-Sixth Amendment	1971	Lowered the minimum voting age to 18.

6. Which person would most likely have been legally prohibited from voting for president?

(1) a 35-year-old white Northern farmer in 1790
(2) a 40-year-old Southern black man in 1860
(3) a 30-year-old Southern black woman in 1925
(4) a 21-year-old black resident of Washington, D.C., in 1968
(5) a 19-year-old white convicted of a traffic violation in 1984

7. What effect have the Constitutional amendments shown in the chart most likely had on voting?

(1) They have given more criminals the right to vote.
(2) There are now increased restrictions on voting.
(3) More politically conservative people are voting.
(4) They have increased the number of potential voters.
(5) More unqualified people are now permitted to vote.

8. In the 1972 presidential election, which of the following people was most likely voting for the first time?

(1) a Virginia black man, age 25
(2) an Ohio black woman, age 25
(3) an Alabama white woman, age 18
(4) a California Hispanic woman, age 21
(5) a convicted murderer, age 28

9. Which conclusion about the relative power of the national and state governments is supported by the passage and chart?

(1) The national government controls the state governments.
(2) The state governments control the national government.
(3) The state governments have become more powerful.
(4) The national government has become more powerful.
(5) There has been no change in the relative power of the national and state governments.

Answers start on page 310.

GED SKILL **Identifying Faulty Logic**

Identifying faulty logic means recognizing errors in reasoning. A person who is presenting an argument might begin with a logical progression of ideas but then draw conclusions from these ideas that are not fully logical. It is important to be aware of faulty logic because a speaker or writer might use such erroneous thinking convincingly. It is up to the reader or listener to note if reasoning has gone wrong and to reject conclusions based on faulty logic.

One example of faulty logic is hasty generalization. This happens when someone makes a broad statement based on inadequate evidence. A common type of hasty generalization is the **stereotype.** You can suspect a stereotype in almost any statement about someone or something that is based on its connection to a larger group. Be especially wary if the group has religion, race, nationality, or gender in common. For example, one stereotype is that males are better than females at math and science. In fact, many women are better than most men in these areas.

A related type of faulty logic is **oversimplification.** This often results when someone links two things that are not directly connected in a cause-and-effect relationship. For example, one common oversimplification is that poverty causes crime. If that were true, then all poor people would be criminals—which, of course, they are not. The causes of crime are much more complicated than whether or not a person is poor.

stereotype
a fixed idea or image of a particular type of person or thing that is often not true

oversimplification
a description of something in terms that make it seem less complicated than it really is

Read the following passage and complete the exercise below.

Carl Jones for Senate! It's time for a change! Senator Brown is responsible for the law that raised your taxes. Carl Jones will work to repeal this tax increase! Politicians are controlled by the interest groups who donate money to their campaigns. But Carl Jones will be the people's senator! Elect Carl Jones to the U.S. Senate!

Mark the oversimplification in this campaign ad with an *O* and the stereotype with an *S*.

_____ a. Politicians are controlled by the interest groups that donate money to their campaigns.

_____ b. Senator Brown is responsible for the law that raised your taxes.

You were correct if you chose *option a* as the stereotype and *option b* as the oversimplification. Not all politicians are controlled by special interests. Saying that one senator is responsible for a tax increase is an oversimplification. For the tax hike to have been approved, many other senators must also have voted for it.

TIP

In looking for faulty logic, ask yourself: Does the information presented support the conclusion? Is more information needed to support this conclusion?

Use the paragraph and the political cartoon to complete the exercise below.

In recent years, the number of eligible Americans who vote has declined by about 20 percent. More than half of nonvoters are people who have seldom or never voted. They tend to come from families that have never voted, and they also tend to be among the poorer and less educated members of society. In addition, more than 20 million Americans who were once frequent voters have completely stopped participating in elections. The result is that the United States—where fewer than half the voters turn out for presidential elections and only about a third for nonpresidential elections—now has the lowest rate of voter participation of any democracy in the world.

Scott Nickel. Reprinted by permission.

1. Put a check mark beside the stereotype about presidential election campaigns that the cartoon presents.

   _____ a. Televised candidate debates are uninteresting and lack excitement.

   _____ b. Presidential candidates hold their debates too late at night for most Americans.

   _____ c. Presidential debates are always very quiet.

2. Put a check mark beside the statement that is an oversimplification of the information in the passage.

   _____ a. Millions of people who used to vote in most elections now never vote.

   _____ b. Many people who don't vote have parents who also do not vote or never did vote.

   _____ c. The tendency not to vote is a trait people inherit from their parents.

Answers start on page 311.

A **political party** is an organization that **nominates** candidates to run for elective office in order to gain control of the government. Most democratic nations have a **multiparty system** in which three or more political parties with widely differing **ideologies,** or basic beliefs about government, compete for power. The United States operates under a **two-party system** in which two political parties dominate the government, although some minor parties may also exist. In the United States, the two dominant parties are the Republican Party and the Democratic Party. The chart below shows the typical organization of both.

Each party's ideology is spelled out in a document, called a **platform,** which represents the basic principles of the party. Although many people complain that there is little difference between the two major parties, their platforms in the 1990s suggest otherwise. Republican platforms have opposed abortion, new taxes, and increases in the minimum wage. Democratic Party platforms have supported abortion, have favored increasing taxes on wealthy Americans, and have called for increases in the minimum wage.

Both major parties are highly organized. Each party functions down to the **precinct** level, a geographic area whose voters all cast their votes at the same polling place. Precinct volunteers distribute information about the party and its candidates. On election day, they encourage the party's supporters in the precinct to vote.

How Political Parties Are Organized			
Level	Party Official(s)	Responsibilities	Connection to Other Levels
precinct	precinct captain (unpaid)	Organizes volunteers to distribute information about party candidates.	The precinct captains for all precincts in a ward are appointed by the ward committee member.
ward	ward committee member (unpaid)	Coordinates party activities in ward; represents ward on county committee.	Each ward committee member is selected by the ward's party members; all committee members in a county form the county committee.
county party	county committee/ county chair (paid)	Coordinates local party activities; determines which local candidates will receive party support; handles county party's daily affairs.	The county committee selects the county chair. All county chairs sit on the state central committee.
state party	state central committee/ state chair (paid)	Raises money; assists local parties and state and local candidates; manages state party's daily operations.	The state committee is composed of county party representatives and other key party members; it selects the state chair.
national party	national committee/ national chair (paid)	Raises money and runs party between party's national conventions/manages national party's daily operations.	The national committee consists of state chairs and other party officials, some state and local elected officials and some members of Congress; it elects the national chair.

Directions: Choose the one best answer to each question.

Questions 1 through 6 refer to the passage and the chart on page 154.

1. According to the passage, what is the real difference between the two major political parties?

   (1) their platforms
   (2) their names
   (3) their financial support
   (4) the success of their candidates
   (5) their organization

2. Which of the following statements is a stereotype?

   (1) Most democratic nations have multiparty systems.
   (2) The Republican and Democratic parties are organized in much the same way.
   (3) The main job of a party's state chair is to manage the organization's daily affairs.
   (4) The national committee of a political party raises money for candidates from the party.
   (5) If a person is a Republican, he or she is against abortion.

3. Which of the following statements is an oversimplification?

   (1) The two-party system is better than a multiparty system.
   (2) Democratic platforms tend to call for increases in the minimum wage.
   (3) The election of a Republican shows that voters oppose higher taxes on the wealthy.
   (4) Precinct captains are unpaid volunteer political party workers.
   (5) Both precinct captains and ward committee members are unpaid volunteers.

4. What assumption can be made from the information in the chart?

   (1) Each ward is made up of a number of precincts.
   (2) County party chair works with the state central committee.
   (3) The national committee of a political party includes members of Congress.
   (4) Each state committee has more members than a party's national committee.
   (5) A party's national committee has more members than any of its state committees.

5. Which function of political parties is less important at the county level than at the state level?

   (1) selecting a chair to manage the party's daily operations
   (2) selecting precinct captains
   (3) helping party candidates get elected
   (4) raising money for the party
   (5) providing representatives to the next higher level of party organization

6. Based on the passage, which generalization can accurately be made about the major political parties in the United States?

   (1) Neither party is truly addressing the issues that concern the average American.
   (2) There is really little if any difference between Republicans and Democrats.
   (3) If the Democrats achieve their tax goals, the nation's economic growth will come to a halt.
   (4) Republicans are inflexible conservatives who stand in the way of the nation's progress.
   (5) The two parties tend to have opposing views on abortion and tax issues.

Answers start on page 311.

GED Practice • Lesson 13

Directions: Choose the <u>one best answer</u> to each question.

<u>Questions 1 through 4</u> refer to the following passage.

Although the Democratic and Republican parties dominate U.S. politics, many third parties have arisen over the years. A **third party** is any political party other than the two major parties.

Third parties often appear when people believe the major parties are not properly addressing an important issue. In the mid-1800s, for example, the Free Soil Party formed to take a stronger stand against the expansion of slavery than either major party was taking. Many third parties have been single-issue parties. Most have disappeared when their issue became less important or was taken up by a major party.

More lasting are ideological third parties that focus on overall changes rather than on specific issues. The Libertarian Party, which calls for drastic reductions in government in order to increase personal freedom, has run a candidate in every presidential election since 1972. Other ideological third parties, such as the Socialist Party, have even longer histories.

Several third parties have captured Senate seats and major state offices. In 1998, Reform Party candidate Jesse Ventura was elected governor of Minnesota. In addition, third-party presidential candidates have influenced the outcome of elections. For example, many political experts credit Bill Clinton's victory over President George Bush in 1992 to the presence of third-party candidate Ross Perot on the ballot. They believe that Perot drew enough votes away from Bush to allow Clinton to become president.

1. What does the passage imply about third parties in the United States?

   (1) They are dangerous to American government.
   (2) Their members do not support them.
   (3) They have been influential in politics.
   (4) Their issues are not truly important.
   (5) They have contributed nothing to the nation.

2. Which of the following best summarizes the third paragraph of the passage?

   (1) The Socialist Party is an example of an ideological third party.
   (2) There have been third-party candidates in all presidential elections since 1972.
   (3) Ideological third-parties arise when the major parties aren't addressing important issues.
   (4) Third parties are in favor of increasing individual freedom.
   (5) Ideological third parties typically live longer than single-issue parties.

3. What is the most likely reason that large numbers of voters support third parties and their candidates?

   (1) Americans are increasingly afraid of taking a stand on political issues.
   (2) Third-party candidates are more exciting than the candidates of the major parties.
   (3) Many Americans want to change the nation to a constitutional monarchy.
   (4) Voters feel that the major parties are not addressing important problems.
   (5) Growing numbers of Americans have become indifferent about politics.

4. Which type of party system would the United States have if the Libertarian Party or the Reform Party became a major force in national politics?

   (1) a democracy
   (2) a republic
   (3) a two-party system
   (4) a third-party system
   (5) a multiparty system

TIP Arguments and conclusions that are based on judgments or opinions are more likely to contain faulty logic than those that are based on facts.

Questions 5 through 8 refer to the following paragraph and chart.

The major characteristic of a republican form of government, such as we have in the United States, is that the people elect officials to represent them in making laws. This principle exists at each level of government, as shown on the following chart.

How the People Are Represented in Government				
Level	Body	Officeholder	Term of Office	Representation Scheme
Municipal	Council	Council member	Usually 2–4 years	May serve by district or "at large" representing all city residents.
State	State Assembly	State representative	Usually 2 years	Represents the people of a small district within the state.
State	State Senate	State senator	Usually 4 years	Represents the people of a large district within the state.
National	House of Representatives	U.S. representative	2 years	Represents the people of a district within a state; number of representatives for each state depends on state population.
National	United States Senate	U.S. senator	6 years	All residents in each state are represented by 2 senators.

Recently, many cities and a number of states have placed **term limits** on their lawmakers. Term limits restrict the length of time an incumbent can serve. Term limits arise from the belief that officials who hold office for long periods of time become less responsive to the will of the people. Some states have attempted also to limit the terms of their national representatives. However, the federal courts have held such state laws to be unconstitutional.

5. Which idea related to the passage demonstrates faulty logic?

   (1) People elect official representatives in a republican form of government.
   (2) The principle of republicanism exists at each level of government.
   (3) Any elected official holding office for a long time becomes unresponsive to the people.
   (4) Many cities and states have limited the number of terms officials can serve.
   (5) State laws that limit the terms of U.S. lawmakers are unconstitutional.

6. Which office demonstrates the principle of at-large representation?

   (1) state representative
   (2) state senator
   (3) member of Congress
   (4) U.S. senator
   (5) justice of the U.S. Supreme Court

7. What do all the officeholders listed on the chart have in common?

   (1) All serve four-year terms.
   (2) All represent the people of specific geographic areas.
   (3) All are limited in the number of terms they can serve.
   (4) All are appointed by the executive branch.
   (5) All are equally qualified to hold office.

8. What does the information in the passage and the chart indicate is valued most highly in a republican form of government?

   (1) order in society
   (2) term limits
   (3) the will of the people
   (4) reelection to office
   (5) levels of government

Answers start on page 311.

Directions: This is a ten-minute practice test. After ten minutes, mark the last question you finished. Then complete the test and check your answers. If most of your answers were correct, but you didn't finish, try to work faster next time. Choose the <u>one best answer</u> to each question.

Questions 1 through 3 refer to the following paragraph.

General political attitudes can be described by a number of terms. A person who wants drastic and basic changes in government and society is often called a radical. A person who believes that government programs can help solve economic and social problems is frequently labeled a liberal. Someone who feels that the federal government is too powerful and has too much control over people's lives is generally considered to be a conservative. A reactionary is someone who wants to return things to the way they used to be. There is nothing bad about having any of these political attitudes. But because some of these beliefs are in opposition, people who think one way often use the other labels to insult those who hold one of the other sets of beliefs.

1. What is true of the political labels described in the paragraph?

   (1) They are positive and complimentary terms.
   (2) They are negative and critical terms.
   (3) They distinguish differences in political beliefs.
   (4) They are not accurate descriptions of how people feel about government.
   (5) Some labels are better than others.

2. According to the paragraph, how are radicals and reactionaries similar?

   (1) Both groups support change.
   (2) Both groups are dangerous.
   (3) Both groups are closer to conservatives than they are to liberals.
   (4) Both groups are closer to liberals than they are to conservatives.
   (5) Reactionaries want to return to the past while radicals want to try something new.

3. Which of the following is an example of a stereotype that many people hold?

   (1) Liberals tend to be against change.
   (2) People differ in political attitudes.
   (3) Radicals never want change.
   (4) Democrats are always liberals.
   (5) Republicans run against Democrats.

4. Third parties often have promoted controversial ideas that later became law. For example, calling for a five-day work week seemed extreme in the late 1880s, when many people worked every day. But this change and other major reforms that guaranteed a minimum wage and unemployment benefits were first proposed by third-party platforms.

   Based on this information, which political label would best apply to members of third parties?

   (1) radical
   (2) conservative
   (3) reactionary
   (4) Republican
   (5) Democrat

5. In some states, if three or more candidates run for the same elective office and no candidate gets a majority of the vote, the law requires a second election to be held between the top two candidates.

   What would such an electoral process prevent?

   (1) an election with more than two candidates
   (2) a third-party candidate from winning
   (3) the election of more men than women
   (4) the election of more challengers than incumbent officeholders
   (5) the election of an officeholder who is supported by fewer than half the voters

Questions 6 and 7 refer to the following paragraph and cartoon.

The two major political parties are often shown as animals: the Republican Party as an elephant; the Democratic Party as a donkey. The cartoon refers to their working relationship in Congress.

BY THE POWERS VESTED, WE DECLARE OURSELVES JOINED AT THE WALLET

SO LONG AS WE BOTH SHALL PROSPER

BALANCED BUDGET

Draper Hill © 1997. Reprinted with permission from *The Detroit News.*

6. What is the main idea of the cartoon?

(1) Republicans control Congress.
(2) Democrats are better than Republicans.
(3) Democrats and Republicans put aside their differences to pass the balanced-budget law.
(4) The Republicans have adopted the Democrats' platform.
(5) Both parties are working together to raise campaign funds for all candidates.

7. What promise is the elephant making in the cartoon?

(1) Republicans and Democrats will work together in the future.
(2) Both parties' leaders are always interested only in the good of the nation.
(3) The two parties will share power.
(4) Republican leaders will not try to block legislation proposed by Democrats.
(5) The parties will cooperate in Congress as long as it is in their best interests.

Questions 8 through 10 refer to the following paragraph.

Funds for most political campaigns come from private sources. No person may contribute more than $1,000 to a candidate for federal office. However, this limit does not apply to state and local races. Political action committees (PACs) of special interest groups may contribute more. PACs cannot give more than $5,000 to a federal candidate, but there is no limit on how many candidates a PAC can support. PACs often contribute to both major-party candidates for important offices. PACs may give unlimited sums of money to the parties themselves, which the parties then use to help their candidates.

8. What do their political contributions suggest that special interest groups value most?

(1) money
(2) influence
(3) competition
(4) Republican principles
(5) Democratic principles

9. How does fundraising by candidates running for Congress differ from fundraising by candidates running for a governor's office?

(1) Congressional campaigns are financed by federal funds.
(2) There are no limits on how much money a candidate for Congress can raise.
(3) PACs contribute to candidates for Congress.
(4) Donations to congressional candidates are limited in size.
(5) PACs contribute to candidates for governor.

10. Why have current laws to reform campaign financing proven to be ineffective?

(1) Special interest groups have formed PACs.
(2) The limits on PAC contributions are too high.
(3) Limits on individual contributions are too high.
(4) PACs have enough money to contribute to many candidates.
(5) There are no limits on contributions.

Answers start on page 312.

Lesson 14

GED SKILL Applying Information to New Contexts

context
the circumstances or setting in which an event occurs

Frequently, things you have already learned in one **context** can be applied to other situations that you encounter. To apply information to a new context means to take information that you learned in one situation and use it to help you understand a related situation. It is a useful life skill as well as an aid in understanding social studies material.

For example, you might read that the Supreme Court has declared that a law must not be enforced because it violates the Constitution. Later, you find out that the local police can no longer enforce another law that was in effect in your community. You can apply what you learned about the first law to conclude that the second law was probably also unconstitutional.

Sometimes information is presented in a general way. If you understand the general idea, you can then apply it to a specific situation. Other times you may learn something through a specific example. You may then find out about another situation. If the two situations are similar, the information you learned about the first situation can be applied to help you better understand the second.

Read the following passage and answer the question below.

Many industries benefit from government programs. For example, agricultural research and crop **subsidies** are paid for by the U.S. government. Each year the government spends millions of dollars on research into soil erosion, pest control, and improving the quality of crops. The results of such research are usually given away free to farmers as part of the government's contribution to the public welfare.

Mark the federal government program that provides similar aid to an industry while also contributing to the nation's welfare.

_____ a. subsidies to a state to build new highways

_____ b. government crash tests on automobile safety

You were correct if you checked *option b*. Like the agricultural research, the crash test results help car makers build a better product. The entire nation benefits from the safety improvements that result. Applying information about how the government aids farmers helps you understand how the crash test program aids the auto industry. The original information cannot truly help you better understand *option a* because the two contexts are not similar.

TIP

The more two contexts are similar, the more information about one situation will apply in helping to understand the other. Knowing the effect of one government program helps you understand the effect of a different program.

Use the paragraph and the chart to complete the exercise below.

To carry out the government's operations, many departments and agencies have been created within the executive branch. Five of the most important executive departments and their main responsibilities are outlined in the chart below.

Some Departments of the Executive Branch and Their Functions	
Department	**Major Functions and Responsibilities**
Department of State	Conduct diplomacy and foreign affairs; maintain U.S. embassies in other countries; carry out U.S. foreign policy.
Department of the Treasury	Produce the supply of paper money and coins; collect duties on goods brought into the U.S. and enforce smuggling laws; collect taxes and enforce federal tax laws; supervise the operation of the nation's banks; supervise federal borrowing and manage the public debt.
Department of Defense	Provide for national security; manage the military services (Army, Navy, Air Force, and Marines) and assure the combat readiness of their equipment and personnel; conduct weapons research and testing; advise the president on military matters.
Department of Justice	Enforce federal criminal and civil laws—including business, drug, and civil rights laws—investigate their violation, and prosecute accused violators; enforce the nation's immigration policies and laws; manage federal prisons; act as the government's attorney in all court cases in which it is involved.
Department of the Interior	Manage the nation's publicly-owned land, water, and other natural resources including fish and wildlife, minerals, and national parks and forests.

1. The United States sends a delegate to represent the country at the United Nations. Put a check mark next to the department that would employ this person.

    _____ a. the Department of Defense

    _____ b. the Department of State

    _____ c. the Department of Justice

2. In the 1960s, the federal government aided African Americans in ending segregation and obtaining voting rights. Put a check mark next to the department involved in protecting African Americans' rights.

    _____ a. the Department of the Interior

    _____ b. the Department of Justice

    _____ c. the Department of State

3. A U.S. vacationer taking a trip to a foreign country may bring back merchandise up to a certain total value without having to pay customs duty. Put a check mark next to the department you would contact for more information about this.

    _____ a. the Department of the Treasury

    _____ b. the Department of State

    _____ c. the Department of the Interior

Answers start on page 313.

The federal government aids state and local governments, businesses, and individual Americans through a wide variety of **subsidy** and **social welfare** programs. Subsidies take several forms. A common type of subsidy is a direct cash payment. Most cash subsidies go to education, transportation, and health programs. The government might provide a grant to a school system to purchase educational materials, for example, or to a state department of transportation to pay the cost of repairing its highway system.

Another type of subsidy is a reduction of taxes for a particular reason. Tax-relief subsidies include tax credits for children's day care expenses and tax reductions for homeowners with mortgages. A business may receive a tax credit for installing energy-efficient machinery. The government also provides low-interest loans to people who have lost their homes or businesses in natural disasters. Low-interest loans to college students are another example.

In addition, the government sells many things and provides many services free or at a minimum cost. For example, it uses surplus farm products to subsidize school lunches throughout the United States. Such subsidies lower school meal costs, making a nourishing lunch affordable for most students. Those who cannot afford these low-cost meals can get a further cost reduction.

The government has other social welfare programs that are designed for special groups. However, a number of such programs affect almost all Americans. Many Americans use the following programs and agencies at one time or another.

Some Social Welfare Agencies and Programs	
Agency or Program	**Social Welfare Function**
Social Security	A federal insurance plan that pays monthly benefits to retirees and workers above a certain age, to disabled workers, and to the surviving spouses of deceased workers.
Department of Veterans Affairs (VA)	Provides people who have served in the armed forces with hospital care and money for education and job training, as well as special rates for home loans and life insurance.
Department of Housing and Urban Development (HUD)	Provides funds for housing for low-income families and for elderly or disabled Americans; also provides funds for rehabilitating urban areas.
Food Stamp Program	Provides free or reduced-cost groceries to persons having serious temporary or long-term financial difficulties.
Medicare	Pays most medical costs for retirees and workers above a certain age who qualify for social security benefits.
Unemployment Insurance	Pays weekly cash benefits to workers who have lost their jobs involuntarily.

Directions: Choose the one best answer to each question.

Questions 1 through 6 refer to the passage and the chart on page 162.

1. The automobile parts company that a woman worked for has laid her off. For which benefits is she most likely to be eligible?

   (1) unemployment insurance benefits
   (2) social security benefits
   (3) VA benefits
   (4) HUD benefits
   (5) food stamps

2. A 45-year-old man who fought in the Vietnam War has quit his job in a small town and moved with his family to a large city. His wife has found a well-paying job, but he has found that he needs more skills to be hired at a local factory. What would be his best course of action?

   (1) apply to the Social Security Administration
   (2) apply for food stamps
   (3) apply for Medicare
   (4) apply for unemployment insurance
   (5) apply to the Department of Veterans Affairs

3. A woman has operated her own business since she was 30. Even though she just turned 68, she remains active in the company. Lately she has been receiving treatment for severe headaches, but her insurance does not cover all the costs. Where should she check first to see if she can get assistance with these costs?

   (1) with unemployment insurance
   (2) with the food stamp program
   (3) with the Medicare program
   (4) with the Department of Veterans Affairs
   (5) with the local government

4. A man who was a construction worker for 45 years died recently. His wife, who is elderly, was employed for only a short time, spending most of her working years taking care of the children. Her son has advised her to apply for government benefits. Whom did the son probably tell his mother to contact?

   (1) the Department of Veterans Affairs
   (2) the Social Security Administration
   (3) the Department of Housing and Urban Development
   (4) the food stamp program
   (5) the unemployment insurance program

5. Which of the following is an example of a give-away subsidy?

   (1) free medical care and hospitalization benefits for veterans
   (2) low-interest, long-term home mortgages for people who fall below a certain income
   (3) property taxes on people's homes that are used to pay for schools
   (4) business tax-credits for buying certain machinery
   (5) federal taxes on alcohol, cigarettes, and gasoline

6. Which of its main missions is the U.S. government aiming to fulfill by providing subsidies and other similar programs?

   (1) It is setting up fair rules for running the government.
   (2) It is providing for the common defense.
   (3) It is promoting the general welfare of its citizens.
   (4) It is ensuring people's freedoms.
   (5) It is ensuring similar freedoms to future generations.

Answers start on page 313.

GED Practice • Lesson 14

Directions: Choose the one best answer to each question.

Questions 1 through 4 refer to the following graph and passage.

The federal government gets the money to pay for its programs and operating expenses in two ways: taxing and borrowing. The main source of revenue is the federal income tax. Americans who receive more than a minimum amount of income must pay part of their earnings to the federal government in the form of income taxes. Other government revenue comes from duties on imported goods and excise taxes on such products as gasoline, tobacco, and alcohol.

The Department of the Treasury borrows from American citizens and from citizens of foreign countries by offering Treasury notes and bonds for sale. Even though the person is "buying" the note or bond, the transaction is really a loan and thus a debt owed by the government. After a set number of years, the government must repay the cost of the bond or note plus pay the buyer interest on the loan. The total amount the government owes to purchasers of its notes and bonds is known as the **national debt.**

FEDERAL SPENDING BY CATEGORY, 1999

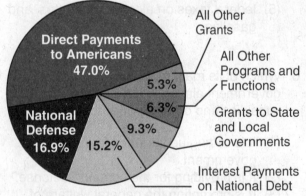

Direct Payments to Americans 47.0%
All Other Grants 5.3%
All Other Programs and Functions 6.3%
Grants to State and Local Governments 9.3%
National Defense 16.9%
15.2%
Interest Payments on National Debt

Source: Office of Management and Budget

1. Which part of the graph would include interest paid to people who buy government bonds?

   (1) National Defense
   (2) Direct Payments to Americans
   (3) Grants to State and Local Governments
   (4) All Other Grants
   (5) Interest Payments on National Debt

2. Which statement is true of government programs and spending?

   (1) All government services are provided to citizens for free.
   (2) The largest portion of money the government spends is paid directly to the people.
   (3) Government programs are supported solely by the taxes Americans pay.
   (4) The interest on the national debt helps pay for government programs.
   (5) The government spends more on defense than it does on social welfare.

3. Which is most likely to happen if the government spends more money than it collects?

   (1) Income taxes will go down.
   (2) Excise taxes will go down.
   (3) Taxes will increase.
   (4) The government will offer fewer bonds.
   (5) Americans will have to earn more money.

4. Which category on the graph would include monthly benefit checks from the Social Security Administration?

   (1) National Defense
   (2) Direct Payments to Americans
   (3) Grants to State and Local Governments
   (4) All Other Programs and Functions
   (5) General Revenues

TIP
When applying information in a new context, ask: What is similar? Are the events similar? Are the results similar?

Questions 5 through 8 refer to the following passage and document.

There are many advantages to living in the United States. However, the most important benefits of being an American are accompanied by and depend on equally important responsibilities. For example, the Bill of Rights guarantees every person a jury trial if he or she is accused of a crime. However, the exercise of this right depends on citizens being willing to serve when called for jury duty. But many citizens do not want to take the time to sit through a trial. So they find some reason to be excused from jury duty.

Much the same is true of voting. One reason people do not register to vote is that some states use voter registration lists to select candidates for jury duty. Other people just don't bother to register. The fewer the voters, however, the less likely it is that elected leaders truly represent the will of the people. This weakens democracy, undermining our system of government.

★ VOTER REGISTRATION CERTIFICATE TRAMMS COUNTY			School District TISD	SMD 4	City SALFP
Certificate Number 000000000	Gender M	Valid from 01/01/2001			
Date of Birth 11/08/1962	Prec No. 220	to 12/31/2002			
Name and Permanent Residence: Michael B. Livens 5098 McMurtry Drive Salinas, KS 55678					
✗ *Michael B. Livens*					

5. Why is it important for citizens to serve on juries when they are called to do so?

    (1) Jury duty is a requirement for voting.
    (2) An innocent person might otherwise be convicted.
    (3) A guilty person might otherwise go free.
    (4) Someday they might be accused of a crime and need to go before a jury.
    (5) Part of the Bill of Rights is threatened when citizens do not serve.

6. To which other common document is a voter registration card most similar?

    (1) a credit card
    (2) a driver's license
    (3) a birth certificate
    (4) a vaccination certificate
    (5) a certificate of insurance

7. Michael B. Livens calls the registrar to find out where he should vote. Which information from his card will help the registrar the most?

    (1) 220
    (2) 55678
    (3) SALFP
    (4) 11/08/1962
    (5) 01/01/2001

8. What important value of our political system is suggested by the requirement that voters must register before they can vote?

    (1) The people in charge of government have control over voting.
    (2) The greatest number of people possible should vote in elections.
    (3) Only a small number of people should get to vote in elections.
    (4) Only the people who meet the eligibility requirements should be allowed to vote.
    (5) The system should appear to be democratic while allowing only the wealthy to hold power.

Answers start on page 314.

Directions: This is a ten-minute practice test. After ten minutes, mark the last question you finished. Then complete the test and check your answers. If most of your answers were correct, but you didn't finish, try to work faster next time. Choose the <u>one best answer</u> to each question.

<u>Questions 1 through 4</u> refer to the following passage and the key document.

Our system of government empowers people to openly work for change in the government and in the society it represents. The most frequent expression of such change takes place in the voting booth on election day. But some of the most sweeping and dramatic changes have occurred in the courts.

One of the most important court cases in American history began after Oliver Brown attempted to enroll his daughter Linda in an all-white grade-school in Topeka, Kansas. He pointed out that the white school was in his neighborhood, while the school that black children were required to attend was on the other side of town. When the school board rejected Brown's request, he sued. The resulting case, *Brown v. Board of Education,* soon reached the Supreme Court of the United States.

In 1954, the Supreme Court struck down the practice of segregation in public schools. It overturned a long-standing principle that separate facilities for African Americans and whites were legal as long as the facilities were of equal quality. In the Court's decision, Chief Justice Earl Warren attacked the "separate but equal" doctrine:

Excerpt from *Brown v. Board of Education*
"Does segregation of children in public schools solely on the basis of race . . . deprive the children of the minority group of equal educational opportunities? We believe that it does. . . . To separate them from others . . . solely because of their race generates a feeling of inferiority . . . unlikely ever to be undone. . . . In the field of public education the doctrine of "separate but equal" has no place. Separate educational facilities are inherently unequal."

1. Why did Brown try to enroll his daughter in the "whites-only" school?

   (1) It was better than the black school.
   (2) It was closer than the black school.
   (3) He was required to do this by law.
   (4) He was a troublemaker.
   (5) He supported the "separate but equal" doctrine.

2. What does Chief Justice Warren's opinion suggest he considered most valuable and important for a child to succeed in school and life?

   (1) a high-quality public education
   (2) equal opportunity to go to college
   (3) effective and caring teachers
   (4) a feeling of equality and self-worth
   (5) a willingness to stand up for one's rights

3. What other civil rights gain most likely resulted from the principles established in the *Brown* decision?

   (1) the end of job discrimination based on race
   (2) passage of laws guaranteeing voting rights for African Americans throughout the nation
   (3) an increase in the number of black voters
   (4) a greater number of black elected officials
   (5) an end to separate seating by race on buses and trains and in movie theaters

4. Based on the passage, how did Linda and Oliver Brown change American society?

   (1) They started the civil rights movement.
   (2) They ended discrimination in America.
   (3) They restored the Supreme Court's power.
   (4) Their case led to the requirement that public schools be racially integrated.
   (5) Their case led more people to use the courts to work for social justice.

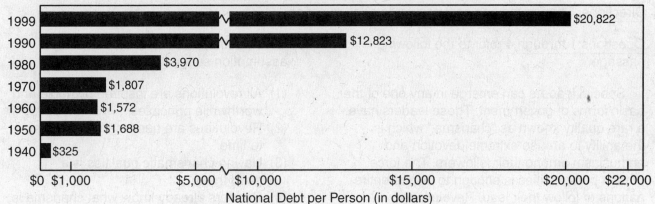

U.S. NATIONAL DEBT PER CAPITA (1940–1999)

Sources: U.S. Bureau of the Census: U.S. Office of Public Debt

5. In 1950, how much did the federal government owe for every person in the United States?

   (1) $ 325
   (2) $ 1,572
   (3) $ 1,688
   (4) $ 1,807
   (5) $12,823

6. Which of the following statements is supported by the information in the graph?

   (1) The per-capita national debt has risen in every decade since 1940.
   (2) The total national debt in 1990 was $3,233,313,000,000.
   (3) In 1960 the government's total national debt was less than it was in 1950.
   (4) Between 1980 and 1990, the national debt per person more than tripled.
   (5) Each year, the federal government spends more money than it collects.

7. To which common financial transaction is the change in the national debt most similar?

   (1) monthly increases in a credit-card balance
   (2) monthly payments on a home mortgage
   (3) paying off an auto loan in advance
   (4) rent payment on an apartment
   (5) investment in a certificate of deposit (CD)

8. In 1999, the federal government took in more money than it spent. This meant that the government had a surplus of money left over in 1999. Yet the total national debt in 1999 was nearly $150 billion higher than it was in 1998.

   What was the most likely cause of the increase in the national debt?

   (1) The government had to borrow money during 1999.
   (2) The government did not pay off any of the national debt during 1999.
   (3) The government's spending exceeded its income during 1999.
   (4) The government spent much more in 1999 than it took in during 1998.
   (5) More interest accumulated on the national debt during 1999 than the government paid off.

9. Poor people are more in favor of social welfare than are rich people. Workers are more in favor of Medicare and Medicaid than are business owners. Executives are more in favor of tax shelters than are clerical workers.

   Which generalization about political opinions does this information best support?

   (1) They are largely shaped by self-interest.
   (2) They express a political party's viewpoint.
   (3) They are related to educational level.
   (4) They are influenced by age and gender.
   (5) They depend on the holder's occupation.

Answers start on page 314.

Unit 3 Cumulative Review Civics and Government

Directions: Choose the one best answer to each question.

Questions 1 through 4 refer to the following passage.

Special leaders can emerge in any one of the basic forms of government. These leaders have a rare quality known as "charisma," which is the ability to arouse extreme devotion and enthusiasm among their followers. The force of their personalities is enough to inspire entire nations to follow their lead. Revolutionary movements sometimes form around charismatic figures who appear to represent or symbolize the principles and ideas they advocate.

Two of the most famous charismatic leaders of history are the visionary Joan of Arc and, later, France's great military leader and ruler Napoleon Bonaparte. In more recent times, notable charismatic figures have included the Nazi dictator Adolf Hitler, India's brilliant Mohandas Gandhi, China's Mao Zedong, Great Britain's Winston Churchill, and Cuba's Fidel Castro.

The nature of American democracy hinders the development of such powerful and popular figures. However, American leaders whose personality and ideas inspired large numbers of devoted followers include Franklin D. Roosevelt, John F. Kennedy, and Ronald Reagan.

1. Which title best summarizes the passage?

   (1) The World's Charismatic Leaders
   (2) The Dangers of Charisma
   (3) How Democracy Limits the Power of Charismatic Leaders
   (4) Why Charismatic Leaders Support Change
   (5) Where Charismatic Leaders Come From

2. Which of the following is an opinion stated in or implied by the passage?

   (1) Joan of Arc claimed to have visions.
   (2) Ronald Reagan was a popular president.
   (3) Adolf Hitler was a Nazi.
   (4) Mohandas Gandhi was a brilliant person.
   (5) Fidel Castro is a dictator.

3. Which of the following is an unstated assumption suggested by the passage?

   (1) All revolutions are inspired by noble and worthwhile principles.
   (2) Revolutions are necessary from time to time.
   (3) Having charismatic qualities is a good thing.
   (4) Readers already know what charisma is.
   (5) The political figures identified will be familiar to readers.

4. Which statement stereotypes charismatic leaders?

   (1) They can arise in any political system.
   (2) They include both men and women.
   (3) They all are revolutionaries.
   (4) They all inspire others to follow them.
   (5) They all arouse devotion from their followers.

5. One result of decentralized government control, some people believe, is that standards of public service vary greatly from area to area. People who live in areas with high standards benefit, while those in areas with low standards suffer as a result. Public education provides an example. Local control of education increases inequality, according to this view. Some school systems maintain high educational standards and others have low standards. The result is that not all citizens have equal educational opportunity.

Which is an example of a centralized government service that does not vary in quality from place to place?

   (1) control of public education by local school boards
   (2) city building codes and zoning restrictions
   (3) federal regulation of the banking industry
   (4) water and sewage treatment districts
   (5) local public housing projects

NON SEQUITUR

by WILEY

©1995 Wiley Miller / Dist. by Universal Press Syndicate

6. Which fact does the cartoonist assume you know to understand the cartoon?

(1) The federal government aids American businesses.
(2) The Internal Revenue Service collects taxes from individuals and businesses.
(3) The Internal Revenue Service welcomes taxpayers to stop by with questions.
(4) The Internal Revenue Service is trying to stop companies from building factories overseas.
(5) Most American businesses are not making a profit.

7. What is the main message of the cartoon?

(1) American business leaders should watch where they walk.
(2) More Americans should start their own businesses.
(3) Most business people are corrupt and must be carefully watched by the government.
(4) Tax collectors should use every method possible to get businesses to pay taxes.
(5) Federal tax laws make it difficult to successfully run a business in America.

TIP Political cartoonists use labels as well as pictures to present their opinions. Pay careful attention to all labels when interpreting a political cartoon.

8. Which of the following is an opinion with which the cartoonist would disagree?

(1) The United States has a free enterprise system.
(2) Some businesses have high incomes.
(3) The Internal Revenue Service is fair in its dealings.
(4) Taxes on businesses are too high.
(5) Businesses that make profits should pay taxes.

9. In 1964, Congress created Medicare, a program that provides government health insurance for elderly Americans. Today the financial health of this program has deteriorated, and there are not enough funds to ensure adequate care for eligible recipients in the future.

Which of the following is the most likely reason for Medicare's financial crisis?

(1) Government leaders do not care about the health of the American people.
(2) The number of elderly citizens has rapidly declined.
(3) There has been a dramatic increase in the number of elderly people.
(4) Americans are healthier because they are getting yearly medical checkups.
(5) Americans cannot rely on government programs.

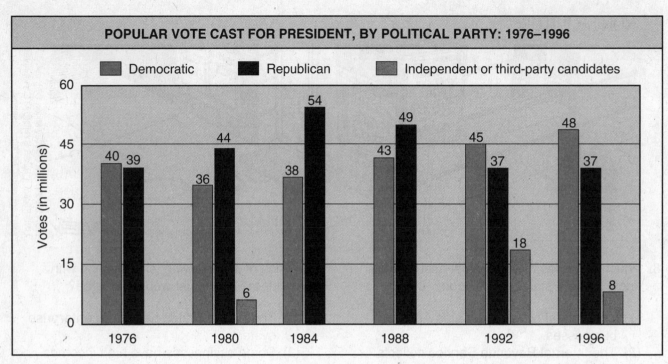

POPULAR VOTE CAST FOR PRESIDENT, BY POLITICAL PARTY: 1976–1996

Source: U.S. Bureau of the Census

10. In which elections did the Democratic candidate get more popular votes than the Republican candidate?

    (1) 1976, 1980, and 1984
    (2) 1980, 1984, and 1988
    (3) 1976, 1992, and 1996
    (4) 1980, 1992, and 1996
    (5) 1976, 1988, and 1992

11. Which of the following statements is supported by the information in the graph?

    (1) The number of people voting for third-party candidates steadily increased from 1976 to 1996.
    (2) From 1976 to 1996, the Republicans won the popular vote only twice in the six elections.
    (3) The Democratic margin of victory was greater in 1980 than it was in 1976.
    (4) Independent and third-party candidates took more votes from the Democratic candidate in 1996 than they did in 1980.
    (5) The Republican candidate had a larger margin of victory in 1984 than in 1988.

12. In which election did the candidate elected president receive less than half of the popular votes cast?

    (1) 1976
    (2) 1980
    (3) 1988
    (4) 1992
    (5) 1996

13. The federal Occupational Safety and Health Administration (OSHA) was created in 1970 and empowered to regulate workplace safety. OSHA sets safety standards, inspects workplaces, and fines companies that violate safety rules.

    Which of the following changes has most likely resulted from the creation of OSHA?

    (1) more dangers in the workplace
    (2) higher pay for workers
    (3) improved safety conditions
    (4) more strikes by labor unions
    (5) fewer part-time workers

Questions 14 through 17 refer to the following paragraph and chart.

In the American system of government and politics, a number of rights are considered basic to individual freedom and the practice of democracy. Some of these rights are spelled out in the Constitution. Others are simply values that most Americans share. The five rights that most Americans consider to be their most fundamental rights are described in the following chart.

Five Fundamental Rights
Freedom of Speech
The First Amendment states that "Congress shall make no law . . . abridging the freedom of speech." Free speech issues generally relate to expression by individuals.
Freedom of the Press
The First Amendment prohibits Congress from "abridging the freedom . . . of the press." Free press issues generally relate to expression by the media, such as newspapers and TV news programs.
Freedom of Association
Although there is no explicit guarantee of freedom of association, the Supreme Court has held that the right to associate is an outgrowth of the freedoms of speech and assembly.
Freedom of Religion
The First Amendment says that "Congress shall make no law respecting an establishment of religion, or prohibiting the free exercise thereof."
Equal Protection of the Laws
Equality before the law means that the law applies to all equally unless there is a clear reason for a distinction (such as a law setting a minimum age for working). This right is protected by the Fourteenth Amendment.

14. In recent years there has been controversy over whether prayer should be permitted in public schools. Which right would both sides be able to turn to for support in the dispute?

    (1) freedom of speech
    (2) freedom of the press
    (3) freedom of association
    (4) freedom of religion
    (5) equal protection of the laws

15. For almost 30 years, it was a crime in the United States to belong to the Communist Party. What right did such laws limit?

    (1) freedom of speech
    (2) freedom of the press
    (3) freedom of association
    (4) freedom of religion
    (5) equal protection of the laws

16. The Civil Rights Act of 1964 prohibited discrimination based on race and gender. What right likely guided the development and passage of this law?

    (1) freedom of speech
    (2) freedom of the press
    (3) freedom of association
    (4) freedom of religion
    (5) equal protection of the laws

17. A commentator on a television news program criticizes an elected government official for giving summer jobs to the children of campaign supporters. When the elected official complains to the television station, what right does the station cite in support of the commentator?

    (1) freedom of speech
    (2) freedom of the press
    (3) freedom of association
    (4) freedom of religion
    (5) equal protection of the laws

18. "For democracy to function, voters need to be well-informed decision-makers." Based on this opinion, which of the following should be most highly valued in a democracy?

    (1) tradition
    (2) wealth
    (3) neighborliness
    (4) individuality
    (5) education

Questions 19 through 21 refer to the following table.

Number of Government Employees, 1997				
Function	Federal	State	Local	Total
Education	11,000	2,114,000	7,095,000	9,220,000
Health and hospitals	299,000	665,000	808,000	1,772,000
Defense (civilians)	854,000	—	—	854,000
Police	95,000	94,000	762,000	951,000
Postal service	854,000	—	—	854,000
Streets and highways	4,000	252,000	297,000	553,000

Source: U.S. Bureau of the Census

19. How many people worked for state governments in education in 1997?

    (1)   11,000
    (2)   299,000
    (3) 2,114,000
    (4) 7,095,000
    (5) 9,220,000

20. Based on the information in the table, which service is most likely provided at state and local levels rather than at the national level?

    (1) building public elementary, middle, and high schools and hiring teachers
    (2) defending the borders of the nation
    (3) paying interest to holders of government bonds to pay off the national debt
    (4) delivering letters to people in cities and suburbs and on farms
    (5) maintaining and repairing the White House and monuments in Washington, D.C.

21. Which of the following statements is supported by the information in the table?

    (1) More government workers are involved in education than in any other field.
    (2) State police forces have grown more slowly than local police forces.
    (3) Government employment in the area of defense is decreasing.
    (4) The best paid federal workers are postal employees.
    (5) Most street and highway workers are employed by state government.

Questions 22 and 23 refer to the following paragraph.

The main purpose of a special interest group is to promote the concerns of its members. One of the methods such groups use to achieve this goal is a practice called "lobbying." This means trying to convince government leaders to support or favor certain causes. Many special interest groups employ paid lobbyists. These professionals work at all levels of government, all across the country.

22. What is the job of a lobbyist?

    (1) to run for political office
    (2) to campaign for specific candidates
    (3) to give volunteer help to government officials on tight budgets
    (4) to convince government leaders to support certain causes
    (5) to travel around the country

23. Which of the following actions is most like lobbying?

    (1) a TV newscaster reporting on the activities of government officials
    (2) writing a letter to a government official that presents your position on a controversial issue
    (3) writing a letter to the editor of your local newspaper about a controversial issue
    (4) a newspaper editor writing a column that takes a position on a controversial issue
    (5) joining a special interest group

Questions 24 through 26 refer to the following passage.

More than any other person, the president is responsible for the nation's foreign policy. As commander-in-chief of the armed forces, the president can send troops all over the world. The president has the power to make treaties and appoint ambassadors to represent the United States in other nations. The president also receives ambassadors to the United States from foreign nations. The president can refuse to recognize another country's officials as its legitimate government.

The president's powers over foreign affairs are supported by the U.S. Constitution as well as by practical considerations. In dealing with other nations, the United States must speak with one voice, and that voice belongs to the president. In addition, overseas events can require a speedy response. One person can react more quickly than can Congress or one of its committees. Finally, foreign policy often requires secrecy. To share national security concerns and overseas plans with all the members of Congress would be risky where secrecy is involved.

24. Which of the following would be a good title for this passage?

(1) Foreign Policy
(2) The President's Role in Foreign Policy
(3) The Importance of Foreign Policy
(4) Congress and Foreign Policy
(5) The National Security of the United States

25. Which of the following is a conclusion stated in the first paragraph?

(1) The president has more responsibility for the nation's foreign policy than anyone else.
(2) The president is commander-in-chief of the armed forces.
(3) The president makes treaties and appoints ambassadors to represent the United States.
(4) The president receives foreign ambassadors who are sent to the United States.
(5) The president can recognize or refuse to recognize another nation's government.

26. At the time of the 1980 Olympic Games, the former Soviet Union had sent troops to invade Afghanistan. President Jimmy Carter decided to refuse to let U.S. athletes take part in the Olympics, which were being held in the Soviet Union. What foreign policy power of the president did this action illustrate?

(1) power as commander-in-chief of the armed forces
(2) power to grant recognition to other governments
(3) power to send and receive ambassadors
(4) power as head of the U.S. Olympic Committee
(5) power to conduct U.S. affairs with other nations

Clay Bennett, North America Syndicate. Reprinted by permission.

27. Which of the following is an opinion expressed in the cartoon?

(1) Members of Congress present themselves as independent even though they follow the advice of special interest groups.
(2) To get elected, members of Congress must raise money to finance their campaigns.
(3) Lobbyists try to persuade members of Congress to vote in ways that favor the goals of the interest groups they represent.
(4) The speech writers that many members of Congress have on their staffs tell the legislators exactly what to say.
(5) Most members of Congress and most lobbyists are middle-aged white men.

In recent years state governments have turned to lotteries for an additional source of income. New Hampshire launched the first of the modern state lotteries in 1964. Since then, 36 other states and the District of Columbia have begun operating lotteries. Many state officials view their lottery as a favorable alternative to raising taxes.

The Top Ten States in Lottery Revenue, 1997		
State	Revenue from Ticket Sales (in millions of dollars)	Proceeds After Prizes and Expenses (in millions of dollars)
New York	$3,644	$1,531
Texas	3,385	1,174
Massachusetts	3,002	696
Ohio	2,445	1,046
Florida	1,965	819
California	1,930	722
Pennsylvania	1,611	683
New Jersey	1,502	663
Michigan	1,487	586
Illinois	1,462	572

Source: U.S. Bureau of the Census

28. How much money did California's lottery provide in 1997 to fund the state's other operations and programs?

(1) $ 722,000
(2) $ 1,930,000
(3) $ 7,220,000
(4) $ 722,000,000
(5) $1,930,000,000

29. Which statement is supported by the information provided about lotteries?

(1) Lotteries provide enough revenue for the states that use them.
(2) Lotteries can supply millions of dollars in revenue for some states.
(3) Ten states operate legal lotteries.
(4) New York has the best state lottery system in the nation.
(5) States now can rely only on lotteries for their revenue.

30. Which of these lotteries is the least efficient in providing operating money for the state?

(1) Massachusetts
(2) Pennsylvania
(3) New Jersey
(4) Michigan
(5) Illinois

31. The president does not have the power to declare war. Only Congress has this power. Yet two major wars, the Korean War and the Vietnam War, were never declared by Congress.

What is implied by this situation?

(1) U.S. presidents can declare war if Congress refuses to do so.
(2) Presidents have sent U.S. forces into combat without a declaration of war.
(3) The Korean War and Vietnam War were not really wars.
(4) North Korea and North Vietnam violated treaties that they had with the United States.
(5) The Korean War led to the Vietnam War.

Answers start on page 315.

Cumulative Review Performance Analysis
Unit 3 • Civics and Government

Use the Answers and Explanations starting on page 315 to check your answers to the Unit 3 Cumulative Review. Then use the chart to figure out the skill areas in which you need more practice.

On the chart, circle the questions that you answered correctly. Write the number correct for each skill area. Add the number of questions that you got correct on the Cumulative Review. If you feel that you need more practice, go back and review the lessons for the skill areas that were difficult for you.

Questions	Number Correct	Skill Area	Lessons for Review
1, **7**, **10**, **19**, 22, 24, **28**, 31	____/8	Comprehension	1, 2, 7
2, 3, **6**, **8**, 9, **12**, 13, 25, **27**, **30**	____/10	Analysis	3, 4, 6, 9, 10, 11, 12
5, **14**, **15**, **16**, **17**, **20**, 23, 26	____/8	Application	14
4, **11**, 18, **21**, 29	____/5	Evaluation	5, 8, 13
TOTAL CORRECT	____/31		

Question numbers in **boldface** are based on graphics.

UNIT 4

Economics

Economics is the study of the decisions involved in the way goods and services are produced, distributed, consumed, or used. Understanding economics equips us to be better consumers and to make wiser choices that will bring us greater satisfaction when we spend our time and money.

Economics is also part of our everyday lives. We deal with economics when we collect a paycheck, shop, or pay taxes. Many of the choices we make involve economics in some way, whether we realize it or not. Economics is also an important part of the GED Social Studies Test, making up 20 percent of the test questions.

High-paying jobs require education and job skills training in today's high-tech economy.

The lessons in this unit include:

THINKING SKILLS

○ Using ideas in new contexts

○ Identifying implications from graphs

○ Assessing the adequacy of supporting data

GED SKILL **Using Ideas in New Contexts**

concept
an idea or principle that applies to many individual circumstances or situations

You already have learned that a piece of information from one specific context or situation can help you understand similar situations. However, you can also apply a general idea called a **concept** to situations that may not even be related. For instance, the concept of "distance" helps determine how long it takes to get somewhere. It also helps you understand that you can increase your mealtime at work if you eat in the lunchroom rather than go out to a restaurant. You are using the concept of distance in analyzing how to spend your lunch break.

Applying concepts from economics to your daily shopping helps you to be a smarter consumer. One such concept in consumer economics is getting value for your money. Perhaps you have considered buying shirts with the logo of a popular sportswear maker. The shirts are attractive, but they cost much more than other shirts. Your clothing budget is limited. But, consider quality. They may be of higher quality and may last longer than less-costly shirts. Thus they may provide more value for the money. You are applying the economic concept of quality versus cost to your shopping.

To use ideas in new contexts, you apply other skills that involve analysis and evaluation. These include identifying cause-and-effect relationships, making comparisons, and drawing conclusions.

TIP

To apply an idea to a situation, look for how the idea helps explain, define, or reveal a cause or effect of the situation.

Read the passage and answer the question below.

Very primitive societies produced everything they needed themselves. As various groups gained different skills and produced different things, a **barter system** arose. In a barter economy, people exchange the products or labor skills they have for those they want. Later, the use of money developed. Money allowed for greater flexibility in the distribution of **goods** and **services.** In a **money economy,** products and services are exchanged for coins, paper money, or checks. This **currency** can then be used to obtain other products and services.

Which of the following transactions involves barter?

_____ a. buying vegetables at a farmer's market

_____ b. giving old furniture to a charity

_____ c. trading a wristwatch for a CD

You were correct if you chose *option c.* This is the only transaction that involves the exchange of one product for another. *Option a* is a transaction that involves money. *Option b* is not barter because no product is received in return.

Use the passage and the diagram to answer the questions.

One reason currency developed in most societies is that barter restricts the distribution of goods and makes it more difficult for people to obtain the products they want or need. The diagram illustrates the advantages of a money economy. Dan's customers want ground beef, but he does not have enough of it to meet the demand. In addition, his customers do not want to buy his broccoli. Dan can get ground beef from Maria, who has more than she needs and sell his extra broccoli to Polly, whose customers have bought all she has in stock and want more.

Imagine how this would work out if there were no money. Dan needs ground beef and Maria has too much. But Dan has nothing that Maria needs to give her in exchange. Maria does not need his broccoli; she needs bread and Dan does not have any bread to spare. Polly has extra bread, but she has no need for Maria's ground beef. Instead, Polly needs broccoli, but Dan does not need the bread she has available in exchange. In a barter system it is more difficult for people to obtain what they need and dispose of goods they do not need.

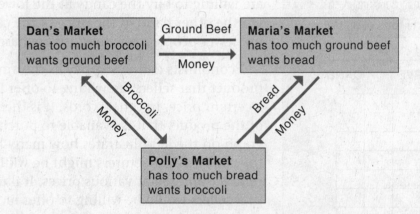

1. Put a check mark next to each way Dan can barter to get ground beef from Maria.

_____ a. Trade broccoli to Polly for bread, and trade bread to Maria for ground beef.

_____ b. Mow Maria's lawn in exchange for ground beef.

_____ c. Ask Maria to give him the ground beef because they are friends.

2. Use a *B* to label each context in which the concepts of the barter system apply. Use an *M* to label each context in which concepts of a money economy apply.

_____ a. Dan lets Polly use his delivery truck in return for 500 pounds of cabbage.

_____ b. Maria sells her store to Polly, and they negotiate the purchase price.

_____ c. Polly borrows money from Maria and uses it to buy Dan's delivery truck.

_____ d. Dan reduces the price of broccoli in order to entice more customers to buy it.

_____ e. Polly repays the loan from Maria by letting Maria use the delivery truck one week each month.

Answers start on page 318.

The main factor that determines the cost of a product is the relationship between demand and supply. In general, if the demand for a product is greater than the supply, the price of the product will rise. If the supply of the product is greater than the demand, the product's price will fall.

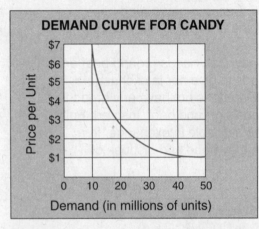

DEMAND CURVE FOR CANDY

To economists, **demand** is the amount of a product that purchasers are willing to buy at a certain price. The graph on the left shows what the demand might be for a special type of candy at various price levels. It illustrates a general principle of economics: As the price of a product changes, so does the demand for it. The graph shows that as the price of the candy declines, the demand for it increases—that is, more consumers are willing to buy the candy at the lower price. On the other hand, if the price of the candy goes up, fewer people are willing to purchase it.

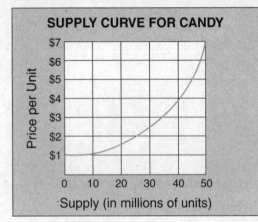

SUPPLY CURVE FOR CANDY

Economists define **supply** as the amount of a product that sellers are willing to offer for sale at a certain price. In other words, it is the amount of the product that is available to purchasers. The graph on the left illustrates how many bars of the candy manufacturers might be willing to produce and sell at various prices. It illustrates that sellers would be willing to offer more of the candy for sale at higher prices than they would at lower prices. At higher prices, however, the supply of the candy may exceed the demand for it, causing sellers to be left with a **surplus** of the product. On the other hand, at low prices, the demand for the candy may exceed the supply, causing a **shortage** of the candy.

The relationship between supply and demand may make it seem like prices are always rising and falling in a continuous cycle of change. However, they do not. This is because of another economic principle called **equilibrium.** Equilibrium occurs when the number of people willing to buy a product at a certain price equals the supply that sellers are willing to provide at that price. Simply put, equilibrium is the point at which supply equals demand. This is the point at which sellers will price their products.

A seller's business will be best at the equilibrium price, where it can earn the most money and not have a surplus of the product left unsold. Buyers will be able to find and buy the product, and sellers will be able to sell most of what they produce.

Directions: Choose the one best answer to each question.

Questions 1 through 6 refer to the passage and the graphs on pages 180 and 181.

1. Based on the passage, what is the main factor that determines a product's selling price?

   (1) how much of the product the seller is willing to offer at a particular price
   (2) how much demand there is for the product compared to the supply available for purchase
   (3) how quickly the product wears out and has to be replaced
   (4) whether the seller provides a warranty or guarantee with the product
   (5) how often the manufacturer of the product produces a new and improved version

2. What will most likely happen when the price of a product goes down?

   (1) Demand for the product will go up.
   (2) Demand for the product will go down.
   (3) Demand for the product will stay the same.
   (4) The supply of the product will go up.
   (5) The supply of the product will stay the same.

3. Based on the supply curve, suppliers are willing to produce the most of a product when the product is being offered under which of the following conditions?

   (1) at a low price
   (2) at a moderate price
   (3) at a high price
   (4) by many producers
   (5) when supply of the product exceeds demand

4. When is a product surplus likely to occur?

   (1) when demand for the product goes down
   (2) when demand for the product goes up
   (3) when the price of the product goes down
   (4) when supply of the product goes down and its price goes up
   (5) when the equilibrium price is reached

5. Based on this graph, what is the equilibrium price for the candy?

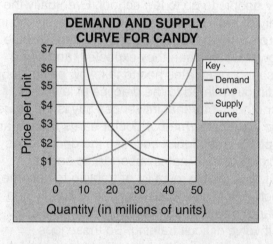

DEMAND AND SUPPLY CURVE FOR CANDY

Price per Unit: $7, $6, $5, $4, $3, $2, $1

Quantity (in millions of units): 0, 10, 20, 30, 40, 50

Key
— Demand curve
— Supply curve

   (1) $1
   (2) $2
   (3) $4
   (4) $5
   (5) $7

6. Imagine that eating the candy is shown to increase the risk for cold sores. How might this affect the demand for the candy and its equilibrium price?

   (1) It would raise demand and raise the equilibrium price.
   (2) It would raise demand and lower the equilibrium price.
   (3) It would lower demand and raise the equilibrium price.
   (4) It would lower demand and lower the equilibrium price.
   (5) It would lower demand but would not change the equilibrium price.

Answers start on page 318.

GED Practice • Lesson 15

Directions: Choose the one best answer to each question.

Questions 1 through 4 refer to the following passage and graph.

The principles of supply and demand also help determine workers' wages. If more people want to work at a certain occupation than there are jobs available, the pay for that work will be lower than if there are a lot of jobs and few people to fill them. If the supply of or demand for workers changes, so may the wages in that occupation. For example, at one time there was a shortage of lawyers, and high pay prompted many people to go to law school. Eventually the supply of lawyers exceeded demand, resulting in a surplus. Many beginning lawyers had to settle for lower wages than they expected, and some law-school graduates had to take low paying jobs not directly related to the practice of law.

Another factor that influences pay is the value of the work performed. A doctor earns more than a doctor's receptionist because the doctor does specialized work that is important to society.

Of course, it takes a lot of training to become a doctor. But training also relates to supply and demand. Fewer people are qualified to fill jobs that involve difficult training. So those jobs generally pay more than jobs that require less training. Unpleasant or hazardous work is the exception. Jobs in plants that process nuclear materials require little training. However, these jobs expose workers to potentially harmful radiation. Thus, these jobs pay well since few people want them.

1. Which two occupations are closest in pay?

   (1) teacher and dental hygienist
   (2) medical illustrator and sales clerk
   (3) messenger and typist
   (4) sales clerk and doctor's office receptionist
   (5) teacher and park naturalist

2. Which is the most likely explanation of why messengers earn more than medical illustrators?

   (1) Medical illustration is a dangerous job.
   (2) There is less demand for medical illustrators.
   (3) Messenger is a more desirable job.
   (4) There are many more messengers than medical illustrators.
   (5) Medical illustrators require more training than messengers.

3. The chart shows that police officers have a high starting pay. What gives the best explanation for the high salary police make?

   (1) The job of police officer is dangerous.
   (2) The demand for police officers is smaller than the supply of people who want the job.
   (3) Training is required for the job.
   (4) Most police officers are men.
   (5) Police officers provide a more valuable service to society than doctors do.

4. What conclusion about the starting pay of lawyers is supported by the information?

   (1) It is better than the pay for teachers.
   (2) It is rising rapidly.
   (3) It is better than the pay of any of the occupations shown on the graph.
   (4) It was better in the past than it is today.
   (5) It is below that of police officers.

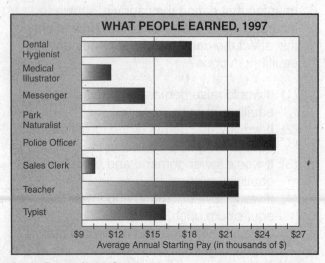

WHAT PEOPLE EARNED, 1997

Dental Hygienist
Medical Illustrator
Messenger
Park Naturalist
Police Officer
Sales Clerk
Teacher
Typist

$9 $12 $15 $18 $21 $24 $27
Average Annual Starting Pay (in thousands of $)

Source: Bureau of Labor Statistics

The American economy is said to go through an eight-to-ten-year **business cycle.** This cycle has four phases: expansion, peak, contraction, and trough. During **expansion,** business activity increases until it reaches a high point, or peak. During **contraction,** business activity decreases until it reaches a low point, or trough. Although minor upswings and downswings happen all the time, the overall pattern of the business cycle is to rise, then fall, and then rise again.

Movement in the economy is classified by many different terms that explain the effects that wages, production, and money supply have on one another—and on the business cycle—at any given time. The chart identifies some of these terms and briefly defines the economic trends they describe.

ECONOMICS TERMS AND DEFINITIONS

Term	Description
inflation	a general increase in prices resulting from a decline in the value of money; occurs when there is more money in the economy than there are goods to buy
demand-pull inflation	an increase in prices that occurs when there is a greater demand for goods than there is a supply; results from too much money and relatively too few goods
cost-push inflation	an increase in prices caused by an increase in the cost of production; often results from a general rise in wages; cost-push inflation related to wages is sometimes called the wage-price spiral
recession	a period of general economic decline; characterized by production declines, rising unemployment, and people having less money to spend
depression	a severe reduction or slowing of business activity and in the flow of money in the economy; many people are unemployed and have little money to spend

5. Which word <u>best</u> describes the American economy?

   (1) positive
   (2) negative
   (3) changing
   (4) unchanging
   (5) large

6. Which economics term relates to <u>both</u> a recession and a depression?

   (1) inflation
   (2) peak
   (3) trough
   (4) expansion
   (5) upswing

7. In the year 2000, it cost $2 to purchase an item that cost $1 in 1990. Which economic condition does this illustrate?

   (1) inflation
   (2) recession
   (3) depression
   (4) expansion
   (5) contraction

8. Which is an unstated assumption the passage makes about the American economy?

   (1) It is currently on the rise.
   (2) Inflation has no effect on it.
   (3) Contraction is preferable to expansion.
   (4) Minor variations in the pattern can lead to recession or depression.
   (5) It is not seriously affected by minor variations in the pattern.

TIP

To apply an idea to a new situation, analyze the situation to make sure the idea clearly relates to it. Look for similarities between the original context and the new situation.

Answers start on page 319.

GED Mini-Test • Lesson 15

Directions: This is a ten-minute practice test. After ten minutes, mark the last question you finished. Then complete the test and check your answers. If most of your answers were correct, but you didn't finish, try to work faster next time. Choose the <u>one best answer</u> to each question.

<u>Questions 1 through 4</u> refer to the following table.

Unemployment as a Percentage of the Labor Force 1929–1943 and 1986–2000			
Year	Unemployment	Year	Unemployment
1929	3.2	1986	7.0
1931	15.9	1988	5.5
1933	24.9	1990	5.6
1935	20.1	1992	7.5
1937	14.3	1994	6.1
1939	17.2	1996	5.4
1941	9.9	1998	4.5
1943	1.9	2000	4.1

Source: U.S. Department of Commerce

1. According to the table, in which year was unemployment the worst?

   (1) 1929
   (2) 1933
   (3) 1941
   (4) 1992
   (5) 1998

2. How did unemployment rates in the 1990s compare with unemployment during the earlier years shown in the table?

   (1) The 1990s rates are lower than any earlier year shown in the table.
   (2) The 1990s rates are higher than any earlier year shown in the table.
   (3) The 1990s rates are about the same as the rates in the 1930s.
   (4) The 1990s rates are lower than the rates during the 1930s.
   (5) The 1990s rates are higher than the rates during the 1930s.

3. To draw an accurate conclusion about the effect World War II had on unemployment, what information do you need?

   (1) only the information in the table
   (2) the dates for the Great Depression
   (3) the year America entered the war
   (4) the causes and effects of the war
   (5) the total size of the available labor force

4. Workers' wages were higher in 1929 than they were in 1939. Which principle of economics does the table suggest was responsible for this difference in wages?

   (1) the relationship of supply and demand
   (2) the operation of the barter system
   (3) the forces of inflation
   (4) the occurrence of equilibrium
   (5) the operation of the money economy

<u>Question 5</u> refers to the following paragraph.

Interest is the amount of money earned on an investment. If an investment pays simple interest, the interest is earned only on the original amount of the investment. If an investment earns compound interest, the interest is earned on the original investment plus its earnings.

5. Alicia is trying to decide where to open a savings account. Alicia will receive the most interest on the $1,000 she intends to deposit from the accounts paying which of following rates and types of interest?

   (1) 4 percent simple interest
   (2) 4 percent compound interest
   (3) 5 percent simple interest
   (4) 6 percent simple interest
   (5) 6 percent compound interest

Businesses are organized in three basic ways. A proprietorship is a business that is owned by one person. The single owner gets all the profits and has to pay all the debts. The owner also has total control of how the company is managed.

A partnership is owned by at least two people. The owners share the management decisions. The profits and debts are also shared, usually according to the percentage of the company that each partner owns. However, each partner is usually legally responsible for all the company's debts if any other partner fails to pay his or her share.

A corporation is owned by one or more people but is itself a legal unit. Each owner holds shares of ownership of the corporation called stock. How much stock each owner holds depends on how much money he or she has invested in the company. The profits of a corporation are divided among the owners according to how much stock each owner holds. Each share receives the same amount. The company itself is responsible for its debts. If a corporation cannot pay its bills, the individual owners (shareholders) cannot be forced to pay.

6. In what way are proprietorships and partnerships alike?

(1) Both are large businesses.
(2) Both are small businesses.
(3) One person makes the business decisions.
(4) Both raise money by selling stock.
(5) The owners of each get the profits.

7. Based on the passage, what is the biggest difference between a partnership and a corporation?

(1) the size of the business
(2) the way business profits are divided
(3) responsibility for business debt
(4) the party who manages the daily operations of the business
(5) the number of people who own the business

8. Dan and Ann are opening a print shop. Ann owns two thirds of the business and Dan owns one third. Dan runs the presses, and Ann takes customers' orders. What do both Dan and Ann most likely assume?

(1) They will share equally in the profits.
(2) Dan's job is more important than Ann's.
(3) Ann will be responsible for all the bills.
(4) They will agree about business decisions.
(5) Ann will manage the business.

One of the most important factors in the economy is the consumer. Sales of items from candy to cars are a major part of what keeps the economy growing. When people have the money to buy more than just what they need to live, businesses profit.

When interest rates go down, the amount of money people borrow and spend goes up. But when consumers begin to feel a pinch in the pocketbook, they spend less. A decrease in spending hurts business. It often results in unemployment so that people have even less money to spend. Then the economy slows.

9. According to the paragraph, which is an effect of declining interest rates?

(1) Business activity slows down.
(2) People borrow more money.
(3) People have less money to spend.
(4) Fewer people buy houses.
(5) Consumers lose confidence in the economy.

10. The owner of Joe's Diner learns that unemployment is rising sharply. Based on this information and on the paragraph, what should he assume will happen to affect his business?

(1) The economy will grow.
(2) The interest rate on his loan will rise.
(3) He will have fewer customers.
(4) Other restaurants will raise prices.
(5) Many of his employees will quit.

Answers start on page 320.

GED SKILL Identifying Implications from Graphs

You have already learned that maps provide information in a visual format. Graphs are another device for presenting information visually. Writers sometimes use graphs to show relationships between things so that they do not need to explain those relationships in writing. It is the reader's responsibility to identify the implications of this graphic material.

Graphs are often used to show changes over time. This allows readers to easily make comparisons and see trends. The bar graph below shows how the **minimum wage** that employers must pay workers has changed since 1975. Setting a minimum wage rate is one way that the government affects the nation's economy.

TIP

To interpret a graph, examine its vertical and horizontal axes to see what kinds of data are shown.

Various dollar amounts are listed on the left side of the graph. Along the bottom of the graph, each year between 1975 and 2000 is indicated. Above each year is a vertical bar. The top of each bar corresponds to a dollar amount on the left side of the graph. For example, the graph shows that the minimum legal wage in 1975 was $2.10 per hour. In 1976 and 1977, it rose to $2.30 an hour.

Study the graph and answer the question below.

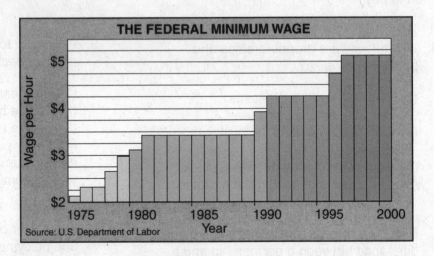

THE FEDERAL MINIMUM WAGE

Wage per Hour

$5
$4
$3
$2

1975   1980   1985   1990   1995   2000

Year

Source: U.S. Department of Labor

Which information is implied by the graph?

_____ a. The minimum wage has risen steadily since 1980.

_____ b. The minimum wage increased the most in the 1990s.

You were correct if you chose *option b*. The graph shows that the rise in the minimum wage was the sharpest during that period. *Option a* is incorrect because, as the graph shows, the minimum wage did not rise steadily—it did not rise at all during most of the 1980s and for several years in the early 1990s.

Use the passage and the graph to answer the questions.

Trade with other nations plays an important role in the American economy. Goods American companies sell overseas are called **exports**. Products from other countries that are sold in this country are called **imports**. The difference between the total value of goods imported and the total value of goods exported to other countries is called the **balance of trade**. Most economists believe that it is important to a nation's economic health to maintain a positive trade balance—that is, for the value of its exports to exceed the value of its imports. Negative trade balances usually tend to reduce employment and slow economic growth.

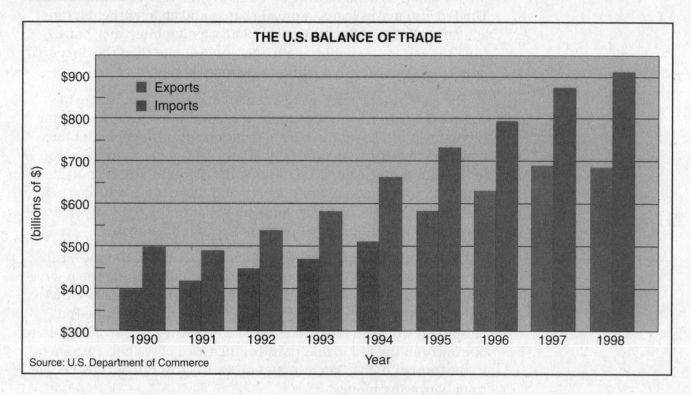

THE U.S. BALANCE OF TRADE

Source: U.S. Department of Commerce

1. Use the graph to find the following information. Circle the best answer.

   a. the value of goods imported into the United States in 1990 ($394 billion, $495 billion)

   b. the value of American exports in 1990 ($394 billion, $495 billion)

   c. the approximate U.S. balance of trade in 1990 (negative $100 billion, positive $100 billion)

2. Complete this sentence to state a conclusion that is implied by the graph.

   The nation had a _____ balance of trade from the year _____ to the year _____.

3. Put a check mark next to each statement that is implied by the data in the graph.

   _____ a. In the 1990s, the United States showed a trend of increasing imports and decreasing exports.

   _____ b. The balance of trade is a problem area in the American economy.

   _____ c. In general, the value of American exports has been rising.

Answers start on page 321.

GED CONTENT The Government and the Economy

The federal government tries to control the economy by controlling the money supply. This is done mainly by the **Federal Reserve System,** which Congress created in 1913 to supervise the operations of private banks. The "Fed," as it is sometimes called, is a bank for banks. Most private banks are required to be members of the Fed and to have savings accounts at one of the 12 Federal Reserve banks across the nation. The amount of money the Fed requires in private banks' Federal Reserve accounts is the **reserve requirement.** The Fed also makes loans to private banks and charges them interest at a rate called the **discount rate.** Banks lend money they borrow from the Fed to the public at a higher interest rate than the discount rate. This is one way that banks make money.

The Fed uses the reserve requirement and the discount rate to control the nation's money supply. If the Fed wants to stimulate the economy, it can lower the reserve requirement or the discount rate. Lowering the reserve requirement allows private banks to loan more of their funds to customers. Lowering the discount rate encourages banks to borrow money from the Fed and make more loans to their customers. Either action puts more money into the economy. This encourages spending, which promotes economic growth.

On the other hand, if the Fed wants to slow the economy, it can raise the reserve requirement or the discount rate. Raising the reserve requirement reduces the amount that banks can lend, because they must keep a greater portion of their money on deposit at the Fed. Raising the discount rate makes it more expensive for private banks to borrow from the Fed. Banks pass this increased cost on to customers in the form of higher interest rates on loans. This discourages people from borrowing money.

The graph shows changes in the prime rate over a 15-year period. The **prime rate** is the interest rate that private banks charge their most credit-worthy customers.

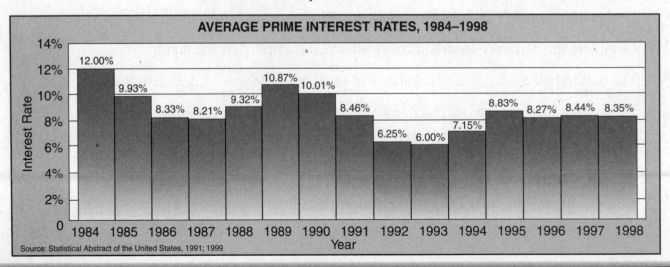

AVERAGE PRIME INTEREST RATES, 1984–1998

Source: Statistical Abstract of the United States, 1991; 1999

Directions: Choose the one best answer to each question.

Questions 1 through 8 refer to the passage and the graph on page 188.

1. According to the passage, what is one way that banks make money?

   (1) by loaning less money to customers
   (2) by increasing the amount of money they keep on reserve in the Federal Reserve Bank
   (3) by borrowing money from the Federal Reserve and loaning it to their customers
   (4) by lowering their reserve requirement
   (5) by lowering their discount rate

2. According to the passage, interest rates on personal loans would go up when which of the following occurs?

   (1) fewer people are applying for loans
   (2) there is an economic depression
   (3) the Fed raises the prime rate
   (4) the Fed lowers its reserve requirement
   (5) the Fed raises the discount rate

3. Which of the following is the most likely result of higher interest rates?

   (1) Consumers borrow money.
   (2) Money is put into the economy.
   (3) Banks lower interest rates on savings.
   (4) The nation's economy expands.
   (5) The number of loans decreases.

4. What trend does the graph suggest about interest rates in the late 1990s?

   (1) Rates on loans rose significantly.
   (2) Rates for savings accounts rose significantly.
   (3) Rates on loans stayed about the same.
   (4) Rates for savings accounts fell significantly.
   (5) Rates on loans fell significantly.

5. What does the graph suggest the Fed did in 1995?

   (1) raised the discount rate
   (2) lowered the discount rate
   (3) lowered the reserve requirement
   (4) required banks to raise the prime rate
   (5) required banks to lower the prime rate

6. What does the information in the graph suggest happened in 1985?

   (1) The amount of money in the economy decreased.
   (2) Banks made fewer loans.
   (3) The Fed tried to slow the economy.
   (4) The amount of money in the economy increased.
   (5) The nation fell into a deep depression.

7. Which of the following does the passage best support as the reason for the Fed's reserve requirement for member banks?

   (1) so the Fed will have money to run the government
   (2) so worn-out paper money can be removed from circulation and replaced
   (3) so money will be readily available to cover a bank's obligations
   (4) so the Fed can make low-interest loans to consumers
   (5) so the federal government can finance presidential election campaigns

8. Based on information in the passage, which of the following would you choose as the best place to put your savings?

   (1) a bank that is a member of the Fed
   (2) a bank that keeps all its money in a vault
   (3) a bank that doesn't make many loans
   (4) a bank that makes a lot of loans
   (5) one of the 12 Federal Reserve banks

Answers start on page 321.

Directions: Choose the one best answer to each question.

Questions 1 through 4 refer to the following passage and graph.

The economy of every country is based on exchange—either through the barter of goods and services or through the payment of money for them. Goods are physical objects like food, cars, or housing. Services refer to work that people do which does not produce new goods. Services include car repair, house painting, and health care.

A common way to measure how well a country's economy is performing is by its **Gross Domestic Product, or GDP.** The GDP is the total monetary value of all goods and services produced in that country during a year.

The American GDP was about twice as large in 1991 as it was in 1975. But this does not mean that the economy had doubled in size or that Americans were twice as well off economically. This is because of inflation and population growth. Prices between 1980 and 1991 rose about 50 percent. So a large part of the GDP increase resulted from higher prices, not increased production. The so-called **real GDP**— the value of annual production adjusted for increases due to inflation—was smaller. In addition, the nation's population increased by 12 percent. So although more goods and services were produced in 1991 than in 1980, they had to be divided among more people.

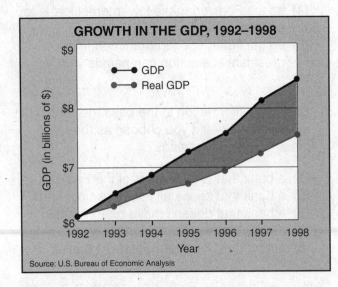

GROWTH IN THE GDP, 1992–1998

GDP (in billions of $)

Year

Source: U.S. Bureau of Economic Analysis

1. What is the real GDP?

    (1) all the goods and services produced and sold in a country in one-year
    (2) the total value of a country's production divided by its population
    (3) a country's overseas trade in goods and services
    (4) the GDP adjusted for price increases that are due to inflation
    (5) the personal income that a country's people earn

2. Which of the following is a good that would be included in the year's GDP?

    (1) a used car, purchased in California
    (2) legal advice from a New York attorney
    (3) an ear of corn grown in Illinois
    (4) an operation on a family pet in Iowa
    (5) a CD player imported from Japan

3. What does the information in the graph imply about the 1990s?

    (1) Most Americans became wealthier.
    (2) The nation's economy grew steadily.
    (3) The value of manufactured goods declined.
    (4) American companies sold more overseas.
    (5) Americans bought more foreign goods.

4. Which conclusion about the U.S. economy is supported by the graph?

    (1) About a third of the growth in the GDP has been due to inflation.
    (2) The nation's economy was healthier in the 1990s than it was in the 1980s.
    (3) The nation's economy was less healthy in the 1990s than it was in the 1980s.
    (4) The nation is changing from a manufacturing economy to an economy that provides services.
    (5) The unemployment rate is declining as the GDP is growing.

One way government is involved in the economy is in its attempts to protect the consumer. In the past, people had little protection. Every store should have posted large signs saying "Buyer, beware!" If a baker bought flour that was full of bugs, he could take the time to sift them out, include them in the products he baked, or toss out the flour and lose money. Today, the Food and Drug Administration (FDA), Consumer Product Safety Commission (CPSC), and other agencies protect consumers from careless or unethical people who might otherwise put profits ahead of public health and safety.

Public awareness of consumer rights, public relations on the part of manufacturers and store owners, and self-policing by various businesses have also increased consumer protection. For example, food stores today replace food that has gone stale or sour or that is contaminated in some way. In fact, they figure in the losses from not being able to sell such food when they decide what prices to charge for the groceries.

THE MAJOR FEDERAL CONSUMER PROTECTION AGENCIES	
Agency	Consumer Protection Functions and Activities
Food Safety and Inspection Service (FSIS)	Inspects meat and poultry to ensure its quality, wholesomeness, and accurate labeling (part of the Department of Agriculture)
Food and Drug Administration (FDA)	Sets and enforces standards for quality and accurate labeling of food and drugs (part of the Department of Health and Human Services)
Consumer Product Safety Commission (CPSC)	Sets and enforces safety standards for consumer products; can require manufacturers to recall unsafe products
Federal Trade Commission (FTC)	Enforces laws that prohibit false advertising, agreements between competitors to fix prices, and mislabeling of products
Federal Aviation Administration (FAA)	Makes and enforces regulations regarding safety on airlines (part of the Department of Transportation)
National Highway Traffic Safety Administration (NHTSA)	Enforces federal laws regarding the safety of passenger cars and trucks (part of the Department of Transportation)

5. Which of the following is implied by the passage and the chart?

   (1) Self-policing protects consumers more effectively than government action can.
   (2) The FDA is a more effective consumer protection agency than the FAA is.
   (3) The most serious product safety issues involve food items.
   (4) Self-policing by industry groups makes government regulation unnecessary.
   (5) Without government protections, companies might knowingly sell products that harm people.

6. Who most likely pays the cost of a manufacturer's recall of a defective product?

   (1) the government
   (2) the manufacturer
   (3) consumers
   (4) the CPSC
   (5) the NHTSA

7. What is the common goal of the agencies described in the chart?

   (1) to keep companies from saying untrue things about their products in their ads
   (2) to keep competitors from fixing prices
   (3) to ensure that food is of high quality
   (4) to set prices on essential products
   (5) to help prevent Americans from buying potentially harmful goods and services

Answers start on page 322.

GED Mini-Test • Lesson 16

Directions: This is a ten-minute practice test. After ten minutes, mark the last question you finished. Then complete the test and check your answers. If most of your answers were correct, but you didn't finish, try to work faster next time. Choose the <u>one best answer</u> to each question.

<u>Questions 1 through 4</u> refer to the following passage.

Three major economic systems exist in the world today: capitalism, communism, and socialism. The main differences in the systems are the ways ownership and decision-making are treated.

Capitalism, the economic system favored by the industrialized western world, allows for private ownership of goods and the means of production. Decisions and planning are in private hands.

Under communism, the economic system of countries like North Korea and Cuba, the state owns the means of production and plans the economy. The basis of communism is that, in theory, all individuals contribute their best effort to the good of the community and in return receive everything they need.

Socialism is similar to communism in that the state owns all major means of production and plans the economy for the good of all. But, socialism encourages competition among small businesses. The state provides certain social services for its citizens, such as free or inexpensive health care.

In the modern world, these economic systems have become confused with political systems. Because communism and socialism depend so much on central planning, they have become associated in people's minds with dictatorship. Capitalism, because it is built around private ownership and free enterprise, is associated with democratic or representative government.

1. According to the passage, how are capitalism and socialism similar?

    (1) The state owns production.
    (2) The state plans the economy.
    (3) Small businesses can compete.
    (4) All people have everything they need.
    (5) People have economic and political freedom.

2. What do capitalism and communism have in common?

    (1) Economic planning is in private hands.
    (2) Individuals work for the common good.
    (3) They require democratic government.
    (4) They are economic systems.
    (5) The state owns all businesses.

3. Which conclusion is supported by the passage?

    (1) Individual freedom is associated with capitalism.
    (2) In the past, socialist economies have failed.
    (3) Under communism, people can get rich.
    (4) Capitalism can do well under a dictatorship.
    (5) Politics and economics have nothing to do with each other.

4. What additional information do you need to draw the conclusion that the theory of communism differs from the reality?

    (1) only what is stated in the passage
    (2) what the theory of communism is
    (3) what the reality of communism is
    (4) more details about communist theory
    (5) how socialism differs from communism

5. Many manufactured products carry a warranty. A warranty promises that, if the product is defective, the manufacturer will repair it. What concept of economics do warranties illustrate?

    (1) capitalism
    (2) consumer protection
    (3) the gross domestic product
    (4) supply and demand
    (5) communism

Questions 6 through 9 refer to the following passage and graph.

Congress has created several regulatory boards and commissions that protect citizens from certain economic problems. Regulatory boards and commissions make rules and come to decisions that affect banking, transportation, communications, and other corporations, as well as their workers These boards and commissions make rules about what businesses can and cannot do. They also help settle disputes between parties.

One regulatory commission is the Federal Communications Commission, or the FCC. The FCC licenses radio and television stations, giving them permission to operate and assigning each a radio frequency or TV channel. This determines which of the limited number of wavelengths the station can use for broadcasting. The FCC also sets the hours when a station may operate and how strong its broadcast signal may be. Because of such regulations, people can tune in a radio or TV station without concern that another station broadcasting on the same wavelength will ruin their listening or viewing pleasure.

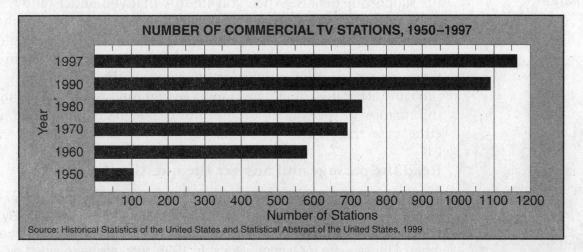

NUMBER OF COMMERCIAL TV STATIONS, 1950–1997

Source: Historical Statistics of the United States and Statistical Abstract of the United States, 1999

6. Which of the following is implied by the graph?

   (1) TV stations shouldn't be regulated.
   (2) There are too many TV stations.
   (3) There were just over 100 TV stations in 1950.
   (4) The FCC is not an important agency.
   (5) The number of TV stations has risen since 1950.

7. What is the most likely reason that Congress formed regulatory commissions?

   (1) Some businesses were operating against the public interest.
   (2) The nation's economy was depressed.
   (3) Congress had to deal with a slow economy.
   (4) The president felt it was important to do so.
   (5) Citizens had too much control over their lives.

8. The FCC might rule in a dispute between which of the following parties?

   (1) citizens and a bank
   (2) state governments
   (3) a bank and a bus company
   (4) citizens and a radio station
   (5) a TV station and TV actors

9. Which conclusion does the information in the passage and graph support?

   (1) TV stations need more regulation than radio stations do.
   (2) The FCC is the government's most powerful regulatory agency.
   (3) Broadcast wavelengths have to be carefully shared.
   (4) The number of radio stations has grown faster than the number of TV stations.
   (5) The FCC never makes an unfair ruling.

Answers start on page 322.

GED SKILL Assessing the Adequacy of Supporting Data

data
facts, statistics, or measurements used as a basis for reasoning, discussion, or calculation

You already know that you must decide whether information presented is really related to the statement it is supposed to support. When you evaluate a conclusion, you must also decide if you have been given *enough* facts to support it. Both concerns apply to conclusions that you draw, as well as to those that you read or hear. They also apply to **data** as well as to other supporting information.

To decide whether the data presented are adequate, or enough, to support a conclusion, you need to understand the main idea and all the supporting details. When you are sure that you understand these ideas and data, ask yourself, "Are these facts enough to support the conclusion?" Be sure to also ask if there is anything else you would need to know in order to logically draw that conclusion. If you find enough solid, relevant supporting information, the conclusion is probably accurate. Sometimes, however, you might not find enough information or the conclusion may not be adequately supported. In either case, the conclusion is probably not valid or accurate.

TIP

After identifying supporting data and other facts, look for unstated assumptions, implications, and stated or unstated cause-and-effect relationships in the information related to the conclusion.

Read the passage and answer the question below.

When labor unions were first established in the 1800s, their power was limited by law and by a general lack of support for striking workers. By the early 1930s, fewer than 900 strikes occurred in the nation each year, and most of these were for higher wages. In 1935, workers were aided by passage of the National Labor Relations Act (NLRA). This act, which is still the law almost 70 years later, recognizes the right of workers to form unions and requires employers to bargain with unions over wages and working conditions. In the first five years following the law's passage, the number of strikes jumped to more than 2,100 a year. More than two-thirds of these strikes resulted from the attempts of workers to form unions.

Which of the following conclusions is supported by adequate data?

_____ a. After the NLRA passed, many employers were unwilling to accept the legal rights of workers.

_____ b. Passage of the National Labor Relations Act resulted in higher wages for workers.

You were correct if you chose *option a*. After the passage of the NLRA, two-thirds of the strikes were a result of employees trying to exercise their right to form unions, indicating that employers had to be forced to accept unions. To conclude *option b* would require additional data that compare wages before and after 1935.

Use the paragraph and the graph to answer the questions.

During the two centuries since the United States was founded, the makeup of the labor force has changed. In the early years, most workers were farm workers, and agriculture was the chief industry. After the United States industrialized in the late 1800s, the number of workers involved in manufacturing grew rapidly. By the 1990s, however, automation had cut deep into the manufacturing sector. Now, the fastest-growing occupations are in the **service sector** of the economy. This sector includes industries like health care, education, and computer services.

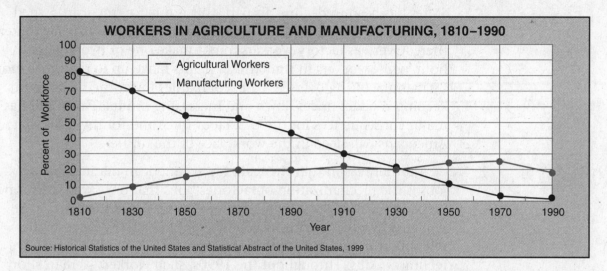

WORKERS IN AGRICULTURE AND MANUFACTURING, 1810–1990

Source: Historical Statistics of the United States and Statistical Abstract of the United States, 1999

1. Interpret the graph to provide the following information.

   a. The approximate percentage of American workers involved in agriculture in 1810 was _____.

   b. The approximate percentage of American workers involved in manufacturing in 1970 was _____.

2. Put a check mark next to each statement that the data in the graph support.

   _____ a. Agricultural workers were a much smaller part of the U.S. labor force in 1990 than one hundred years before.

   _____ b. People are giving up agriculture today at the fastest rate in the nation's history.

3. Mark a *T* next to statements supported by the graph. Mark an *F* to those the graph shows to be false. Mark an *X* next to those not adequately supported by the graph.

   _____ a. During the two centuries since the United States was founded, the makeup of the labor force has changed.

   _____ b. Until the late 1800s, most U.S. workers were agricultural workers.

   _____ c. After the United States industrialized in the late 1800s, most of the nation's workers were in manufacturing industries.

   _____ d. By the 1990s, automation had cut deep into the manufacturing sector.

   _____ e. Now, the fastest-growing occupations are in the service sector of the economy.

Answers start on page 323.

The development of the **global economy** in the 1980s and 1990s has had a tremendous effect on Americans both as consumers and as workers. From athletic shoes to washing machines, the products of American companies are increasingly being manufactured overseas. It has become difficult to know whether goods are American-made because more and more U.S. businesses own and operate factories in distant parts of the world.

For years, the total number of manufacturing jobs in the United States has been in decline. In part, this is due to American-owned companies building factories overseas and hiring lower-paid workers there. Overseas factory workers might make one or two dollars an hour, while workers in similar U.S. plants make up to ten times more. By manufacturing overseas, U.S. companies lower their labor costs, keeping product prices down and increasing profits. This trend has major consequences for the U.S. labor force and for the skills that Americans will need in the workplace of the future.

Another reason that there are fewer American manufacturing jobs is the mechanization of factories. Jobs that once were performed by hand are now done by machine, and machines that used to be operated by people are now run by computers. This suggests that job opportunities will continue to exist for U.S. workers who have technical skills. Throughout the 1990s, such workers were in short supply. Thus, many health care, research lab, and computer programming jobs have been filled by people trained in other countries. American employers have received permission from the U.S. government to recruit people from overseas to meet the need for workers in many technical areas.

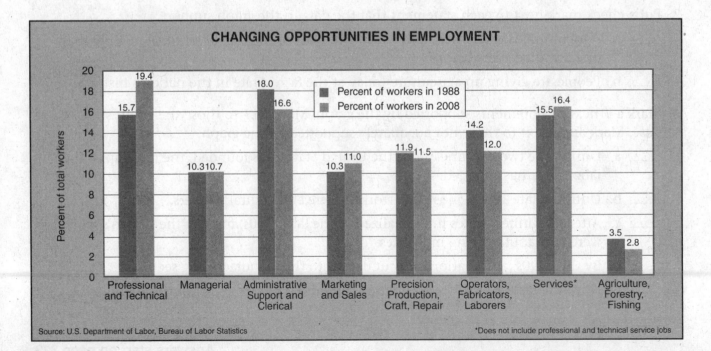

CHANGING OPPORTUNITIES IN EMPLOYMENT

Percent of workers in 1988
Percent of workers in 2008

Percent of total workers

Category	1988	2008
Professional and Technical	15.7	19.4
Managerial	10.3	10.7
Administrative Support and Clerical	18.0	16.6
Marketing and Sales	10.3	11.0
Precision Production, Craft, Repair	11.9	11.5
Operators, Fabricators, Laborers	14.2	12.0
Services*	15.5	16.4
Agriculture, Forestry, Fishing	3.5	2.8

Source: U.S. Department of Labor, Bureau of Labor Statistics

*Does not include professional and technical service jobs

Directions: Choose the one best answer to each question.

Questions 1 through 7 refer to the passage and the graph on page 196.

1. Why have many U.S. companies moved their manufacturing operations overseas?

   (1) Overseas plants are more automated.
   (2) Labor costs are lower overseas.
   (3) There are not enough U.S. workers.
   (4) Goods sold overseas are made there.
   (5) Other countries do not have labor unions.

2. Which of the following occupations is projected to offer in 2008 the fewest job opportunities to American workers?

   (1) auto repair
   (2) factory worker
   (3) file clerk
   (4) farm worker
   (5) salesperson

3. Which of the occupations shown on the graph is expected to show the greatest drop in percentage from 1988 to 2008?

   (1) administrative support and clerical
   (2) marketing and sales
   (3) precision production, crafts, and repair
   (4) operators, fabricators, and laborers
   (5) agriculture, forestry, and fishing

4. What effect has the transfer overseas of manufacturing jobs had on the U.S. economy?

   (1) American stores have fewer products to sell.
   (2) American wages are falling.
   (3) American manufacturing jobs are becoming more technical.
   (4) Consumers have more choices in brands of products.
   (5) The need for operators, fabricators, and laborers is shrinking.

5. What is the best explanation for why so many "high-tech" jobs are now performed by immigrants to the United States?

   (1) The government has allowed recruiting workers overseas.
   (2) Not enough native-born workers have the needed technical skills.
   (3) Immigrant workers are better trained than native-born workers of the same profession.
   (4) Workers overseas are paid less than workers in the United States.
   (5) Immigrants are smarter than native-born Americans.

6. What conclusion can be supported by the information in the passage and on the graph?

   (1) The wages of overseas employees of U.S. companies are rising.
   (2) The size of the managerial sector of the labor market is getting smaller.
   (3) Manufacturing jobs are becoming less important in the U.S. economy.
   (4) Mechanization has reduced the number of jobs in agriculture.
   (5) The service sector is the slowest-growing part of the U.S. economy.

7. Which statement has the strongest support, based on the information in the passage and on the graph?

   (1) People currently involved in fishing, agriculture, or forestry should find another occupation.
   (2) Health care offers better employment opportunities than does the computer industry.
   (3) The size of the American labor force is shrinking.
   (4) Current workers in U.S. factories will probably lose their jobs.
   (5) The best job to prepare for is one that requires professional and technical skills.

Answers start on page 324.

GED Practice • Lesson 17

Directions: Choose the one best answer to each question.

Questions 1 through 4 refer to the following passage and table.

Mergers between companies and **takeovers** by one company of part or all of another have become facts of American economic life. These actions occur when companies large and small run into trouble and put themselves up for sale. Even some businesses that are not for sale can be the targets of **hostile takeovers** by competitors or other buyers who find the business attractive.

Workers who are employed by companies that are taken over often worry about job security, fearing that the new owners might hire new staff or eliminate their jobs. The new owners may decide to stop producing or selling some of the products of the company they purchased.

Nearly 50 percent of the people who lost their jobs in 1998 became unemployed because their company moved or closed a plant. Another third were let go because their positions were eliminated.

Even so, some workers benefit from the shifting business scene. Stable companies sometimes take advantage of shake-ups elsewhere by offering good jobs to the skilled employees of companies in transition.

MERGERS AND BUYOUTS IN THE 1990s					
Activity	1990	1992	1994	1996	1998
Mergers	1,907	1,598	2,005	2,423	3,304
Foreign purchases of U.S. companies	773	361	NA	73	48
U.S. purchases of foreign companies	392	456	207	364	746

Source: Statistical Abstract of the United States, 1999

TIP To support a conclusion, imagine having to explain the conclusion to someone else. Ask "Will these facts convince another person that the conclusion is correct?"

1. According to the passage, when does a hostile takeover always occur?

   (1) when the company being bought does not wish to be purchased
   (2) when the buyer is a competitor of the company it is buying
   (3) when the buyer is a foreign company
   (4) when the buyer has no real interest in the company it is purchasing
   (5) when the buyer eliminates jobs in the company it acquires

2. What would be the most likely effect of one company buying a competitor?

   (1) Workers' wages will go down.
   (2) More jobs will become available.
   (3) Consumers will have fewer product choices.
   (4) The new company will put itself up for sale.
   (5) Both companies' prices will drop.

3. What information would you need to determine the accuracy of the conclusion drawn in the first sentence of the passage?

   (1) names of big companies that have merged
   (2) the number of hostile takeovers
   (3) the percentage of workers who have lost their jobs through mergers
   (4) the unavailable table data for 1994
   (5) only the information in the table

4. Which information presents the best evidence for answering the question "Should employees of companies that are taken over worry about their jobs?"

   (1) the information in paragraph two
   (2) the information in paragraph three
   (3) the information in paragraph four
   (4) the data on mergers in the table
   (5) the data on foreign purchases in the table

Questions 5 through 8 refer to the following passage and table.

Income in America is distributed unequally. Although the United States is considered a middle-class nation, the richest 20 percent of our population earn nearly 50 percent of the income. In contrast, the poorest 20 percent of Americans earn less than 5 percent of the income. In 1998, some 10 percent of U.S. families and 19 percent of U.S. children lived below the poverty line. Many such people lack the education and training necessary to hold jobs in this increasingly technological society.

The difference in income between the rich and the poor is increasing. Between 1991 and 1996, the share of the nation's income held by the richest fifth increased by 10 percent, while the share held by the poorest fifth decreased by almost 20 percent. As prices increase for necessities like food and shelter, the poor have become less able to pay for them.

PERCENTAGE OF FAMILIES LIVING IN POVERTY							
Year	Percent	Year	Percent	Year	Percent	Year	Percent
1979	9.2	1984	11.6	1989	10.3	1994	11.6
1980	10.3	1985	11.4	1990	10.7	1995	10.8
1981	11.2	1986	10.9	1991	11.5	1996	11.0
1982	12.2	1987	10.7	1992	11.9	1997	10.3
1983	12.3	1988	10.4	1993	12.3	1998	10.0

Source: U.S. Census Bureau

5. In which of the following years was the poverty rate for families in the United States the highest?

(1) 1979
(2) 1991
(3) 1993
(4) 1996
(5) 1998

6. Wealth in the United States is distributed unevenly. What would you expect to find in a country where wealth is distributed more evenly?

(1) All people would spend similar proportions of their income on food and housing.
(2) Most people would purchase the same make and model of car.
(3) All families would have the same number of children.
(4) Everyone would have the same amount of education.
(5) People would spend their money on the same kind of leisure time activity.

7. There are more children living in poverty than families living in poverty. What is the most likely reason?

(1) Children are poorer than their parents.
(2) Most families in poverty have more than one child.
(3) Raising a child costs money.
(4) Children in poverty are more likely to drop out of school than are other children.
(5) It is not legal for children under age 15 to work at most jobs.

8. Would a claim that poverty rates are rising be believable?

(1) Yes, because the table shows that poverty rates generally rose between 1979 and 1993.
(2) No, because the passage fails to relate rising prices to rising poverty rates.
(3) Yes, because the passage shows that the distribution of income has become more unequal.
(4) No, because the table shows that poverty rates have generally been lower in recent years.
(5) Yes, because the passage establishes that 19 percent of children lived in poverty in 1998.

Answers start on page 324.

Directions: This is a ten-minute practice test. After ten minutes, mark the last question you finished. Then complete the test and check your answers. If most of your answers were correct, but you didn't finish, try to work faster next time. Choose the one best answer to each question.

Questions 1 through 3 refer to the following passage.

In 1986, the International Ladies Garment Workers Union (ILGWU) became concerned about what it called "sweatshop" conditions in rural Iowa. It accused Bordeaux, Inc., of Clarinda, Iowa, of violating the federal regulations that outlaw women's wear from being manufactured in workers' homes.

The company began manufacturing decorated sweatsuits in 1980 and had sales in the three-million-dollar range within six years. It employed from 100 to 150 women who worked at home using their own sewing machines and the company's material. The company paid about $2.45 per piece if the work passed inspection, and $1.12 if it did not.

Some workers figured that they earned from $4.00 to $9.00 an hour. In this economically depressed farm area, they were pleased to have the work. Other workers complained to the ILGWU that the hourly rate was more like $1.85, which was illegal under the minimum wage laws.

The Department of Labor investigated the claims. At first, the government officials proposed a system in which Bordeaux and other employers of home workers would register with the department, providing it with lists of workers so that on-the-spot inspections could be made. Labor Department officials felt that fair employers should be allowed to operate. The ILGWU felt that piecework at home could not be monitored effectively and wanted the department to uphold the federal regulations on home workers.

Later, the Labor Department filed suit against Bordeaux. While the case was in court, the company opened a factory, hired workers, and stopped using home employees. Eventually, the court ruled against Bordeaux and ordered the company to pay back wages to the home workers it had employed before the suit.

1. What does the passage imply about how the Labor Department saw this dispute?

   (1) as a dispute between two competing labor unions
   (2) as an issue of union labor versus non-union labor
   (3) as an issue of fair management versus unfair management
   (4) as a issue of sweatshop conditions versus piecework
   (5) as a conflict involving employment discrimination against women

2. Which economic activity is most like piecework?

   (1) a painter who paints a mechanic's house in return for a repair on his car
   (2) a manufacturer who lowers the price of a product in order to sell a larger quantity
   (3) a fast food worker who is paid the minimum wage
   (4) a salesperson whose income is a percentage of the price of what she sells
   (5) a store owner who holds a sale to get rid of surplus merchandise

3. What is the most likely reason that the ILGWU complained to the government about the Bordeaux company?

   (1) It wanted to put the company out of business.
   (2) It wanted to force the company to pay its workers an hourly wage rather than by the piece.
   (3) It wanted the Labor Department to sue the company.
   (4) It wanted to raise the pay of home workers above the minimum wage.
   (5) It wanted to end the manufacture of women's wear by home workers.

Questions 4 through 6 refer to the following passage and graph.

Many believe that teenage unemployment is a serious problem in the United States. Many teenagers drop out of high school. Many high-school graduates do not go on for further training or degrees. Although the statistics vary somewhat from region to region, they give cause for concern. About 15 percent of teenagers who are not in school are unemployed, and a number of these have children. Many of the young women are not part of the workforce because they need to work in their own homes cooking, cleaning, and caring for their young children. Lack of paying jobs can cause financial hardship for these families.

For other teenagers who drop out of school, fast-food restaurants or motel housekeeping provide short-term employment solutions. But few teenagers look forward to a lifetime of waiting on or cleaning up after other people. The looming question is how these teenagers will support themselves and others who depend on them financially.

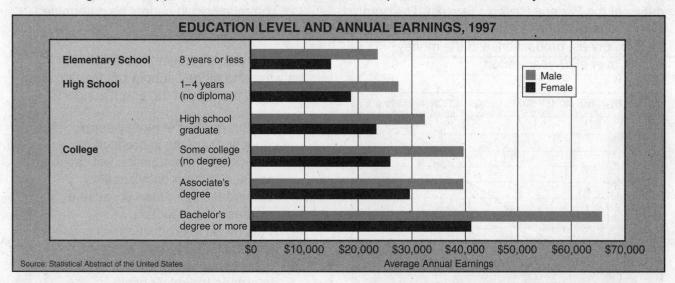

EDUCATION LEVEL AND ANNUAL EARNINGS, 1997

Source: Statistical Abstract of the United States

Average Annual Earnings

4. Which information would best support the conclusion that the teenage dropout rate is cause for alarm?

(1) that provided in the graph
(2) that in the first paragraph of the passage
(3) that about teenage mothers
(4) that in the passage and graph together
(5) more about what becomes of teenagers who drop out of school

5. Based on the information, what factor is most important in determining whether a person will get a well-paying job?

(1) gender
(2) previous work experience
(3) level of education
(4) marital status
(5) a high school diploma

6. Which of the following is a likely effect of teenagers dropping out of high school?

(1) more teenage mothers
(2) more children in poverty
(3) higher wages for high school graduates
(4) fewer workers for fast-food industries
(5) fewer motel housekeepers

7. About 15 percent of all adults 55 or older enroll in adult education courses. Data for enrollment for adults 17–34 and 35–54 are 43 percent and 40 percent, respectively.

Which conclusion do these statistics support?

(1) Adults take courses to learn new skills.
(2) Most adult students are under age 35.
(3) Young adults earn the most money.
(4) Adult education is popular in America.
(5) Older adults are busier than younger adults.

Answers start on page 325.

Unit 4 Cumulative Review Economics

Directions: Choose the one best answer to each question.

Questions 1 through 3 refer to the following paragraph and graph.

The amount of money that consumers, businesses, and the government have available to spend is known as the money supply. Rapid changes in the money supply can cause economic problems, so it is important to keep it under control. This responsibility is among the duties of the Federal Reserve System. The graph illustrates the money supply's importance by tracking prices, production, and the money supply over a 20-year period.

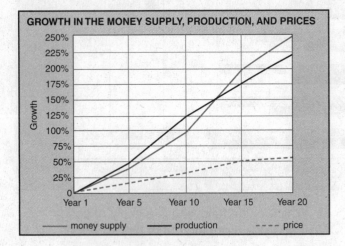

GROWTH IN THE MONEY SUPPLY, PRODUCTION, AND PRICES

—— money supply   —— production   - - - - price

1. During the first 10 years shown on the graph, what happened to prices when the amount of money in the economy increased?

   (1) They rose sharply.
   (2) They rose, but more slowly than the increase in the money supply.
   (3) They rose at the same rate as the increase in the money supply.
   (4) They fell.
   (5) They did not change.

TIP To identify relationships in a graph, analyze how a change in one element compares to changes in the other elements the graph is measuring.

2. When the supply of money grows faster than the rate at which the economy produces goods and services, what happens to prices?

   (1) Inflation causes prices to rise sharply.
   (2) Prices fall.
   (3) Prices rise, then fall, and then rise again.
   (4) Prices are not affected by this development.
   (5) The relationship cannot be determined.

3. What conclusion about the relationship between the money supply, production, and prices do the data in the graph support?

   (1) An increase in the money supply will cause a decrease in production.
   (2) An increase in production will cause an increase in the money supply.
   (3) An increase in prices will cause a decrease in production.
   (4) A decrease in production will cause an increase in the money supply.
   (5) There is not enough information to determine the relationship.

4. In 1997, the average full-time female worker earned 74¢ for every $1 earned by the average full-time male worker.

   What is the most likely result of the difference in the earning power of women and men?

   (1) Women have more buying power than men.
   (2) Fewer women are working full-time than men.
   (3) Households headed by women have a lower standard of living.
   (4) Women pay more income taxes than men.
   (5) Women drop out of the workforce when they have children.

Questions 5 through 8 refer to the following passage.

When more goods are being made, we say that the economy is expanding. In an expanding economy, manufacturers must find more people to buy their goods. The practice of promoting, advertising, and presenting a product in order to increase its sales is called marketing.

Marketing professionals use advertising to convince consumers that there is something special about their product. They also develop coupon offers to lower a product's price, making consumers feel that they are getting a bargain. Rebate promotions are another way marketing attracts customers. A rebate is a refund of part of the purchase price. Buyers who take the time to obtain rebates feel that they are spending their money wisely.

Marketing professionals also find new customers by directing products to other markets. One way to do this is to change the product's packaging so it will appeal to other groups of people. Food manufacturers, for example, traditionally packaged products for couples and families. But in the 1970s, many single people began to establish their own households. Companies recognizing this trend began to sell food in single-serving packages in order to attract this new market.

5. Which techniques for expanding markets are most alike?

(1) advertising and packaging
(2) coupons and rebates
(3) advertising and coupons
(4) packaging and rebates
(5) coupons and packaging

6. With what new cost should a manufacturer in an expanding economy be most concerned?

(1) the cost of potential labor problems
(2) packaging costs
(3) the costs of producing the good
(4) the cost of raw materials
(5) the costs of finding new markets

7. What assumption is the writer making about selling products in the U.S. economy?

(1) Marketing is an economic fact of doing business.
(2) Advertising is how manufacturers trick consumers.
(3) New packaging is wasteful and ineffective.
(4) Manufacturers need more customers when the economy is expanding.
(5) Advertising has no effect on sales.

8. Which of the following is the best example of a manufacturer finding a new market for a product?

(1) mail a special offer to loyal customers
(2) advertise a product in local newspapers
(3) advertise office products to home users
(4) give a rebate to someone who buys a product
(5) change and update the design of a product

Question 9 refers to the following cartoon.

"The meek will inherit the earth, but NEVER the market."

Cartoon by Dean Vietor. Copyright 1989, *USA TODAY*. Reprinted with permission.

9. What does the creator of this cartoon assume readers know about "the market"?

(1) It is a grocery store.
(2) It is the stock market.
(3) It refers to natural resources.
(4) It refers to an advertising promotion.
(5) It refers to inherited property.

Questions 10 through 14 refer to the following passage.

A lone worker has only one small voice. But workers who speak as a group through a labor union have a loud and powerful voice. When these workers threaten to stop production by striking, their employer is forced to pay attention to them.

To balance the power of the company and its workers, Congress passed the Labor-Management Relations Act of 1947, which is better-known today, as the Taft-Hartley Act. This law requires labor unions to negotiate their demands with employers, thus setting the stage for collective bargaining.

Collective bargaining is the discussion between company managers and union leaders who speak for the company's employees. The two groups negotiate and attempt to come to agreement on a contract setting the workers' wages and conditions of employment. Often both sides will give up something that is important to them to get something else that they want even more.

Since the 1930s, collective bargaining has improved wages and salaries, health and vacation benefits, working and safety conditions, and company liability for accident and health hazards. If, after collective bargaining, the labor union and management cannot agree on a contract, the union may choose to strike. Often, the mere threat of a strike will cause management to agree to workers' demands. Sometimes, however, even a long strike does not help workers get their way.

10. What would probably happen first if a school board did not want to increase teachers' salaries?

(1) The teachers would strike.
(2) The teachers would take a cut in pay.
(3) The teachers would quit.
(4) The school board would close the schools.
(5) The teachers' union would bargain with the school board.

11. Which statement about labor unions is an opinion?

(1) They are too powerful.
(2) They improved the lives of workers.
(3) They engage in collective bargaining.
(4) They give workers a voice in their jobs.
(5) They negotiate about work safety and other issues.

12. Which value is most strongly related to the use of collective bargaining in resolving labor disputes?

(1) power
(2) wealth
(3) control
(4) compromise
(5) freedom

13. Which of the following statements is a generalization based on faulty logic?

(1) Unions are responsible for the good wages and conditions that many workers enjoy today.
(2) Prices would be lower if unions didn't exist.
(3) Unions don't truly represent workers' best interests because union leaders are corrupt.
(4) A strike is a powerful tool of labor unions.
(5) Employers would prefer it if their workers did not belong to unions.

14. Many people believe that the power of labor unions is in decline. Which of the following provides the best evidence for determining if this assumption is correct?

(1) the number of strikes that have occurred in recent years
(2) the percentage of workers who are union members now and in previous decades
(3) the wages of nonunion workers
(4) the number of on-the-job accidents suffered by workers today and in previous decades
(5) the speeches of union leaders to their members

Questions 15 through 18 refer to the following cartoon.

"We plan to bargain all night until an agreement is reached."
From *The Wall Street Journal*—Permission, Cartoon Features Syndicate.

15. What is the main idea of this cartoon?

(1) Collective bargaining is a long, hard, and exhausting process.
(2) Employers always lie to the media to make it appear that they are bargaining hard.
(3) Union leaders always lie to the media to make it appear that they are bargaining hard.
(4) The public and the media have a right to know the facts in an important labor dispute.
(5) Negotiators falsely maintain the image of marathon negotiations.

16. Based on the details of the cartoon, which of the following is most likely happening in the negotiations shown?

The negotiators

(1) are not making progress.
(2) have fallen ill.
(3) are near an agreement.
(4) are taking a lunch break.
(5) have just signed a contract.

17. What does the cartoonist assume the reader will recognize?

(1) which company is negotiating with the union
(2) which union is negotiating with the company
(3) that the man with the notebook is a reporter
(4) the identity of the speaker with the pillow
(5) the issue being negotiated

18. The cartoon's message is intended to have an effect on the public. Which of the following is the message most like in terms of its intent?

(1) crying "Fire" in a crowded theater
(2) saying "The check is in the mail."
(3) publicly criticizing a popular politician
(4) a suspected criminal saying "No comment."
(5) admitting that no agreement is possible

19. Work stoppages in the last half of the 20th century peaked in 1970. That year almost 2.5 million workers stopped work or went on strike. In 1998 only 387,000 were involved in work stoppages.

What is implied by this information?

(1) There were more work stoppages in 1965 than in 1970.
(2) The number of workers involved in work stoppages has remained steady.
(3) There has been a decline in the number of work stoppages since 1970.
(4) Workers usually have good reasons for stopping work.
(5) People do not get paid during work stoppages.

TIP

If a cartoon has a caption, analyze how it relates to the cartoon. Identify whose point of view the caption is expressing—that of the cartoonist, a cartoon figure, or some other person.

Questions 20 through 22 refer to the following information.

All economic systems must answer five basic questions in using resources to satisfy people's needs. These questions underlie typical business decisions. The five basic questions are:

- What is to be produced?
- How much should be produced?
- How is it to be produced?
- Who is to receive it?
- How can the economy adapt to change?

20. Last year Sam's company made a profit on baseballs, but now he's wondering whether footballs might sell better next year. Which question is Sam asking?

   (1) What is to be produced?
   (2) How much should be produced?
   (3) How is it to be produced?
   (4) Who is to receive it?
   (5) How can the economy adapt to change?

21. Parker's company has been selling machine parts to U.S. companies for years. Now they are thinking of selling their parts overseas. Which question is Parker's company asking?

   (1) What is to be produced?
   (2) How much should be produced?
   (3) How is it to be produced?
   (4) Who is to receive it?
   (5) How can the economy adapt to change?

22. Patricia's low-fat chips have really caught on. They are crispy, tasty, and good for you. She is thinking of expanding her factory so she can sell more chips next year. What question is Patricia asking?

   (1) What is to be produced?
   (2) How much should be produced?
   (3) How is it to be produced?
   (4) Who is to receive it?
   (5) How can the economy adapt to change?

Questions 23 and 24 refer to the following paragraph.

Congress passed the Fair Labor Standards Act in 1938. The law established a minimum wage of 25 cents an hour and an increase to 40 cents after seven years. In the decades that have followed, many additional increases have pushed the minimum wage much higher. However, not all workers are covered by the minimum wage law. For example, restaurant waitstaff, hairdressers, taxi drivers, and others who receive tips can legally be paid less than the minimum wage if their tips make up the difference. Nevertheless, the minimum wage law is an attempt to guarantee that the standard of living of American workers will not fall below a certain level.

23. Which statement best summarizes the information in the paragraph?

   (1) American workers in restaurants and hair salons are not covered by a minimum wage.
   (2) In 1938, a new law created the federal minimum wage.
   (3) A minimum wage law has applied to most U.S. workers for more than 60 years.
   (4) The minimum wage has risen over time.
   (5) The minimum wage law has been controversial.

24. Which of the following statements from the paragraph is a conclusion?

   (1) Congress passed the Fair Labor Standards Act in 1938.
   (2) The law established a minimum wage of 25 cents an hour.
   (3) Not all workers are covered by the minimum wage law.
   (4) Waitstaff, hairdressers, taxi drivers, and others who receive tips can legally be paid less than the minimum wage if their tips make up the difference.
   (5) The minimum wage law guarantees that the standard of living of American workers will not fall below a certain level.

Answers start on page 326.

Cumulative Review Performance Analysis
Unit 4 • Economics

Use the Answers and Explanations starting on page 326 to check your answers to the Unit 4 Cumulative Review. Then use the chart to figure out the skill areas in which you need more practice.

On the chart, circle the questions that you answered correctly. Write the number correct for each skill area. Add the number of questions that you got correct on the Cumulative Review. If you feel that you need more practice, go back and review the lessons for the skill areas that were difficult for you.

Questions	Number Correct	Skill Area	Lessons for Review
1, 6, **15**, 19, 23	____/5	Comprehension	1, 2, 7, 16
2, 4, 5, 7, **9**, 11, **17**, 24	____/8	Analysis	3, 4, 6, 9, 10, 11, 12
8, 10, **18**, 20, 21, 22	____/6	Application	14, 15
3, 12, 13, 14, **16**	____/5	Evaluation	5, 8, 13, 17
TOTAL CORRECT	____/24		

Question numbers in **boldface** are based on graphics.

UNIT 5

Geography

Over the course of human history, people have spread over all of Earth's usable land. Understanding the planet and its resources has always been essential to human survival. People need to know where there is sufficient water, where the land will provide enough food, and where materials needed for shelter can be found.

Geography is the study of the physical environment, the human environment, and how each of these environments affects the other. Knowing about geography helps us understand the land we occupy and how we can make better use of it. Geography is also an important part of the GED Social Studies Test, making up 15 percent of the test questions.

Location, location, location—cities like Chicago thrived because of access to excellent transportation routes.

The lessons in this unit include:

Lesson 18:   Places and Regions
Every place in the world is unique. To better understand these places, geographers organize them into regions. The world's many regions and their characteristics have shaped the way people live.

Lesson 19:   Resources Affect Where People Live
All people live where they do for a reason. This reason is almost always related to the resources that are there. In many ways, Earth's resources shape where and how people live.

Lesson 20:   How People Change the Environment
People shape their natural environment as much as it shapes them. In this process, people have sometimes abused the resources on which they depend. This abuse has caused many environmental problems, and people are now trying to correct these problems.

THINKING SKILLS

○ Restating information from maps

○ Distinguishing conclusions from supporting details

○ Recognizing values

Lesson 18

GED SKILL Restating Information from Maps

restatement
information that is provided in another way

legend
the map tool that explains the meaning of the map's symbols

compass rose
the map tool that indicates the four cardinal directions—north, south, east, and west—on the map

Suppose you are hosting a party and not all the guests know where you live. Some of them want a map to your home, and others prefer written directions. People learn in different ways. Verbal **restatements** help some people better understand the content of visual material. When you write out directions, you are restating the map's visual information in a verbal format.

Maps give information about land. This information may include the way the land is shaped; the location, direction, and distance of objects; and even the land's climate, resources, and population. To accurately restate information from maps, you must be able to read them.

To find out what is in a map, first look at the map's title. On many maps, a list of symbols—called a **legend**—explains information that is shown on the map. A map tool called a **compass rose** indicates north and the other directions. Distance measurements are given in a map scale.

Read the map and answer the question below.

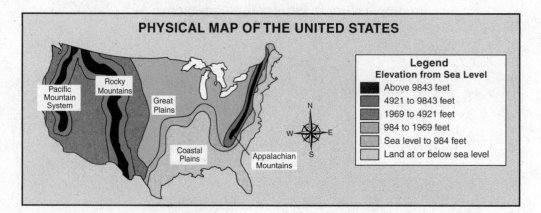

Which statement accurately restates information from the map?

_____ a. The largest and highest region in the United States is the Great Plains.

_____ b. The Rocky Mountains run in a generally southeastern direction, starting at the northern border of the United States.

You were correct if you chose *option b*. The orientation of the Rocky Mountains can be determined from the map's compass rose. The legend shows that the Great Plains do not have the highest elevation.

TIP

Before using a map, read its title and study the legend. This helps you determine what you can learn from the map.

Use the following map to answer the questions.

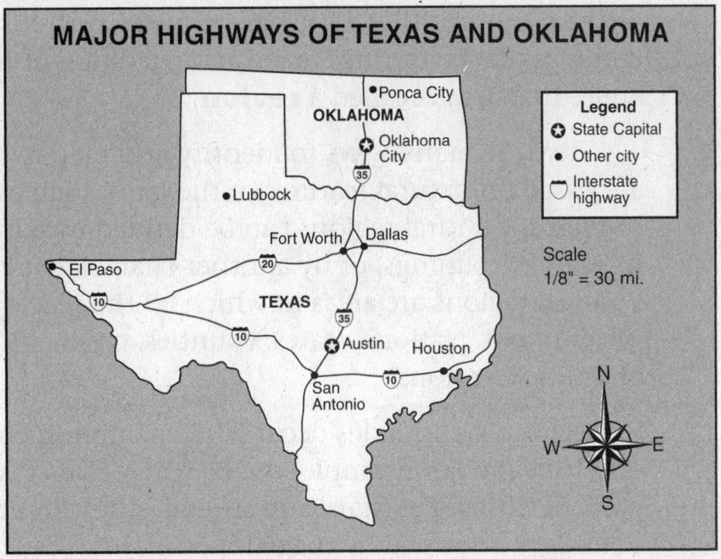

MAJOR HIGHWAYS OF TEXAS AND OKLAHOMA

1. Put a check mark next to the statement that restates information contained in the map.

_____ a. The map shows where Texas and Oklahoma are located in the United States.

_____ b. The map shows major cities and interstate highways in Texas and Oklahoma.

_____ c. The map shows the major rivers and mountain ranges of Texas and Oklahoma.

2. The following statements are based on information contained in the map. Use a *T* to label those that are accurate restatements of map information and an *F* to label those that are not.

_____ a. San Antonio is located at the junction of Interstate Highway 20 and Interstate Highway 35.

_____ b. Austin is the capital of Texas and is located west of Houston and south of Dallas.

_____ c. Lubbock is a city in Texas that is located about halfway between Oklahoma City and El Paso.

_____ d. Forth Worth, Texas, is closer to El Paso, Texas, than it is to Ponca City, Oklahoma.

_____ e. San Antonio, Texas, is located about 200 miles southwest of Houston.

_____ f. The state of Texas is more than twice the size of the state of Oklahoma.

_____ g. Dallas is on Interstate Highway 35 about midway between Austin and Oklahoma City.

3. Using information from the map, write directions that include approximate mileage and that tell a driver how to get from Oklahoma City, Oklahoma, to El Paso, Texas.

_____

_____

_____

Answers start on page 328.

The world is made up of places. Each **place** has characteristics that make it different from every other place. However, most places that are near one another also share some characteristics. When these common characteristics make an area different from surrounding areas, that area is called a **region.**

There are many ways to identify and map regions. Physical regions are based on natural features of the land, such as deserts, mountains, or plains. Cultural regions can be defined by a language, by racial or ethnic groupings, or by another characteristic of human culture. Political regions are areas in which all the places have the same government. Nations, states, counties, cities, and towns are examples of political regions.

Regional boundaries occur where common characteristics end and others begin. For example, the Plateau of Tibet is a region that covers parts of China, Pakistan, and several other countries. Its southern boundary is formed by rugged mountains, the Himalayas. South of these mountains, another region called the Gangetic Plain begins. This region is defined by flat, low-lying land through which the Ganges River and its tributaries flow.

Because regions are classified in many ways, the same place can be in several regions. The boundaries of different types of regions can also overlap. Study the regions shown on the following map.

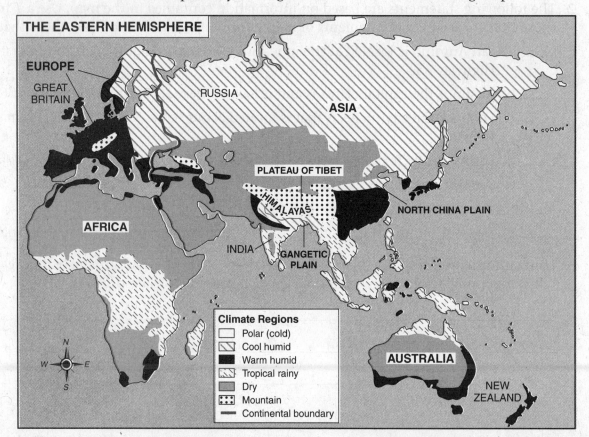

THE EASTERN HEMISPHERE

EUROPE
GREAT BRITAIN
RUSSIA
ASIA
PLATEAU OF TIBET
HIMALAYAS
NORTH CHINA PLAIN
AFRICA
INDIA
GANGETIC PLAIN
AUSTRALIA
NEW ZEALAND

Climate Regions
- Polar (cold)
- Cool humid
- Warm humid
- Tropical rainy
- Dry
- Mountain
- Continental boundary

Directions: Choose the one best answer for each question.

Questions 1 through 7 refer to the passage and the map on page 212.

1. Which of the following must always be true in order for an area to be considered a region?

   (1) Its people must all have the same religion and speak the same language.
   (2) Its land must be all mountains, all desert, or all plains.
   (3) It must be inhabited by people.
   (4) Its places must have some characteristic or feature in common.
   (5) Its boundaries must fall within the borders of a single nation.

2. Which of the following can be used to define a cultural region?

   (1) a common government
   (2) a common regional boundary
   (3) common physical characteristics
   (4) a common language or religion
   (5) common long-term weather patterns

3. Which of the following features labeled on the map is a political region?

   (1) Russia
   (2) the North China Plain
   (3) the Eastern Hemisphere
   (4) Asia
   (5) the Himalayas

4. What kind of climate does the region along the eastern coast of Australia have?

   (1) a dry climate
   (2) a cool, humid climate
   (3) a tropical, rainy climate
   (4) a mountain climate
   (5) a warm, humid climate

5. Which of the following accurately restates information from the map?

   (1) Most of Africa consists of hot and rainy tropical forests.
   (2) In terms of climate, Great Britain and New Zealand are vastly different.
   (3) People who live on the Plateau of Tibet get more rain than do people who live on the North China Plain.
   (4) Central India has a dry climate while the coasts get a lot of rain.
   (5) Both northern Asia and northern Africa have the same type of climate.

6. Based on the map, how does northeastern Europe contrast with most of the rest of Europe?

   (1) Places in northeastern Europe are dry, while places in the rest of Europe are rainy.
   (2) Northeastern Europe has a cool climate, while the rest of Europe has a warm climate.
   (3) A polar climate predominates in northeastern Europe while a mountain climate predominates elsewhere on the continent.
   (4) People of northeastern Europe are fair skinned while people in the rest of Europe have darker complexions.
   (5) Northern Europe contains more countries than southern Europe does.

7. If you wanted to determine how natural features and climate affect the location of major cities in Asia and Africa, what additional types of maps would you need?

   (1) cultural and physical maps
   (2) physical and political maps
   (3) cultural and political maps
   (4) cultural and road maps
   (5) political and road maps

Answers start on page 329.

GED Practice • Lesson 18

Directions: Choose the one best answer to each question.

Questions 1 through 4 refer to the following map.

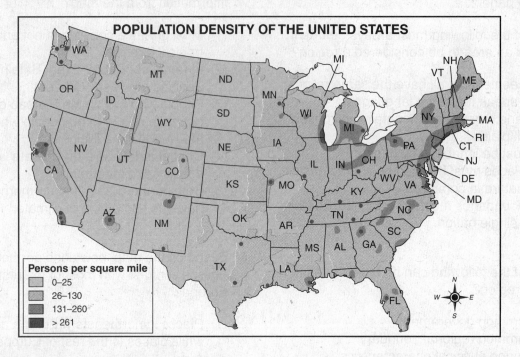

POPULATION DENSITY OF THE UNITED STATES

Persons per square mile
- 0–25
- 26–130
- 131–260
- > 261

1. On average, which of the following states has the highest population density?

   (1) Arizona
   (2) Illinois
   (3) Montana
   (4) Oklahoma
   (5) South Dakota

2. Which statement accurately reports information shown by this map?

   (1) The eastern United States is more densely populated than the western United States.
   (2) The largest area of high population density is on the West Coast.
   (3) The South is the fastest-growing region.
   (4) More people live in Utah than in Idaho.
   (5) The best place to live is in the North.

3. Which reason best explains why some areas on the map show very high population density?

   (1) Many tourists visit these areas.
   (2) They are mountainous areas.
   (3) The climate in these areas is warm.
   (4) They are good farming areas.
   (5) Major cities are located in these areas.

4. Suppose that you wanted to open a chain of restaurants across a state. Based on the information given, which of the following states would be the best choice in which to do this?

   (1) Arizona
   (2) Arkansas
   (3) Ohio
   (4) Utah
   (5) Washington

Questions 5 through 8 refer to the following passage and map.

Some countries are made up of islands. One such country is Japan, which consists of 4 large islands and about 3,000 small ones. The nation's climate varies. Hokkaido, in the north, is very cold in winter. On the other hand, Kyushu, the southern island, has subtropical summers.

More than 70 percent of Japan is mountainous. The longest mountain range runs through Japan's largest island of Honshu. About 50 of Japan's mountains are active volcanoes. Periodic eruptions and earthquakes have damaged cities and destroyed villages, killing thousands of Japan's people.

Plains make up only about 20 percent of Japan's area. So not much land is available for farming or for building sprawling cities like those in the United States. Japan's cities are among the most densely populated in the world.

THE MAIN ISLANDS OF JAPAN

Major cities
Mountain regions
Coastal plains

Sapporo
HOKKAIDO
Sea of Japan
HONSHU
Sendai
PACIFIC OCEAN
Kyoto
Osaka
Hiroshima
Nagoya
Tokyo
Kitakyushu
Kobe
Yokohama
Fukouka
Nagasaki
SHIKOKU
KYUSHU
East China Sea
Philippine Sea

SCALE
0   200   400
Miles

5. What does the passage imply about Japan's climate?

(1) It is influenced by volcanic eruptions.
(2) It is always very mild.
(3) It makes farming difficult.
(4) It varies from north to south.
(5) Japan's major cities are in warm regions.

6. Which of the following statements expresses an opinion about Japan?

(1) Japan is a mountainous nation.
(2) Tokyo is a more important city than Kobe.
(3) Some parts of Japan get cold.
(4) Volcanoes and earthquakes pose a danger to the Japanese.
(5) The nation of Japan consists of many islands.

7. Which of the following restates the information shown on the map?

(1) Japan is an island nation surrounded by the East China Sea.
(2) The nation of Japan consists of six main islands and a couple of smaller ones.
(3) Japan's main islands are formed of mountain ridges ringed by coastal plains where most of the people live.
(4) Japan is one of several island nations that are located in Asia.
(5) There are many volcanoes in Japan and most of these are located on the largest island, Honshu.

8. What conclusion about Japan does the map support?

(1) Japan's highest mountains are found on Hokkaido.
(2) Kyushu is Japan's smallest main island.
(3) There are fewer farms on the western coasts of Japan's main islands than on the eastern coasts.
(4) Industry is more important than agriculture to Japan's economy.
(5) More Japanese live on Honshu than on any of the other islands.

TIP To restate information from a map, use the legend, scale, and compass rose to help you put the data into words accurately.

Answers start on page 329.

GED Mini-Test • Lesson 18

Directions: This is a ten-minute practice test. After ten minutes, mark the last question you finished. Then complete the test and check your answers. If most of your answers were correct, but you didn't finish, try to work faster next time. Choose the <u>one best answer</u> to each question.

<u>Questions 1 through 4</u> refer to the following passage and map.

Of all the continents, only Antarctica has not attracted permanent settlers. Antarctica is one of the most difficult places in the world to live. The average temperature is 56 degrees below zero.

Even though it is a cold land covered by snow and ice, Antarctica is considered a desert. Only a small amount of precipitation falls every year. It falls in the form of snow. The snow almost never melts, and over the centuries, the light snowfalls have built up to form a sheet or "cap" of ice that is thousands of feet thick.

Only a few types of plants survive in the rare, rocky places that are not covered by ice. Except for a few insects, animals are able to live only on the edges of this vast frozen continent. Penguins and seals gather food in Antarctica's offshore waters, which, although studded with icebergs, are warmer than the land.

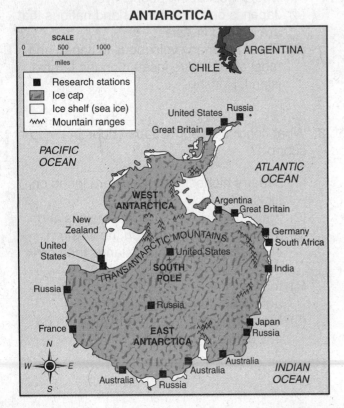

ANTARCTICA

1. Which of the following correctly restates information about Antarctica from the map?

   (1) Because of its location at the South Pole, it does not have seasons.
   (2) Many nations have research stations, but the United States has the most.
   (3) The Transantarctic Mountains divide it into eastern and western regions.
   (4) It consists mostly of shelf ice, but with mountain ranges and an ice cap too.
   (5) The highest point is found at the South Pole in the continent's interior.

2. What does the passage imply about deserts?

   (1) Deserts exist only in Africa and Asia.
   (2) A place that is cold cannot be a desert.
   (3) Snow almost never occurs in a desert.
   (4) Deserts have sand, even if covered by ice.
   (5) Places with little precipitation are deserts.

3. Why do Antarctica's largest animals live along the coasts, not in the interior, of the continent?

   (1) The interior is too cold.
   (2) The interior is too mountainous.
   (3) Most of the interior is covered with ice.
   (4) The interior has no good food source.
   (5) Researchers in the interior have hunted large animals to extinction.

4. Which value has most likely caused nations to establish research stations in Antarctica?

   (1) curiosity—to learn more about the continent
   (2) courage—lack of fear of the climate
   (3) compassion—to help the people there
   (4) love of nature—to save its animals
   (5) efficiency—to build industry on unused land

Questions 5 through 7 refer to the following passage and map.

Like other major land masses, the United States has climates that are in large part the result of the shape of the land. Major mountain ranges run from north to south near the eastern and western edges of the nation. These ranges form barriers that channel cool air from the north and warm air from the south in between them.

The climate on the outer edge of the mountain ranges is different from the climates between the ranges. On the West Coast in particular, ocean air moving inland is blocked by the high Cascade and Sierra Nevada mountain ranges. This gives much of California and the northwest coast climates that are found nowhere else in the United States.

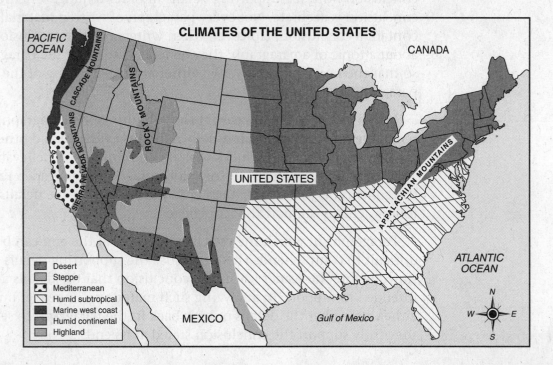

5. Which sentence summarizes the passage?

   (1) Like weather, climate is unpredictable.
   (2) Climate varies because of land features.
   (3) Mountain ranges block air movement.
   (4) Climate depends on ocean patterns.
   (5) Climate becomes warmer farther south.

6. Which sentence accurately restates information from the map?

   (1) The climates along the West Coast and along the East Coast are similar.
   (2) The mountains of the West are higher than the Appalachians in the East.
   (3) The Rocky Mountains are the highest mountains in the United States.
   (4) The Atlantic Ocean has a greater influence on climate than the Pacific Ocean does.
   (5) Much of the climate is either humid subtropical or humid continental.

7. If the mountain ranges ran east and west instead of north and south, how would the weather most likely be affected?

   (1) Days would be warmer and nights cooler.
   (2) The region with a desert climate would become larger.
   (3) The oceans would have a greater effect.
   (4) The weather would become hot and unbearable.
   (5) There would be no change.

8. What features would be least likely to appear on a map of physical regions?

   (1) mountains
   (2) lakes
   (3) plains
   (4) roads
   (5) deserts

Answers start on page 330.

GED SKILL Distinguishing Conclusions from Supporting Details

As you have already learned, it is important to be able to tell a conclusion from its supporting details in order to judge whether the conclusion is accurate. Not every paragraph of written material will contain a conclusion. However, when writers reach a conclusion about a topic of a paragraph, they generally structure the paragraph so that their conclusion is stated either at the beginning of the paragraph or at the end.

When a conclusion appears at the beginning of a paragraph, the remainder of the paragraph usually contains evidence and other details that the writer includes to make the conclusion believable. This paragraph structure has some advantages for the reader. Knowing the conclusion first makes it easier to judge whether the details that follow actually support that conclusion.

Paragraphs in which the conclusion occurs at the end can be more difficult to comprehend. This is because the supporting details are stated before the reader learns the conclusion that the details are intended to support. In analyzing such materials, the reader must either remember the details or look back in the paragraph to see if they truly support the conclusion stated at its end.

TIP

When a paragraph contains information about a cause-and-effect relationship, the conclusion will likely be stated at the end of the paragraph.

Read the paragraph and answer the question below.

Resources play an important role in determining where people live. In the early 1800s, Americans referred to the Great Plains as the Great American Desert. This is because the region seemed barren, providing few of the things necessary to support life or to conduct economic activities. There were few trees to provide lumber for houses. The lack of large lakes and rivers made it appear that water was also in short supply. The thick prairie sod was difficult to plow. These conditions caused the Great Plains to be one of the last areas settled in the United States.

Which sentence from the paragraph states its conclusion?

_____ a. Resources play an important role in determining where people live.

_____ b. These conditions caused the Great Plains to be one of the last areas settled in the United States.

You were correct if you chose *option a*. The rest of the paragraph shows how this statement is true. *Option b* is a fact that supports the opinion that resources are important in determining where people live.

Use the passage and the map to answer the questions.

A small town can grow into a major city if it is located in the right place. Trade flourishes when good transportation is available. Thriving trade draws more people to the area, where they can find jobs or open new businesses, increasing trade even more. Places like New York City and San Francisco attracted trade because they had good harbors where ships could dock. The Great Lakes formed an inland water transportation system that helped the growth of cities like Chicago. New Orleans became a trade center because of its location at the mouth of the Mississippi River, one of the major waterways in the United States. Atlanta's location at the junction, or meeting point, of railroad lines helped it grow into one of the major cities of the South. The major cities of the United States exist because traders, merchants, and workers could get to them easily.

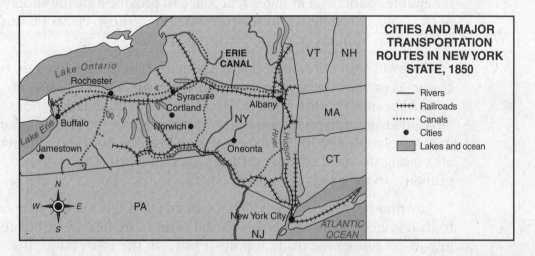

CITIES AND MAJOR TRANSPORTATION ROUTES IN NEW YORK STATE, 1850

1. Put a check mark beside any statement that is a supporting detail in the passage.

   _____ a. A small town can grow into a major city if it is located in the right place.

   _____ b. Trade flourishes when good transportation is available.

   _____ c. Thriving trade draws more people to the area, where they can find jobs or open new businesses.

2. Put a check mark beside the conclusion in the passage.

   _____ a. Places like New York City and San Francisco attracted trade and settlers because they had good harbors where ships could dock.

   _____ b. The major cities of the United States exist because traders, merchants, and workers could get to them easily.

3. Put a check mark beside the city that would have the least amount of trade based on the map's supporting details.

   _____ a. Albany

   _____ b. Buffalo

   _____ c. Jamestown

Answers start on page 331.

Resources Affect Where People Live

Some six billion people share Earth. They depend on the planet's supply of natural resources for their survival. These resources can be grouped into two basic categories: nonrenewable resources and renewable resources. **Nonrenewable resources** are resources that are not replaced by Earth's natural processes, or are replaced at an extremely slow rate. **Renewable resources** can be replaced by natural processes. The chart on this page lists some important renewable and nonrenewable resources

Fortunately, the resources that are most critical for survival are all renewable. Plants and animals reproduce to provide a steady supply of food. Water is renewed in the form of rain or snow. Plants produce oxygen that humans and animals require to live.

The availability of resources has affected where people live. Air, of course, is present everywhere on the planet's surface. But that is not true of the other basic resources. For example, the first civilizations developed along rivers because they provided water for drinking, for irrigating crops, and for keeping livestock healthy. Even today, deserts are among the most sparsely settled places on Earth. This is due primarily to their lack of water resources.

The number of people who live in an area is often directly related to its resources. Many of Earth's coastal regions are heavily populated, in part because of the ready supply of fish. On the other hand, the polar regions of America and Asia are home to relatively few people. Although plenty of water and game are available, the absence of trees deprives residents of wood for shelter and fuel.

In the modern world, transportation and technology have reduced the importance of resources in determining where people live. Coal and oil deposits provide electricity and fuel—as well as jobs in the industries they power—for populations far from where the deposits are located. No longer must people live near a coast to have access to fish. A nearby store provides this resource.

This change in how resources affect where people live has also had negative consequences. The increased availability of resources has increased their use. Even the majority of renewable resources can be exhausted if people consume them at a faster rate than they can be renewed.

RENEWABLE AND NONRENEWABLE NATURAL RESOURCES					
Some Renewable Resources			**Some Nonrenewable Resources**		
plants	soil	solar energy	coal	nuclear fuel
forests	water	geothermal energy	petroleum	iron ore
animals	air		natural gas	copper

Directions: Choose the <u>one best answer</u> to each question.

<u>Questions 1 through 6</u> refer to the passage and the chart on page 220.

1. Which statement <u>best</u> summarizes the contents of the passage?

   (1) There are two basic types of resources— renewable resources and nonrenewable resources.
   (2) Resources help determine where people live, but technology has made them less important as a factor.
   (3) Renewable resources are being exhausted much more rapidly than nonrenewable resources.
   (4) Air, food, and water are the basic resources necessary for the survival of humankind.
   (5) People who live far from coal and oil deposits tend to have industrial or agricultural jobs.

2. Which of the following is a nonrenewable resource?

   (1) cotton
   (2) fish
   (3) wool
   (4) wood
   (5) gold

3. Which of the following statements from paragraph three is a conclusion?

   (1) The availability of resources has affected where people live.
   (2) The first civilizations developed along rivers.
   (3) Rivers provided water for drinking, for irrigating crops, and for keeping livestock healthy.
   (4) Even today, deserts are among the most sparsely settled places on Earth.
   (5) This is due to their lack of water resources.

4. Which of the following is an unstated assumption necessary for understanding the conclusion in paragraph four of the passage?

   (1) Most people who live on the world's coasts earn their living by fishing.
   (2) Coastal regions tend to have mild climates, so people to want to live there.
   (3) Fish are a major source of food for many of the world's people.
   (4) There are no trees in the polar regions.
   (5) Many of the world's polar regions are rich in oil resources.

5. Which conclusion about resources is supported by the details provided in the passage and/or the chart?

   (1) Nonrenewable resources are more crucial to life than are most renewable resources.
   (2) Air is the most important of the renewable resources.
   (3) Nuclear fuel is the most important nonrenewable resource.
   (4) Few people will live in a place if an important resource cannot be provided.
   (5) Any renewable resource can be exhausted by heavy use.

6. The following conclusions are based on information in the passage. Which conclusion results from the use of faulty logic?

   (1) Coal, oil, and other fuel resources have encouraged the development of industry.
   (2) People in desert and polar regions live in primitive and isolated conditions.
   (3) Soil is an important resource because it enables people to grow food.
   (4) One way to conserve resources is to use them wisely.
   (5) Resources can be moved long distances and made available where they are locally scarce.

Answers start on page 331.

GED Practice • Lesson 19

Directions: Choose the one best answer to each question.

Questions 1 through 5 refer to the following passage.

The landscape of America is littered with towns that failed to achieve their dreams. In the 1800s, many people believed that Nelsonville, Ohio, would become a major city. Excited citizens built an opera house in preparation for their town's expected glory. But in the 1900s, the coal production that brought great prosperity to the area began to decrease. As coal deposits were exhausted and mines closed, the town also declined. Today, few people outside southern Ohio have ever heard of Nelsonville.

The history of Virginia City, Nevada, provides an even more dramatic example of how resources and their depletion can affect where people choose to live. In 1859, the Comstock Lode, a rich vein of silver and gold, was discovered in western Nevada. People rushed to the area and set up camps nearby. Miners in one camp built permanent structures, founding Virginia City.

Over the next twenty years, the Comstock Lode yielded more than $300 million worth of gold and silver, and Virginia City grew rapidly. By 1875, it was home to 20,000 people and a center of great wealth. Luxurious hotels and restaurants sprang up. The citizens of Virginia City also built an opera house. But as in Nelsonville, the good times in Virginia City did not last. In the 1880s, production in the mines started to decline. By 1898, the gold and silver were nearly gone. Most of the mines were abandoned, and Virginia City became a virtual ghost town. Today, only 700 people live where thousands once looked forward to a glorious future.

1. Which title expresses the topic of this passage?

   (1) The Tragic History of Virginia City, Nevada
   (2) How Resource Depletion Affects Settlement
   (3) Nelsonville, Ohio, and Virginia City, Nevada
   (4) The Discovery of the Comstock Lode
   (5) The History of Mining in the United States

2. Which sentence from the first paragraph is a conclusion?

   (1) The landscape of America is littered with towns that failed to achieve their dreams.
   (2) In the 1800s, many people believed that Nelsonville would become a major city.
   (3) In the 1900s, the coal production that had brought prosperity began to decrease.
   (4) As coal deposits were exhausted and mines closed, the town also declined.
   (5) Today, few people outside southern Ohio have ever heard of Nelsonville.

3. How are Virginia City and Nelsonville alike?

   (1) They both started out as mining camps.
   (2) Mining was the basis of each economy.
   (3) They both became ghost towns.
   (4) Each is in the southern part of its state.
   (5) Nelsonville citizens moved to Virginia City.

4. What evidence best supports the conclusion that Virginia City was "a center of great wealth"?

   (1) The town was founded by miners.
   (2) Some 20,000 people lived there in 1874.
   (3) Many fancy restaurants were built there.
   (4) Mining netted $300 million in gold and silver.
   (5) Many people left after the mines closed.

5. Which event is most similar to what happened to Nelsonville and Virginia City?

   (1) A labor union goes on strike, and the company they work for shuts down.
   (2) A person invents a new production process and becomes rich.
   (3) A business buys its competitors and gains control of its entire industry.
   (4) A city raises taxes to build more fire stations and hire more police officers.
   (5) A factory lays off workers because people no longer use the only product it makes.

Questions 6 through 8 refer to the following passage and map.

The Pacific and Gulf coasts of the United States are home to many cities. In the East, however, few cities between New York City and Charleston, South Carolina, are actually located on the coast. Most cities are found miles inland, on a **fall line** that separates the highlands of the interior from the plains that line the East Coast. All along the fall line, rivers that begin in the Appalachian Mountains rush through rapids and over waterfalls as they flow toward the sea.

The fall line marks the farthest point inland that boats on these rivers can reach. In early times, settlers heading upriver stopped and built towns in many of these places. Later, when American industry developed, the first machines were driven by water power. Places near rapids and waterfalls were ideal locations for factories. The jobs factories created caused towns on the fall line to grow faster than those on the coast. Water resources thus created most of the cities that exist along the eastern seaboard today.

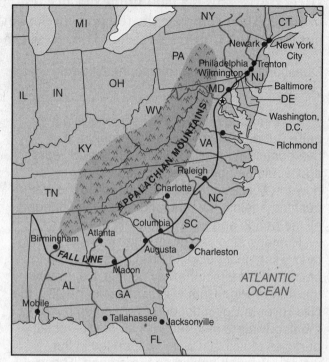

SETTLEMENT PATTERNS IN THE ATLANTIC COAST REGION

6. Which sentence from the passage best restates the map's information about eastern cities?

   (1) The Pacific and Gulf coasts of the United States are home to many cities.
   (2) Most cities are found miles inland, on a fall line separating the highlands of the interior from the plains of the East Coast.
   (3) In early times, settlers heading upriver stopped and built towns in many of these places.
   (4) All along the fall line, rivers that begin in the Appalachian Mountains rush through rapids and over waterfalls as they flow toward the sea.
   (5) The jobs factories created caused towns on the fall line to grow faster than those on the coast.

7. What information about the eastern seaboard is implied in the passage?

   (1) Early settlers built roads across the Appalachian Mountains.
   (2) The region lacks sufficient water resources to support a large population.
   (3) Travel by land from the coast into the interior was difficult in early times.
   (4) Most industry developed elsewhere.
   (5) No important cities developed there.

8. Which statement is the conclusion in the second paragraph of the passage?

   (1) The fall line marks the farthest point inland boats on these rivers can reach.
   (2) When American industry developed, the first machines were driven by water power.
   (3) Places near rapids and waterfalls were ideal locations for factories.
   (4) The jobs factories created caused towns on the fall line to grow faster than those on the coast.
   (5) Water resources created most of the cities that exist along the eastern seaboard today.

TIP

Often a conclusion contains words like, *consequently, thus, therefore,* or *as a result.* Look for such words to identify conclusions.

Answers start on page 332.

Directions: This is a ten-minute practice test. After ten minutes, mark the last question you finished. Then complete the test and check your answers. If most of your answers were correct, but you didn't finish, try to work faster next time. Choose the <u>one best answer</u> to each question.

Questions 1 through 3 refer to the following passage.

On a map, a river looks like it follows a set path. But a river can change its course. A riverboat captain who lived one hundred years ago would be able to detect many changes in how the Mississippi River looks today. The water pushing against the mud and trees has changed all the bends and small islands in the river.

Humans also can change the course of a river by digging channels and building dams, and the changes can affect the way people live. Before the Aswan High Dam was completed in 1970, the Nile River in Egypt flooded every autumn. As the floodwaters receded, a layer of silt—small particles of soil that were suspended in the water—was left behind on the ground. These silt deposits enriched the land, increasing the harvests and profits of farmers.

Since the dam ended flooding, farmers along the Nile have had to replenish their land with expensive chemical fertilizers. Some of these chemicals get into the river, killing fish on which other Egyptians depend for their living. However, damming the Nile has also brought electricity into homes and businesses of millions of Egyptians.

1. How did the flooding of the Nile River affect Egyptian farmers?

   (1) The floods made farming more difficult.
   (2) Frequent flooding required them to use expensive fertilizer on their farmland.
   (3) The floods made it impossible for farmers to harvest their crops during the summer months.
   (4) The flooding allowed farmers to produce more crops.
   (5) The floods washed away the land's rich top layer of soil.

2. Which detail supports the conclusion that changes in a river can affect how people live?

   (1) A river can change its course.
   (2) Humans can change the course of a river by digging channels and building dams.
   (3) Before the Aswan High Dam was completed in 1970, the Nile River flooded every year.
   (4) Silt deposits enriched the land, increasing the harvests and profits of farmers.
   (5) Farmers along the Nile have had to enrich their soil with expensive chemical fertilizers.

3. Which conclusion is supported by the passage?

   (1) Rivers can be dangerous and deadly.
   (2) Rivers are economically important.
   (3) The Nile flooding made travel and trade more difficult.
   (4) Egyptian farmers use more fertilizer than U.S. farmers do.
   (5) The fishing industry in Egypt is growing.

4. Large parts of Earth are very different now from the way they used to be. Many of the changes, like climate changes, have natural causes. Others are caused by people. For example, much of the eastern United States was farmland in the 1800s. Today, much of it is urban or forested.

   What is the main idea of this paragraph?

   (1) The United States was mainly farmland in the 1800s.
   (2) Cities now stand where farms used to be.
   (3) Changes in Earth are caused by nature and by people.
   (4) Although Earth has changed in the past, it no longer does so.
   (5) Much of the eastern United States is forested or urban today.

Questions 5 through 8 refer to the following passage and map.

Each autumn, monarch butterflies across the eastern and central United States fly south for the winter. They reappear every spring. In 1975, a Canadian scientist located the winter home of the monarchs in the Sierra Madre Mountains of central Mexico. In just 60 square miles there are 14 colonies of monarchs, or about 150 million of these regal creatures. They turn the sky orange and black and cover the trunks of trees, and branches bend under their weight.

When word of this wondrous place spread, it began to attract sightseers. By the early 1980s, thousands of tourists were visiting the area every weekend from December through March. They filled the monarchs' home with litter and stuffed butterflies into plastic bags as souvenirs. Local residents, seeing an economic opportunity, began to supply small wood and glass cases with monarchs mounted inside.

As tourism brought development, the threat to the monarchs became even more severe. The region's growth created a need for wood, and local residents increased logging in the forest where the monarch colonies lived. In 1986, Mexico's government created a preserve to protect 5 of the 14 colonies. But the owners of the land received little compensation for the loss of their timber resources; illegal logging continues today in the area that is supposed to shelter the monarchs.

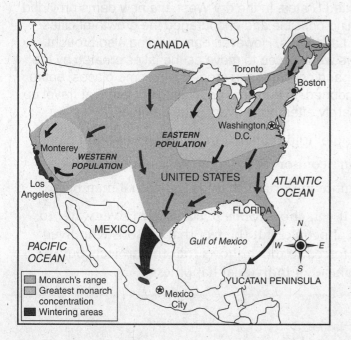

5. According to the map, in what other region besides central Mexico do monarch butterflies spend the winter?

(1) Canada
(2) Central America
(3) Mexico City
(4) the West Coast of the United States
(5) Mexico's Yucatan Peninsula

6. Which of the following is an unstated fact important for understanding the first paragraph of the passage?

(1) Butterflies are smaller than birds.
(2) The monarchs' winter home is in Mexico.
(3) Air quality in the monarch preserve is poor.
(4) Birds also fly south for the winter.
(5) A monarch has orange-and-black wings.

7. If the U.S. government wanted to protect monarch butterflies along the West Coast, what might it establish that would be similar in intention to Mexico's monarch preserve?

(1) a zoo
(2) a wildlife refuge
(3) a farm
(4) a tourist resort
(5) a national recreation area

8. What cause-and-effect relationship is implied by the information in the passage?

(1) Logging the forest threatens the well-being of the monarchs.
(2) The government created the preserve at the request of the tourists.
(3) Economic growth has brought an end to logging in the area.
(4) Establishing the preserve has increased the number of monarchs.
(5) Most of the damage to the forest is caused by the monarchs themselves.

Answers start on page 332.

GED SKILL **Recognizing Values**

You have already learned that values are principles, qualities, and goals people think are desirable and worthwhile. People often make decisions about what to do based on their values.

You have also previously learned that the values people share are among the things that hold a society together. These shared values—as well as the values of the individual members of a society—affect the decisions that people make about the use and conservation of the society's resources. For example, many people make an effort to conserve water during a shortage. But some people continue to soak their lawns with little apparent concern about whether others will have enough water. These two approaches toward using this resource result from very different sets of values.

Two types of values can be present in written material—the values of the people being written about and the writer's values. Being able to recognize the values of the people being written about helps us understand why they act as they do. It is also important to recognize the writer's values in order to be aware of any **biases** in his or her writing. Look for words in the material that provide clues about the writer's attitude toward the subject.

bias
a strong opinion that a person holds about a topic, sometimes unfairly or without good reason.

Read the passage and answer the question below.

The first half of the twentieth century was a period of unprecedented dam building on the rivers of the United States. The Grand Coulee Dam in Washington State, the Hoover Dam in Nevada, and hundreds of other dams built during this period brought flood control and electric power to large areas of the United States. In the dry West, the new dams provided water that made farming possible and encouraged the growth of cities like Los Angeles and Las Vegas. However, dam building also brought problems. Landowners were forced to move as the lakes created by the dams filled with water and covered their property. In some places, entire towns had to be abandoned. In addition, populations of fish that travel up rivers to breed fell sharply after those rivers were dammed.

Which belief did people hold that encouraged them to build dams?

_____ a. Each person's comfort and happiness is important.

_____ b. Society is more important than its individual members.

You were correct if you chose *option b*. Dams used river water to benefit large groups of people. But the fact that persons who lived near the dams were forced to move shows that the projects put the benefits for society ahead of individual happiness.

TIP

To recognize values in written materials, pay close attention to accounts of people's actions as well as to accounts of their words. How people behave often reveals more of their values than what they say.

Use the passage and the chart to answer the questions.

In our throw-away society, the average person produces 1,500 pounds of garbage per year. For generations, nearly everything we discarded ended up in the local dump. But in recent years, as dumps grew to cover hundreds of acres, some Americans sought better ways of dealing with all this trash. Today, about 27 percent of our garbage is **recycled,** or processed to be used again. Most recycled trash is **inorganic waste**—plastic and steel, for example, and other garbage that comes from things that were never alive. The most easily and commonly recycled products are those that are made of one material, rather than of a mix of materials. Recycling is a good way to conserve energy and other resources. The chart lists ways recycled materials are used.

Many communities ask residents to separate recyclable trash from the rest of their garbage. Some enlightened states require deposits on metal and glass drink containers. This encourages the thoughtless public to return these items rather than discard them.

THE RECYCLING OF COMMON MATERIALS		
Material	**The Recycling Process**	**Examples of Uses**
Plastic bottles	Shredded and reformed as a fiber	Fiberfill
Plastic foam	Melted, compacted and shaped under pressure	Building materials, furniture frames, trash cans
Glass	Separated by color, then melted and reused	Nearly all new glass products
Metals	Separated by type, then melted and reformed	Nearly all new metal products
Office paper	De-inked, reshredded, and repulped	Newspaper, cardboard boxes, paper bags

1. Put a check mark next to the statement that reflects the values of people who recycle their trash.

   _____ a. People who recycle are wasteful and uncaring about the nation's resources.

   _____ b. People who recycle are concerned about conserving the nation's resources.

2. Put a check mark next to all sentences from the passage that provide clues to the writer's values.

   _____ a. In our throw-away society, the average person produces 1,500 pounds of garbage per year.

   _____ b. Today, about 27 percent of our garbage is recycled, or processed to be used again.

   _____ c. Some enlightened states require deposits on metal and glass beverage containers.

   _____ d. This encourages the thoughtless public to return these items rather than throw them away.

3. Put a check mark next to the item a person who supports recycling would most likely purchase.

   _____ a. apple juice in a bottle made of glass capped with a metal lid

   _____ b. apple juice in a cardboard box with an aluminum foil lining glued inside

4. Put a check mark next to the statement that best summarizes the writer's values and beliefs.

   _____ a. People who waste resources are behaving badly; those who do not are behaving well.

   _____ b. Recycling is a good idea, but it is better to conserve resources by producing less garbage.

Answers start on page 333.

How People Change the Environment

One way that people have changed the **environment**—the natural conditions in which organisms live—is by **polluting** it. Much of the technology that produces the food we eat, the products we buy, and the power we consume contributes to the contamination of our air, land, and water resources.

Rain washes fertilizers, weed killers, and pesticides into city storm sewers and rural ditches. These chemicals eventually end up in streams, rivers, and lakes. Industrial and animal wastes and sewage also poison our waters. Signs have been posted at many lakes warning fishers against eating their catch. Tests have shown that the fish in these lakes are full of harmful chemicals.

Another serious threat to our resources is **acid rain,** a form of pollution produced by burning **fossil fuels**—that is, coal and petroleum products. When coal is burned, it releases a waste gas called sulfur dioxide. The gasoline burned in car engines produces a waste gas called nitrogen oxide. As these gases combine with water vapor in the atmosphere, sulfuric acid and nitric acid are formed. These return to Earth as acid rain. Acid rain forms in clouds primarily over the Midwest. It is blown eastward by westerly winds. When it falls, it pollutes lakes and damages forests.

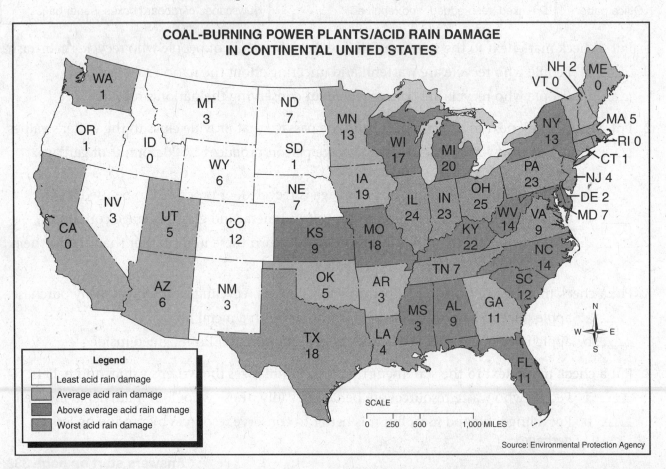

COAL-BURNING POWER PLANTS/ACID RAIN DAMAGE IN CONTINENTAL UNITED STATES

WA 1
OR 1
MT 3
ND 7
MN 13
NH 2
VT 0
ME 0
NY 13
MA 5
RI 0
CT 1
ID 0
SD 1
WI 17
MI 20
PA 23
NJ 4
DE 2
MD 7
NV 3
WY 6
NE 7
IA 19
IL 24
IN 23
OH 25
WV 14
VA 9
CA 0
UT 5
CO 12
KS 9
MO 18
KY 22
NC 14
AZ 6
NM 3
OK 5
AR 3
TN 7
SC 12
TX 18
LA 4
MS 3
AL 9
GA 11
FL 11

SCALE
0   250   500   1,000 MILES

Legend
Least acid rain damage
Average acid rain damage
Above average acid rain damage
Worst acid rain damage

Source: Environmental Protection Agency

Directions: Choose the one best answer to each question.

Questions 1 through 7 refer to the passage and the map on page 228.

1. According to the map, which part of the nation has the most acid rain damage?

   (1) the Northeast
   (2) the Southeast
   (3) the Southwest
   (4) the Northwest
   (5) the West Coast

2. Which information is implied by the passage?

   (1) Driving cars produces a waste gas.
   (2) All technology is bad for humankind.
   (3) Acid rain contains nitric acid and sulfuric acid.
   (4) Our air is more polluted than our water.
   (5) Some chemical wastes harm people.

3. Which of the following is a source of acid rain?

   (1) storm sewers and ditches
   (2) coal mining and oil drilling
   (3) coal-burning power plants
   (4) the manufacture of chemicals
   (5) toxic chemicals in rivers and streams

4. Which conclusion is supported by the information in the passage and on the map?

   (1) Water pollution is not a serious problem in the United States.
   (2) Pollution can spread long distances.
   (3) Coal should be outlawed as a source of energy.
   (4) The worst water pollution is in the West.
   (5) Acid rain is the greatest pollution problem faced by the United States.

5. The passage states that warning signs have been posted at many lakes in the United States. What value is expressed by the posting of these signs?

   (1) Conservation is not important.
   (2) Animals should be protected.
   (3) Public health is important.
   (4) Fishing is not a worthwhile activity.
   (5) People who pollute the water are bad.

6. Which of the following actions would people who truly value a clean environment be least likely to take?

   (1) collect and recycle aluminum cans
   (2) work in a factory
   (3) buy a used car
   (4) use chemicals on their lawns
   (5) make their living by farming

7. Does the map support the passage's claim that acid rain is carried east by the wind?

   (1) No, because most of the states with the worst acid rain damage are also those with the highest number of coal-burning power plants.
   (2) Yes, because states east of those with large numbers of coal-burning power plants tend to have above-average acid rain damage.
   (3) No, because some states to the west of those with large numbers of coal-burning power plants have above-average acid rain damage.
   (4) Yes, because the states with the greatest acid rain damage are located in the nation's major coal-mining regions.
   (5) No, because the western states have very few coal-burning power plants and the states to their east have the most acid rain damage.

Answers start on page 333.

GED Practice • Lesson 20

Directions: Choose the one best answer to each question.

Questions 1 through 4 refer to the following passage.

One of the greatest challenges to our environment is water pollution. For years, industries across the United States buried harmful chemicals or dumped them into streams. Most water pollution cannot be seen. Only its effects on plants and animals provide evidence of poor water quality.

Water pollution is not confined to places where the contamination actually happens. In the cycle of nature, the water supply is used and reused. **Surface water** evaporates and later returns to Earth in the form of rain or snow. Some of this water soaks through the soil and slowly seeps down between cracks in rocks to become part of large pools, lakes, and rivers of water that exist beneath Earth's surface. Eventually this **groundwater** returns to the surface in the springs that create streams. Because of this cycle, the pollution of any water becomes the pollution of all water.

Groundwater is also tapped by wells and provides drinking water for about half the population of the United States. Many people use water filters or drink bottled water because they question whether their household water is safe. Older homes often have lead pipes. Lead from these pipes can sometimes get into the water that passes through them. Lead is absorbed very slowly by the body. But if high levels build up, damage to the brain and central nervous system can result.

1. Which of the following expresses the main idea of the passage?

   (1) Lakes and rivers are being polluted.
   (2) Water pollution is hazardous to human health.
   (3) Water pollution is a widespread problem.
   (4) There is no solution for water pollution.
   (5) People should start drinking bottled water.

2. Which of the following is a conclusion supported by the passage?

   (1) Polluted water can be detected by its appearance.
   (2) Groundwater is more polluted than water from rivers and lakes.
   (3) Water from rivers and lakes is more polluted than groundwater.
   (4) People who get their drinking water from wells should have it periodically tested.
   (5) People will become seriously ill if they drink water from the pipes of older homes.

3. What do people who drink bottled water value most?

   (1) their health
   (2) impressing their neighbors
   (3) old houses
   (4) conserving resources
   (5) a clean environment

4. According to the passage, should the burying of harmful chemicals be considered a source of water pollution?

   (1) Yes, because water pollution is one of the greatest challenges to our environment.
   (2) No, because these chemicals are buried on land, not dumped into bodies of water.
   (3) Yes, because the chemicals are harmful to humans.
   (4) No, because when the chemicals were buried, it was not against the law to do so.
   (5) Yes, because seepage from rainwater could carry these chemicals into the groundwater.

TIP Remember that the things considered to be important indicate people's values.

Questions 5 through 8 refer to the following passage and diagrams.

Tremendous growth has occurred along the nation's coasts in recent decades. Shores that were once deserted are now covered with homes and businesses. From a geographical standpoint, these shores often are not good places for such development.

Over time, waves and currents reshape shorelines and beaches. Waves that strike a beach "head on" wash the sand directly out to sea. This produces islands called **sand bars** just off shore. Where the waves hit the shore at an angle, they create a current, called a **longshore current,** that flows parallel to the coastline. Sand washed from the beach is carried by this current and deposited elsewhere along the coast.

To resist these natural forces, property owners and communities have constructed **breakwaters, jetties,** and **seawalls.** Breakwaters are barriers placed offshore; jetties jut out from the shore. The diagrams show how these structures work. Seawalls can be thought of as on-shore breakwaters. They are often a last-ditch effort to save buildings. While seawalls protect land behind them, they accelerate **erosion** on their seaward side, causing beaches to rapidly disappear.

Breakwaters and jetties slow the erosion of nearby beaches. Breakwaters can even create new beach by keeping sand deposited by the longshore current from being washed away. But neither prevents the shoreline from changing, and some experts believe that they increase long-term erosion by interfering with the natural cycles.

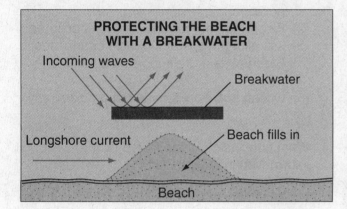

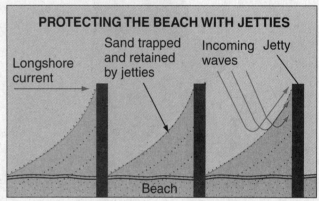

5. Based on the diagram, what do jetties do?

(1) break the energy of incoming waves
(2) change the angle of incoming waves
(3) trap the sand
(4) create the longshore current
(5) create sand bars

6. Which sentence expresses a value that <u>best</u> relates to the construction of breakwaters, jetties, and seawalls?

(1) Protecting property is important.
(2) Natural environment must be preserved.
(3) People should accept forces of nature.
(4) Natural beauty is worth preserving.
(5) People have a responsibility to help others.

7. Which of the following is most similar in function to the breakwater in the diagram?

(1) a ski lift on a mountainside
(2) a bridge over a river
(3) a TV station's transmission tower
(4) a guardrail along a highway
(5) an underground bomb shelter

8. Which of the following is an opinion?

(1) The shoreline is constantly changing shape.
(2) Waves can wash beach sand away.
(3) Jetties and breakwaters function differently.
(4) The building of seawalls destroys beaches.
(5) Breakwaters and jetties accelerate erosion.

Answers start on page 334.

Directions: This is a ten-minute practice test. After ten minutes, mark the last question you finished. Then complete the test and check your answers. If most of your answers were correct, but you didn't finish, try to work faster next time. Choose the one best answer to each question.

Questions 1 through 4 refer to the following cartoon.

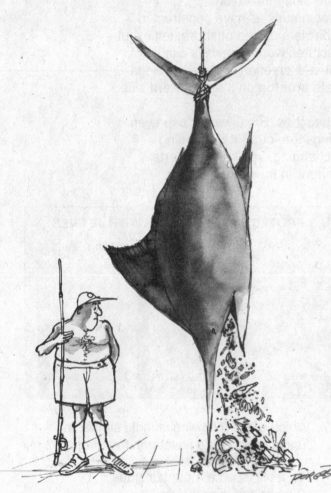

Cartoon by Peter Porges. © 1975. Reprinted by permission.

1. Which statement best describes what is happening in the cartoon?

   (1) A fisherman has caught the largest fish on record.
   (2) A fish is being prepared for processing and eating.
   (3) A fish is hanging over a dock or the deck of a boat.
   (4) A fisherman has caught a fish that has eaten people's trash.
   (5) A large fish was used to help clean up the ocean.

2. What opinion is the cartoon expressing about how people are changing the environment?

   (1) Fishing is exhausting the supply of fish.
   (2) The world's oceans are polluted.
   (3) Fishing is cleaning up the environment.
   (4) Pollution is causing birth defects in fish.
   (5) Fishing is polluting the environment.

3. What does the cartoon suggest are some polluters' values and attitudes about pollution?

   (1) Sports fishing kills more fish than pollution.
   (2) Fishermen are among the worst polluters.
   (3) It is all right to litter if people cannot see it.
   (4) Clean air is more important than clean water.
   (5) Ocean pollution is not a big problem.

4. What conclusion is supported by the information in the cartoon?

   (1) It is not safe to eat fish.
   (2) Pollution of the oceans kills fish.
   (3) Fishing with a pole is less harmful to the environment than fishing with a net.
   (4) The government should regulate fishing.
   (5) Pollution affects the ocean's animals.

5. Natural barriers like oceans and deserts have long slowed the movement of ideas. Today, satellites allow telephones and the Internet to reach almost anywhere in the world, to spread ideas and reduce differences among societies.

   Which of the following is most like a communications satellite?

   (1) a wall
   (2) a floor
   (3) a window
   (4) a room
   (5) a ceiling

Questions 6 through 10 refer to the following passage.

The environment we live in is not just air, land, and water. It also includes cities and towns. Much of the world's population lives in cities. In the United States, about 75 percent of people live in urban areas.

Unfortunately, the nation has not prepared well for urban growth. Even though the majority of Americans live in cities, the space they occupy is only about 1 percent of the land. Cities face problems related to overcrowding, air pollution, trash disposal, water supply and treatment, inadequate housing, and more. The problems that cities face result from many people being concentrated in a small area. If the urban environment does not get more attention, these problems are likely to get worse.

Recently, more and more Americans have come to understand and appreciate cities' problems. Politicians have begun to pay attention to cities, too. Some are beginning to pass laws that help make cities better places to live.

6. What is the main idea of the first paragraph of the passage?

(1) The environment includes all land as well as air and water.
(2) More people live in suburbs than in cities.
(3) Cities take up more land than farms do.
(4) Cities and suburbs are part of the environment, but farms are not.
(5) Most Americans live in urban areas, which are part of the environment.

7. Which of the following statements from the passage is a conclusion?

(1) Much of the world's population now lives in cities.
(2) The majority of Americans live in cities.
(3) The problems cities face result from many people being concentrated in a small area.
(4) Urban problems include overcrowding, air and water pollution, and inadequate housing.
(5) The majority of Americans live on only 1 percent of the land.

8. Which is the most likely cause of the water supply problems that cities face?

(1) not enough rain
(2) too many people
(3) polluted wells
(4) too much rain
(5) urban flooding

9. Which information is the writer's opinion?

(1) About 75 percent of Americans live in urban areas.
(2) Trash disposal is an issue affecting cities.
(3) Urban growth has not been well planned.
(4) Some politicians work to help cities.
(5) New laws address some issues cities face.

10. Which cause-and-effect relationship is suggested by the passage?

(1) As more Americans move to cities, the amount of land cities occupy decreases.
(2) Americans have become aware of urban problems because the news media are paying more attention to cities.
(3) As Americans have become more aware of urban problems, government has come under more pressure to improve cities.
(4) Because cities have so many problems, most of the people living are unhappy.
(5) Politicians know about urban problems because the problems are worldwide.

11. America's worst oil spill in history occurred in 1989. An oil tanker struck a reef off Alaska's coast, and 11 million gallons of oil leaked into the sea. More than 1,200 miles of coastline was polluted and 100,000 birds died.

What conclusion is supported here?

(1) The oil spill was an environmental disaster.
(2) Transporting oil by ship should be outlawed.
(3) Many birds died from drinking the oil.
(4) The ship was not operating safely.
(5) People can clean up their environment.

Answers start on page 335.

Unit 5 Cumulative Review **Geography**

Directions: Choose the one best answer to each question.

Questions 1 through 3 refer to the following passage.

All Americans have ancestors who came from somewhere else. Native Americans' ancestors are believed to have come across the Bering Sea between Asia and Alaska. They followed migrating animals on which they depended for food. Until recently, most people who came to the United States were from Europe or Africa. Recent movements of people have been from Asia and Latin America to the United States.

Most Asians come to the United States from South and Southeast Asia. More than one-third settle in California. Immigrants from Mexico and Central America tend to settle in the Southwest.

1. What information about immigrants is implied by the passage?

    (1) Most immigrants settle in the Southwest.
    (2) Immigrants sometimes enter the United States illegally.
    (3) Many immigrants live in Asia, Latin America, and Africa.
    (4) Most immigrants to the United States in recent years have been wealthy.
    (5) Immigrants are people who were not born in the country where they currently live.

2. Which of the following statements from the passage is a conclusion?

    (1) All Americans have ancestors who came from somewhere else.
    (2) Native Americans' ancestors came across the Bering Sea between Asia and Alaska.
    (3) Until recently, most of the people who came to the United States were from Europe or Africa.
    (4) Recent movements of people have been from Asia and Latin America to the United States.
    (5) Most Asians who move to the United States are from South and Southeast Asia.

3. Mark lives in California. He has a neighbor who has recently moved to the United States. He has not met her yet and is trying to guess where she is from. Based on the passage alone, which country would Mark most easily rule out as her country of origin?

    (1) Japan
    (2) Mexico
    (3) Canada
    (4) France
    (5) Vietnam

Question 4 refers to the following graph.

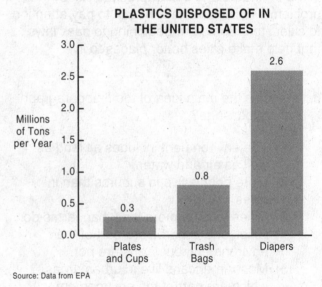

PLASTICS DISPOSED OF IN THE UNITED STATES

Source: Data from EPA

4. Which of the following statements about life in the United States is implied by the graph?

    (1) Americans are having too many babies.
    (2) Americans use more plastic plates and cups than nonplastic plates and cups.
    (3) Americans buy a lot of disposable plastic items.
    (4) Americans do not use anything that is made of plastic.
    (5) Americans are unwilling to waste anything.

"Have you given any thought to what you'll do with your Saturdays when the world's fossil fuels are used up?"

Fossil fuels include all fuels derived from underground deposits of coal, oil, and natural gas. Fossil fuels have been formed over millions of years from the buried remains of plants and animals. The burning of fossil fuels provides most of the world's energy. Less than 10 percent of the energy used is produced by other methods. The increasing demand for energy has begun to exhaust the supply of fossil fuels. Some experts estimate that coal will be gone in 250 years, and that the world's known oil reserves may last only another 30.

5. What fact does the cartoonist assume you know to understand the point of the cartoon?

   (1) Washing cars depletes water resources.
   (2) Most Americans use commercial car washes.
   (3) Most Americans do not work on Saturdays.
   (4) Gasoline, which powers automobiles, is a fossil fuel.
   (5) Coal supplies most of the world's energy.

6. Which conclusion is supported by the information in the paragraph and the cartoon?

   (1) We are too dependent on fossil fuels.
   (2) People should conserve water resources.
   (3) Fossil fuels will not run out soon.
   (4) New forms of transportation will be invented.
   (5) People will walk more in the future.

7. Temperatures of places are affected by their latitude and elevation. Latitude is the distance of a place from the equator. The sun's heat is strongest at the equator. Elevation affects temperature because the higher a place is, the cooler it will be.

   Which of these places would be the coldest?

   (1) close to the equator with a high elevation
   (2) far from the equator with a low elevation
   (3) close to the equator with a low elevation
   (4) far from the equator with a high elevation
   (5) on the equator with a high elevation

Questions 8 through 12 refer to the following paragraph.

The wide range of geographical features in the United States provides a broad choice of beautiful vacation spots. A trip to Vermont can satisfy the person who wants crisp air and white slopes for skiing or hiking. For nature lovers who prefer gently rounded mountains with wildflowers, good fishing, and the smell of pine trees, the Apache Tribal Enterprises allows camping in the White Mountains of Arizona. Sun-lovers might go to sandy beaches in either southern California or Florida. The Black Hills of South Dakota are full of caves sparkling with the mineral deposits that more than a century ago brought European Americans to the region to seek their fortunes. Modern-day adventurers can travel down the white waters of the Colorado River. And for the backpacker, there is the long hike down to the bottom of the Grand Canyon.

8. Which statement is the best summary of the paragraph?

(1) The varied landscapes of the United States provide vacations for everyone.
(2) Great excitement can be had on vacations to the Colorado River and the Grand Canyon.
(3) Beaches and coastlines are geographic features.
(4) Vacations can be taken in the mountains at any time of year.
(5) A beach vacation is recommended over any other vacation.

9. Based on the passage, which vacation destinations have the most similar geography?

(1) Florida beaches and Vermont
(2) the Black Hills and the Grand Canyon
(3) Vermont and Arizona's White Mountains
(4) the Colorado River and California beaches
(5) the Grand Canyon and Florida beaches

TIP To summarize first look for the topic sentence. This sentence will state a paragraph's main idea.

10. Which of the following states a fact?

(1) White-water rafting is very exciting.
(2) Outdoor vacations are the most enjoyable.
(3) The best U.S. beaches are in Florida and California.
(4) Skiing is a dangerous and costly sport.
(5) Camping generally costs less than staying in a hotel.

11. Based on the passage, what did the early European-American visitors to the Black Hills likely value the most?

(1) beauty
(2) challenge
(3) isolation
(4) wealth
(5) caves

12. Which statement involves faulty logic?

(1) Beaches offer sun, sand, and water.
(2) People vacation outdoors because they love adventure.
(3) Some skiers like to vacation in Vermont.
(4) Many people find camping a fun activity.
(5) Physical fitness is critical for backpacking.

Question 13 refers to the following table.

LIFE EXPECTANCY AT BIRTH, 1999		
Country	Male	Female
United States	73	80
Brazil	59	69
Sweden	77	82
Japan	77	83
Egypt	60	64

Source: The CIA World Fact Book

13. Which conclusion is supported by the table?

(1) Americans have the longest life expectancy in the world.
(2) U.S. men live longer than Japanese men
(3) Women tend to live longer than men.
(4) Climate affects life expectancy.
(5) Brazil has the longest life expectancy in South America.

236   Unit 5: Geography

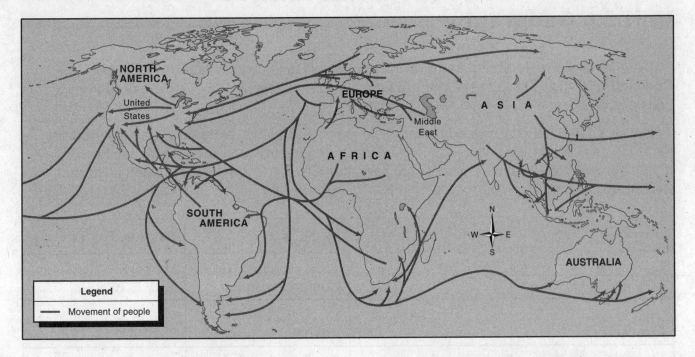

14. What would be the best title for this map?

(1) The Worldwide Movement of People
(2) Immigration in the 1800s
(3) Immigration to the United States
(4) Future Population Trends
(5) Patterns of European Settlement

15. According to the map, which continents had very few people leave for other continents?

(1) South America and Europe
(2) Europe and Africa
(3) Africa and Asia
(4) Asia and North America
(5) North America and Australia

16. Which statement best restates information from the map?

(1) The number of immigrants has increased.
(2) U.S. immigration peaked in the 1900s.
(3) Immigration affects all continents.
(4) African immigrants mainly go to Europe.
(5) People move to gain better lives.

17. As countries became more industrialized, the standard of living improved. Labor-saving devices were invented that required energy to run, but that made people's lives easier. People began to see comfortable lives as a basic right. Much of the land was mined and stripped of its minerals and forests. Air and water pollution began to poison plant and animal life. Gradually, people began to realize that many activities that hurt the planet were bad for their own lives.

What cause-and-effect relationship is suggested by the paragraph but not explicitly stated in it?

(1) The invention of labor-saving devices is responsible for air and water pollution.
(2) Much environmental damage has resulted from people's pursuit of more comfortable lives.
(3) Air and water pollution are responsible for damage to plants and animals.
(4) Labor-saving devices have caused people to think they have a right to comfortable lives.
(5) Industrialization produced an improved standard of living for many people.

Answers start on page 336.

Cumulative Review Performance Analysis
Unit 5 • Geography

Use the Answers and Explanations starting on page 336 to check your answers to the Unit 5 Cumulative Review. Then use the chart to figure out the skill areas in which you need more practice.

On the chart, circle the questions that you answered correctly. Write the number correct for each skill area. Add the number of questions that you got correct on the Cumulative Review. If you feel that you need more practice, go back and review the lessons for the skill areas that were difficult for you.

Questions	Number Correct	Skill Area	Lessons for Review
1, **4**, 8, **14**, **15**, **16**	____/6	Comprehension	1, 2, 7, 16, 18
2, **5**, 9, 10, 17	____/5	Analysis	9, 10, 11, 12, 19
3, 7	____/2	Application	14, 15
6, 11, 12, **13**	____/4	Evaluation	8, 13, 17, 20
TOTAL CORRECT	____/17		

Question numbers in **boldface** are based on graphics.

SOCIAL STUDIES

Directions

This Social Studies Posttest is intended to measure your knowledge of general social studies concepts.

The questions are based on short readings or on graphs, maps, charts, cartoons, and illustrations. Study the information given and then answer the questions that follow. Refer to the information as often as necessary in answering the questions.

You should spend no more than 70 minutes in answering the 50 questions on this test. Work carefully, but do not spend too much time on any one item. Do not skip any items. Make a reasonable guess when you are not sure of an answer. You will not be penalized for incorrect answers.

When time is up, mark the last item you finished. This will tell you whether you can finish the real GED Test in the time allowed. Then complete the test.

Record your answers to the questions on a copy of the answer sheet on page 361. Be sure that all required information is recorded on the answer sheet.

To record your answers, mark the numbered space on the answer sheet that corresponds to the answer you choose for each item on the test.

Example:

Early pioneers of the western frontier looked to settle on land that had adequate access to water. To ensure access to water, many early pioneers settled on land near which type of geographic feature?

(1) forests
(2) grasslands
(3) rivers
(4) glaciers
(5) oceans
①　②　●　④　⑤

The correct answer is <u>rivers</u>; therefore, answer space 3 should be marked on the answer sheet.

Do not rest the point of your pencil on the answer sheet while you are considering your answer. Make no stray or unnecessary marks. If you change an answer, erase your first mark completely. Mark only one answer for each question; multiple answers will be scored as incorrect. Do not fold or crease your answer sheet.

When you finish the test, use the Performance Analysis Chart on page 256 to determine whether you are ready to take the real GED Test, and, if not, which skill areas need additional review.

Directions: Choose the one best answer to each question.

Questions 1 through 3 refer to the following paragraph and cartoon.

JOIN, or DIE.

In 1754, Benjamin Franklin drew this cartoon in support of a plan to establish a union of colonies that could negotiate with Great Britain. The image was so successful that it was used again in 1765 during the colonists' dispute with Britain over the taxes imposed by the Stamp Act. In 1774, Franklin's snake appeared again, this time on the masthead of a Massachusetts newspaper.

1. What does the snake in this cartoon represent?

    (1) the potential power of the united colonies
    (2) the colonies' great differences
    (3) the unity of the New England colonies
    (4) the evil of the British government
    (5) the great variety of immigrants in the colonies

2. What opinion was the Massachusetts publisher expressing by putting this cartoon on the masthead as the symbol of the newspaper?

    (1) The Stamp Act put a tax on newspapers, legal documents, and other printed materials.
    (2) New England was in the northernmost region of the colonies.
    (3) Massachusetts was part of New England.
    (4) The colonies should unite against Britain.
    (5) Massachusetts is better than the rest of the colonies.

3. Which of the following events is most like the ideas expressed in this cartoon?

    (1) The government forces a manufacturer to recall a defective product.
    (2) Workers at a company form a labor union and demand changes from their employer.
    (3) A chain of fast food restaurants lowers its price in order to attract its competitors' customers.
    (4) Environmentalists launch a campaign to save an endangered species of snake.
    (5) A homeowner hunts down and kills all the snakes in her neighborhood.

Questions 4 through 6 refer to the following graph.

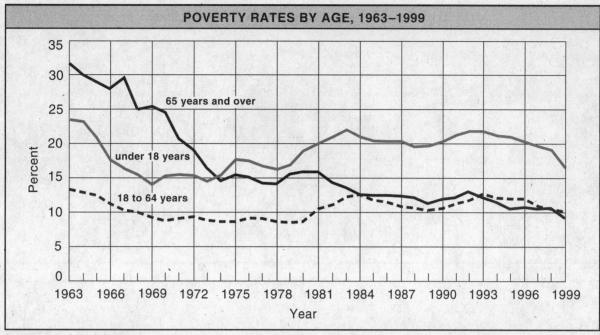

POVERTY RATES BY AGE, 1963–1999

65 years and over

under 18 years

18 to 64 years

Source: U.S. Census Bureau

4. What percentage of children lived in poverty in 1971?

(1) fewer than 10 percent of children
(2) about 15 percent of all children
(3) over 20 percent of all children
(4) about 25 percent of all children
(5) about 35 percent of children

5. Which of the following statements is supported by the evidence in the graph?

(1) The poverty rate in 1999 was lowest among children.
(2) In general, young and middle-aged adults have the highest rate of poverty.
(3) The poverty rate for elderly Americans has shown the most improvement over time.
(4) The number of people in poverty has declined steadily since 1966.
(5) The poverty rate for children has steadily improved since 1966.

6. Which of the following developments is most likely related to the trends shown in the graph?

(1) U.S. involvement in the Vietnam War ended in 1973.
(2) President Johnson launched a series of antipoverty programs in 1964.
(3) Tax rates for wealthy Americans have generally declined since 1966.
(4) More people graduate from college today than in years past.
(5) The average life expectancy of Americans continues to increase.

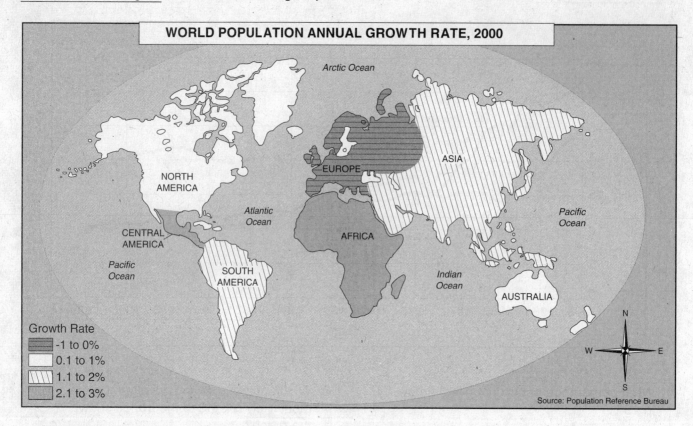

WORLD POPULATION ANNUAL GROWTH RATE, 2000

Source: Population Reference Bureau

Growth Rate
- -1 to 0%
- 0.1 to 1%
- 1.1 to 2%
- 2.1 to 3%

7. Which of the following continents has the lowest rate of population growth for the year 2000?

(1) North America
(2) South America
(3) Africa
(4) Asia
(5) Europe

8. Which of the following people would be most interested in this map?

(1) a director of a United Nations social services agency
(2) a historian studying the development of ancient civilizations
(3) a scientist predicting earthquakes worldwide
(4) a psychologist studying human personality
(5) a geographer specializing in ocean resources

9. Which of the following statements is supported by the map?

(1) Europe and North America are the continents with the slowest population growth.
(2) The populations of Central America and Africa are rising faster than those of other regions.
(3) The population of Asia is growing faster than the population of South America.
(4) Fewer people live in Australia than in Europe.
(5) More people live in Asia than on any other continent.

Questions 10 through 12 refer to the following passage.

The U.S. government tries hard to protect Americans against consumer fraud and dangerous products or practices. The Food and Drug Administration (FDA) works to prevent the sale of dangerous foods, drugs, and cosmetics. The Federal Aviation Administration (FAA) sees to the safety of air travelers. The Federal Trade Commission (FTC) protects consumers from false or misleading advertising. For example, the FTC has investigated the environmental claims of certain products: disposable diapers that the maker claimed would decompose in landfills, "biodegradable" plastic bags, and "ozone-friendly" hairsprays, to name a few.

10. Which of the following statements from the paragraph is a conclusion?

    (1) The U.S. government tries hard to protect Americans against consumer fraud and dangerous products or practices.
    (2) The Food and Drug Administration (FDA) works to prevent the sale of dangerous foods, drugs, and cosmetics.
    (3) The Federal Aviation Administration (FAA) sees to the safety of air travelers.
    (4) The Federal Trade Commission (FTC) protects consumers from false or misleading advertising.
    (5) The FTC has investigated the environmental claims of certain products.

11. Which of the following is an example of a situation that the FTC would investigate?

    (1) an eyeliner that causes allergic reactions
    (2) defects in a brand of microwave oven
    (3) reports of deaths from a new prescription drug
    (4) reports that an airline is not performing the maintenance required on its planes
    (5) TV commercials claiming that a breakfast cereal prevents heart disease

12. What does the existence of these federal agencies suggest that the federal government values highly?

    (1) minority rights
    (2) free enterprise
    (3) citizens' safety
    (4) individual responsibility
    (5) free speech

Question 13 refers to the following maps.

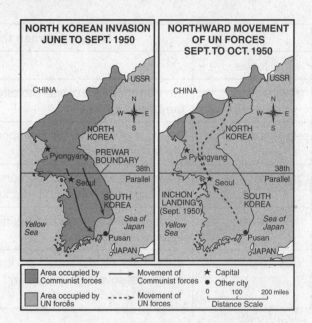

13. Which of the following is a conclusion about the Korean War that can be made from comparing the information on both maps?

    (1) North Korea invaded South Korea in June 1950.
    (2) After the Communist occupation of South Korea, UN forces pushed the invaders back to the Chinese border.
    (3) Invading Communist troops drove south almost to the city of Pusan.
    (4) The United Nations intervened in the Korean War on the side of the South Koreans, landing at Inchon in September 1950.
    (5) Before the Korean War began, the 38th Parallel was the dividing line between North and South Korea.

Questions 14 through 16 are based on the following passage and chart.

In the first half of the 1800s, great changes swept through the United States. In the North, industrialization turned towns into manufacturing centers. As people flocked to them seeking factory jobs, these towns grew into cities. In the South, the invention of the cotton gin saved the plantation system and slavery. The cotton gin mechanically removed the seeds from cotton fibers, which allowed a plantation's slaves to prepare more cotton for sale than they could by hand. This development encouraged southerners to grow more cotton, and the plantation system spread.

The differences in their development led to disagreement between the North and the South on several issues. Conflict over the issues summarized in the following chart eventually led to the Civil War in 1861.

Issues Between the North and the South	
Issue	**Summary**
abolitionism	the view that slavery was morally wrong and should be abolished wherever it existed in the United States
slavery extension	the issue of whether slavery should be allowed to spread into new territories acquired by the United States
tariff policy	the issue of whether goods manufactured in other countries should be taxed so they would cost more than U.S.-manufactured goods
nullification	the theory that a state had the right to declare null and void any federal law it believed to be unconstitutional
secession	the withdrawal of a state from the Union, based on the belief that the Constitution created a union of sovereign states, and that this sovereignty gave each state the right to withdraw from the Union at any time

14. In 1820, Congress passed the Missouri Compromise. It admitted Missouri to the Union as a state that allowed slavery but required that slavery be banned in any new states that formed north or due west of Missouri. Which type of issue between North and South was the Missouri Compromise addressing?

    (1) abolitionism
    (2) slavery extension
    (3) tariff policy
    (4) nullification
    (5) secession

15. Which two issues between North and South were most alike in their nature?

    (1) abolitionism and slavery extension
    (2) slavery extension and tariff policy
    (3) tariff policy and nullification
    (4) abolitionism and secession
    (5) secession and tariff policy

16. What conclusion can be drawn from the information in the passage and chart?

    (1) Most northerners hated slavery.
    (2) White southerners generally favored the extension of slavery into western territories.
    (3) Southern slaves did not work as hard as northern factory workers.
    (4) Abolitionism led to secession.
    (5) Slavery was the cause of the Civil War.

Questions 17 and 18 refer to the following cartoon.

17. What does the cartoon imply is the biggest obstacle faced by people running this race?

(1) having enough time
(2) having enough money
(3) making it to the starting line
(4) getting past Iowa
(5) getting past New Hampshire

18. What does the cartoonist assume readers understand about the subject of the cartoon?

(1) It is about qualifying for the Olympics.
(2) It refers to being appointed to the Supreme Court.
(3) It is about improving the balance of trade.
(4) It refers to the interstate highway system between Iowa and New Hampshire.
(5) It is about gaining a political party's nomination for president of the United States.

Question 19 refers to the following information.

Price-fixing is a formal or informal arrangement among a group of sellers to set a certain price for an item they all produce, thus avoiding competition. In most countries, price-fixing without government approval is illegal.

19. Which of the following is the most likely result of price-fixing?

(1) lower prices for consumers
(2) lower profits for the seller
(3) higher prices for consumers
(4) an improved product
(5) too many items on the market

Question 20 refers to the following map.

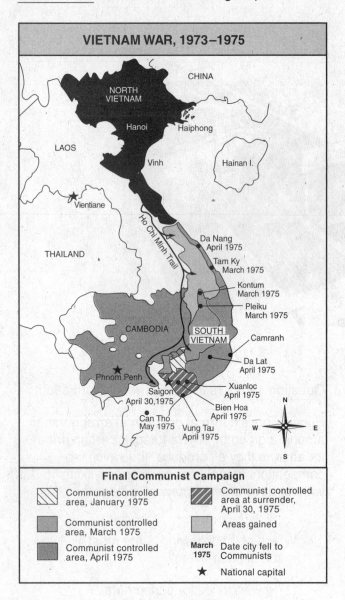

VIETNAM WAR, 1973–1975

CHINA

NORTH VIETNAM

Hanoi

Haiphong

LAOS

Vinh

Hainan I.

Vientiane

Ho Chi Minh Trail

Da Nang
April 1975

Tam Ky
March 1975

THAILAND

Kontum
March 1975

Pleiku
March 1975

CAMBODIA

SOUTH VIETNAM

Camranh

Da Lat
April 1975

Phnom Penh

Xuanloc
April 1975

Saigon
April 30, 1975

Bien Hoa
April 1975

Can Tho
May 1975

Vung Tau
April 1975

N
W   E
S

Final Communist Campaign

Communist controlled area, January 1975

Communist controlled area at surrender, April 30, 1975

Communist controlled area, March 1975

Areas gained

Communist controlled area, April 1975

March 1975 Date city fell to Communists

★ National capital

20. Which of the following statements does the map support?

(1) Like Laos and Cambodia, Vietnam was once governed by France.
(2) A war of independence divided the country into Communist and non-Communist sectors.
(3) By 1973, the United States had withdrawn its forces from South Vietnam.
(4) By mid-1975, North Vietnamese troops had overrun South Vietnam.
(5) Vietnam has had difficulty rebuilding its war-shattered economy.

Question 21 refers to the following passage from the Preamble to the Constitution of the United States.

"We the People of the United States, in Order to form a more perfect Union, establish Justice, insure domestic Tranquillity, provide for the common defense, promote the general Welfare, and secure the Blessings of Liberty to ourselves and our Posterity, do ordain and establish this Constitution for the United States of America."

21. According to the Preamble, what did the writers of the Constitution hope to achieve from the document?

(1) a stronger and more stable nation
(2) independence from Great Britain
(3) the conquest of foreign nations
(4) to create the United States
(5) an end to slavery in the United States

Question 22 refers to the following paragraph.

"A politician in this country must be the man of a party," wrote John Quincy Adams in 1802. Five years after President George Washington left office, political parties had become a fact of American life. There were two major parties in the early 1800s, as there are today. In the past, Republican candidates challenged Federalists; later Democrats ran against Whigs. Today, Republicans and Democrats vie against each other. Third parties first appeared in 1832.

22. Which statement best summarizes the paragraph?

(1) Third parties have always existed in the American political system.
(2) Third parties have failed to offer popular candidates for president.
(3) Through most of its history, the United States has had a two-party political system.
(4) American voters tend to cast their ballots for candidates from the two major parties.
(5) A candidate for office cannot get elected without the support of a political party.

Questions 23 through 25 refer to the following chart.

HOW A BILL BECOMES A LAW

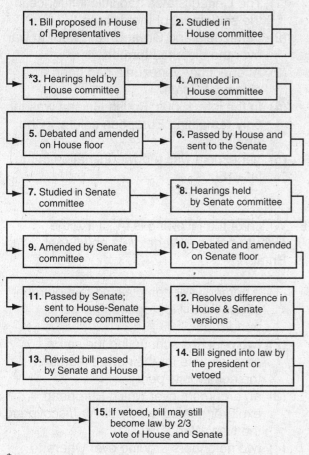

1. Bill proposed in House of Representatives
2. Studied in House committee
*3. Hearings held by House committee
4. Amended in House committee
5. Debated and amended on House floor
6. Passed by House and sent to the Senate
7. Studied in Senate committee
*8. Hearings held by Senate committee
9. Amended by Senate committee
10. Debated and amended on Senate floor
11. Passed by Senate; sent to House-Senate conference committee
12. Resolves difference in House & Senate versions
13. Revised bill passed by Senate and House
14. Bill signed into law by the president or vetoed
15. If vetoed, bill may still become law by 2/3 vote of House and Senate

*Optional step

23. Representative A introduces a bill to lower government price supports for milk. Representative B, from a dairy state, would like the bill changed. During which of the following processes can Representative B first influence this bill?

(1) Senate committee hearings
(2) the Senate debate on the bill
(3) the House debate on the bill
(4) the House vote on the bill
(5) conference committee discussions

24. What must legislators value most highly for step 12 in the chart to be successful?

(1) the views of the president
(2) the spirit of compromise
(3) the will of the House
(4) the will of the Senate
(5) the will of the people

25. According to the chart, a bill might still become law even after failing to be approved by which of the following?

(1) a House committee
(2) a Senate committee
(3) the full House
(4) the full Senate
(5) the president

Questions 26 through 29 refer to the following passage and map.

In the late 1800s, Great Britain and Venezuela argued over the border between Venezuela and the small colony of British Guiana. Tensions increased in the 1880s when gold was discovered on land that both countries claimed.

The United States wanted to weaken British influence in South America, so they sided with the Venezuelans in the controversy. After bickering and threats of war, the dispute was settled in 1899. An international commission set the boundary between Venezuela and British Guiana. This border still exists today, between the nations of Venezuela and Guyana.

THE VENEZUELA BOUNDARY DISPUTE

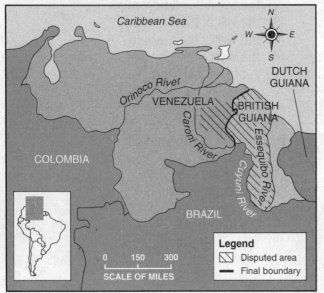

26. What boundary did Venezuela claim in the dispute?

(1) the Orinoco River
(2) the Caroni River
(3) the Essequibo River
(4) the border with Dutch Guiana
(5) the border with Colombia

27. Which of the following statements is supported by evidence from the passage and map?

(1) The United States had little influence in the settlement of the dispute.
(2) Venezuela and Great Britain went to war over the disputed territory.
(3) At one time, Venezuela had been a colony of Spain.
(4) In the late 1800s, British Guiana was the only remaining European colony in the Americas.
(5) Venezuela was a powerful nation in the late 1800s.

28. Which of the following is most like the dispute between Venezuela and Great Britain?

(1) a homeowner complaining to a plumber about the bill for repairs that were performed
(2) two coaches scheduling the same practice time for their swim teams in the community pool
(3) an argument over which European explorer should get credit for discovering the New World
(4) two neighbors arguing over where to erect a fence to separate their backyards
(5) a driver whose car is towed after being parked in the lot of a store that is closed

29. What assumption can be made from the information in the map and passage?

(1) British Guiana eventually became part of Venezuela.
(2) Dutch Guiana was also a British colony at one time.
(3) The gold discovery made Venezuela a wealthy nation.
(4) Brazil and Great Britain also had a land dispute.
(5) The South American nation of Guyana was once a British colony.

Question 30 refers to the following information.

There are two types of costs involved in producing a product. The first type is fixed costs. This includes such things as rent for the building or the cost of production equipment. Fixed costs are the same no matter how much of the product is produced. The second type of cost is variable costs. Variable costs, which include materials, increase when more product is produced and decrease when less is produced.

30. Suppose that you own a business and are preparing the annual budget for your company. Which of the following budget assumptions would illustrate faulty logic on your part?

When the quantity of product

(1) increases, the supplies budget will increase as well.
(2) increases, the mortgage payment will remain the same.
(3) decreases, property taxes will remain the same.
(4) decreases, the advertising budget will increase.
(5) decreases, the raw materials budget will decrease.

Question 31 refers to the following chart.

DIFFERENCES BETWEEN THE HOUSE AND SENATE	
House	**Senate**
• 435 members	• 100 members
• Members organized into 22 permanent committees	• Members organized into 16 permanent committees
• Elected from districts in states	• Elected from entire states
• 2-year terms	• 6-year terms
• Entire body elected every 2 years	• One-third of body elected every 2 years
• Headed by an elected Speaker	• Headed by the Vice President
• Less attention from news media	• More attention from news media

31. Which of the following is a way in which the House and Senate are similar, according to the chart?

(1) the length of term that members serve
(2) the number of committees in each
(3) that members represent geographical areas
(4) how the leadership of each is selected
(5) when members come up for reelection

Question 32 refers to the following information.

Acid rain forms when the industrial pollutants sulfur dioxide and nitrogen oxide combine with water vapor in the air. The resulting harmful substances are carried by the wind and fall back to Earth in rain. Acid rain damages forests, rivers, and lakes. It corrodes buildings and poisons fish.

32. Which type of region is most likely to have an acid rain problem?

(1) a region where the wind blows in from the ocean, like the West Coast of the United States
(2) an area with very little rainfall, such as the Sahara of North Africa
(3) a region with heavy industry and average rainfall, like Germany and central Europe
(4) a heavily forested area with little or no industry, like northern Canada
(5) an area surrounded by large bodies of water, such as the Italian peninsula in southern Europe

Questions 33 through 35 refer to the following passage and map.

People sometimes use the terms *weather* and *climate* interchangeably. But weather and climate are not the same thing. *Climate* refers to the general atmospheric conditions that characterize a region over a long period of time. *Weather* refers to daily conditions in the atmosphere, including temperature, cloudiness, and precipitation. Weather can change from day to day as atmospheric fronts move from west to east across the United States.

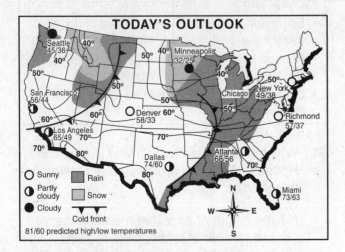

33. In which cities is the weather predicted to be most similar today?

(1) Seattle and San Francisco
(2) San Francisco and New York
(3) Richmond and Chicago
(4) Los Angeles and Atlanta
(5) Dallas and Denver

34. What is the most likely effect of today's weather?

(1) Snow delays flights at Minneapolis airport.
(2) The Denver school system announces a snow day.
(3) Pollution closes beaches in the Los Angeles area.
(4) Smog disrupts air travel in New York City.
(5) Hurricane Alice threatens Miami and the rest of South Florida.

35. Which of the following conclusions is supported by the information presented?

(1) There is little difference between a region's weather and its climate.
(2) The higher a place's altitude, the colder its climate.
(3) Precipitation often occurs when cold air and warm air meet along cold fronts.
(4) The eastern half of the United States has a wetter climate than the western half.
(5) Temperatures tend to be warmer in the northern half of the United States.

Question 36 refers to the following maps.

EUROPE BEFORE WORLD WAR I, 1914

EUROPE AFTER WORLD WAR I, 1919

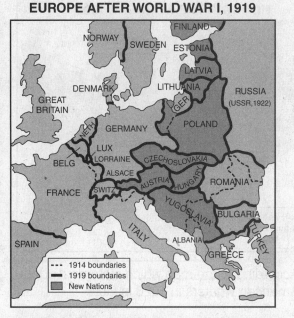

- - - 1914 boundaries
——— 1919 boundaries
▨ New Nations

36. Which of the following statements is a conclusion based on these maps?

(1) Austria and Hungary were joined as an empire before World War I.
(2) World War I resulted in the break-up of Austria-Hungary.
(3) After World War I, Czechoslovakia became an independent nation.
(4) The republic of Austria was established after the war.
(5) Hungary became an independent nation when World War I ended.

Question 37 refers to the following quotation.

"The truth is, we've got advantages over the Japanese in every car we make—but nobody knows it! . . . I think America's getting an inferiority complex about Japan: 'Everything from Japan is perfect, everything from America is lousy.' . . . Americans just don't understand the quality of our cars. We gotta get people to wake up to the truth."

—Lee Iacocca, former Chairman, Chrysler Corporation

37. If the speaker's view is correct, which of the following would best help American automakers sell more cars?

(1) better technology
(2) better quality cars
(3) lower prices for cars
(4) better advertising and marketing
(5) higher wages for auto workers

Question 38 refers to the following map.

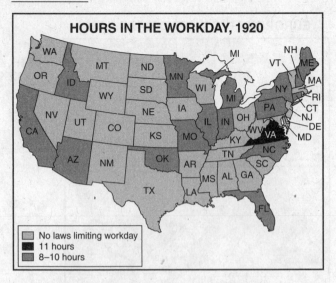

HOURS IN THE WORKDAY, 1920

No laws limiting workday
11 hours
8–10 hours

38. According to the map which statement about American workers in 1920 is fact?

(1) Employees who worked 11-hour days were worse off than those who worked 8 hours.
(2) Employers in states without limits on the workday had no concern for their employees.
(3) Strong labor unions probably existed in states with laws that limited the workday.
(4) Employees in western states were better workers than those in New England.
(5) Most southern workers were required to work as long as their employer demanded.

Question 39 refers to the following information.

Industrialization led to the growth of towns and cities in the United States. America's urban population jumped from about 3 percent in 1790 to about 16 percent by 1860. However, urban growth was not spread evenly across the United States, as the following graph illustrates.

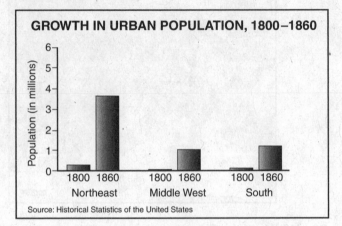

GROWTH IN URBAN POPULATION, 1800–1860

Source: Historical Statistics of the United States

39. What is the most likely reason for the Midwestern urban growth shown on the graph?

(1) an increase in immigration to the Northeast
(2) the growth of industry in the Midwest
(3) the decline of slavery in the South
(4) the failure of Midwest farms due to droughts
(5) the decline of American Indian populations

Question 40 refers to the following chart.

POPULAR VOTE IN THE 2000 PRESIDENTIAL ELECTION

Percentage of Votes Received by the Democratic and Republican Candidate in the Five Most Populous States		
State	**Bush**	**Gore**
California	42%	54%
Florida	49%	49%
Illinois	43%	55%
New York	35%	60%
Texas	59%	38%

40. Which of the following best summarizes the information in this chart?

(1) George W. Bush won the popular vote in all of the five most populous states.
(2) Albert Gore won the popular vote in all of the five most populous states.
(3) Gore overwhelmingly won three of the states, Bush overwhelmingly won one of the states, and the fifth was closely contested.
(4) Gore and Bush each won two of the most populous states, and the fifth state was closely contested.
(5) Gore won the popular vote but lost in the Electoral College.

Question 41 refers to the following graph.

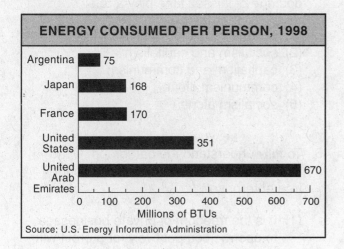

ENERGY CONSUMED PER PERSON, 1998

Argentina 75
Japan 168
France 170
United States 351
United Arab Emirates 670

Millions of BTUs

Source: U.S. Energy Information Administration

41. Which of the following statements is a conclusion related to the graph?

(1) The United States consumed 351 million BTUs of energy per person in 1998.
(2) The United Arab Emirates consumed 670 million BTUs of energy per person in 1998.
(3) Argentina consumed 75 million BTUs of energy per person in 1998.
(4) France consumed 170 million BTUs of energy per person in 1998.
(5) Per person energy use varies widely among the nations of the world.

Question 42 refers to the following chart.

IMPORTANT EVENTS IN ANCIENT ATHENS	
Date	Event
621 BC	a code of laws is drawn up
594 BC	debt slavery is abolished; a court of appeals is established
508 BC	a governing council is created, formed of members from local government units
461– 429 BC	all male citizens become eligible to hold government offices

42. Which development does this chart summarize?

(1) the growth of democratic institutions in ancient Athens
(2) the growth of the military in ancient Greece
(3) the establishment of representative government in modern Greece
(4) the abolition of tyranny in ancient Athens
(5) the development of the Athenian judicial system

Question 43 refers to the following information.

In a survey of more than one million families in 1998, the U.S. Department of Labor found the average family's income to be about $41,600 per year. The following graph shows how the average American family spent that money.

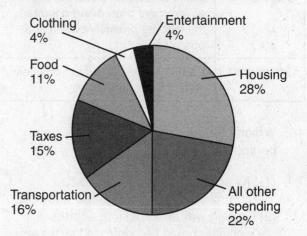

Clothing 4%
Entertainment 4%
Food 11%
Housing 28%
Taxes 15%
Transportation 16%
All other spending 22%

43. Which of the following statements about the graph information is a conclusion?

(1) Americans spend about 4 percent of their income on entertainment.
(2) The single largest expense for most American families is housing.
(3) More than one dollar of every ten that Americans earn is spent for food.
(4) About 16 percent of what families earn is spent on transportation.
(5) Americans spend most of what they earn on the basic necessities of life.

Questions 44 through 46 refer to the following paragraph and chart.

In economic planning, a central public authority tries to control and direct economic activity. Economic planning is the opposite of the laissez-faire doctrine, which holds that a nation's economy does best when there is little government interference. However, economic planning plays a role even in nations devoted to free enterprise. In such nations, economic planning becomes especially important during periods of war and recession.

THREE MAJOR ECONOMIC SYSTEMS	
System	Theory Behind the System
Communism	All productive resources are government owned and operated
Socialism	Basic productive resources are government owned and operated; the rest are privately owned and operated
Capitalism	Productive resources are privately owned and operated

44. Which of the following restates the theory behind socialism?

(1) All economic activity should be controlled by a central public authority.
(2) During war or recession, economic activity should be controlled by a central public authority.
(3) The government should own and operate all productive resources.
(4) The government should own and operate basic productive resources.
(5) Private businesses should own and operate all productive resources.

45. In which type of economic system would the doctrine of laissez faire play a role?

(1) communism and socialism
(2) socialism and capitalism
(3) capitalism and communism
(4) communism alone
(5) socialism alone

46. To fully understand the paragraph, what assumption do you need to make about free enterprise?

(1) It is the freedom of private businesses to operate competitively for a profit with little government regulation.
(2) It is the freedom of government to set prices and wages and to make economic decisions it deems best for all citizens.
(3) It is a law that allows some private businesses to receive financial aid from the government.
(4) It is most popular in socialist nations.
(5) It is most popular in Communist nations.

Question 47 refers to the following quotation.

"The time has come for the Congress of the United States to join with the executive and judicial branches in making it clear to all that race has no place in American life or law."
—President John F. Kennedy

47. Which of the following was the desired outcome of Kennedy's plea to Congress?

(1) the Peace Corps
(2) increased aid to education
(3) increased foreign aid to Latin America
(4) the Civil Rights Act of 1964
(5) the Trade Expansion Act of 1962

In the early 1900s, the United States played a major role in the economic development of several Latin American countries. U.S. companies invested billions of dollars in countries in Central and South America and the Caribbean. Because of their economic importance, these companies often had political power as well. Their support of dictators in countries where they had investments earned the United States the lasting resentment of many Latin Americans.

U.S. INVESTMENT IN LATIN AMERICA, 1929

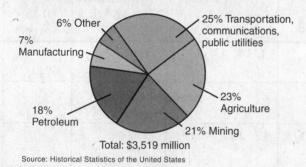

Total: $3,519 million

Source: Historical Statistics of the United States

48. Which of the following is the most likely reason for the U.S. investment in transportation in Latin America?

(1) because there were very few profits to be made by investing in this sector of the economy
(2) to increase tourism income for the Latin American countries
(3) to move the products of U.S. companies there for export and sale to the United States
(4) because Latin American leaders resented American investment in this sector of the economy
(5) to help the people of a Latin American nation better move around their country

As the nation's population has increased, the population center of the United States has shifted westward. When the first census was taken in 1790, the population center of the United States was near Baltimore, Maryland. Two centuries later it was southwest of St. Louis, Missouri.

CENTERS OF U.S. POPULATION, 1790–1990

Source: U.S. Census Bureau

49. Which of the following conclusions is supported by the paragraph and map?

(1) The U.S. population center has moved steadily eastward.
(2) Since 1910, population in the South and West has grown faster than in the North and East.
(3) Baltimore, Maryland, was the largest U.S. city in 1790.
(4) The population of the United States has been steadily increasing because of immigration to American cities.
(5) In 1990, most of the nation's people lived near St. Louis, Missouri.

INITIATIVE
Process by which citizens can, by petition, propose new state or local laws and submit them to a vote of the people

REFERENDUM
A direct vote by the people to accept or reject a law proposed or already passed by a state or local government

50. How are the initiative and referendum similar?

Both allow citizens to

(1) bypass their elected representatives.
(2) repeal state laws.
(3) propose state laws.
(4) remove state legislators for corrupt behavior.
(5) repeal federal laws.

Answers start on page 337.

Posttest Performance Analysis Chart
Social Studies

This chart can help you determine your strengths and weaknesses in the content and skill areas of the GED Social Studies Test. Use the Answers and Explanations starting on page 337 to check your answers to the test. Then circle on the chart the number of test items you answered correctly. Put the total number correct for each content area and skill area in each row and column. Look at the total items correct in each column and row and decide which areas are difficult for you. Use the page references to study those areas. Use a copy of the Social Studies Study Planner on page 31 to guide your review.

Thinking Skill / Content Area	Comprehension (Lessons 1, 2, 7, 16, 18)	Analysis (Lessons 3, 4, 6, 9, 10, 11, 12, 19)	Application (Lessons 14, 15)	Evaluation (Lessons 5, 8, 13, 17, 20)	Total Correct
U.S. History (Pages 32–93)	**1**, 22	**2, 15, 38, 39, 48**	**3, 14**, 47	**16, 49**	_____/12
World History (Pages 94–133)	**26, 42**	**13, 29, 36**	28	**20, 27**	_____/8
Civics and Government (Pages 134–175)	**17**, 21, **40**	10, **18, 25, 31, 50**	11, **23**	12, **24**	_____/12
Economics (Pages 176–207)	**4, 44**	6, 19, **43**, 46	37, **45**	**5**, 30	_____/10
Geography (Pages 208–238)	**7**	**33, 34, 41**	**8**, 32	**9, 35**	_____/8
Total Correct	_____/10	_____/20	_____/10	_____/10	_____/50

1–40 → Use the Study Planner on page 31 to organize your review.
41–50 → Congratulations! You're ready for the GED! You can get more practice with the Simulated Test on pages 257–274.

Boldfaced numbers indicate questions based on charts, graphs, diagrams, and drawings.

For additional help, see the ***Steck-Vaughn GED Social Studies Exercise Book.***

SOCIAL STUDIES

Directions

This Social Studies GED Simulated Test is intended to measure your knowledge of general social studies concepts.

The questions are based on short readings or on graphs, maps, charts, cartoons, and illustrations. Study the information given and then answer the questions that follow. Refer to the information as often as necessary in answering the questions.

You should spend no more than 70 minutes in answering the 50 questions on this test. Work carefully, but do not spend too much time on any one item. Do not skip any items. Make a reasonable guess when you are not sure of an answer. You will not be penalized for incorrect answers.

When time is up, mark the last item you finished. This will tell you whether you can finish the real GED Test in the time allowed. Then complete the test.

Record your answers to the questions on a copy of the answer sheet on page 361. Be sure that all required information is recorded on the answer sheet.

To record your answers, mark the numbered space on the answer sheet that corresponds to the answer you choose for each item on the test.

Example:

Early pioneers of the western frontier looked to settle on land that had adequate access to water. To ensure access to water, many early pioneers settled on land near which type of geographic feature?

(1) forests
(2) grasslands
(3) rivers
(4) glaciers
(5) oceans

① ② ● ④ ⑤

The correct answer is <u>rivers</u>; therefore, answer space 3 should be marked on the answer sheet.

Do not rest the point of your pencil on the answer sheet while you are considering your answer. Make no stray or unnecessary marks. If you change an answer, erase your first mark completely. Mark only one answer for each question; multiple answers will be scored as incorrect. Do not fold or crease your answer sheet.

When you finish the test, use the Performance Analysis Chart on page 274 to determine whether you are ready to take the real GED Test, and, if not, which skill areas need additional review.

Directions: Choose the one best answer to each question.

Questions 1 through 4 refer to the following paragraph and graphs.

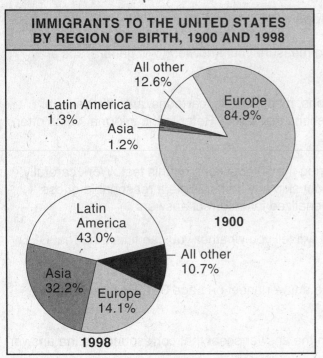

IMMIGRANTS TO THE UNITED STATES BY REGION OF BIRTH, 1900 AND 1998

All other 12.6%
Latin America 1.3%
Asia 1.2%
Europe 84.9%
1900

Latin America 43.0%
All other 10.7%
Asia 32.2%
Europe 14.1%
1998

Source: U.S. Census Bureau and Immigration and Naturalization Service

For much of the nation's history, most immigrants to the United States came from the nations of Europe. In 1892, the U.S. government opened a center on Ellis Island in New York Harbor to process these immigrants. In 1910, the government opened a second center on Angel Island in San Francisco Bay. Before Ellis Island closed in 1954, more than 16 million immigrants had arrived there. Today, Ellis Island is a national historic site, while Angel Island is a California state park.

1. From which region of the world did the largest group of immigrants arrive in 1998?

   (1) Asia
   (2) Latin America
   (3) Europe
   (4) Africa
   (5) It cannot be determined from the information provided.

2. Which of the following statements is a fact based on the paragraph and graph?

   (1) The percentage of immigrants coming from Asia greatly increased during the 1900s.
   (2) The percentage of immigrants coming from Latin America greatly decreased during the 1900s.
   (3) Angel Island should be made into a national historic site similar to that at Ellis Island.
   (4) Immigrants who came to the United States 100 years ago had more difficulties adjusting than recent immigrants have had.
   (5) Encouraging large numbers of people to immigrate is good for our nation's economy.

3. How have the developments discussed in the passage and illustrated by the graphs most likely affected the nation?

   (1) The government has dropped all limits on the number of people who come to the United States.
   (2) Immigrants no longer arrive in California and New York.
   (3) The United States has become a more ethnically and culturally diverse nation.
   (4) Immigration from Asia has fallen as a result of the closing of Angel Island.
   (5) Immigration from Latin American has increased due to closing of Ellis Island.

4. Which statement is best supported by the paragraph and graphs?

   (1) Most Asian immigrants live on the West Coast of the United States.
   (2) Europe is no longer the most important source of immigrants to the United States.
   (3) The total number of immigrants to the United States has risen since 1900.
   (4) Ellis Island attracts more visitors than Angel Island does.
   (5) Ellis Island closed before Angel Island did.

Question 5 refers to the following paragraph.

Until about 1500, the Maya people of what is now southern Mexico and Guatemala occupied large city-states, which were the unit of government in the region. These governments directed building, maintained armies, and collected taxes. They maintained roads and conducted trade over long distances. In addition, they had systems of writing and mathematics and developed a highly accurate calendar.

5. What does this evidence suggest the Maya valued highly?

   (1) war
   (2) family
   (3) simple living
   (4) organization
   (5) competition

Question 6 refers to the following cartoon.

Reprinted with permission of the *Denver Rocky Mountain News*.

6. What assumption do readers need to make to understand this cartoon?

   (1) The Second Amendment is part of the Constitution.
   (2) Women have the right to vote.
   (3) The Second Amendment gives people the right to bear arms.
   (4) National crime rates are declining.
   (5) The Second Amendment protects against unreasonable searches and seizures.

Question 7 refers to the following map.

7. Based on the information in the map, which of the following is most likely to happen?

   (1) The average temperature of North America will become cooler.
   (2) The East Coast of the United States will experience severe earthquakes.
   (3) The population of the United States will increase.
   (4) The population of the United States will decrease.
   (5) The present-day coastal cities of the eastern United States will be flooded.

Questions 8 through 10 refer to the following passage and chart.

The highest official in state government in the United States is the governor. In every state, the holder of this office is elected by the people of the state. The governor's executive powers include enforcing state laws and heading the National Guard and the state police forces. The following chart lists the other major executive offices that exist in most states, along with their main functions and powers. In some states, many or all of these officials are appointed by the governor. In other states, they are elected by the people.

Office	Main Functions
lieutenant governor	serves as governor when the governor is out of state; becomes governor if the elected governor leaves office before his or her term is up
attorney general	legal officer who advises the governor on matters of law and represents the state in important court cases
secretary of state	the chief clerk of the state who keeps the documents of the state and records all official actions taken by the state government
comptroller	the chief financial officer of the state who keeps track of the accounts of those offices that collect and spend state money; makes sure that state money is being spent legally
treasurer	receives and keeps state money and maintains accurate records of all money received and spent

8. Which official in the federal government has duties and functions most like those of a state governor?

   (1) the president
   (2) the vice president
   (3) the secretary of state
   (4) a U.S. senator
   (5) a member of the House of Representatives

9. Which state offices are the most similar in their duties and functions?

   (1) lieutenant governor and attorney general
   (2) secretary of state and comptroller
   (3) treasurer and secretary of state
   (4) attorney general and comptroller
   (5) comptroller and treasurer

10. What is the most likely reason for requirements in many state constitutions that the officials listed in the chart be elected by the people?

   (1) to lower the cost of running the government at the state level
   (2) to make sure that the governor does not have too much power
   (3) to make sure that all groups in society are represented in government
   (4) to make sure that the governor does not spend too much money
   (5) to encourage more citizens to become interested in voting

Questions 11 through 14 refer to the following passage and graph.

In 1995, a federal study found that years of affirmative action had failed to help women and minorities achieve equality in the workplace. The study revealed that white men, who made up less than a third of the workforce, held 95 percent of top management jobs. In contrast, white women, who made up about 40 percent of the workforce, held less than 5 percent of the top jobs. Only 3 percent of top executives were minorities, and nearly all of them were men.

The study found that while many women and minorities gained middle-management jobs, their careers usually stopped there. Although in theory they could reach the top jobs, they often hit an invisible barrier that blocked their progress. The commission concluded that the fears and prejudices of white men were largely responsible for the "glass ceiling."

Five years after the federal Glass Ceiling Commission revealed its findings, government data showed the following about average annual earnings of groups of Americans.

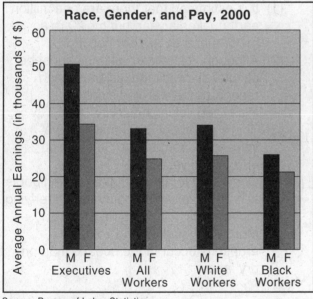

Race, Gender, and Pay, 2000

Source: Bureau of Labor Statistics

11. According to the graph, which group is the lowest paid?

(1) white female executives
(2) white male workers
(3) white female workers
(4) black male workers
(5) black female workers

12. What does the passage imply is the definition of the "glass ceiling"?

(1) the prejudices and fears that white men harbor about women and minorities
(2) the practice of not promoting women or minority employees beyond a certain level
(3) a federal commission that did a study of racial and gender equality in the workplace
(4) the pay difference between male and female executives
(5) the inability of women and minorities to become part of the workforce

13. According to the information, what characteristic do white women workers and Black women workers have in common?

(1) Both groups are equally unlikely to hold top executives jobs.
(2) Both groups work many more hours than men do.
(3) Most workers in each group have jobs in middle management.
(4) Both groups earn less on average than male workers of the same race.
(5) Neither group is greatly affected by the glass ceiling.

14. The graph data are for 2000, five years after the commission's study. What evidence from the graph suggests that the glass ceiling still existed for women in 2000?

(1) The average annual earnings of female executives were greater than those of male workers.
(2) The average annual earnings of white workers were still higher than those of Black workers.
(3) The earnings of white male workers and female executives were about equal.
(4) Female executives earned much more than any other female workers.
(5) The pay difference for male and female executives was greater than for the other groups on the graph.

Questions 15 through 17 refer to the following map.

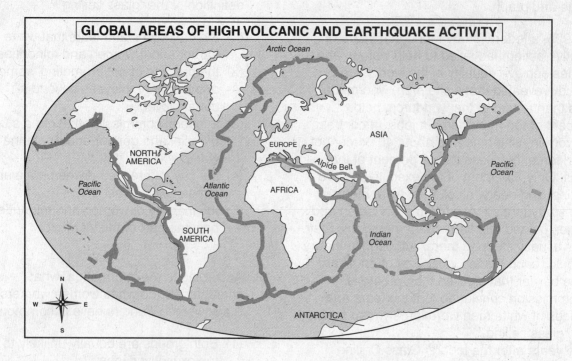

GLOBAL AREAS OF HIGH VOLCANIC AND EARTHQUAKE ACTIVITY

15. In which of the following regions would you most expect an earthquake to occur?

    (1) the east coast of South America
    (2) the west coast of South America
    (3) northern Africa
    (4) northern Europe
    (5) Australia

16. Which of the following is an opinion based on the map, rather than a statement of fact?

    (1) A large earthquake will soon occur along the West Coast of the United States.
    (2) There have been many volcanic eruptions and earthquakes on the islands of East Asia.
    (3) Concentrations of volcano and earthquake activity have been recorded in Central America.
    (4) There have been few volcanic eruptions in the Great Lakes region of the United States.
    (5) Central Asia is relatively free of earthquake activity.

17. All of the following statements are true. Which one is supported by evidence from the map?

    (1) It is estimated that there are one million earthquakes a year, but most are so minor that they are not noticed.
    (2) Although volcanic eruptions cannot be accurately predicted, scientists can recognize the warning signs of increased volcanic activity.
    (3) There are about 500 known active volcanoes, some 20 to 30 of which erupt each year.
    (4) Compared to dry land, the ocean floor is thin and easily pierced by the underlying molten rock.
    (5) More earthquakes and volcanic eruptions occur in the oceans than on dry land.

Question 18 refers to the following paragraph.

Third parties have been common in the United States since the mid-1800s. But no third-party candidate has ever become president. Some former presidents have become third-party candidates after having served as Republicans or Democrats. Their failure as third-party candidates suggests that voters will not vote for a person or a party they see as having little chance of victory.

18. Which statement is the conclusion reached by the writer of this paragraph?

(1) Third parties have been common in the United States since the mid-1800s.
(2) No third-party candidate has ever become president.
(3) Some former presidents have been third-party candidates.
(4) Former presidents have failed as third-party candidates.
(5) Voters will not vote for someone they see as having little chance of victory.

Question 19 refers to the following map.

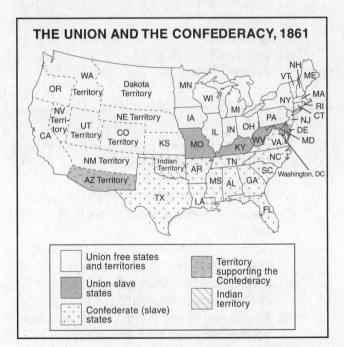

THE UNION AND THE CONFEDERACY, 1861

Union free states and territories

Union slave states

Confederate (slave) states

Territory supporting the Confederacy

Indian territory

19. Which information based on the map of the Union and Confederacy best supports the argument that slavery was not the only issue in the Civil War?

(1) Texas and the Arizona Territory supported the Confederacy.
(2) Indian Territory was not yet the state of Oklahoma.
(3) The southern states formed a separate nation called the Confederacy.
(4) Slavery existed in states that remained in the Union.
(5) There were 18 free states and 15 slave states in 1861.

Question 20 refers to the following map.

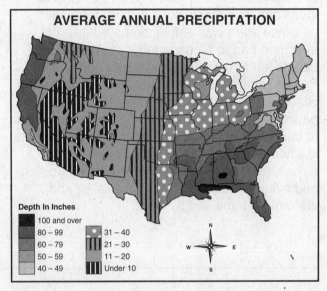

AVERAGE ANNUAL PRECIPITATION

Depth In Inches

100 and over
80 – 99
60 – 79
50 – 59
40 – 49
31 – 40
21 – 30
11 – 20
Under 10

20. Types of wheat grown in certain parts of the world are resistant to drought and use water economically. In which U.S. region is such wheat most likely grown?

(1) the eastern United States
(2) the western United States
(3) the southeastern United States
(4) the northeastern United States
(5) the Great Lakes region

The first great civilizations of the world developed along the banks of rivers. In river valleys, early people first worked out rules for living together in communities. The earliest laws dealt with irrigation. People worked together to build systems of dams and canals. Leaders supervised the building, and laws were required to ensure fair use of materials and water.

From the beginning, conditions in the Nile Valley in Egypt were favorable for agriculture. The well-watered soil produced abundant harvests. The valley was so fertile that farmers could produce more than enough food for themselves and their families. As a result, surplus food could be sold. Commerce expanded, and people from different regions exchanged ideas and inventions along with trade goods.

Since there was ample food available, not everyone had to be engaged in farming. Some people left farming to develop arts and crafts. Potters learned to shape clay to make decorative vases; weavers learned to make fabrics and patterns of intricate designs. Carpenters learned to build different types of furniture, and architects learned to construct elaborate buildings for government and worship. In this way, civilization and culture flourished in the Nile Valley and elsewhere in the Middle East.

21. For what reason were the first laws established?

    (1) to provide adequate housing for people
    (2) to limit the production of goods
    (3) to create a water distribution system
    (4) to govern commerce and trade
    (5) to build temples for worship

22. Which of the following was the basic reason that civilization flourished in the Nile Valley?

    (1) It became a major trade center in the region.
    (2) The fertile soil produced abundant harvests.
    (3) A wide variety of arts and crafts developed.
    (4) Government buildings were constructed.
    (5) The area had a large and diverse population.

23. Which of the following does the passage suggest that the ancient Egyptians valued most highly?

    (1) cooperation
    (2) education
    (3) competition
    (4) generosity
    (5) independence

Question 24 refers to the following paragraph.

The Fifth Amendment to the United States Constitution says in part that no person "shall be compelled in any criminal case to be a witness against himself, nor be deprived of life, liberty, or property without due process of law."

24. Which of the following ideas is implied in this part of the Fifth Amendment?

    (1) The death penalty is cruel and unjust.
    (2) People are free to worship as they please.
    (3) A person is innocent until proven guilty in a court of law.
    (4) Elected leaders are the basis of democratic government.
    (5) All citizens have the right to petition the government with their grievances.

Question 25 refers to the following advertisement.

25. Which applicant is best qualified for one of the jobs described in the ad?

(1) Brenda has a year of experience doing lawn and yard maintenance.
(2) Glen graduated with honors from a local trade school.
(3) Bob has done some roofing, but he does not have a driver's license.
(4) Maria has worked as a carpenter for three years and has her own tools and a car.
(5) Jan likes to work with his hands, has a car, and lives in the south suburbs.

Question 26 refers to the following graph.

ACID RAIN: A Danger to Plant and Animal Life

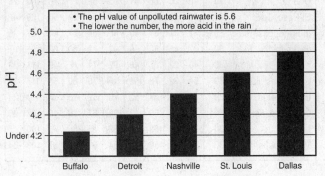

26. In which city would a vegetable garden suffer the least effects from acid rain?

(1) Buffalo
(2) Detroit
(3) Nashville
(4) St. Louis
(5) Dallas

Question 27 refers to the following graph.

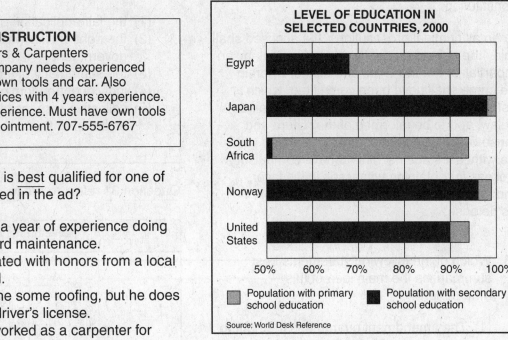

27. Which of the following conclusions is supported by the graph?

(1) The Japanese are the most highly educated people in the world.
(2) South Africa spends less money on education than Egypt does.
(3) Schools in Japan are better than schools in the United States.
(4) The average Egyptian is poorer than the average Norwegian.
(5) The population of Norway is better educated than the population of the United States.

Questions 28 through 30 refer to the following passage from the Sixth Amendment to the U.S. Constitution.

"In all criminal prosecutions, the accused shall enjoy the right to a speedy and public trial, by an impartial jury of the State and district wherein the crime shall have been committed, which district shall have been previously ascertained by law, and to be informed of the nature and cause of the accusation; to be confronted with the witnesses against him; to have compulsory process for obtaining witnesses in his favor, and to have the Assistance of Counsel for his defense."

28. Which of the following statements best summarizes the main idea of this amendment?

(1) The amendment guarantees the right to a speedy and public trial.
(2) The amendment sets forth the rights of people being tried for crimes.
(3) The amendment protects defendants against cruel and unusual punishments.
(4) The amendment sets out the procedures for police to follow in making arrests.
(5) The amendment establishes a defendant's right to trial by jury.

29. Which legal principle most likely resulted from a Supreme Court decision in a case involving an alleged violation of the Sixth Amendment?

(1) Uttering words that create a clear and present danger to others is a crime and is not protected by the right to free speech.
(2) Police officers must inform criminal suspects of their rights before questioning them.
(3) If a person accused of a crime cannot afford a lawyer, the court will appoint one at no cost to the accused person.
(4) Evidence obtained in an illegal search may not be used against an accused person in a trial.
(5) Each legislative district in a state must have approximately the same number of voters.

30. The Sixth Amendment affirms which basic value of American democracy?

(1) the fair application of the law
(2) the right of citizens to petition the government
(3) the supremacy of federal law
(4) individual freedom of all citizens
(5) collective responsibility for the environment

Question 31 refers to the following table.

TEMPERATURE TABLE											
		AVERAGE DAILY TEMPERATURE								EXTREME	
		JANUARY		APRIL		JULY		OCTOBER			
	LENGTH OF RECORD	MAXIMUM	MINIMUM	MAXIMUM	MINIMUM	MAXIMUM	MINIMUM	MAXIMUM	MINIMUM	MAXIMUM	MINIMUM
CITIES	YEAR	°F	°F	°F	°F	°F	°F	°F	°F	°F	°F.
Bismarck, N. D.	30	20	0	55	32	86	58	59	34	114	-45
Boise, Idaho	30	36	22	63	37	91	59	65	38	112	-28
Brownsville, Tex.	30	71	52	82	66	93	76	85	67	104	12
Buffalo, N. Y.	30	31	18	53	34	80	59	60	41	99	-21
Cheyenne, Wyo.	30	37	14	56	30	85	55	63	32	100	-38
Chicago, Ill.	30	33	19	57	41	84	67	63	47	105	-23
Des Moines, Ia.	30	29	11	59	38	87	65	66	43	110	-30
Dodge City, Ks.	30	42	20	66	41	93	68	71	46	109	-26
El Paso, Tex.	30	56	30	78	49	95	69	79	50	109	-8
Indianapolis, Ind.	30	37	21	61	40	86	64	67	44	107	-25
Jacksonville, Fla.	30	67	45	80	58	92	73	80	62	105	10
Kansas City, Mo.	30	40	23	66	46	92	71	72	49	113	-22
Las Vegas, Nev.	30	54	32	78	51	104	76	80	53	117	8
Los Angeles, Ca.	30	64	45	67	52	76	62	73	57	110	23
Louisville, Ky.	30	44	27	66	43	89	67	70	46	107	-20
Miami, Fla.	30	76	58	83	66	89	75	85	71	100	28
Minneapolis, Mn.	30	22	2	56	33	84	61	61	37	108	-34

31. Based on this table, which two cities have the most similar annual weather patterns in terms of temperature?

(1) Bismarck and Indianapolis
(2) Brownsville and Las Vegas
(3) Buffalo and Chicago
(4) Cheyenne and El Paso
(5) Los Angeles and Miami

Questions 32 and 33 refer to the following passage and map.

When the first Europeans reached North America's shores in the 1500s, the continent was teeming with people. Modern-day scholars estimate the continent's Native American population between 8 million and 40 million people. Many of the Europeans thought that these native peoples were uncivilized savages. But Native Americans had developed a number of sophisticated cultures. The following map shows the basic culture groups into which the first Americans were organized.

NATIVE AMERICAN CULTURAL AREAS

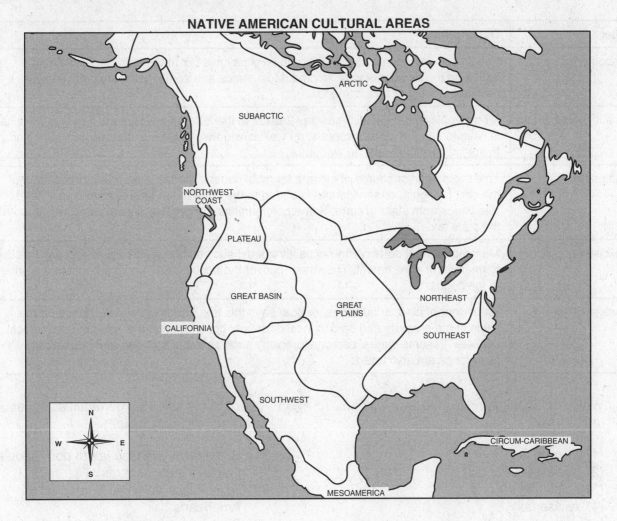

32. According to the map, how are most Native American culture areas named?

(1) for names of leaders
(2) for famous chieftains
(3) for objects
(4) for geographical characteristics
(5) for bodies of water

33. Which statement is a fact, according to the information provided?

(1) Native American societies were very disorganized.
(2) Many Europeans felt they were culturally superior to Native Americans.
(3) The eastern Native American cultures were superior to those in the west.
(4) The most advanced Native American cultures were located in the southeast.
(5) European cultures were better than Native American cultures.

Taxes are paid to all levels of government in order to support the services they provide. These taxes can be classified into two categories: direct taxes and indirect taxes. When you pay direct taxes, you know the amount you are paying. Indirect taxes are built into the larger price or cost of something, and the exact amount of the tax is unknown to the consumer of the item or service. The following chart lists the five basic types of taxes and a brief description of each type.

Tax	Description
income tax	People with an income above a certain level pay this tax to the federal government, based on the amount of their income. Most states and some local communities also require payment of an income tax.
social security tax	Most people who have incomes pay this tax to the federal government. The money raised is used to support retired workers, as well as widows, widowers, disabled workers, and minor children of deceased workers.
sales tax	This tax is a major source of income for most states. The tax is a certain percentage of the cost of a good or service and is added to the price at the time of purchase. The tax rate varies from state to state. Some communities "piggyback" a local sales tax on top of the state tax.
excise tax	Manufacturers of certain non-necessity goods, such as liquor and cigarettes, pay this tax to the federal government. They then recover the tax by including its amount in the price of the goods.
property tax	The owner of land, or buildings, or both pays this tax. The tax is usually based on the value of the property and paid to local or county governments. It is used to pay for local services. In some states, personal property such as motor vehicles and household furnishings are also taxed.

34. Which of the following is an example of an indirect tax?

(1) income tax
(2) social security tax
(3) sales tax
(4) excise tax
(5) property tax

35. Which of the following generalizations about taxes shows faulty logic?

(1) Sales taxes are less fair to poor people than are income taxes.
(2) Taxes place an unfair burden on all Americans.
(3) Social security taxes help elderly Americans in their retirement years.
(4) When property values in a community go up, revenues from taxes usually also go up.
(5) A national sales tax would increase the income of the federal government.

Questions 36 and 37 refer to the following paragraph and map.

In the 1500s Portuguese traders began capturing and purchasing slaves in Africa and transporting them to North and South America for sale. In less than a century, enslaved Africans were performing much of the labor that enabled some English and Spanish colonists to become fabulously wealthy in the New World. Meanwhile, the Netherlands and Britain joined Portugal as countries that profited from trading in human beings.

THE AFRICAN SLAVE TRADE, 1600s –1700s

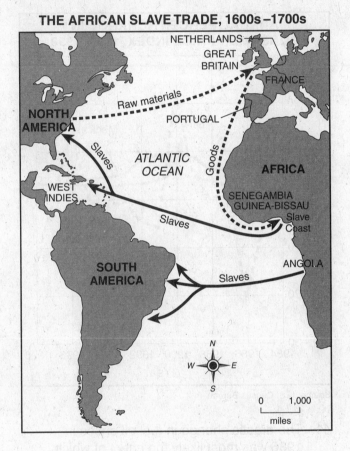

36. Where, besides North and South America, does the map or paragraph indicate that enslaved Africans were transported?

    (1) Portugal
    (2) the Netherlands
    (3) Great Britain
    (4) France
    (5) the West Indies

37. How did the South American slave trade differ from the slave trade with North America?

    (1) More slaves went to North America than went to South America.
    (2) Spanish ships carried slaves to South America, and Portuguese ships carried slaves to North America.
    (3) Slaves taken to South America were from a different part of Africa than those taken to North America.
    (4) Slaves sold in South America cost less than those sold in North America.
    (5) The trip to South America was longer than the trip to North America.

Question 38 refers to the following graph.

REASONS WOMEN HOLD TWO JOBS

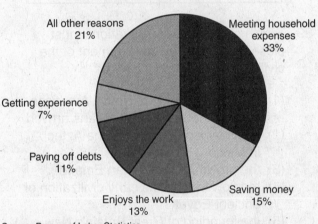

Source: Bureau of Labor Statistics

38. What does this graph suggest is the most likely reason that many women have more than one job?

    (1) Many women are single parents and are struggling to raise families.
    (2) Women are not as well-educated as men.
    (3) The male unemployment rate is highest among married men.
    (4) Most women have a great interest in saving for their future.
    (5) Women enjoy the additional work.

Question 39 refers to the following map.

EARLY CIVILIZATION IN SOUTH ASIA

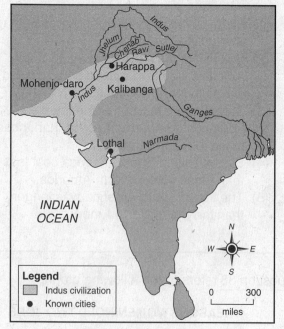

39. Which of the following situations most closely parallels the development of the civilization shown on the map?

    (1) the diversification of Native American cultures before the Europeans arrived
    (2) the Spanish conquest of the Aztec in Mexico
    (3) the growth of the Roman Empire
    (4) the flowering of the early civilization of ancient Egypt
    (5) the founding of Great Britain's New England colonies

Question 40 refers to the following paragraph.

The First Amendment to the U.S. Constitution states that Congress shall make no law regarding an official or "established" religion, or prohibiting the free practice of religion; or limiting freedom of speech or of the press; or the right of the people to assemble peacefully and to present their complaints to government.

40. What does Congress's decision in 1789 to add the First Amendment to the Constitution suggest that its members valued highly?

    (1) a free-market economy
    (2) the power of the president
    (3) the rights of the states
    (4) the rights of individual citizens
    (5) the division between federal and state government

Question 41 refers to the following graph.

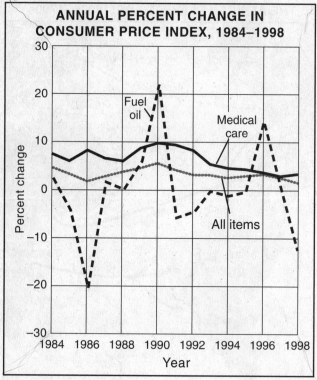

Source: U.S. Census Bureau

41. The drastic change in fuel oil prices in 1986 was most likely the effect of which development?

    (1) a slight decrease in the overall cost of living
    (2) a war in the Persian Gulf
    (3) an increase in U.S. fuel oil production
    (4) an Arab embargo on oil shipments to the U.S.
    (5) a slight increase in the cost of medical care

Questions 42 through 44 refer to the following paragraph and chart.

During the 1900s the United States gradually became both a world power and a world leader. At first, U.S. international involvement concentrated on the Americas. But as time passed, events in Europe caused the United States to become more active in the world at large. The following chart summarizes some major U.S. foreign policies and programs in the twentieth century and illustrates the nation's growing involvement in world affairs.

Foreign Policy	Description
Big Stick	a policy developed by President Theodore Roosevelt calling for the United States to use the threat of force if necessary to achieve its goals when dealing with other nations
Dollar Diplomacy	a policy developed by President William Howard Taft calling for the United States to use trade and overseas investments to achieve its goals with other nations
Good Neighbor Policy	a policy developed by President Franklin D. Roosevelt calling for the U.S. to respect the rights and independence of other nations in the Americas
Marshall Plan	a policy begun by President Harry S. Truman to provide U.S. supplies, equipment, and loans to rebuild nations devastated by World War II
Truman Doctrine	a policy developed by President Harry S. Truman that the United States would provide military and other aid to nations threatened by internal Communist revolutions or by aggression from other Communist countries

42. In the 1980s, President Ronald Reagan sent military advisors and arms to El Salvador to help its government put down a Communist revolution there. Which policy does this action illustrate?

(1) the Big Stick
(2) Dollar Diplomacy
(3) the Good Neighbor Policy
(4) the Marshall Plan
(5) the Truman Doctrine

43. In 1933, the president withdrew U.S. military forces from Nicaragua and Haiti, where they had been protecting U.S. property since the 1920s. Which policy brought about this withdrawal?

(1) the Big Stick
(2) Dollar Diplomacy
(3) the Good Neighbor Policy
(4) the Marshall Plan
(5) the Truman Doctrine

44. In the 1950s, President Dwight D. Eisenhower announced the policy of containment. This policy pledged the United States to block the spread of communism from countries where it already existed. To which earlier U.S. foreign policy was Eisenhower's policy of containment most closely linked?

(1) the Big Stick
(2) Dollar Diplomacy
(3) the Good Neighbor Policy
(4) the Marshall Plan
(5) the Truman Doctrine

Questions 45 and 46 refer to the following cartoon.

© 1995 by Mike Luckovich. Reprinted by permission of Mike Luckovich and Creators Syndicate, Inc.

45. Who is <u>most likely</u> driving the pickup truck?

(1) a trash collector
(2) a terrorist
(3) a National Park Service ranger
(4) a police officer
(5) a local rancher

46. Which of the following is an unstated assumption you need to make to understand this cartoon?

(1) Terrorism is most common in rural areas.
(2) Criminals hide in wilderness areas.
(3) Most terrorists use car bombs in their attacks.
(4) These hikers would prefer to be in a city, where there are more activities to choose from.
(5) The people hiked to this isolated place to get away from terrorism and crime.

Question 47 refers to the following graph.

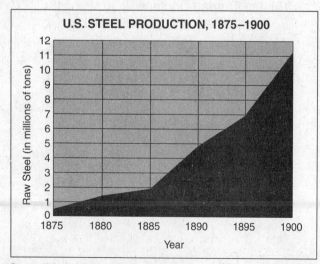

U.S. STEEL PRODUCTION, 1875–1900

Raw Steel (in millions of tons) vs. Year (1875–1900)

Source: Historical Statistics of the United States

47. Which of the following was the <u>most likely</u> direct effect of the developments shown in this graph?

(1) The first high-rise buildings were built in U.S. cities.
(2) The United States became a strong leader in international diplomacy.
(3) U.S. industry went into decline.
(4) Gas and oil production increased.
(5) Agricultural production increased.

Question 48 refers to the following photo.

Question 49 refers to the following graph.

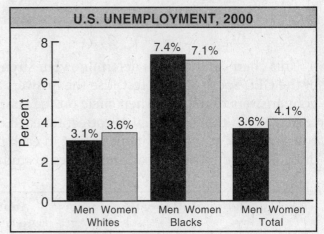

U.S. UNEMPLOYMENT, 2000

Source: U.S. Bureau of Labor Statistics

48. In February 1945, a photojournalist caught the moment when American troops, after six weeks of intense fighting, secured the Pacific Island.

Which is the most likely reason this photo became a national symbol of pride?

(1) The photo was used immediately for Navy recruitment.
(2) The photo appeared staged.
(3) The photo showed an important and strategic victory for the Allies.
(4) The photo was the first taken during World War II.
(5) The photo revealed teamwork.

49. Which of the following is a conclusion based on the graph?

(1) About 3 percent of white males are unemployed.
(2) Over 7 percent of black males are unemployed.
(3) Unemployment is much lower among whites than among blacks.
(4) Nearly 4 percent of white women are unemployed.
(5) More than 7 percent of black women are unemployed.

Question 50 refers to the following map.

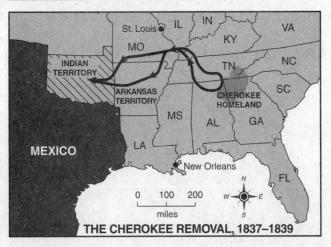

THE CHEROKEE REMOVAL, 1837–1839

50. Which of the following is a conclusion related to the information on the map?

(1) In the 1830s, the Cherokee lived in four southern states.
(2) The Cherokee followed more than one route to the West.
(3) The Cherokee traveled through Tennessee and Kentucky.
(4) The new home of the Cherokee was in Indian Territory.
(5) The Cherokee of the Midwest today are descended from the Cherokee of the South.

Answers start on page 342.

Simulated Test Performance Analysis Chart
Social Studies

This chart can help you determine your strengths and weaknesses in the content and skill areas of the GED Social Studies Test. Use the Answers and Explanations starting on page 342 to check your answers to the test. Then circle on the chart the number of test items you answered correctly. Put the total number correct for each content area and skill area in each row and column. Look at the total items correct in each column and row and decide which areas are difficult for you. Use the page references to study those areas.

Thinking Skill / Content Area	Comprehension (Lessons 1, 2, 7, 16, 18)	Analysis (Lessons 3, 4, 6, 9, 10, 11, 12, 19)	Application (Lessons 14, 15)	Evaluation (Lessons 5, 8, 13, 17, 20)	Total Correct
U.S. History (Pages 32–93)	**1, 32**	**2, 3**, 33, **47, 50**	**42, 43, 44**	**4, 19**	____/12
World History (Pages 94–133)	21, **36**	22, **37, 48**	39	5, 23	____/8
Civics and Government (Pages 134–175)	24, 28, **45**	**6, 9, 10**, 18, **46**	**8**, 29	30, 40	____/12
Economics (Pages 176–207)	**11**, 12	**13, 38, 41, 49**	**25, 34**	**14, 35**	____/10
Geography (Pages 208–238)	**15**	**7, 16, 31**	**20, 26**	**17, 27**	____/8
Total Correct	____/10	____/20	____/10	____/10	____/50

1–40 → You need more review.
41–50 → Congratulations! You're ready for the GED!

Boldfaced numbers indicate questions based on charts, graphs, diagrams, and drawings.

For additional help, see the *Steck-Vaughn GED Social Studies Exercise Book.*

Answers and Explanations

PRETEST (Pages 14–29)

1. **(1) a gradual rise in the sea level** (Analysis) Slow warming will gradually melt the polar ice, thereby gradually raising the sea level. Option (2) is incorrect because slow warming will not produce a sudden increase in sea level. Options (3) and (5) are the opposite of the likely result. Option (4) is not an effect of global warming or the level of the sea.

2. **(3) North America and Africa** (Analysis) The map shows that both these continents are threatened by flooding at numerous sites along most of their coastlines. Options (1), (2), (4), and (5) are incorrect because the coastlines of South America and Australia have fewer affected areas and the threat of coastal flooding is concentrated on only one side of each continent.

3. **(2) coastal cities** (Application) As the map shows, many areas along the coastlines all over the world are likely to be flooded when the sea level rises. Options (1) and (3) are incorrect because the map shows that fewer places are threatened in Europe and Australia than on other continents. Option (4) is incorrect because the west coast of South America does not have any areas that are likely to be affected. Option (5) is incorrect because seas will rise all over the world and although people who live in some places along the Arctic coast near the North Pole will be affected, they will not be affected any more than people along the coasts of other oceans.

4. **(1) electrical machinery** (Comprehension) Electrical machinery heads the lists of both imports and exports in 1994. Options (2), (3), (4), and (5) are incorrect because the sum of the amount imported plus the amount exported for each is lower than the sum for electrical machinery.

5. **(2) NAFTA has reversed the trade relationship between the United States and Mexico.** (Evaluation) The graph shows that, before NAFTA went into effect, the value of U.S. exports to Mexico exceeded the value of goods imported from Mexico. Since NAFTA took effect in 1994, the reverse is true, and the value of imports from Mexico now exceeds the value of U.S. exports to Mexico. Options (1), (3), and (5) cannot be determined from the graph because there is no comparison of Mexico with Canada or other sources of clothing. Option (4) is not supported by the graph.

6. **(3) U.S. exports to Canada and imports from Canada have both increased.** (Application) The graph shows that overall U.S. trade with Mexico—imports as well as exports—has increased since 1994, when NAFTA began to remove trade barriers between the two countries. Since the paragraph states that NAFTA removed barriers on trade with Canada as well, it is logical that overall trade between the U.S. and Canada would also increase. Nothing in the graph or paragraph suggests that the direction of change of imports and exports differs, so options (1) and (2) are incorrect. The graph information suggests that the opposite of option (4) would likely be true of U.S. trade with Canada. There is no support for option (5) in either the paragraph or the graph.

7. **(4) a limited war in Korea to drive communist invaders of South Korea back into North Korea** (Application) The United States and its allies were content to keep communism contained in North Korea rather than attempting to overthrow it there. Options (1), (2), and (3) do not illustrate the element of containment. Option (5) illustrates the spread of communism, not the containment of it.

8. **(5) members of the Tammany Ring** (Comprehension) This is shown by the "Tammany Ring" label and the circle of figures in the cartoon. Nothing in the cartoon indicates that option (1) or (3) is the answer. The fancy clothing worn by some of the figures at the front of the ring suggests that option (2) is incorrect. The labels on the figures at the back of the ring indicate that they are businesspeople (carpenter, gas pipe company, awning company, etc.), making option (4) incorrect.

9. **(1) They know the Tammany Ring is considered corrupt.** (Analysis) Unless the readers assume that the Tammany Ring is corrupt, the cartoon—the point of which is that each member is proclaiming his innocence and blaming another member—makes no sense. The cartoon's point would also make no sense if option (2), (3), or (4) were true. If option (5) were correct, the cartoonist would have labeled these figures as he did all the others (with names on the figure's back or hat band.)

10. **(3) amending the Constitution to abolish slavery** (Application) The practice of slavery was contrary to the principles expressed in the Declaration of Independence that all people are created equal and entitled to life, liberty, and the pursuit of happiness. Option (1) improved people's lives and helped to create more

educational equality, but it did not address people's rights to life and liberty. Options (2) and (4) have to do with the nation's growth, not with the principles expressed in this excerpt from the Declaration of Independence. Option (5) is contrary to these principles, not an example of them.

11. **(5) 45 percent** (Comprehension) Senators with more than two terms have served more than 12 years (more than two 6-year terms). According to the top graph, this is 45 percent of the senators; add 20 percent and 25 percent to come up with the figure for all senators with more than 12 years in Congress. Option (1) is incorrect because it accounts for only the 20 percent who were in their third term (13–18 years of service) in 1995. Option (2) accounts for only the 25 percent who had served more than three terms (19 or more years). Option (3) is incorrect because it is the percent who were in their second terms and thus had served only between 7 and 12 years. Option (4) is the percentage of first-term senators.

12. **(5) Members of Congress did not want term limits applied to themselves.** (Analysis) The clue to this is in the writer's reference to the graphs. The data show that most members of each house of Congress have been there for two or more terms. Option (1) is incorrect because the writer states that public opinion favored the proposal. Options (2) and (3) are arguments for and against term limits, but the passage's final paragraph makes it clear that the writer assumes that the vote was more influenced by self-interest than by these arguments. Option (4) is true but is not relevant to the issue or the vote.

13. **(4) In the 1995 Congress, the Senate had a higher proportion of members serving more than a dozen years than the House did.** (Evaluation) You can see this by comparing the two pie graphs. They show that 45 percent of Senators served 13 or more years, compared with 31 percent of House members. Options (1) and (2) are both true but cannot be concluded from the information provided. Option (3) is contradicted by the information in both the passage and the graphs. The bottom graph shows that option (5) is untrue.

14. **(1) Land disputes would erupt between the colonists and the French.** (Application) The map shows that the territory between the Mississippi River and the Appalachian Mountains was claimed by both France and the colonies. Using this information, you could predict that there would be disputes. Options (2), (3), (4),

and (5) describe real historical events, but these could not have been predicted from the information on the map.

15. **(3) He has worked as a bookkeeper.** (Application) Of his qualifications, this experience is the most directly related to what the employer is looking for in the person to be hired. Option (1) is incorrect because the advertisement does not mention the need to speak a second language. Options (2) and (4) have nothing to do with the job requirements. Although a high school diploma is required, the advertisement says nothing about grades, so option (5) is incorrect.

16. **(4) A person without payroll experience probably won't be hired.** (Analysis) The word *probably* marks this as an opinion. Also, the advertisement indicates that payroll experience is helpful, but not required. Options (1), (2), (3), and (5) are facts that can be verified by reading the ad.

17. **(2) Bosnia-Herzegovina was occupied by various armies.** (Comprehension) Bosnia-Herzegovina is shaded on the map to show where the various forces were located in 1995. The map also shows where UN peacekeeping troops were located. While option (1) is true, the map does not provide any information indicating that this event had taken place. Option (3) cannot be determined from the map. Although the map shows a ship carrying U.S. Marines off the coast of the region, the map does not indicate that the Marines had landed in Bosnia-Herzegovina, so option (4) is incorrect. Option (5) is contradicted by the map.

18. **(1) The price of a taxi ride is high.** (Comprehension) The taxi company is a monopoly, a business with no competition and therefore with complete control over the selling of its service. Since there is no transportation alternative to take away business by offering lower prices and/or better service, ABC can keep its prices high. Options (2) and (3) are incorrect because there is no incentive for the company to provide low prices or good service when there is no competition. Options (4) and (5) are very unlikely given the monopoly that ABC enjoys.

19. **(4) older people with some college education** (Comprehension) The three lines showing the highest percentage of voters (between 60 and 80 percent) are those of the college educated. These lines tend upward, indicating an increase in percentage along the age line, reaching their highest point in the 70–80 age range. Options (1), (2), (3), and (5) are

incorrect because the graph shows that that the likelihood of voting increases with both education and age.

20. **(5) The United States has a two-party political system.** (Analysis) The passage assumes that you know that the Democratic and Republican parties dominate American politics. Without this knowledge, all the references to voter registration and party-line voting would be difficult for readers to comprehend. Options (1), (3), and (4) are incorrect because this information is stated directly in the passage. Option (2) is incorrect because this information is not necessary to understanding the main points of the passage.

21. **(3) Third-party and independent candidates benefit from the erosion of party loyalty.** (Evaluation) Since many people no longer vote strictly along party lines, candidates who are not from either major political party have a better chance of gaining voter support, and some third-party and independent candidates have been elected in the recent past. Option (1) is contradicted by the passage. Option (2) is incorrect because the passage does not indicate whether the trend is likely to continue. Option (4) is true, but nothing in the passage connects the outcome to shifts in party loyalty or voter behavior. Option (5) is incorrect because no such cause-and-effect relationship is suggested.

22. **(1) Temperatures vary with the season, and there is little rain and snow.** (Evaluation) The graph supports this statement because it shows cold winters with temperatures well below freezing, cool summers with temperatures in the 60s, and monthly precipitation of less than two inches, even in the wettest months. Option (2) may be true, but the graph does not support any conclusions about the town's population. Option (3) is incorrect because it is contradicted by the graph. Options (4) and (5) are incorrect because they refer to conditions during a 24-hour period, while the graph presents information month by month.

23. **(3) Women could vote in all elections in Oregon but in no elections in Virginia.** (Analysis) The map shows that Oregon granted full voting rights to women in 1912, but that women in Virginia had no voting rights as of 1919. This fact about Virginia women makes options (1), (2), (4), and (5) incorrect. Options (1) and (2) also incorrectly state the voting rights of women in Oregon.

24. **(2) Women gained full voting rights in the West before they did in the East or South.** (Evaluation) This can be concluded by comparing the number of western states where women had full voting rights with the number of such states in the East or South. The fact that women had full or partial voting rights in most northern states and no voting rights in most southern states suggests that option (1) is incorrect. Options (3) and (5) cannot be determined from the map. Option (4) is incorrect because the fact that fewer southern states granted women voting rights is not evidence that southern women were less desirous of such rights than northern women.

25. **(5) Understanding the history of a region requires understanding the region's geography.** (Comprehension) This is the best statement of the main idea of the paragraph. Option (1) is an incorrect interpretation of the paragraph's point because the paragraph does not say that a geographer must know the history of a place. Options (2), (3), and (4) are true but are details that help explain why knowing the history of a region also requires a knowledge of the region's geography.

26. **(4) the power to appoint federal judges** (Comprehension) The president can influence the judicial branch, or the judiciary, by appointing judges who hold certain views. Option (1) is not a check but is rather a power of the legislative branch. Options (2) and (3) are checks by the judicial branch, not on it. Option (5) is a check that the president has on the legislative branch, not on the judiciary.

27. **(1) Congress can propose to amend the Constitution to make burning the flag a crime.** (Application) The chart shows that Congress has this power. If the Constitution were to be amended, the law against flag burning would no longer be unconstitutional. Options (2) and (3) are incorrect because veto and enforcement are executive powers, not powers of the legislative branch, and the veto is used against bills passed in the legislature, not against Court decisions. Option (4) would do no good because the Court would just rule the law unconstitutional a second time. Option (5) is not true.

28. **(2) The division of powers and the system of the checks on those powers keep a balance of power among government's three branches.** (Analysis) This is the main point of the chart and passage. Options (1), (4), and (5) are examples of how the system of checks and balances operates. Option (3) is a detail that helps explain how the system works.

29. **(3) agriculture** (Comprehension) The graph for 1870 shows that more than half of U.S. workers were engaged in this type of work. The graph indicates that options (1), (2), and (5) all involved

smaller percentages of the workforce than did agriculture. Option (4) is incorrect because this is not one of the categories in this graph.

30. **(5) As agriculture's economic importance declined, more people took up factory work and other jobs.** (Analysis) The graphs show a decrease in the number of agricultural jobs between 1870 and 1920 and an increase in jobs in manufacturing and other sectors. Options (1), (2), and (4) are details that support this conclusion. Option (3) is incorrect because fewer people were employed in farming in 1920 than in 1870.

31. **(4) Ads can appear in print or electronic formats.** (Analysis) This is a fact related to the paragraph, which mentions that companies use various forms of advertising to promote their goods or services; print ads can be found in magazines and newspapers and on billboards, while advertising in an electronic format takes places on television, radio, and the Internet. Options (1), (2), (3), and (5) are all opinions, which may or may not be true.

32. **(1) Production of coal, oil, and natural gas exceeds their consumption every year.** (Evaluation) This is faulty logic because the graph shows data only for 1998, not for any other years, and it does not provide any reason to conclude that 1998 was typical of other years. Options (2), (3), (4), and (5) are all facts supported by data on the graph, so they are not faulty logic.

33. **(4) Republicans opposed slavery in most of the nation's western territory.** (Analysis) This can be determined by comparing the two maps. The top map shows that slavery would be allowed in the territories and the bottom map shows that the Republicans wanted slavery to be illegal there. The paragraph indicates that option (1) is incorrect; disagreement with Whigs and Democrats about slavery was the reason for the formation of the Republican party. Options (2) and (3) are both contradicted by the bottom map, which indicates that Republicans accepted the existence of slavery in the South but not in the West. The paragraph and bottom map both contradict option (5) because both indicate that slavery was an important issue to Republicans in the 1850s.

34. **(5) the increasing use of computer technology** (Analysis) All five of the fastest-growing occupations involve the use of computers. Option (1) would not cause an increased need for such workers and, in fact, would likely have the opposite effect. Options (2), (3), and (4) are incorrect because there is no cause-and-effect relationship between these conditions and the need for more computer services workers.

35. **(4) The Cold War pitted the United States and its allies against the Soviet Union and its allies.** (Analysis) Unless you realize this, you will not be able to understand the last sentence of the passage—the connection between the collapse of the Soviet Union, the end of the Cold War, and the reference to how it "split the world," and continued existence of Communism. Options (1) and (2) are incorrect because they are untrue, but even if they were accurate, they would be details that would not aid in understanding the main point of the passage. Option (3) is incorrect because it is stated in the passage. Option (5) is incorrect because it is directly implied by the passage.

36. **(4) It led to pro-democracy movements starting in many countries.** (Analysis) The passage indicates that the freedom granted by Gorbachev's policies of the mid-1980s inspired people to throw off Communism and work toward more democratic governments in many parts of the world. Options (1) and (3) are incorrect because the passage indicates they are the opposite of what happened as a result of Gorbachev's policy. Option (2) is incorrect because this was the Chinese government's response to the demand for democracy in China not their response to the Soviet's policy of glasnost. There is no indication in the passage that option (5) was an effect of Gorbachev's policy.

37. **(1) the policy of glasnost** (Comprehension) The passage states that in hopes of revitalizing the Soviet Union, Gorbachev launched a policy of reforms called "glasnost" in the mid-1980s. Options (2), (3), (4), and (5) are incorrect because these events occurred years after the cartoon was published and because they don't make sense as possible ways to revive the Soviet Union, which the cartoonist pictured as dead.

38. **(5) Gorbachev would not be able to save the Soviet Union.** (Analysis) That the Soviet Union is represented by a tombstone indicates that that nation is beyond resuscitation; with the intravenous line into the tombstone, the cartoonist implies that Gorbachev's policies are too little too late. Options (1), (3), and (4) are incorrect because they are details from the passage that help support the conclusion. Option (2) is incorrect because it is a detail implied in the passage that is not related to the cartoon's conclusion.

39. **(5) control by the government** (Evaluation) The fact that the Chinese leaders used the

army against students shows that crushing this challenge to their authority and maintaining control was most important to Chinese leaders. Their brutal response shows that they had little regard for option (1) or (3). The action has no relationship to option (2) or (4).

40. **(3) the South** (Application) All the southern states failed to ratify the ERA. Options (1), (4), and (5) are incorrect because these states were nearly all in favor of the amendment and would probably be so again. Option (2) is incorrect because support in these states was weaker than in New England, the Northwest, and the Great Lakes states but stronger than support in the South.

41. **(2) large numbers of people from Great Britain migrating to Australia** (Application) Just as in North America, European settlers drove native Australian peoples out of their territory. Option (1) is incorrect because the moon is uninhabited and the Americans did not settle there. Option (3) is an economic development that has nothing to do with displacement of people. Options (4) and (5) are incorrect because they involve only temporary presence in a territory, not permanent settlement and displacement of inhabitants.

42. **(5) Pure democracy is a better form of government than representative democracy.** (Analysis) This is the only statement that is based on a personal judgment with which not everyone would agree. Options (1), (2), (3), and (4) are facts expressed or implied by the chart.

43. **(4) representative democracy** (Application) A senator is elected by and represents the people of his or her state. Responding to the electorate in deciding whether to support laws is a characteristic of representative democracy. These characteristics rule out options (1), (2), (3), and (5).

44. **(1) desire for control** (Evaluation) By definition, a dictator holds all governing power in his or her country. Dictators are not necessarily cruel, so option (2) is incorrect. Option (3) is incorrect because freedom is seldom found in a dictatorship. Option (4) is incorrect because it is not related to a specific form of government. Preserving wealth for a small group is usually more closely associated with oligarchy than with a dictatorship, so option (5) is incorrect.

45. **(5) Crowds at the park will get larger.** (Analysis) The graph shows that lower prices correlate with increased attendance, so setting a lower price for children should have this effect. Option (1) is incorrect because the lower price

should attract more, rather than fewer, children. Option (2) is incorrect for much the same reason; with more children going to the park, general attendance should go up. There is no support for option (3) or (4) on the graph.

46. **(1) It will continue to increase.** (Analysis) Since the trend has been steady, it is reasonable to assume that population will continue to increase over time. Options (2), (3), (4), and (5) do not logically follow from the trend shown in the graph.

47. **(2) an increase in urban crime** (Analysis) The paragraph states that Prohibition was weakest in cities, where it led to illegal liquor sales, increasing urban crime. The paragraph rules out option (1) as an effect. There is no evidence suggesting option (3). Option (4) was the cause of Prohibition, not an effect of it. Although option (5) was an intent of Prohibition, the paragraph establishes that it was not an actual effect.

48. **(2) the nation's highway system** (Analysis) The nation's system of state and interstate highways has resulted from the power to build roads shared by the national (derived from its power to maintain a mail-delivery system) and state governments. Option (1) is not a result of concurrent powers because control of elections is solely a state function. Option (3) is a result of the states' power to establish schools. Option (4) results solely from the national government's power to coin money. Option (5) is incorrect because the two-party system was not created by any level of government.

49. **(3) Most U.S. businesses are proprietorships, but corporations have the highest total revenues.** (Evaluation) This conclusion is supported by the graph, which shows that more than 70 percent of U.S. businesses are proprietorships, while only 20 percent are corporations, but that this 20 percent of businesses produces nearly 90 percent of revenue, compared to less than 5 percent for proprietorships. Option (1) is contradicted by the graph, which shows that the percentage of business that are partnerships and their percentage of all business revenue are about the same, while many more proprietorships produce less revenue than partnerships. Option (2) is also contradicted by the graph, which shows that partnerships are much less common than corporations. Options (4) and (5) cannot be determined from the graph. The fact that the volume of revenue is lowest among proprietorships seems to contradict the conclusion that revenues increase when the owner does the selling.

50. (5) Benjamin Franklin was the author of the Declaration of Independence. (Evaluation) This statement is an example of a hasty generalization. Although the passage indicates that Franklin was in favor of signing the Declaration of Independence, there is nothing in the passage to support the idea that he wrote it; in fact the Declaration was written by Thomas Jefferson. Options (1), (2), (3), and (4) are all implied by the passage and so are not examples of faulty logic.

UNIT 1: UNITED STATES HISTORY
Lesson 1
GED Skill Focus (Page 35)

1. **a.** A variety of factors accounted for the differences in American Indian cultures.

2. **b.** American Indian cultures differed greatly from region to region.

3. Your answer may be similar to the following: I looked for the idea that ties all the sentences together because the topic is not stated directly in one sentence.

4. **b.** There were nine American Indian cultural regions in North America.

GED Content Focus (Page 37)

1. **(3) how Europeans became interested in the New World** (Comprehension) This is the only option that is broad enough to include all the ideas covered in the three paragraphs. Each of the other options is too specific to be the main idea of the first three paragraphs.

2. **(5) European countries colonized different areas of the Americas.** (Comprehension) This is the only option that is general enough to cover all the information in the paragraph. Option (1) is incorrect because motives are not mentioned in the paragraph. Options (2) and (4) are incorrect because even if they are true, they are details, not the main idea. Option (3) is incorrect because the paragraph does not mention competition.

3. **(1) The colonization of the New World benefited many European countries, but it had a tragic effect on the land's original inhabitants.** (Comprehension) This is the only option that is general enough to cover all the information in the passage. All the other options are mentioned, but each focuses on only one part of the passage: (2) the voyages of Columbus, (3) the mistreatment of American Indians, (4) the definition of colonization, and (5) European motives for colonization.

4. **(4) Between 1620 and 1750, the American Indian population diminished to almost nothing while the population of**

European settlers grew. (Comprehension) This is the only option that is general enough to cover all the information in the graph. Options (1) and (2) accurately restate some information from the graph, but neither conveys the whole idea. Options (3) and (5) may be true, but neither is supported by data in the graph.

5. **(1) the decline of the American Indian population** (Comprehension) This is the only option that is a focus of both the graph and the last paragraph. Option (2) is incorrect because the paragraph does not discuss the population of the colonists. Option (3) is incorrect because New England is not discussed in the paragraph. Option (4) is incorrect because the graph does not give information about why the American Indian population declined, although the paragraph does. There is no information about option (5) in the graph.

GED Practice (Pages 38–39)

1. **(4) to make plans for governing the colony** (Comprehension) In the document, the signers agree to take the actions needed to set up a government. Option (2) explains why they are establishing the colony. The document does not mention options (1), (3), or (5).

2. **(3) There was no English government where they landed.** (Analysis) Since the passage states that the Pilgrims landed far north of England's only other colony, it can be assumed that no English government existed there. Option (1) is not correct because, while the Pilgrims may have been lost, there is no evidence that they were afraid. There is no discussion in the paragraph or the Compact to support options (2), (4), or (5).

3. **(2) the growth of self-government** (Application) The *Mayflower Compact* expresses the Pilgrims' plan to form their own government. Option (1) is incorrect because they achieved religious freedom by coming to America. Options (3), (4), and (5) are not mentioned in the document.

4. **(5) Men had to belong to the church in order to take part in government.** (Evaluation) This shows one way that the church and the government were connected. The other options are all true, but none of them explains or illustrates the close relationship between the church and the government in the Massachusetts Bay Colony.

5. **(2) Geographic differences caused people in the colonies to make their living in different ways.** (Comprehension) This paragraph focuses on how soil and climate conditions affected the ways that people in the

colonies earned a living. Option (1) is true but is not the focus of the paragraph. Options (3), (4), and (5) are facts that support or relate to the main idea.

6. **(1) England's North American colonies were grouped into three categories.** (Comprehension) This can be seen in the map's content and key. The other options present information from the map, but this information is not the main focus of the map.

7. **(5) The New England colonies were the farthest north.** (Evaluation) Option (5) is based on the map showing that the New England colonies were the farthest north and therefore had a relatively colder and harsher climate for farming. Options (2) and (4) are based on the map but have nothing to do with climate or farming. Options (1) and (3) cannot be determined from the map and have nothing to do with farming.

8. **(4) Massachusetts** (Application) Option (4) is correct because the map shows that Massachusetts has a longer coastline than New Hampshire, option (1). Therefore, Massachusetts is most likely the colony in which people made their living by fishing. Options (2), (3), and (5) are incorrect because the passage states that the New England colonies had good harbors and those colonies are not in New England.

GED Mini-Test (Pages 40–41)

1. **(4) the establishment of the mission system** (Comprehension) Most of the paragraph discusses the spread of the mission system. Options (3) and (5) are details that support this topic by explaining the events leading up to it. Option (2) is only implied but not directly discussed in the paragraph, and no mention is made of option (1).

2. **(5) slaves** (Application) The whippings and forced obedience are clues that mission Indians were treated like slaves. This description would not apply to any of the other options.

3. **(4) Mission Indians were forced to obey the priests' orders and to give up their religions.** (Evaluation) This is the only option that would make their lives harsh. Options (1) and (5) are true, but they are not directly related to the conditions under which mission Indians lived. Options (2) and (3) are also true, but do not by themselves make life harsh.

4. **(4) Most missions in the United States were in Florida, Texas, and the Southwest.** (Evaluation) This statement could be verified by locating Spanish mission buildings in North America. The other options are dependent on the records kept at the time. Records can raise

questions about accuracy, and they may express only one person's opinion. Thus, because options (1), (2), (3), and (5) can be known only by memoirs and other records of the time, they would be harder to verify than option (4).

5. **(3) French traders traveled mainly by water.** (Analysis) The paragraph indicates the importance of rivers and lakes in getting French fur traders into the interior of the continent. Option (1) is not supported by the paragraph, and options (2), (4), and (5) are not addressed.

6. **(4) more than 250,000** (Comprehension) The label on the graph states that population figures are in thousands, so a graph value of 250 is actually 250,000. Options (1), (2), and (3) are figures based on an incorrect interpretation of the graph. Option (5) is the white population in 1760.

7. **(3) The black population increased at a greater rate than the white population between 1720 and 1760.** (Evaluation) The graph shows the black population increasing at a greater rate than the white population. The graph does not include any information about the population of other colonies, so options (1) and (5) are not correct. Option (2) is incorrect because the graph does not distinguish between the free and enslaved black populations. Option (4) would result from misinterpreting the information on the graph.

8. **(3) Systems of Colonial Government in America** (Comprehension) The passage describes and compares the three systems of government used in the colonies. This makes options (1) and (5) incorrect because they address only one or two systems. Option (2) is not discussed in the passage. Option (4) is the subject of the first paragraph only.

9. **(4) Rhode Island** (Analysis) Rhode Island was the most democratic (defined as people ruling themselves) of the colonies listed because it was a completely self-governing colony, electing both its governor and all members of both houses of its legislature. Options (1) and (5) are not correct because Georgia and Virginia are not among the four colonies discussed in the passage, making them royal colonies with appointed governors and one appointed legislative house. Although Pennsylvania elected both houses of its legislature, both Pennsylvania and Maryland had appointed governors, making them proprietary colonies; thus options (2) and (3) are incorrect.

Lesson 2
GED Skill Focus (Page 43)
1. **a.** After nine years of fighting, France lost most of its American territory.

2. Your answer may be similar to the following: From 1754 to 1763 (*when*), the British and French (*who*) fought a war (*what*) (called the French and Indian War) against each other for control over colonies (*why*) in North America (*where*). The British won this war but soon faced many conflicts with the colonists. These conflicts eventually led to the American Revolution.

3. These maps show that **France** lost most of its land in **North America** between the years **1700** and **1763**. All **France** had left was a small territory in the **Caribbean Sea.**

GED Content Focus (Page 45)

1. **(1) Britain had trouble governing the American colonies after the French and Indian War.** (Comprehension) This option accounts for all the information in the paragraph. Option (2) is an example of the trouble between Britain and its American colonies. Option (3) is not supported by information in the paragraph. Option (4)—a rewording of the phrase, "Taxation without representation is tyranny"—is just one example of the colonists' complaints against the British. Option (5) is discussed in the second paragraph, not the first.

2. **(4) Reaction of Americans to the loss of the right to self-government led to the outbreak of the Revolutionary War.** (Comprehension) This is the only option that is general enough to cover all the information in the paragraph. Options (1), (2), and (3) are examples of the increasing conflict. Option (5) is a detail mentioned in the paragraph, not a summary of it.

3. **(5) Governments that do not protect rights of the people should be replaced.** (Comprehension) This is the only option that is general enough to cover all the information in the paragraph. Options (1) and (4) represent ideas mentioned in the paragraph but they are too specific to stand as a summary of the whole. Options (2) and (3) are inaccurate restatements of ideas in the paragraph or the document.

4. **(5) The British abolished the legislature of one or more of the colonies.** (Comprehension) The third paragraph of the passage indicates the colonists considered the abolition of the Massachusetts legislature an outrage. This is also one of the objectionable acts listed in the Declaration. Option (1) is a misstatement of information in the passage. The Americans boycotted British goods; not the other way around. Options (2) and (3) are mentioned in the Declaration as British injustices, but the passage does not label either of these as the final outrage that led to war. Option (4) is mentioned in the Declaration but

not in the passage, so it was not likely to be considered the worst outrage.

5. **(2) They were unhappy about the treaty.** (Analysis) This is the only option supported by the painting and the explanatory text for this question. Nothing in the text or painting addresses options (1), (4), and (5). Option (3) cannot be correct because the explanation says that the British *did* sign the treaty.

GED Practice (Pages 46–47)

1. **(1) with specifying citizens' rights** (Analysis) The discussion of state constitutions and the list of freedoms in the first paragraph support this conclusion. Options (2) and (3) are contradicted by the passage. There is no information in the passage about options (4) or (5).

2. **(2) an agreement to form a new nation** (Comprehension) The purpose of the Articles of Confederation is set forth in the first two sentences of the first paragraph. Options (1) and (5) were left to the states. Option (3) is incorrect because this freedom was addressed in state constitutions. Option (4) is incorrect because the Declaration of Independence accomplished this goal.

3. **(3) It would be hard for states with different money systems to conduct trade.** (Analysis) The passage establishes that lack of uniformity in several areas led to trade problems. No information in the passage suggests options (1), (4), and (5). Option (2) is not very likely because people would get used to the appearance of the money.

4. **(5) the United Nations, where each country is represented in a General Assembly of independent nations** (Application) Like the states under the Articles of Confederation, the member countries of the UN work together but are largely independent in their actions. Option (1) is incorrect because this organization eases trade restrictions and promotes cooperation. Option (2) is incorrect because it is a military alliance. Option (3) is a police organization. Option (4) has no relationship to how the states functioned under the Articles of Confederation.

5. **(4) to present an example of how all sections in a township could be divided** (Analysis) This answer is suggested by the structure of the diagram, which focuses on ever-smaller portions of the region to give an increasingly detailed explanation of how the survey system worked. Although options (1) and (2) are illustrated in the diagram, they are not the main reason for focusing on section 13. Nothing in the paragraph or diagram suggests that voting

was involved in the survey system, so option (3) is incorrect; nor is anything suggested about desirability, so option (5) is incorrect.

6. **(5) Education was valued since the government set aside land for schools.** (Evaluation) The question establishes that the law required one section in each township of the Northwest Territory to be reserved to support education. This suggests that education was important. Nothing in the passage suggests that land was not valued, so option (1) is incorrect. Options (2) and (3) require a comparison with other areas and this is not addressed in the passage. There is nothing in the passage to support the idea in option (4) that the government built all the schools—only that they set aside the land.

GED Mini-Test (Pages 48–49)

1. **(2) states with large populations and those with small populations** (Comprehension) The information establishes that states are represented in the House according to their population, and equally in the Senate. This arrangement suggests that a compromise was required because of population differences among the states. Options (1), (3), (4), and (5) are incorrect because the compromise plan was not based on any of the factors mentioned in these options.

2. **(5) a government that would work for all states** (Evaluation) The fact that the writers (called "the framers") of the Constitution were willing to compromise indicates their desire to make the new government work for all states. Option (1) is the opposite of the way they worked. Nothing in the passage addresses options (2) or (3). Option (4) is incorrect because the number of representatives in the House varies from state to state.

3. **(3) desire for wealth and prestige** (Evaluation) Owning a large amount of land and slaves to grow cash crops on it suggests that Cherokee leaders valued wealth and prestige. The fact that they held slaves makes options (1) and (4) incorrect. Nothing in the information relates to option (2). Option (5) is incorrect because loyalty is unrelated to owning plantations and slaves.

4. **(4) They were brave, courageous warriors.** (Analysis) While one person may think that certain actions make a group brave and courageous, another person may not. Options (1), (2), (3), (5) are facts, not opinions, because they can be proven from historical records and other evidence.

5. **(1) People accused of crimes have specific rights.** (Comprehension) These amendments list a wide range of rights held by people who are suspected of, arrested, tried, and punished for criminal acts. Option (2) is contradicted by the information for Amendment 4. Option (3) relates to the free speech and right-of-assembly guarantees of the First Amendment. Option (4) applies to only Amendments 6 and 7. Option (5) applies only to Amendment 5.

6. **(4) the Fourth Amendment** (Application) The Fourth Amendment is the only one that deals with searches. The amendments listed in options (1), (2), (3), and (5) address other types of rights and protections.

7. **(1) the First Amendment** (Application) Magazine publication is both a free speech and freedom of the press issue, which are First Amendment rights. The amendments listed in options (2), (3), (4), and (5) address other types of rights and protections.

8. **(3) the Fifth Amendment** (Application) In this scenario, you would be protected by the Fifth Amendment right to not speak against yourself at a trial. Option (1) is incorrect because this is not a freedom of speech matter. The amendments listed in options (2), (4), and (5) do not deal with trial-related rights.

Lesson 3
GED Skill Focus (Page 51)

1. **a.** where the Appalachian Mountains and the Mississippi River are

2. **b.** European countries had the right to give away or sell lands in North America.

3. **c.** The Louisiana Purchase opened the door to westward expansion.

GED Content Focus (Page 53)

1. **(3) It had been owned by other countries.** (Comprehension) Aside from the original thirteen colonies, almost every section of the map indicates that it was acquired by purchase or agreement with France, Great Britain, Spain, or Mexico. The map doesn't indicate anything about whether the land was inhabited (option 1) or settled (option 5). Neither does it mention anything about warfare (option 2) or American Indians (option 4).

2. **(2) They didn't need to honor their agreement to live under Mexican law.** (Analysis) This is the only assumption supported by the facts presented in paragraph 2. The settlers originally agreed to live by Mexican law, but later decided they didn't want to. Nothing in the passage supports options (1), (4), or (5). Option

(3) is incorrect because the passage does not relate the idea of manifest destiny to political independence but to the occupation of land.

3. **(3) The gold rush spurred population growth, business development, and better transportation.** (Comprehension) This is the only option that is general enough to cover all the information in the paragraph. Options (1), (2), and (4) are too limited. Option (5) goes beyond the facts of the paragraph.

4. **(4) opposition to the seizure of their lands** (Analysis) The passage shows that the American Indians had to be pushed off their land to make way for the settlers to mine, farm, and ranch. Options (1), (3), and (5) were all results of relocation of American Indians, not the cause. Option (2) does not relate to standing in the way of so-called "progress."

GED Practice (Pages 54–55)

1. **(3) Good transportation systems are important to a region's economic growth.** (Analysis) The passage states that newly settled regions needed roads, canals, and railroads to prosper. Options (1) and (4) are not assumptions because they are directly stated in the paragraph. No information provided in the paragraph suggests options (2) and (5).

2. **(1) their willingness to work hard** (Evaluation) According to the passage, work was what brought most immigrants to the growing United States. Although it is true that many immigrants came to the United States for religious, political, and personal freedom, options (2), (3), (4), and (5) are not supported by the passage.

3. **(4) the Highway Act of 1956, which authorized the building of an interstate highway system** (Application) It took action by the federal government to create another transcontinental transportation system. Option (1) has no relationship to the passage, while options (2) and (5) relate to immigration, not transportation. Option (3) is incorrect because the Interstate Commerce Act oversaw the completed railroads, not their creation.

4. **(5) the Ft. Smith-Santa Fe and Old Spanish trails** (Application) The map shows this to be the most direct route from the southern United States to California. Options (1), (3), and (4) begin in Missouri, which would be less convenient for people in the South. Option (2) does not reach California.

5. **(1) Trails followed rivers when they could because of the water the rivers provided.** (Analysis) People moving through remote areas would need a dependable supply of water.

Moving westward beside a river would provide this, and the map shows that the trails followed rivers whenever possible. Options (2) and (4) are contradicted by information on the map. Nothing on the map suggests that options (3) and (5) are correct.

6. **(2) There was conflict between American Indians and travelers on the Oregon Trail.** (Comprehension) The fact that the treaty guaranteed wagon trains safe passage and allowed the government to build forts suggests that relations between American Indians and travelers on the trail was an ongoing problem. Option (1) is incorrect because the Senate, not the treaty negotiators, changed the treaty. And although changing the treaty may have been dishonorable, it does not necessarily suggest lying. Nothing in the paragraph suggests options (3) and (5). Option (4) cannot be assumed because, although the tribes received supplies from the government, this does not necessarily indicate that they were starving.

GED Mini-Test (Pages 56–57)

1. **(3) Businesses could send and receive orders more quickly than by letter.** (Analysis) The telegraph provided much quicker communication than the mail did. Options (1) and (5) are incorrect because this innovation did not affect how many employees a business needed or the productivity of the workforce. Even though options (2) and (4) would make businesses more efficient, they are not related to the telegraph.

2. **(5) to tell the station if a train would be late** (Application) A telegraph operator at one railroad station could inquire, or send status reports, about a train's progress as it traveled along the railroad line. This would permit people to know whether the train was on schedule. The telegraph would not assist in the functions listed in options (1), (2), (3), and (4).

3. **(2) the telephone** (Application) This is the only other device that transmits messages and information over a wire. Option (1) is a means of transportation. Option (3) provides power, but does not transmit information. Option (4) also provides messages and information, but cannot transmit them over long distances. Option (5) is an entertainment and storage device.

4. **(4) Before 1861, communication between California and the eastern states was very slow.** (Analysis) This is suggested by the first and last sentences of the passage. Options (1) and (2) are directly stated in the passage. Nothing in the information indicates that options (3) and (5) are true.

5. (2) The telegraph helped connect the nation. (Comprehension) The passage focuses on construction of telegraph lines—in particular, a line connecting the East and the West. Options (1) and (3) are implied, but the passage is not primarily about Morse or the efficiency of American business. Nothing in the passage supports options (4) and (5).

6. (3) The land that formed the Gadsden Purchase lay south of the Gila River. (Evaluation) This is shown on the map and indicated by the last sentence of the first paragraph. Nothing in the passage suggests options (1), (2), and (4) are true. Because the map shows no towns at all, it is impossible to determine whether option (5) is true.

7. (1) It became part of the New Mexico Territory. (Comprehension) This is shown on the map. The map also shows that option (2) is incorrect. There is nothing in the passage or on the map to support option (3). Option (4) is incorrect because the passage shows that it was in the interests of southerners, not northerners, to obtain the land. Option (5) is incorrect because the passage states that Gadsden went to Mexico in 1853 to negotiate a deal, and the map shows that California became a state in 1850.

8. (1) the Mexican Cession (Comprehension) The information on the map and the second sentence in the passage make this connection. Options (2), (3), and (4) are incorrect because the map shows they are only part of the land ceded in the treaty. Option (5) is incorrect because it is the name of the land purchased in 1853 by the United States.

9. (4) Long-term residents suffered losses under U.S. law. (Comprehension) The passage explains that many residents in the territory acquired from Mexico lost their land because U.S. courts did not recognize their land titles. Options (1), (3), and (5) are not addressed by the paragraph. Nothing in the passage supports option (2).

Lesson 4
GED Skill Focus (Page 59)
1. **b.** Missouri sought to enter the Union as a slave state.

2. California **became a free state as a result of the Compromise of 1850.**

 Utah and New Mexico **voters could decide whether to become free or slave territories.**

3. Concern in the North about slavery was an important **cause** of the Missouri Compromise.

One **effect** of the Compromise of 1850 was that life became more difficult for runaway slaves.

GED Content Focus (Page 61)
1. **(1) They seceded from the Union.** (Comprehension) The map key indicates that these states seceded after the attack on Ft. Sumter. The map does not indicate anything about voting or secession from the Confederacy, so the other options are incorrect.

2. **(5) They remained with the Union even though they were slave states.** (Comprehension) This fact is shown on the map. Options (1), (2), and (3) are incorrect because the map shows that these states stayed with the Union. Option (4) is incorrect because the map shows nothing about joining the Union, which in fact was relevant only to the newly formed state of West Virginia.

3. **(2) They had to import most manufactured goods from the North and from Europe.** (Analysis) This is an important point made in the first paragraph. The passage does not mention options (1), (3), or (4) as possible effects of having little industry. Option (5) is incorrect because the passage states that southerners considered the election of Lincoln to be a threat to their way of life and so seven states seceded.

4. **(4) the 1860 election and Southern secession** (Analysis) These factors are discussed in paragraphs 3 and 4 as two important sparks for tension between North and South that led to war. Option (1) is an effect of the war. Option (2) is a cause for a turning point of the war. Option (3) is mentioned as a cause of tension between North and South but not as the most important causes of the war. Option (5) is incorrect because economic tension is mentioned but land scarcity is not.

GED Practice (Pages 62–63)
1. **(5) The South's war effort was weakened.** (Comprehension) The facts presented in the paragraph support this statement. Options (1), (2), (3), and (4) are the opposite of what is stated and implied in the paragraph.

2. **(2) They would not help protect slavery.** (Comprehension) The paragraph states that England had outlawed slavery in 1833. Options (1), (3), (4), and (5) are not mentioned in the paragraph.

3. **(5) The Emancipation Proclamation of 1863 did not end all slavery in the United States.** (Analysis) The fact that an amendment to the Constitution was required to outlaw slavery suggests that it continued to exist after the Emancipation Proclamation. No information

in the chart provides a basis for assuming options (1), (2), or (3). Option (4) is not correct because the chart shows that the 15th Amendment guaranteed voting rights for males, regardless of race, not to females.

4. **(3) Some states were not allowing former slaves to vote.** (Comprehension) That an amendment to the Constitution was needed suggests that African Americans were being deprived of the right to vote. Options (1) and (4) are incorrect because the amendment does not address land ownership or age. Option (2) is incorrect because the chart shows that slavery had been ended by the 13th Amendment. Option (5) cannot be supported by the information on the table.

5. **(4) the effort to reunite the nation and rebuild the South** (Comprehension) This definition is stated in the first paragraph. None of the other options gives an accurate definition of the term.

6. **(1) Radical Congressmen took over Reconstruction.** (Evaluation) The passage states that the radicals wanted to punish the South and deprive traditional leaders of their power, while Lincoln pardoned Southerners for rebelling and wanted to reunite the nation. Options (2), (3), and (4) are incorrect because they do not relate to how the South was to be treated. Option (5) does not in itself support the conclusion because the passage says nothing about why the president was assassinated.

7. **(3) a federal disaster relief agency** (Application) Providing emergency relief was the agency's only wartime function. Options (1) and (4) are incorrect because the Freedmen's Bureau did not focus on jobs and education until after the war, plus it never was a job placement agency. Option (2) is incorrect because medical care was only one part of the organization's function. Option (5) is incorrect because the Freedmen's Bureau was a public relief organization, not a private religious one.

8. **(3) White Southerners owned most of the land but had little money to pay farm workers.** (Analysis) The passage shows this to be a cause of the development of the sharecropping system. Options (1) and (4) are the opposite of what is stated in the passage. Nothing in the passage states or suggests that sharecropping developed for the reason in option (2), and there is no information presented about former slaves' moving to the North, making option (5) incorrect.

GED Mini-Test (Pages 64–65)

1. **(4) to remind Northerners of the ideals for which they were fighting** (Comprehension) Lincoln's speech drew people's attention to the principles on which the nation was founded, which were the underlying reasons for the war. This is implied in the paragraph and the excerpt from Lincoln's speech. Nothing in the excerpt supports option (1) or (3) as the main purpose of Lincoln's remarks. Option (2) is incorrect because Union prisoners held in the South would be unlikely to learn of the speech from their Southern captors. Option (5) is incorrect because the speech's tone is inspiring, not discouraging.

2. **(1) the Declaration of Independence** (Application) The statement that "all men are created equal" is the best-known phrase from the Declaration of Independence. None of the documents in options (2), (3), (4), and (5) includes this phrase.

3. **(3) They made it easier for Lee to surrender.** (Analysis) Grant's generous terms made it easier for Lee to surrender than would harsh terms, which might have encouraged Lee to hold out longer. Therefore, option (4) is incorrect. Although the passage describes Lee as grateful, no information supports either option (1) or option (2). Option (5) is contradicted by the last sentence of the passage.

4. **(4) Lee knew his army was in trouble.** (Comprehension) If Lee had been planning to fight on or escape, he would likely not have requested a meeting with Grant. Options (2) and (5) are therefore incorrect. No evidence is provided to indicate option (1) or (3).

5. **(2) The federal government lost interest in the welfare of Southern African Americans.** (Analysis) The passage shows that the federal government did not object to the steps taken by Southern whites to deny rights to African Americans. Options (1), (3), and (4) are the opposite of what is stated in the passage. Nothing in the passage suggests option (5).

6. **(3) Southern African Americans did not share equally in the region's growing prosperity.** (Analysis) Because white Southerners blocked African Americans from sharing political power and social equality, it can be reasonably assumed that they did not share equally in the South's economic growth either. Options (1), (2), and (4) are incorrect because they are contradicted in the passage. No information in the passage supports option (5).

7. **(4) number of factories** (Comprehension) The graphs show that the North had a major advantage over the South in each area, but the

difference is greatest in the number of factories. Therefore, the other options are incorrect.

8. **(3) It helps explain why the North eventually won the war.** (Evaluation) Farms and factories provide food, weapons, and supplies for armies. A country's troops come from its population. Railroads facilitate the movement of these troops and goods to where they are needed. This information does not explain options (1), (4), and (5), however. Option (2) is incorrect because the inequities would suggest a short war rather than a long one.

Lesson 5
GED Skill Focus (Page 67)
1. **a.** Factory owners valued the efficient production of goods.

2. **b.** In the late 1800s, more and more women took jobs as a way to help their families survive.

3. **a.** *T:* After the Industrial Revolution, society valued manufacturing more than farming.

   b. *F:* After the Industrial Revolution, handmade goods were valued more than factory-made products.

GED Content Focus (Page 69)
1. **(5) They raised large sums of money to develop industries and reduced individual financial risk.** (Comprehension) This is stated directly in the second paragraph. Options (1), (2), (3), and (4) may be true of corporations, but none of these is mentioned in the passage as a contribution of corporations to industrial growth.

2. **(3) innovations in manufacturing and the use of electricity** (Analysis) Both of these are mentioned in the first paragraph as contributing to economic development. Options (1) and (4) are possible effects of economic development. Option (2) is mentioned as part of the pre-Civil War economy, not a cause of the new economy. Neither item in option (5) is mentioned as a cause of economic development.

3. **(4) Workers who negotiate as a group could bargain more effectively than individual workers.** (Evaluation) This is the only option supported by the passage. It is demonstrated in the last paragraph. Though all the other options might improve conditions for workers, they do not summarize the basic value underlying the labor union movement, as described in the passage.

4. **(2) an interest in technological innovation** (Evaluation) This is the only statement that accurately reflects the information presented in

the graph. Patents are concerned with inventions and innovation, and the graph indicates enormous growth in the number of patents approved by the government. The graph does not indicate anything about big business (option 1), worker safety (option 3), education (option 4), or government regulation (option 5).

GED Practice (Pages 70–71)
1. **(3) The union would lose members.** (Application) When unions lose strikes, they lose members. As the passage points out, a series of unsuccessful strikes was part of the reason for the decline of the Knights of Labor. It stands to reason that workers would become discouraged about unions if the actions of the unions did not help the workers. Option (1) is incorrect because losing strikes would not lead to higher wages. Nothing in the passage suggests that option (2), (4), or (5) is generally true about labor unions.

2. **(5) passage of the National Labor Relations Act** (Analysis) The graph shows that union membership went up during this period. The passage states that the act was passed in 1935 and that it gave workers the legal right to join unions. Options (1) and (3) are incorrect because they occurred well before 1935. Option (2) is not correct, because failure of strikes probably would have caused union membership to fall rather than rise. Nothing in the passage suggests that option (4) was a cause of the growth of unions.

3. **(4) They were discouraged by violent strikes.** (Evaluation) The passage states that membership in the Knights declined after a series of violent strikes. This suggests that workers were discouraged by strikes and violence. The passage also suggests that the AFL's success was due to stressing cooperation over confrontation. Nothing in the passage supports options (1), (3), and (5). Option (2) is contradicted by the information about the Knights.

4. **(2) job opportunities** (Analysis) According to the passage, job opportunities lured people to the cities. Nothing in the passage suggests that option (1), (3), or (5) was related to the growth of cities. The unhealthy conditions that resulted from overcrowding were effects of the rapid growth of large cities, not the cause of them, so option (4) is incorrect.

5. **(3) 1920** (Comprehension) Just over 50 percent of Americans were urban residents in 1920. Options (1) and (2) are incorrect because the graph shows fewer Americans living in cities at those times. Options (4) and (5) are later years in which city dwellers outnumbered rural residents.

6. **(4) World War II** (Analysis) The graph shows a major increase in urban population during

that decade, and the passage suggests that African-American urban migration occurred during World War II because of wartime job opportunities. Option (1) relates to the late 1800s. Options (2) and (5) are incorrect because they were events of World War I and the 1920s. Nothing in the passage supports option (3) as a cause of urban growth.

7. **(1) Jobs were important to African Americans.** (Evaluation) According to the passage, the Great Migration was inspired by the job opportunities that existed in Northern industries during World War I and in the 1920s, when immigration was restricted. This suggests that the people who moved North did so because good jobs were important to them. Option (3) is incorrect because the Great Migration occurred despite overcrowded living conditions in urban areas. The Great Migration was the relocating of African Americans, not of immigrants, so options (2) and (4) are incorrect. Option (5) is incorrect because transportation systems are not mentioned in the passage.

GED Mini-Test (Pages 72–73)

1. **(5) The Development of Mass Production** (Comprehension) The passage focuses on the ideas and manufacturing processes that made possible the rapid production of large quantities of goods—in other words, mass production. Option (1) is incorrect because the passage is not solely about Whitney. Option (2) is one part of the explanation of mass production, and option (3) is only casually mentioned. Although option (4) may be true, it is not discussed in the passage.

2. **(2) Efficiency was important.** (Evaluation) This is the only conclusion that is supported by the passage. Mass production was more efficient than was making products by hand. The information in the passage does not suggest that owners held the values expressed in options (1), (3), (4), or (5).

3. **(1) power** (Evaluation) The evidence in the passage indicates that Rockefeller valued power most of all. Options (2) and (4) cannot be established from the information presented. The information strongly indicates that options (3) and (5) are incorrect.

4. **(4) Rockefeller established an oil trust.** (Analysis) The discussion of trusts and their tendency to result in monopolies is followed by the information that Rockefeller controlled nearly 90 percent of the oil business, making this conclusion a reasonable one. The passage does not charge Rockefeller with theft, so option (1) is incorrect. No information in the passage supports options (2), (3), or (5).

5. **(5) shoes** (Application) Leather goods would need a heavy needle and strong pressure to make the holes for the thread. Options (1) and (2) are lightweight products. Options (3) and (4) are not made by sewing and are also lightweight.

6. **(2) The power of trusts is threatening the American way of life.** (Comprehension) In the cartoon, all the trusts on the Statue of Liberty are about to sink the symbol of the people's liberty. Option (1) is not correct because the cartoon's message is that the trusts are responsible for this condition. Option (3) is not expressed in the cartoon. Options (4) and (5) are incorrect because the trusts are causing the Statue of Liberty to sink.

7. **(3) unhealthful meat-packing practices** (Comprehension) The references to filthy plant conditions and the Pure Food and Drug Act substantiate this conclusion. Nothing in the passage suggests options (1), (4), and (5). Option (2) refers to the work of another author.

8. **(2) making people aware of serious problems** (Analysis) The passage shows that the work of the muckrakers made government officials and citizens aware of problems in industry and government. Information presented in the passage shows that options (1), (3), and (5) are not correct. There is no evidence presented that the muckrakers' work caused riots, so option (4) is incorrect.

9. **(1) a TV news investigation of a major polluter** (Application) This is the only example of the muckrakers' technique of investigating and reporting on serious problems. Option (2) is incorrect because a police investigation is a formal government investigation. Option (3) is the result of scientific research, not investigative reporting. Options (4) and (5) are not muckraking. They are the likely effects of muckraking.

Lesson 6
GED Skill Focus (Page 75)

1. **a.** The United States won the Spanish-American War in 1898 and became known as a world power.

2. **b.** The war lasted only three months and few U.S. soldiers died.

3. Possible answers should include two of the following: The U.S. dominated Cuba; the U.S. took over Puerto Rico, Guam, and the Philippines; the U.S. expanded its import-export markets.

GED Content Focus (Page 77)

1. **(3) why it was hard for the United States to remain neutral during World War I** (Analysis) This is the only statement that is

explained in the paragraph. Three reasons are given for U.S. involvement in the war. Options (1), (2), (4), and (5) are important issues about the war, but none is explained in the first paragraph.

2. **(4) The war caused massive destruction.** (Analysis) This statement is a judgment about the war supported by many facts and details. It draws together the details in the passage. Options (1), (2), and (3) are details that support the conclusion that the war caused massive destruction. Option (5) is a fact about the war that does not relate to the conclusion.

3. **(2) business interests and concerns about human lives** (Evaluation) These values are mentioned in the first paragraph (interference with trading relationships; concern for the loss of innocent lives). Option (1) is not discussed in he passage. Option (3) is a reason World War II broke out, and option (4) describes Germany's aim prior to and during World War II. Option (5) is a reason for the Cold War.

4. **(4) The United States and the Soviet Union each believed its political system was the better one.** (Analysis) This assumption underlies the idea, stated in the fourth paragraph, that each country tried to spread its influence wherever it could. Option (1) is not unstated and also is not connected with the Cold War in the passage. The passage offers no support for options (2), (3), or (5).

5. **(1) Together, the allied nations controlled Berlin.** (Analysis) This is the big idea, or conclusion, that the details of the map add up to. Options (3) and (4) are incorrect because the map shows West Berlin divided between French, British, and American sectors. It does not indicate that any one or two of the nations dominated. Option (2) is incorrect, since the map does not show West Germany. Option (5) is not supported because the map focuses only on Berlin and does not show East Germany as a whole.

GED Content Focus (Page 79)

1. **(5) what some of the country's biggest environmental problems are** (Analysis) The passage states that the EPA was established to enforce environmental protection laws. Because the EPA focuses on these particular environmental problems, you can conclude that they are among the biggest ones. Options (1), (2), and (4) are incorrect because the information in the table doesn't answer any "why" questions. It merely lists the laws and what they are intended to accomplish. Options (3) and (4) are incorrect because the table covers more than just hazardous waste sites or air and water pollution.

2. **(2) Suburban growth contributes to congestion, pollution, and economic segregation.** (Analysis) This is a judgment based on the facts and details in the passage. It's the broader statement that the details add up to. Options (1), (3), (4), and (5) are incorrect because they are the facts or details that support the conclusion.

3. **(3) the belief that all people are equal and deserve decent food, shelter, and health care** (Evaluation) These values underlie the Civil Rights Act and the War on Poverty. Option (1) reflects FDR's reaction to the Great Depression; it is not related to these programs. Option (2) is incorrect because it relates to the environmental protection laws. Options (4) and (5) are values underlying the Civil Rights Act but are not directly related to the War on Poverty.

4. **(1) polluted air, water, and land** (Analysis) The passage says the public was becoming anxious about pollution of the environment, and the table focuses on air and water pollution and solid and hazardous waste as types of environmental problems. Options (2), (3), and (4) are incorrect because neither the passage nor the table links these concerns to Nixon or the EPA. Option (5) is incorrect because neither the passage nor the text mentions the effectiveness of environmental protection laws.

GED Practice (Pages 80–81)

1. **(5) One out of four workers was unemployed.** (Evaluation) Only this detail is characteristic of a depression. Option (1) is incorrect because prosperity is the opposite of depression. Options (2), (3), and (4) are all true, but none suggests that the United States was in a depression in the 1930s.

2. **(2) Hitler and Mussolini planned to restore prosperity at the expense of other countries.** (Evaluation) The passage suggests that to solve their nations' problems, Hitler and Mussolini took actions in the 1930s that threatened other countries. Any leader's actions that threaten to lead to war can be viewed as "extreme." The other options are true, but none of them provides evidence to support the writer's conclusions about Hitler and Mussolini.

3. **(3) a major decrease in spending by Americans** (Analysis) The passage states that decreased spending led to reduced production, which was responsible for layoffs and high unemployment. The end result of this cycle of economic slowdown is a depression. According to the passage, options (1), (4), and (5) were effects of the depression, not causes of it. Option (2) is true, but the passage does not show a cause-and-effect relationship between it and the depression.

4. **(1) The war effort required troops and manufactured goods, which created many jobs.** (Analysis) As the war escalated, Americans joined the military and got jobs in the booming war industries manufacturing the supplies needed for the troops to fight the war, unemployment fell, and Americans again had money to spend pulling the American economy out of the depression. Options (2) and (3) are incorrect because, although true, they would have no major effect on employment and the nation's economy. Nothing in the passage suggests that option (4) is the answer. Option (5) is contradicted by the information presented.

5. **(5) the National Recovery Administration** (Comprehension) The chart shows that this program established codes of fair competition for companies in various industries. Competition would break down monopolies. None of the programs listed in options (1), (2), (3), and (4) deal with the issues of monopoly or competition.

6. **(2) Many New Deal programs were so effective that they were retained after the Great Depression.** (Evaluation) The information in the passage best supports this conclusion; in fact, several of the programs on the chart still exist today. Option (1) is incorrect because the chart shows that each of Roosevelt's stated goals for the New Deal was addressed by at least one of the programs listed. There is not enough information to determine if options (3), (4), and (5) are true.

7. **(3) the Federal Emergency Relief Administration** (Analysis) Only this program provided direct handouts to people for nothing in return. This would have troubled critics who were concerned about the New Deal's effect on Americans' self-reliance. Options (1) and (4) are incorrect because those programs involved work and jobs. Options (2) and (5) are incorrect because the passage and chart establish that those programs were not related to self-reliance, the issue the critics were concerned about.

8. **(2) the Federal Emergency Relief Administration** (Application) The chart shows that this program provided money and other charity to people in need. Options (1), (4), and (5) are incorrect because these programs relate to the way business operates. Option (3) is not correct because the program provided employment for only one category of worker and did not provide other types of aid.

GED Mini-Test (Pages 82–83)

1. **(3) Before the nation could enjoy better times, it had to deal with problems resulting from the war.** (Evaluation) The supporting statements detail the difficulties of the shift from war to peace. The 1920s was marked by competition for jobs and retooling of industries, so option (1) is not true. Option (2) is a broad generalization that cannot be made from the details in the passage. Option (4) is incorrect because the paragraph does not refer to the entire decade, only the early 1920s. Option (5) cannot be supported from the information provided.

2. **(1) Unemployment was high for a few years after World War I.** (Analysis) This conclusion is supported by the statement that returning soldiers were seeking jobs at the same time industries were laying off wartime workers. Nothing in the paragraph suggests option (2), (3), (4), or (5) is true.

3. **(5) demands of women and minorities for equal job opportunity in the 1970s** (Application) In both cases, groups of people were struggling to achieve economic opportunity and success. Options (1), (3), and (4) are not correct because these were political struggles rather than economic ones. Option (2) is incorrect because the 1920s conflict was not over slavery and freedom.

4. **(2) Strikes were part of a communist plot.** (Analysis) The "Red" flag arising from the strike at the steel mill, coupled with the stated information linking strikes, communism, revolution, and the Red Scare support this conclusion. Nothing in the cartoon or the information presented suggests that option (1), (3), (4), or (5) is correct.

5. **(3) Mississippi** (Comprehension) The map shows that only 4 percent of African Americans in Mississippi were registered to vote in 1960, and 6 percent in 1964. This was by far the lowest rate of all the Southern states. Options (1), (2), (4), and (5) are not correct because significantly higher percentages of African Americans in each of those states were registered to vote.

6. **(5) Texas** (Analysis) The passage states that the 24th Amendment ended the poll tax in 1964. The map shows that 14 percent more African Americans in Texas were registered to vote that year than were registered in 1960. Options (1), (2), and (3) are not correct because the map shows that those states did not have a poll tax. Option (4) is incorrect because the end of the poll tax in Virginia increased African American voter registration by only 6 percent.

7. **(2) North Carolina had no poll tax.** (Analysis) The map shows that Alabama had a poll tax, but that North Carolina did not. Consequently African Americans in North Carolina had a longer history of voter participation, as the map data indicate. Options (1) and (4) are incorrect because they both

describe events that occurred in 1965, and so have no bearing on voter registration in 1960 or 1964. Options (3) and (5) are true but have no relationship to why fewer African Americans in Alabama were registered to vote.

Unit 1 Cumulative Review (Pages 84–92)

1. **(3) Christopher Columbus and His Work** (Comprehension) This title sums up the main idea of these paragraphs. Options (1) and (5) are incorrect because they are too broad to be the titles of this passage. Options (2) and (4) are minor points of information that are not the focus of the passage.

2. **(5) Columbus's voyages were crucial to history.** (Analysis) In the last sentence of the passage, the writer concludes that no matter what your opinion of Columbus, his voyages changed the course of history. Options (1), (2), (3), and (4) are all facts stated in the passage.

3. **(4) France, England, and Spain were major European colonizers of eastern North America.** (Analysis) The map shows that these three nations established colonies in eastern North America in the late 1500s and the early 1600s, supporting the conclusion that these nations were major colonizers of the region. Options (1), (2), and (3) are not conclusions but are facts that support the conclusion in option (4). Option (5) is a conclusion that cannot be supported from the information given on the map.

4. **(2) religious** (Evaluation) Wanting to convert other people reflects one type of religious value. The values listed in the other options do not relate to the situation and so are incorrect.

5. **(1) economic** (Evaluation) Wanting to find gold and other resources reflects motivation by economic values. Such goals have nothing to do with the values mentioned in option (2), (3), (4), or (5).

6. **(5) social** (Evaluation) The main purpose of this relocation was to get away from the problems of city life and live in a better society which reflect social values. The values listed in options (1), (2), (3), and (4) do not relate to such goals.

7. **(3) They wanted religious freedom.** (Analysis) This option is correct because the first paragraph states that the Quakers were persecuted for their religious beliefs. Options (1), (2), and (5) are incorrect because they were details related to the Quakers' settling in America, but not the cause of it. Option (4) is not supported by any information in the passage.

8. **(2) Penn got land in repayment of a royal debt.** (Analysis) Although all the options are true, only this one provides strong evidence of

the Quakers' special luck. Other groups also moved to America, so option (1) does not make the Quakers especially lucky. Options (3) and (5) are incorrect because the Quakers worked at keeping the peace and being tolerant; it was not a matter of luck. Option (4) relates to what happened after the Quakers arrived and is not related to luck.

9. **(4) defending himself from a group of colonists** (Comprehension) The paragraph states that some colonists protested having to pay the taxes. The cartoon shows that sometimes their protests took the form of violent attacks against a tax collector. Here the excise man is being attacked and is trying to defend himself. Options (1), (2), and (3) are incorrect because a group (the Bostonians) is acting on an individual figure (the tax collector), not vice versa. Option (5) is not correct because although the cartoon shows something coming out of the tax collector's mouth, nothing suggests that the tax collector is becoming intoxicated.

10. **(4) The Bostonians look like they are cruel.** (Analysis) The cartoonist gives the colonists' faces leering, cruel expressions. This is the best indication that the cartoonist is sympathetic to the tax collector. Options (1), (2), and (3) indicate that the Bostonians are treating the tax collector harshly, but do not indicate how the cartoonist feels about the situation, either way. The hats seem realistic in terms of colonial dress and do not appear to be symbolic of evil or of anything else, so option (5) is incorrect.

11. **(2) respect for the law** (Evaluation) Since the cartoonist shows, by the leering, cruel faces of the colonists, that he or she is not sympathetic with the colonists and dislikes their lawless actions, you can infer that the cartoonist is trying to inspire the opposite value—respect for the law. There is no evidence in the cartoon that the cartoonist is trying to inspire the values listed in option (1), (3), (4), or (5).

12. **(1) They were helped by some colonists.** (Analysis) Since some colonists remained loyal to the king, it is reasonable to assume that these colonists would have helped the British. No information in the paragraph supports option (2). Options (3), (4), and (5) are incorrect assumptions because the British and loyalists were on the same side, and because the war was between the patriots and the British.

13. **(2) They fought against the British.** (Analysis) The paragraph states that the colonists were divided during the war into loyalists and patriots. It further states that the loyalists supported the British king and the patriots favored independence. Taken together, these sentences imply that the patriots were fighting

against the British. Option (1) is incorrect because the last two sentences of the paragraph state that fewer than half the colonists were patriots and the others were either loyalists or did not take sides. So patriots must have taken a side in the war. Options (3) and (4) would have been true of loyalists, not patriots. The patriots favored independence, which makes option (5) incorrect.

14. **(5) The war caused deep divisions in America.** (Analysis) The paragraph provides no information about the relative proportion of loyalists to uncommitted colonists, except that together they make up more than half of the population, so options (1) and (3) are incorrect. Option (2) is incorrect because it is contradicted by the statement that fewer than half the colonists were patriots. The passage states that during the war, the colonists split into three groups and that no side had a large majority. These statements support the conclusion that the war divided the nation and contradict option (4) that the war united the colonists.

15. **(2) Writers of the Constitution compromised to plan a government that all states would accept.** (Comprehension) This is the emphasis of the paragraph. Options (1) and (3) are facts in the paragraph that support the main idea. Option (4) is the implied goal of writing the Constitution, but this goal was not the main focus of the paragraph. Option (5) is an opinion about the Constitution that the writer of the paragraph might agree with, but it is not a summary of the information presented.

16. **(2) slavery** (Comprehension) The paragraph says that the delegates compromised on many issues but left slavery unresolved for fear that if they tried to address this issue, they risked the rejection of their new plan for government. Options (1), (3), and (4) are incorrect, since these issues are not discussed in the paragraph. The issue in option (5) was the main goal of the delegates, and the paragraph states that they successfully met this goal with the writing and acceptance of the Constitution.

17. **(4) respect for open debate** (Evaluation) The publication of editorials representing both sides of the ratification issue indicates a strong respect for open debate. Although option (1), love of language, is a value reflected in the publication of many types of writing, it is not the strongest value because editorials focus on presenting opinions. Option (2) is incorrect because the publishing of editorials was not a new practice. Option (3) is incorrect because editorials, by definition, are not objective. Option (5) is incorrect because the publishing of clashing editorials indicates the opposite of a wish for conformity.

18. **(5) Ratification was easy in the first five states but difficult in the last eight.** (Analysis) The chart shows that the Constitution passed unanimously in three of the first five states and with a two-thirds majority or more in the other two of the first five. This information supports the first half of the conclusion. The chart also shows that the vote was much closer in five of the last eight states, supporting the idea that in these states, debate was more fierce, the last part of the conclusion. Option (4) is the opposite of what the chart shows. Options (1), (2), and (3) are facts given in the chart, with options (2) and (3) supporting the conclusion given in option (5).

19. **(5) Union army generals** (Comprehension) The clue to this is the name tag on the doll representing McClellan. Options (1) and (2) are incorrect because the dolls represent people. Options (3) and (4) are incorrect because ordinary soldiers were not famous enough to be recognized by name.

20. **(3) President Lincoln** (Comprehension) The cartoon's caption gives the clue to the figure's identity. Options (1), (2), (4), and (5) are not supported by the paragraph or the cartoon and its caption.

21. **(1) The Union suffered unnecessary defeats early in the war.** (Analysis) The fact that Lincoln cast so many generals aside like dolls on the shelf suggests that the war did not go well for the Union at first. The paragraph also confirms this conclusion with the statement about lost opportunities to stop the Confederates. The paragraph and cartoon give no information about feelings of Union or Confederate soldiers, so options (2) and (3) are not supported. Option (4) is contradicted by the paragraph, and the paragraph gives no information related to option (5).

22. **(5) to reinstate a labor system similar to slavery** (Analysis) The Black Codes denied basic human rights and freedoms, setting up a labor system that resembled slavery. Option (1) is not the best choice, because, although the Black Codes related to jobs for former slaves, they put limits on their opportunities for employment. Option (2) is incorrect, because the Black Codes were set up in the South, not in the North. Option (3) was an effect of the Black Codes, but certainly not their original intent. Option (4) is incorrect because the Black Codes were designed to prevent the changes Reconstruction would bring.

23. **(4) a concern for justice** (Evaluation) Since the Black Codes did away with basic rights for former slaves, nullification of the Black Codes by

the federal government reflects a concern that former slaves be treated justly and recover their basic rights. Option (1) is incorrect because in abolishing the Black Codes, the federal government overruled local law and customs. Options (2) and (3) are incorrect because neither religion nor education was regulated by the Black Codes. Option (5) is incorrect because in this instance, the federal government did not compromise with white Southerners who drew up the codes.

24. **(4) a part of the Sioux nation** (Analysis) The writer's use of the terms "Lakota Sioux" and "Lakota warriors" implies that Lakota was a part of the Sioux nation. Nothing in the passage suggests that option (1), (2), or (3) is correct. Option (5) is incorrect because the passage's use of "Cheyenne and Lakota warriors" makes it clear that they are distinct groups.

25. **(3) Sitting Bull and Crazy Horse fought to preserve the lands and ways of their people.** (Comprehension) The passage focuses on ways that both leaders tried to resist white encroachment on their lands and their lives. Options (1), (2), (4), and (5) are all facts that are found in the passage, but they are not its central idea.

26. **(5) the Sioux ways of life** (Evaluation) Sitting Bull resisted government attempts to force his people to live like whites. This resistance clearly shows options (2), (3), and (4) to be incorrect. Nothing in the passage supports option (1).

27. **(1) Some cities had mass transit by the 1890s.** (Analysis) The table's information about street railway, or streetcar, workers provides the evidence for this option. Since the table gives information only about average pay of people in the occupations listed, not about numbers of people employed, option (3) is incorrect. Option (4) is contradicted by the figures in the table. There is no information in the table to support options (2) and (5).

28. **(3) City jobs generally paid better wages.** (Analysis) Most of the jobs listed are in the city and pay more than farm labor. There is no support in the table for options (1) and (2). The table does not indicate whether the teacher wages are for urban or rural teachers, so there is no evidence for option (4). Option (5) is incorrect because the table does not suggest how many postal positions (the only government job listed) were available.

29. **(2) African Americans were not generally admitted to colleges attended by white students.** (Analysis) The passage implies that

Washington was addressing a need for black colleges. Options (1) and (5) are the opposite of what is implied in the passage. The passage offers no information to support option (3), and nothing in the passage indicates that option (4) had occurred at this time.

30. **(4) skilled factory work** (Analysis) Together with academic subjects, Tuskegee students learned a skilled trade that they could use to get jobs in industry. Options (1), (2), (3), and (5) are possible but are not supported by the information in the passage.

31. **(3) The 1916 election was close, with Democrats winning over Republicans and two small parties.** (Comprehension) This option sums up the main idea about the outcome of the presidential election of 1916 as illustrated by the graph. Options (1) and (2) are details that are included in the graph, but they are not the main idea. Option (4) is an incorrect summary of the information the graph presents. Option (5) is not the main idea of the graph.

32. **(5) Neither Party had very much support.** (Analysis) The small percentage of voters for each Party shown on the graph indicates neither Party had much support. Options (1) and (4), although they may be accurate, cannot be determined from the information on the graph. Options (2) and (3) are both inaccurate, based on the information on the graph.

33. **(4) A bushel of corn bought much less in 1921 than it did in 1919.** (Analysis) This fact indicates that farmers faced hard times, since their crops could not buy as much as they did in the previous decade. Options (1), (2), (3), and (5) are true but support the opposite conclusion, since they indicate prosperity.

34. **(5) The prosperity of the 1920s was not shared by all Americans.** (Analysis) The passage identifies three groups—New England factory workers, farmers, and coal miners—that did not do well. Option (1) cannot be determined from the passage. Options (2), (3), and (4) are contradicted by the information provided.

35. **(5) The war ended in a stalemate and Korea remained divided.** (Comprehension) This option is supported by the last paragraph, which states that after three years of fighting, the war ended by a negotiated settlement that maintained the border close to what it was before the war (implying a stalemate) and that the nation was still split in two. Options (1), (2), (3), and (4) are not correct because there was no clear winner of the war and Korea did not come under control of a single government.

36. **(3) South Korea was not a democracy before the Korean War.** (Analysis) This is suggested by the last sentences of the first and third paragraphs. No evidence is offered to support options (2) and (4). Options (1) and (5) are contradicted by information in the passage.

37. **(1) The French were fighting the communists.** (Comprehension) This reason is given in the first paragraph. Option (2) is the opposite of what the paragraph states. Options (3) and (4) are not true and are not reasons the passage states that the United States supported France. Option (5) may well have been true, but the United States supplied France only with equipment and supplies, not soldiers, so this would not be a reason the United States supported France.

38. **(3) U.S. involvement increased gradually.** (Analysis) The passage shows that involvement grew from providing military supplies in the years after World War II and a few advisers in the 1950s to providing a half-million combat troops by 1968. Nothing in the passage supports option (1), although it is true. Options (2) and (4) are contradicted by information in the passage. Since the passage says that Americans were sharply divided over the war, option (5) would not be a valid conclusion.

39. **(4) about 400,000** (Comprehension) The graph shows that about 600,000 Americans were killed or missing in World War II and about 200,000 in World War I, a difference of about 400,000. Options (1) and (2) both involve a misreading of the graph, which measures casualties in hundreds of thousands, not in thousands. Options (3) and (5) are incorrect because they are the numbers killed or missing in each of the two wars, not the difference between the two.

40. **(4) the Vietnam War** (Comprehension) You can determine the proportion of dead or missing to the total casualties by comparing the black part of the bar graph (representing the dead or missing) to the total bar (representing total casualties). The graph shows that for the Vietnam War, the black section is the smallest both absolutely and proportionately when compared with the total. The other four options are incorrect.

41. **(3) World War II was the most costly U.S. war of the twentieth century in terms of human lives.** (Analysis) The graph shows that more Americans died in this war than in the others. Option (1) is contradicted by the graph information. Options (2), (4), and (5) cannot be determined from the information on the graph.

UNIT 2: WORLD HISTORY
Lesson 7
GED Skill Focus (Page 97)

1. **a.** *D:* The Nile Valley's floods were caused by rains falling near the Nile River's source.

   b. *I:* A pharaoh's popularity and power depended on the flooding of the Nile.

2. **a.** *I:* Most Egyptians lived along the Nile River.

   b. *I:* Most of ancient Egypt was desert.

3. **c.** *I:* Ancient Egyptian civilization centered along the Nile.

GED Content Focus (Page 99)

1. **(2) War chariots gave the invaders an advantage over the people of the region.** (Comprehension) By noting that the invaders had war chariots, the writer suggests that the chariots were a major factor in their conquest. Options (1) and (3) are not implications because the sentence provides this information directly. Option (4) is not an implication because the sentence contradicts it by stating that the Shang were rulers, not a people. Nothing in the sentence suggests the conclusion in option (5).

2. **(3) The Sumerians fought over water because floods were unpredictable and water was scarce.** (Comprehension) The writer connects flooding and fighting in a single sentence, suggesting that they were related. Options (1), (2), and (4) are not implications because they are directly stated in the paragraph. Nothing in the paragraph hints at option (5).

3. **(5) River valleys were critical to the development of early civilizations.** (Comprehension) The fact that all the civilizations on the map were located in river valleys, and that no other civilizations are shown, suggests the importance of this type of location. Option (1) is directly stated by the map title. Option (2) is correct, but the map provides no clue about what river valley people did for a living. Nothing about the map suggests option (3) or (4).

4. **(2) Mohenjo-Daro and Harappa had water and sewer systems.** (Analysis) The implication is that the two cities shown on the map are "the two great cities" noted in the passage. There is no information in the passage or on the map about where people migrated from, so option (1) is incorrect; where the majority of people lived, so option (3) is incorrect, or what jobs they worked at, so options (4) and (5) are incorrect.

5. **(1) Some of the population were city dwellers.** (Application) The map establishes that all three river valley civilizations had cities, suggesting that this was a common characteristic of early advanced civilizations. Option (2) is not likely because it was not even common to all of the civilizations discussed. Options (3), (4), and (5) are not mentioned in or implied by the passage as characteristic of these civilizations either.

6. **(2) Establishing agriculture was an important early step in developing an advanced culture.** (Evaluation) The passage states that agriculture was important in the early development of all four of the ancient cultures. This suggests that it was important to the development of civilization in general. Option (1) is incorrect because the map and passage show that all four civilizations started along rivers, suggesting the general importance of water to the development of early civilizations. The discussion of irrigation in the passage contradicts option (3). Option (4) is incorrect because nothing in the information suggests that early peoples practiced democracy or that democracy and advanced culture were related. Information in the passage about invaders in Sumeria and China contradicts option (5).

GED Practice (Pages 100–101)
1. **(2) The English word *democracy* comes from the Greek term meaning "the people."** (Comprehension) By providing the Greek term *demos* and its meaning as a lead-in to discussing Greek democracy, the author hints at the word's origin rather than directly stating the connection. Nothing in the passage suggests that option (1) is true. The passage does not touch on the size of the city-states, so option (3) is incorrect. Option (4) is a judgment, and there is no statement in the passage that hints that the writer holds this opinion. Option (5) is contradicted by information in the passage.

2. **(5) The early Greeks influenced modern science.** (Analysis) The chart states the important scientific contributions of Democritus and Hippocrates. Option (1) is wrong because the chart does not tell where the playwrights came from. Nothing in the chart suggests or supports option (2), (3), or (4).

3. **(3) its democratic form of government** (Comprehension) The writer hints at this relationship by connecting Athens as the greatest Greek democracy and Athens as the center of the Golden Age. There is no mention of option (1) in the passage. There is nothing to suggest that option (2) is true. Option (4) is incorrect because the passage states that such rivalries helped end

Athens' leadership rather than promoting it. No information in the passage connects option (5) to Athens.

4. **(1) It was located in North Africa.** (Comprehension) The statement that Rome gained control of North Africa by defeating Carthage suggests the city's location. Option (2) is incorrect because it is directly stated in the passage. Nothing in the passage suggests option (3). Option (4) is incorrect because the passage suggests that the conquests in Greece, Spain, and present-day Turkey were even more responsible for this outcome. The passage directly contradicts option (5).

5. **(4) the justices of the Supreme Court, who determine if laws agree with the Constitution** (Application) The chart states that the praetors interpreted questions about the law. None of the officials described in options (1), (2), (3), and (5) perform this type of legal function: the consuls were most like the U.S. President; the Senate and popular assemblies were most like Congress; and there were no officials in Rome like the members of the state legislatures or governors.

6. **(2) political and military power** (Evaluation) The information in the chart and passage leads to the conclusion that control of their leaders and creation of an empire were important to Romans. No information supports options (1) and (4). Option (3) is contradicted by the passage. Although it is true that the Romans did value Greek art and culture, nothing in the chart or passage supports option (5).

GED Mini-Test (Pages 102–103)
1. **(4) Some rulers of Egypt were black.** (Comprehension) The passage states that Kush, which was a kingdom of black Africans called Nubians, conquered and ruled Egypt for a time. This means that Egypt's rulers would have been Nubians (who were black) during that period. Option (1) is incorrect because it is directly stated in the passage. The information in the passage provides no hint of options (2) and (5). Option (3) is contradicted by the passage.

2. **(3) The Nok were more advanced than other peoples in West Africa.** (Comprehension) The passage states that the Nok were the exception in West Africa because of their agriculture, their first manufacture of iron, and their art. This implies that they were more advanced than their neighbors. Option (1) is not an implication because it is directly stated in the passage. Option (2) is not an implication because it is contradicted by the stated information. Nothing in the passage suggests option (4) or (5).

3. **(5) It was heavily forested in most areas, but there were some farmers and herders.** (Comprehension) The passage indicates that lack of forest-cleaning tools slowed farming in the interior of Africa, but that there was some farming and herding in the Sahel and among the Nok. Option (1) is incorrect because only the Nok had manufacturing, and nothing indicates that they traded with other societies. Option (2) is contradicted by the mention of forests, grasslands, and farming by the Nok. The settlements of the Nok and in the Sahel indicate that option (3) is also incorrect. Because grasslands and herding are mentioned only in the context of the Sahel, and farming only occurred in the Sahel and among the Nok, option (4) is also incorrect.

4. **(2) Those regions were the home of the tsetse fly.** (Application) The Europeans were slowed in areas where they could not use animals. This suggests the tsetse fly as the reason, since the passage establishes that its presence was deadly to livestock. Nothing in the passage suggests options (1) and (3) as a cause of the inability to use animals for transportation. The passage also provides no basis for option (4) as an answer. Option (5) cannot be correct because these events occurred many centuries after the Nok and Kush cultures existed.

5. **(3) Farming was important in each culture.** (Analysis). Farming is the only topic in the passage that is common to all three cultures. Option (1) is incorrect because it was only noted about the Maya. The passage states that the Moche had an extensive system of roads and implies that Maya may have had roads, because they had extensive trade. But nothing about Nazca roads is stated or implied, so option (2) is incorrect. Option (4) is contradicted by information in the passage because the Mayan civilization existed in Central America, not South America. Option (5) is not the correct answer, since no information about the decline and disappearance of the Nazca and Moche is given in the passage.

6. **(2) The Aztec and Inca empires existed at the same time.** (Evaluation) The map key shows that the Aztec and Inca empires were both in existence in A.D. 1500. Option (1) is incorrect because there is no evidence on the map that there were roads between the cities or that trade went on among them. Option (3) is incorrect because the Moche roads were in South America only, while Copán was in Central America. Option (4) is not correct because the map shows

that the Aztec empire was north of Tikal. The map key shows that the Maya were active in A.D. 400, while the date for the Aztec is A.D. 1500, so option (5) is incorrect.

7. **(5) trade** (Evaluation) Roads would have made it easier for the Moche to conduct trade, so their road-building shows that trade was important to them. No connection exists between roads or road-building and the importance of options (1), (3), and (4) in a culture. Roads might have encouraged people to move to cities, but neither the passage nor the map suggest that large cities were a feature of Moche culture, so option (2) is incorrect.

Lesson 8
GED Skill Focus (Page 105)

1. *S:* This system of land in exchange for support is called feudalism.

2. *S:* The serfs performed the day-to-day work of the estate.

3. *S:* Serfs farmed the land, tended the livestock, and provided the food for the lord's table.

4. *N:* In Russia, the serfs were not freed until 1861.

5. Yes; it illustrates the relationship between king, nobles, knights, and serfs that the passage describes.

GED Content Focus (Page 107)

1. **(1) After the fall of the Roman Empire, trade in western Europe nearly disappeared.** (Evaluation) This information supports the generalization by providing an example of how trade declined when central authority disappeared. Options (2), (3), (4), and (5) are all true but have nothing to do with the relationship between trade and stable governments.

2. **(4) Lords were interested in the valuable Asian trade goods being sold throughout Europe.** (Analysis) Lords who were interested in this trade would have encouraged the development of towns as trade centers. Option (1) is incorrect because self-sufficiency is the opposite of the interdependency that trade centers create. Option (2) describes what happened in these towns later, but does not explain why lords encouraged their development in the first place. Option (3) is wrong because the declining number of serfs is an effect of town development, not a reason for it. Option (5) might help explain how an increase in trade was able to occur in the Middle Ages, but it does not explain why it centered in towns.

3. **(2) Yes, the maps illustrate French kings gaining control over French nobles.** (Evaluation) The passage states that kings formed nations by gradually gaining control over the nobles and their lands. The maps illustrate this process at work in one country. The information in options (1), (3), (4), and (5) is not presented on the maps and would not support the generalization even if were shown.

4. **(5) The growth of trade helped nations form by increasing the power of kings.** (Evaluation) This passage focuses on how the growth of towns and trade weakened feudalism and the power of feudal lords while increasing the power of kings. Kings then used this power to gain control of the lords and their land, forming nations in the process. While option (1) is true, it is incorrect because it is a detail and not the focus of the passage. Options (2) and (3) are not correct because information in the passage establishes they are untrue. No information in the passage supports option (4) as a conclusion and it is incorrect, because taxes had been levied in many places since ancient times.

GED Practice (Pages 108–109)

1. **(3) Ancient Romans were the Italians' ancestors.** (Analysis) This is an unstated connection that the writer assumes the reader will be able to make. Options (1) and (5) are incorrect because they are not true and no information in the passage would cause the reader to assume them. Option (2) is not an assumption because it is directly stated in the paragraph. Option (4) is incorrect, because paragraph 1 does not mention these artists; the information concerning da Vinci and Michelangelo is directly stated in paragraph 2.

2. **(1) The Renaissance started in Italy.** (Comprehension) The paragraph suggests this by tying the beginnings of the Renaissance to the curiosity of Italian merchants about their ancestors and to the work of the Italian humanists. No information in the passage suggests that option (2) or (5) is true. Option (3) is contradicted by information in the first paragraph. Option (4) is not implied because it is directly stated in the paragraph.

3. **(5) It explains how the Renaissance spread.** (Analysis) The passage reveals that the Renaissance began in Italy and spread across Europe. This detail helps the reader understand how that spread occurred. Options (1), (3), and (4) are incorrect because the paragraph does not provide these details. Option (2) is incorrect because knowing this detail does not help in understanding the Renaissance.

4. **(2) Venice became a Renaissance center.** (Analysis) The passage establishes that Italy was a Renaissance center and that it connected artists with wealthy merchants. Since the map establishes that Venice was a starting point for trade routes, it can be assumed that Venice was a center of trade and of the Renaissance. There is no evidence in the map or the passage for options (1) and (3). Options (4) and (5) are also wrong because the same reasoning that makes option (2) correct would lead to the assumption that Naples and Florence were Renaissance centers too.

5. **(3) the creation of the Internet** (Application) The main effect of the printing press was to spread ideas and information. Options (1) and (2) can also spread ideas and information, but not with anywhere near the scope and effect of the printing press and the Internet. Options (4) and (5) do not have this effect: shopping malls do not spread ideas, but rather make products available, and the performance of Renaissance music provides entertainment for a select audience.

6. **(2) The Growth and Spread of Islam, 650–1550** (Comprehension) The passage documents the growth and spread of Islam, establishing that Arab and Ottoman Muslims controlled the Middle East, North Africa, Spain, part of India, and eastern Europe at various times between the mid 600s and 1550. Option (1) is incorrect because the passage is about political domination and mentions only one religion, Islam. Options (3) and (4) are incorrect because the Arabs and Ottomans are both covered in the passage. Option (5) is incorrect because a larger geographical region is involved, not just North Africa.

7. **(4) The arts flourished in the Ottoman Empire.** (Evaluation) The passage talks about how important the arts, science, and learning were to Muslim culture. Since the Ottomans were Muslims, it follows that the arts flourished in the Ottoman Empire. The passage does not mention how the Turks treated the Arabs and Christians, so options (1) and (5) are incorrect. Option (2) is incorrect because the passage indicates that the Ottoman Empire did not stretch to Spain and that Arab Muslims ruled Spain centuries before the Ottoman Empire came into being. Option (3) is incorrect because the passage does mention the Renaissance in Europe.

8. **(4) knights** (Application) Like samurai, knights were feudal warriors who fought for their lords. Options (1) and (3) are wrong because merchants and kings were not professional warriors. Option (2) is wrong because the daimyos, not samurai, were the landowning nobles in

Japan. Option (5) is incorrect because although, like samurai, serfs were required to fight for their lord, samurai were not peasants.

9. **(3) A system similar to European feudalism existed in Japan.** (Evaluation) The information in the passage supports the conclusion that Japan had a feudal-like system of government. Option (1) is wrong because the information in the passage shows it to be clearly untrue. The passage establishes that the Tokugawa rulers were shoguns not emperors, so option (2) would not be a correct conclusion to draw. No information in the passage supports option (4). The passage says that the government began establishing authority over the daimyos after 1600 and that the emperor was restored to leadership by 1868, implying that the daimyos lost power, so option (5) is not a valid conclusion.

GED Mini-Test (Pages 110–111)

1. **(5) How Spain Became a Nation** (Comprehension) The passage briefly traces why Spain was divided and then goes on to detail the process by which Spain was unified. Option (1) is not discussed in the passage. Options (2) and (4) are briefly noted details, not the main idea. Option (3) is not broad enough to cover all the content presented in the passage.

2. **(2) They helped Christians unite against Muslims.** (Analysis) These marriages brought Christian kingdoms together. Nothing in the passage suggests that option (1), (4), or (5) was an effect of the marriages. Option (3) is incorrect because it is the opposite of what the passage indicates actually happened.

3. **(3) Columbus made his voyage for Spain in the same year that the last Muslim kingdom fell.** (Evaluation) Columbus' voyage does not help explain how Spain became a nation. Options (1) and (4) help explain how and why the Christians were able to unite against the Muslims. Option (2) helps explain why the Christians were successful, and option (5) might help explain why the rivalries described in option (2) existed.

4. **(1) Spain, because of the Muslims** (Application) Like Spain, Portugal had to drive out the Muslims in order to create its current national territory. Options (2) and (3) are incorrect because nothing in the passage suggests that the presence of nobles or professional soldiers like samurai had anything to do with the creation of Portugal. Options (4) and (5) are incorrect because there is no evidence in the passage that culture or trade relations were involved either.

5. **(3) the growth of the Mongol Empire** (Comprehension) The passage describes the growth of the Mongol Empire, and the map illustrates its huge span. Options (1), (4), and (5) are details that support the main idea of the passage and map. Option (2) is incorrect because the map shows the empire and makes no mention of the leaders.

6. **(4) A Mongol invasion of Japan did not succeed.** (Analysis) The passage indicates an attack on Japan, but the map shows that Japan was not part of the Mongol Empire. This leads to the assumption that the attack failed. No evidence on the map supports option (1), (2), or (3). Nothing in the passage or on the map suggests that option (5) is true.

7. **(5) The Mongols had a major impact on world history.** (Evaluation) The Mongols ruled much of Asia and all of Russia, so their influence on history was immense in its scope. Option (1) is incorrect because the size of the empire suggests that, if anything, the Mongols were good at government. Option (2) is wrong because while the passage establishes their ferocity, it does not prove that they were the fiercest of all time. Nothing in the passage suggests that the Mongols had superior technology, so option (3) is wrong. Option (4) is incorrect because the empire grew after Genghis Khan's death.

Lesson 9

GED Skill Focus (Page 113)

1. **a.** *C:* creation of the compass

   c. *C:* Europe's continuing trade with Asia

   d. *C:* development of the astrolabe

2. **b.** *I:* Europeans became more interested in the writings of ancient geographers.

3. **a.** *I:* Changes made to ships caused them to be safer and more stable in open seas.

GED Content Focus (Page 115)

1. **(4) Horses and guns were unknown to the Aztec.** (Analysis) The implied reason that Cortés was able to conquer the Aztecs rapidly is that he had horses and guns and the Aztec did not. Option (1) is contradicted by information in the passage. There is nothing in the passage to suggest that either option (2) or (5) is true. The information in option (3) is not suggested as a reason.

2. **(1) Enslaved Africans were brought to the Americas.** (Analysis) The passage states that enslaved Africans were brought to the Americas to provide labor after the native Indians died. The Columbian Exchange was a cause of the death of the American Indians, not its effect, so option (2) is incorrect. The passage does not state or suggest that option (3), (4), or (5) was a consequence of the death of so many Indians.

3. **(3) Yes, to break the Italians' monopoly on trade between Europe and Asia** (Comprehension) This cause is stated in the first paragraph of the passage. Option (1) is not stated as a cause for the voyage, although Columbus did claim and colonize lands once he had encountered them. Option (2) is incorrect because it was a result of the invasion, not a cause. Option (4) is shown on the chart as an effect of the Columbian Exchange, not as a reason for Columbus's first voyage. Option (5) is the opposite of what is stated in the first paragraph of the passage.

4. **(5) His men had guns.** (Analysis) Because Pizarro had few men and quickly conquered the Incas, it can be assumed that, like Cortes, he had guns. Option (1) is contradicted by the dates in the passage. Nothing in the passage suggests options (2) and (3). Option (4) cannot be an assumption because it is stated in the passage.

5. **(2) the introduction of tobacco to Europe, Africa, and Asia** (Analysis) The chart shows that tobacco was native to the Americas. Options (1) and (5) are wrong because the chart shows that corn and syphilis originated in the Americas. Options (3) and (4) are wrong because the chart shows that coffee and malaria came to the Americas from the continents of the Eastern Hemisphere.

6. **(3) to conquer and colonize lands for Spain** (Analysis) This cause is suggested in the first paragraph of the passage. Options (1) and (2) were some effects, not causes, of the expeditions. Nothing in the passage suggests either option (4) or (5) as a reason for these expeditions.

7. **(2) It became easier to conquer the Indians.** (Analysis) The many deaths caused by disease would have weakened the Indians' ability to fight the Spanish effectively. No cause-and-effect relationship exists between the deaths and options (1) and (4). Option (3) is wrong because disease was part of the Columbian Exchange. Option (5) is wrong because the chart and the passage establish that Europeans introduced horses to the Americas.

GED Practice (Pages 116–117)

1. **(5) imperialism in world history** (Comprehension) The passage summarizes the causes and effects of imperialism. Options (1), (2), and (4) are incorrect because they are details that provide examples of imperialism. Option (3) is wrong because it is a detail that states a cause of increased European imperialism in the 1800s.

2. **(2) Europeans felt superior to other peoples.** (Analysis) This connection is suggested by the placement of these two ideas in the paragraph. Option (1) is wrong because nothing in the passage suggests that the Europeans spread their culture because the Greeks and Romans had done so. Imperialism does not require culture to be spread, and many forms of imperialism do not involve the spread of culture, so option (3) is incorrect. Option (4) has to do with the effects of the Industrial Revolution, not with spreading culture and religion. Option (5) is incorrect because nothing in the passage suggests the people the Europeans met had no culture, and in fact they all had their own cultures.

3. **(1) Spanish soldiers conquer the Inca Empire in the 1500s.** (Application) This fits the definition of imperialism that is stated in the passage. Outright conquest is the most extreme form of imperialism. Options (2) and (4) are wrong because declaring independence and protecting the economic power of one's country do not qualify as imperialism. Option (3) is not an attempt to take over weaker nations, but instead to join with them. Option (5) is incorrect because the United States and its allies freed Kuwait and allowed it to return to its self-governing status.

4. **(2) the Industrial Revolution and the need for more markets to sell goods** (Analysis) The passage establishes that the Industrial Revolution created a need for more markets which, in turn, encouraged further imperialism. Options (1) and (5) are incorrect because nothing in the passage indicates that the other nations were lacking armies or religion. (In fact, they were lacking neither.) Option (3) is incorrect because the subjugation of Africans was an effect, not a cause, of imperialism. The European nations did not have an excess of raw materials but instead needed them, so option (4) is incorrect.

5. **(4) Industrialized countries became more powerful than nonindustrial countries.** (Analysis) This is suggested by Britain's victory over China in the Opium War and by China's subsequent domination by the industrial powers. There is no support in the passage for option (1), (2), (3), or (5).

6. **(2) Germany** (Comprehension) This can be determined by studying the map. Options (1), (3), and (5) are incorrect because the map shows that France, Great Britain, and Russia had the three largest spheres of influence. Option (4) is wrong because the map shows that Japan's two combined spheres of influence accounted for more territory than Germany's sphere.

7. **(3) controlling trade coming into China** (Evaluation) The passage suggests that the cause of the Opium War was Britain's refusal to stop selling opium in China. Option (1) is incorrect

because the passage does not suggest that China wanted or received any profits from the drug trade. Option (2) is incorrect because Japan is not mentioned in the passage and there is no reason to believe that China was trying to prove anything to Japan. Option (4) is wrong because the passage does not suggest that China wanted all trade with India stopped. Option (5) cannot be true because the spheres of influence were established in the decades following the Opium War, not preceding it.

8. **(5) Japan was an industrial nation in 1912.** (Evaluation) Spheres of influence met the needs of the industrialized nations for additional markets and sources of raw materials for their industries. That Japan had such a sphere in 1912, as shown on the map, suggests that it had become an industrial nation. Option (1) cannot be determined from the map and passage; in fact, although Japan was not the enemy of England and France during this period, no formal alliance existed. Option (2) also cannot be determined from the map and the passage, although Japan had recently defeated Russia in a war that ended in 1905. Also, nothing on the map or in the passage supports options (3) and (4), although Japan did have these foreign policy goals.

GED Mini-Test (Pages 118–119)

1. **(2) to show how imperialism affected Central America** (Comprehension) The passage is a general discussion of imperialism in Central America. Option (1) is a detail that explains one of the causes of imperialism in the region. Option (3) is a major part of the passage, but is not the main point. Option (4) is incorrect because U.S. investment is mentioned only briefly and is also not the cause of imperialism. Although civil war and unrest is mentioned as one effect of imperialism, describing it is not the main purpose of the passage, so option (5) is also wrong.

2. **(5) the ultimate failure of the communists in Nicaragua** (Analysis) The passage states that U.S. involvement with the contras eventually forced the communists to hold new elections, which they lost. The death of innocent citizens was an effect of events in El Salvador and Guatemala, and the passage does not provide any information about the fate of civilians in Nicaragua, so option (1) is not correct. Option (2) was a result of the Nicaraguan communists' actions, not those of the United States. The passage contains no information about options (3) and (4).

3. **(1) concern for Panama Canal security** (Analysis) The passage states that U.S. concern over the canal increased after the 1977 agreement to turn control of it over to Panama—at about

the same time that communist revolutions gained strength in the region. Nothing in the passage suggests option (2) as a cause. Option (3) is wrong because the passage suggests that bananas and coffee are important to American companies with investments there, not to consumers. The passage implies that the nations of Central America are weak, but the passage does not suggest that as a reason for U.S. involvement there, so option (4) is incorrect. There is no support in the passage for option (5).

4. **(3) Cuba and the United States** (Application) Imperialism occurs when one nation extends its control over another one. When Cuba and the United States intervened in revolutions in independent nations in Central America, both were practicing imperialism. A nation that puts down internal rebellion against its own legitimate government, such as occurred in El Salvador and Nicaragua, is not acting imperialistically, so options (1), (2), (4), and (5) are incorrect.

5. **(4) strengthening democracy in Central America** (Evaluation) The passage points out that the United States supported governments in Central America in the 1970s and before that were not democratic. The passage suggests that ensuring stable governments in Central America, whether or not they were democratic, in order to protect American investments and the Panama Canal was the major goal of U.S. policy in the region. Thus, options (1), (2), (3), and (5) are incorrect because these factors were important to the U.S. government.

6. **(2) cultural imperialism** (Application) Introducing a religion fits the definition of cultural imperialism. Neoimperialism is economic imperialism, so option (1) is wrong. Since Hawaii did not become part of the United States until much later, option (3) is also incorrect. Options (4) and (5) are wrong because the information indicates that Hawaii was then an independent kingdom and not an official colony of the United States.

7. **(5) military intervention** (Application) The chart indicates that this involves sending troops to influence the internal affairs of another nation, which is what Cuba did. Since Angola did not become part of Cuba, options (1) and (2) are incorrect. Since the situation does not fit the chart's description of formation of a protectorate, option (3) is also wrong. Also, the information contains no suggestion of cultural imperialism, so option (4) is incorrect.

8. **(3) colonialism and cultural imperialism** (Application) According to the chart, one country's rule over another is colonialism. The information about the writing, religious,

and government systems suggests cultural imperialism as well. The information does not indicate which type of colonies the Chinese established there, so options (1) and (5) cannot be correct. No information establishes that military intervention took place, so option (2) is not correct. Because economic imperialism is not discussed, option (4) is also incorrect.

9. **(4) neoimperialism and settlement colony** (Application) The trade treaty is evidence of economic imperialism, and the large number of Japanese who relocated to Korea suggest settlement colonies there. The Japanese settlement eliminates option (1) as the answer, since dependent colonies involve rule by the colonizer over a predominantly native people, without large numbers of colonizers. Although a protectorate may have been formed and cultural imperialism may have occurred, the information does not indicate them, so options (2), (3), and (5) are wrong.

Lesson 10
GED Skill Focus (Page 121)
1. **b.** Iraq's president Saddam Hussein

2. **b.** Kuwait

3. **b.** that you know it is taking place in Kuwait

4. The cartoonist is telling the reader that Iraq is willing to destroy Kuwait in order to seize its **oil.**

GED Content Focus (Page 123)
1. **(3) The United States and Soviet Union competed in an arms race and for the loyalty of nonaligned nations.** (Comprehension) The Cold War competition of the United States and the Soviet Union is addressed throughout the passage. Option (1) explains a reason the competition existed. Option (2) provides background information; the passage is focused on events after the wars. Option (4) is an example of the competition, and option (5) is a detail about the nonaligned nations, neither of which is the main focus of the passage.

2. **(5) the nonaligned nations** (Comprehension) This is evident from the label on the wall in the cartoon, which indicates that the setting is a conference of nonaligned nations. Option (1) is wrong because none of these nations were named in the passage as members of the Communist bloc. Option (2) is incorrect because the focus of the cartoon is clearly on other nations, not on the Soviet Union. No visual clues in the cartoon indicate that either option (3) or (4) is correct.

3. **(2) The characters are portrayed as puppets.** (Comprehension) Each character has strings running from his body to an overhead

controlling device—just like a puppet. Option (1) is wrong because the characters clearly are not tied up. The artist provides no clues in the cartoon to suggest that option (3) or (4) is true. Option (5) is incorrect because the characters are not connected to each other, but to the controlling device.

4. **(1) what the hammer and sickle symbolize** (Analysis) The cartoon's message cannot be understood without knowing that the hammer and sickle are the symbol of the Soviet Union. This information is central to the cartoon. Knowing the names of the individuals who are depicted is not necessary because the artist has provided labels to explain which country each represents. So options (2) and (3) are incorrect. Option (4) also contains information that is not needed to understand the cartoon. In fact, knowing that Cuba is a communist country might confuse the message, since the cartoonist has included Cuba among the nonaligned nations. Option (5) is also unrelated to the cartoon's message.

5. **(5) These so-called nonaligned nations are actually controlled by the Soviet Union.** (Comprehension) The puppets in the cartoon are attached to and being manipulated by the hammer and sickle. With the understanding of what the hammer and sickle represent, the cartoon's message is clear. Option (1) has nothing to do with the cartoon's message. There are no visual clues to suggest that the artist holds the view expressed in option (2). Option (3) is information given in the cartoon, but it is not the central focus of the cartoon. There is no information in the cartoon to suggest that option (4) is true. In fact, the point of the cartoon is that these so-called nonaligned nations were not really nonaligned.

6. **(4) The launching of *Sputnik* makes Americans worry about the arms race.** (Comprehension) This is indicated by the caption, which connects the launching of *Sputnik* with tranquilizers, which are drugs that calm worried people. Although the cartoon is set in a bar and one man has mentioned tranquilizers, there are no clues to suggest that option (1), (2), or (5) is the message the cartoonist intends to convey: The cartoon is not preaching that mixing drugs and alcohol is dangerous, although it is; nor does it state or imply anything about alcohol consumption or indicate that taking tranquilizers is the right thing to do when worried. Option (3) is wrong because although the characters in the cartoon are talking, there are no clues that this is the cartoon's message either.

1. **(1) to express the view that agreements between the two sides have been shaky** (Comprehension) If you know, as the passage indicates, that the other agreements between the two sides have collapsed, the cartoon's symbolic reference to a "house of cards" becomes clear. There is no evidence in the passage or clue in the cartoon to imply that option (2) is true. Option (3) is wrong because nothing in the cartoon connects the cards to gambling. There are also no clues in the cartoon to imply that the cards are visual symbols for options (4) and (5), so they are also incorrect.

2. **(3) They both lay claim to the same land.** (Comprehension) The passage states that since ancient times, Arabs and Jews have been competing intermittently for the land called Palestine. Option (1) is incorrect because religious differences are not mentioned in the passage. Although it is true that some Arab rulers supported the Germans during World War II, option (2) is not given as a reason in the passage either. Option (4) is incorrect because the passage makes no mention of the Ottomans stirring up conflict and in fact states that conflicts were not common during the rule of the Ottoman Turks. Although the British did aggravate the conflict between the Arabs and Jews, they did not cause it, so option (5) is also wrong.

3. **(4) Most agreements between Israel and the PLO have not been fully carried out.** (Analysis) Without this knowledge, the significance of the symbol of the "house of cards" and caption will be more difficult to recognize. It is important to understand who each character represents, but knowing their names is not important to interpreting the cartoon, so options (1) and (2) are incorrect. The information contained in option (3) also does not help make sense of the cartoon. Option (5) is wrong because knowing the name of Israel's Parliament is not necessary to understand this cartoon.

4. **(4) to promote world peace** (Comprehension) This is a restatement of the point that the UN was created in the hope of preventing future wars. Option (1) is incorrect because, as the passage states, the UN was created just as World War II was drawing to a close; so the UN could not have ended the war. Options (2) and (3) are UN activities that promote peace, but they are not the reason that the UN was formed. Option (5) was a mission that the UN later undertook, but it was not the reason that it was formed.

5. **(2) The Muslims were experiencing atrocities.** (Analysis) According to the passage, the reason the UN's peacekeeping force was sent to Bosnia was to protect the Muslim population from attacks from the Christian Serbs. Option (1) is incorrect because, although the French and Canadians were a part of the UN's peacekeeping force in Bosnia, they were not fighting each other. Option (3) is incorrect because the Muslims were not attacking the Christian Serbs; the passage explains that the opposite was happening. Options (4) and (5) are not supported by the passage.

6. **(5) empty threats by UN personnel in Bosnia** (Comprehension) The hair dryer is being held like a weapon, but it isn't really one. The term *hot air* means that someone makes a fuss about something but actually does very little about it. The cartoonist is using this symbol to show that the UN peacekeepers' threats to the Serbs were nothing more than hot air. Option (1) relates literally to a hair dryer and so is not correct. Option (2) is about hot air, as in the temperature, but it is not related to peacekeeping efforts. Options (3) and (4) relate to the general topic of ethnic violence in Bosnia, but neither is the cartoonist's central point.

7. **(3) hearing a teacher threaten to suspend a bully but not following through** (Application) This is another example of hot air, that is, making threats but not following through. The other options are not examples of empty threats.

8. **(4) The UN should be able to enforce its missions.** (Evaluation) Both the passage and the cartoon support this conclusion. The passage explains that UN peacekeeping missions are not effective, and the cartoon shows the UN peacekeepers as bluffing and not really threatening the Serbs. Options (1), (2), and (3) are incorrect because nothing in the cartoon or passage suggests that the UN should be disbanded, have its own army, or get out of Bosnia. Option (5) is incorrect because there is no discussion of Bosnian refugees.

GED Mini-Test (Pages 126–127)

1. **(5) The Pro-democracy Movement in China** (Comprehension) Both the cartoon and most of the passage are devoted to this topic. Option (1) is incorrect because this information is historical background that explains the development of the movement for democracy and the government's reaction to it. Option (2) is incorrect because only a minor reference is made to it in the passage. Option (3) is incorrect because it is not described in the passage or depicted in the cartoon. Option (4) is incorrect because it helps explain why the pro-democracy movement developed; it is not the central focus of the material.

2. **(3) The world community criticized China.** (Analysis) The cartoon symbolizes China's use of the army against the protesters. The passage indicates that this and other actions against the pro-democracy movement caused the world to condemn China for violating the human rights of its people. The cartoonist's use of irony in the obvious lie coming from the government soldier also implies criticism of the Chinese government. Options (1) and (5) were among the causes that led to the event illustrated in the cartoon, not effects of it. Option (2) is wrong because the passage states that Mao died before the pro-democracy movement began. Option (4) is incorrect because it is contradicted by the passage.

3. **(4) the protesters who demanded democracy** (Comprehension) The passage states that the army attacked and killed the pro-democracy protesters, and the cartoon shows a dead figure clutching a flag labeled democracy. Options (1) and (3) are incorrect because it is clear from the information in the passage that the Chinese army did not kill Mao or China's leaders at the time of the unrest. Although the flag in the cartoon resembles a U.S. flag, nothing in the passage suggests that option (2) could be correct. Neither the passage nor the cartoon provides any reason to believe that option (5) is the case.

4. **(1) control** (Evaluation) Using the army to crush a protest and continuing political suppression of the Chinese people despite world condemnation of their actions establishes that China's leaders value control of China more than the other options. The fact that the soldier in the cartoon is telling a lie disproves option (2). The dead Chinese protester as well as information in the passage about other government acts of oppression make options (3), (4), and (5) incorrect as well.

5. **(2) The desire for democracy is alive in China.** (Comprehension) The content of the text balloon over the flag implies that the soldier's claim about the protester actually applies to democracy in China after the army's attack on the pro-democracy movement. The caption over the flag does not support option (1) as the correct answer. Nothing in the cartoon suggests that option (3) or (5) is true. Option (4) is contradicted by the blood shown coming from the protester's head, flowing out on the ground at the feet of the soldier.

6. **(4) East Berlin was controlled by a communist government.** (Analysis) This assumption can be made because of the statement that East Berlin was separated from democratic West Berlin. No information supports option (1), (2), or (5) as an assumption. In fact, the information about the collapse of communism in general—and the wall in particular—strongly suggests that all three statements are untrue. Option (3) is incorrect because this information is contained in the passage.

7. **(3) North Korea and South Korea** (Application) Like East and West Germany, North and South Korea had been part of one country that was divided after World War II, restricting travel from one part of the country to the other and splitting up families. Option (1) is incorrect because, although the United States and Canada are neighboring countries, they were not formerly one country as were East and West Germany. Option (2) is not correct because Great Britain and the United States had a relationship of colonizer and colony, not the same relationship as East and West Germany. Options (4) and (5) are incorrect because there is free movement between all states, including between North Carolina and South Carolina and between West Virginia and Virginia, while there was not free movement between the two parts of Germany.

8. **(1) The dinosaur represents European communism, under Soviet leadership.** (Analysis) The hammer and sickle appears on the Soviet flag, and the Soviets dominated Eastern Europe, installing harsh communist governments there and influencing them as satellite nations. Since the hammer and sickle appears on the dinosaur's side and since the tail of the dinosaur is the Berlin Wall (in Europe), it is implied that the dinosaur represents Soviet-supported communism in Europe. Since West Berlin was not under a communist government, option (2) is incorrect. Options (3) and (5) are wrong because they are contradicted by the passage. Option (4) is true but doesn't help you understand the message of the cartoon.

9. **(3) European Communism Becomes Extinct** (Comprehension) This is why the cartoonist has chosen to depict communism in Europe as a dinosaur. Option (1) is wrong because the Berlin Wall was torn down, not moved. Option (2) is incorrect because although the wall is represented by the dinosaur's tail, the tail is only an element of the cartoon, not its central focus. Option (4) is not correct because the cartoon deals with the wall as related to the fall of Soviet-supported communism in Europe; the fall of the Soviet Union came slightly later. Option (5) is wrong because, since the dinosaur is extinct, it symbolizes that European communism is dead.

Unit 2 Cumulative Review (Pages 128–132)

1. **(1) Trade moved more easily in Rome's empire.** (Analysis) A system of paved roads would have made it easier for trade goods to move from one place to another. Option (2) is based on a misunderstanding of the saying "All roads lead to Rome"; the passage states that road system went throughout the entire Roman Empire, so roads to other cities were built up, not neglected. Option (3) is a cause for building Rome's road system, not an effect of it. Option (4) resulted from the road system but not as a direct effect of the system, nor was it as important a consequence as improved trade. Option (5) is a description of the road system, not an effect of it.

2. **(3) power** (Evaluation) This is suggested by the creation of a road system that allowed the Romans to send troops throughout their empire and by the erection of the huge stone tablet to celebrate that system. Options (1), (2), and (5) are incorrect because there is nothing in the passage that indicates that spirituality, honesty, or humor were especially valued by the Romans. The quality of compassion would be unlikely to be valued in an empire, where one people dominates and controls other peoples, so option (4) is incorrect.

3. **(5) A major reason for the road system was to move troops rapidly and easily within the empire.** (Evaluation) This is implied by the first and last sentences of the passage, which both refer to army personnel. So the best conclusion is that Rome built the road system to facilitate troop movement. No information in the passage is appropriate evidence to support option (1) or (2) as a conclusion. Option (3) is contradicted by the evidence in the passage. Option (4) is wrong because the passage states that the project took 20 years to complete, so it is not likely that the project was simple.

4. **(4) Spain was once part of the Roman Empire.** (Comprehension) This is the most likely reason that Spanish would be based on Latin. Nothing in the passage suggests option (1). Options (2) and (3) are contradicted by the passage, which states that the Romance languages are modern languages. Option (5) is wrong because the passage gives no evidence that the ancient Romans crossed the Atlantic (they didn't); in fact, Latin America was part of Spain's (not Rome's) empire, coming into existence about 1000 years after the fall of the Roman empire.

5. **(2) as part of a trade mission** (Comprehension) This can be inferred from the description of Polo's father and uncle as Venetian merchants. The trip made Polo a world explorer, but there is no indication in the passage that becoming one was a reason for the trip, so option (1) is incorrect. Options (3) is also not supported by the information given. Option (4) is incorrect because Polo could not have known he would be traveling around the region until after he got to China and was assigned the job by the khan. There is no information in the passage related to option (5).

6. **(5) Pagan** (Comprehension) The map shows that Polo reached this city during his travels in China. Option (1) is incorrect because Venice is the city from which Polo began his trip and to which he returned. Polo visited Nanjing and Malacca, but this was on his return home, when he would not have been a representative of the khan, so options (2) and (3) are not correct. Option (4) is incorrect because it cannot be determined whether Polo visited Shanghai since this city is not shown on the map.

7. **(3) Kublai Khan admired and trusted Marco Polo.** (Analysis) This can be assumed from the information that the khan appointed Polo to represent him. Option (1) is incorrect because if the khan had feared Polo, it is unlikely that he would have made Polo his representative. There is no evidence in the passage to support option (2) or (4). Option (5) is incorrect because the passage states that Polo's book was written while he was in Italy, not China.

8. **(5) The trip home was mainly over water, while the trip to China was mainly over land.** (Evaluation) Because ships travel faster than people who are walking or riding on animals or in wagons, traveling over water would have allowed the Polos to travel much faster on their return trip than on their trip to China, which was mainly over land. Option (1) does not support the idea because the Polos traveled through Persia on both trips. Option (2) is incorrect because the map shows that the trip home was not along a more direct route. Option (3) is incorrect because the trip to China did not cover a greater distance than the return trip. The Polos did not cross Tibet on their return trip, so option (4) is incorrect.

9. **(5) Trade was important to Great Zimbabwe.** (Evaluation) The size of the market and the variety of goods from far-away places suggest that trade was important to Great Zimbabwe. This is the only conclusion that can be reached from the information presented. There is no support in the passage for option (1), (2), (3), or (4).

10. **(4) Islam was not very important in Ghana before the Muslim Berber invasion.** (Comprehension) The passage says that the

invasion of the Muslim Berbers brought religious conflict. This suggests that Islam was not very influential in Ghana before the Berber invasion. Option (1) is incorrect because, although Ghana did eventually become part of the Mali empire, the passage suggests that its power declined as a result of the religious conflict that developed before its conquest by Mali. Nothing in the passage implies option (2) or (3). The passage also provides no clues about where the three empires were located in relation to one another, so option (5) is not implied.

11. **(4) The economy of each was based on trade.** (Evaluation) Trade is the only activity that the passage describes for all three cultures. No evidence is presented that Ghana had schools or a university, so options (1) and (5) are incorrect. Option (2) is wrong because the passage does not indicate that Songhay was conquered by Ghana or Mali. (It was not.) Weak kings were the reason for only Mali's decline. Ghana declined due to religious civil war, and Songhay's decline is not discussed. Therefore, option (3) is also incorrect.

12. **(1) human rights** (Evaluation) This value could not have been very important because the passage indicates that the people of Songhay traded in slaves. Options (2) and (5) are incorrect because Timbuktu contained many Islamic schools and three Islamic universities that offered religious training. Option (3) is wrong because the passage implies that Songhay was a wealthy trading empire. Option (4) is incorrect, because poetry is listed as one of the subjects taught at the universities in Timbuktu under the Songhay.

13. **(3) Many Russians did not want to have a Communist government.** (Analysis) This is a conclusion that can be drawn based on the fact that the Bolsheviks had to fight and win in order to come to power. Option (1) is incorrect because the civil war occurred after the czar resigned, not before. Nothing in the passage supports options (2) and (5), and in fact, they are incorrect statements. Option (4) is a detail in the passage that supports the conclusion in option (3).

14. **(2) How Spain Lost Its South American Empire** (Comprehension) This is the only title that accurately summarizes the content of the passage. Option (1) is incorrect because the passage is about more than the effect of European wars. Option (3) is wrong because this topic is not covered in the passage. Options (4) and (5) are incorrect because the passage does not compare revolutions or revolutionary leaders.

15. **(5) It was originally called the United Provinces of the Rio de la Plata.** (Analysis) The passage establishes that the United Provinces of the Rio de la Plata became independent in 1816. The only nation to have an 1816 independence date on the chart is Argentina. The assumption can thus be made that they are the same country. Option (1) is incorrect because it cannot be determined from either the passage or the chart. (It is also not true.) Option (2) is true but is a wrong answer because it cannot be assumed from the information provided. Options (3) and (4) are incorrect because they are contradicted by information in both the passage and the chart.

16. **(4) Wars in Europe consumed too many of Spain's military resources.** (Analysis) The passage notes that the Spanish were preoccupied and weakened by the wars that were occurring in Europe while their colonies were in revolt. This would have helped the rebels achieve victory. Option (1) is incorrect because the example of the American Revolution was a cause of the rebellion, not of Spain's defeat. There is no support in the passage for option (2) or (5). Option (3) is incorrect because independence was the effect of Spain's defeat, not the cause of it.

17. **(2) Most of South America was free by 1830.** (Comprehension) The chart shows that except for Panama, which was part of Columbia until 1903, all of Spain's South American empire had won independence and reorganized as a number of separate nations by 1830. Option (1) is incorrect because it is neither true nor a summary statement. Option (3) is a summary statement, but it is not true because Panama became independent later than that. Option (4) is true, but it is not a summary statement. Option (5) is incorrect because the chart does not provide information about the number of colonists involved in the rebellion.

18. **(3) The introduction of apartheid caused protests, which brought government crackdowns against black South Africans.** (Comprehension) This sentence touches on all the main points of the paragraph. Options (1) and (2) are incorrect because the paragraph does not discuss racial policies or protests in the United States. Option (4) is true but incorrect because it focuses on details not mentioned in the paragraph. Option (5) is also true but is not the answer because the focus of the paragraph is on what apartheid was and the reactions to it, not on why it was adopted.

19. **(4) Opposition to apartheid grew.** (Comprehension) The paragraph is about opposition to apartheid that arose both in South Africa and around the world. Option (1) is a detail that explains an effect of that growing opposition. Options (2) and (3) are details that serve as examples of the main idea of opposition

to apartheid. Option (5) establishes a cause-and-effect relationship that is not supported by the paragraph.

20. **(5) apartheid** (Comprehension) The wrist iron and chain is a symbol of control or bondage, and it represents the control of black South Africans by the policy of apartheid. Option (1) is incorrect because black South Africans are represented by the hand that is breaking free of the chain. Option (2) is incorrect because low wages were only one of the types of oppression under apartheid. Option (3) is incorrect because the subject of the cartoon, people standing in line to vote, shows peaceful, not violent, change. Option (4) is incorrect because the ANC is not portrayed or symbolized in the cartoon.

21. **(3) The 1994 election was the first in which black South Africans had the right to vote.** (Analysis) Unless you know this, you will not understand the message of the cartoon, which is that getting the vote broke the last link in the chain of apartheid, setting black South African free. Option (1) is incorrect because the passage establishes that the white population does not outnumber the black population. Option (2) is incorrect because knowing whether people traveled long distances will not help you understand the message of the cartoon. Options (4) and (5) are true, but events from Nelson Mandela's life do not help explain the cartoon.

UNIT 3: CIVICS AND GOVERNMENT

Lesson 11

GED Skill Focus (Page 137)

1. **a.** *F:* Governments have five basic functions in a social system.

   b. *O:* Theft is acceptable in some situations.

   c. *F:* If two groups have a dispute, the government can be called in to help resolve the issue.

   d. *O:* The government should help all people and groups achieve their goals.

2. **b.** Teenage drivers are unsafe and a menace on the highways.

GED Content Focus (Page 139)

1. **(4) law** (Comprehension) The second principle of modern government is legal authority, or law. Options (1), (2), and (3) are incorrect because power, wealth, and military force were the basis of authority in traditional systems, not in modern government. Option (5) is incorrect because personal whim was one way some leaders governed in traditional societies, rather than a principle of government or a feature of modern government.

2. **(2) to compare authoritarian and democratic governments** (Comprehension) The chart compares two forms of authoritarian government with three forms of democratic government. Option (1) is incorrect because the chart does not list the principles of modern government. Option (3) is incorrect because the comparison of autocracy and oligarchy is a detail in the overall comparison of the types of government. Direct democracy is not compared with constitutional monarchy on the chart, so option (4) is incorrect. Option (5) is incorrect because the definitions are details, not the main purpose of the chart.

3. **(5) a republic** (Application) Russia's reforms led to the establishment of a government in which the people elect representatives and give them the power to govern—that is, a republic. Option (1) is incorrect because Russia's government functions through elected representatives. Option (2) is incorrect because Russia has no king or queen. Option (3) is incorrect because autocracy is based on the rule of a dictator or absolute monarch. Option (4) is incorrect because oligarchy was the form of government before the legislature and president were elected, when Communist party leaders were in control.

4. **(3) a constitutional monarchy** (Application) The chart establishes that in this form of government the role of the monarch is largely ceremonial and that the real power is held by the elected legislature. Option (1) is incorrect because only a small group holds power in an oligarchy. Options (2) is incorrect because there is no monarch in a republic. Option (4) is incorrect because a direct democracy does not involve an elected legislature. Because the queen does not hold all power, option (5) is also incorrect.

5. **(3) Mass participation is the most important principle of modern government.** (Analysis) The passage indicates that mass participation is one of three principles of modern government, but it does not state that it is the most important nor does it provide any evidence to support such a statement, so the statement is an opinion. Option (1) is a restatement of the second principle of modern government, legal authority, and is therefore a fact. Option (2) is a fact that is supported by the passage. The chart lists New England town meetings as an example of direct democracy and Cuba as an example of an autocracy, so options (4) and (5) are not correct.

6. **(2) The government will be in chaos.** (Analysis) Because all the power was in that one person's hands, the government would likely be in chaos as rivals struggle to assume power. Therefore, option (1) is incorrect. Options (3) and (5) are incorrect because, although they could

happen, they would not occur immediately on the death of a dictator; it takes planning for an authoritarian government to become a democracy and hold elections. Option (4) is wrong because this type of automatic succession is characteristic of a monarchy, not of a dictatorship.

7. **(2) facts about each government's basic principles** (Evaluation) Each description is based on how the principles fit into the government structure. There are no opinions stated about how well the systems work or about citizens' role in each system, so options (1) and (3) are incorrect. Option (4) is incorrect because names of political offices or leaders are not given as examples for every system. Option (5) is wrong because historical details are not included consistently in the chart.

8. **(1) The nature of government has changed over time.** (Evaluation) The discussion of the basic principles of government supports this conclusion. Option (2) is incorrect because the passage states that the principles are relatively new in world history. The chart disproves option (3). These is no information in the passage or the chart to support option (4) or (5).

GED Practice (Pages 140–141)

1. **(3) Legitimate power results in better government than does illegitimate power.** (Analysis) This is a judgment by the writer and therefore an opinion that may or may not be true. Options (1), (2), (4), and (5) are all statements of fact that are established by the information in the passage.

2. **(4) authority** (Application) In a monarchy, the royal family is recognized as having the legitimate power to rule. Having the eldest child become the ruler when the monarch dies is a recognized method for the legitimate transfer of power in a monarchy. Options (1) and (3) are incorrect because the king rules by virtue of his position, not from personal influence or persuasion. Option (2) is wrong because Albert did not come to power by force. Option (5) is incorrect because elections are not mentioned in the passage, and monarchs are not generally elected.

3. **(2) People's support is necessary for power to be legitimate.** (Comprehension) The passage states that the people must accept their leaders' power as proper in order for that power to be legitimate. Therefore, the support of the people is necessary for government to be legitimate. Thus, option (1) is not correct. There is no support in the passage for option (3) or (5) as an explanation of why people's opinions are important to the exercise of power. Behavior can be influenced by

force, but the passage implies that it does not change opinions, so option (4) is incorrect.

4. **(5) It makes people behave in ways that government leaders desire.** (Comprehension) The passage states that force or fear of it can change behavior, so option (1) is incorrect. Option (2) is incorrect because people's support must be willingly given for power to be legitimate. There is no information in the passage to suggest that option (3) or (4) is true.

5. **(4) the legislature** (Comprehension) This is illustrated by the diagram and implied in the second paragraph of the passage. Option (1) is wrong because the president is the chief executive in the presidential system. Option (2) is incorrect because the diagram shows that the voters select the legislature, not the prime minister. The diagram also shows that the prime minister and legislature choose the cabinet, which then chooses the judges, so options (3) and (5) are not correct.

6. **(3) The parliamentary system is a better form of government than the presidential system.** (Analysis) This statement is a judgment that does not have any direct support from the information in the passage or diagram. Option (1) is incorrect because the legislature in a parliamentary system has the power to choose the chief executive, while the legislature in a presidential system does not have this power, so the statement is a fact. Options (2), (4), and (5) are also statements of fact that are proven by information in the passage and diagram.

7. **(1) the cabinet** (Comprehension) This is established by the diagram. The diagram shows that options (2), (3), (4) and (5) are not true in a parliamentary system.

8. **(2) The prime minister must resign if he or she loses an important vote in the legislature.** (Evaluation) This is the best evidence that the prime minister is less independent, because the president is not required to resign if a proposal he or she supports is defeated in Congress. Options (1) and (5) are wrong because, although they are accurate statements, they have nothing to do with the prime minister's level of independence. Option (3) is incorrect because the diagram shows that the president, with the input of Congress, also appoints a cabinet. Option (4) is wrong because the prime minister is directly responsible to the legislature, not to the voters.

GED Mini-Test (Pages 142–143)

1. **(1) freedom of speech** (Application) Like freedom of religion, freedom of speech is an example of a personal freedom, or liberty, that

is part of natural rights. Option (2) is incorrect because a public trial is a civil right, not a natural right. Option (3) is incorrect because people need to meet certain requirements to obtain a license to practice medicine, so obtaining such a license is not a natural right. Option (4) is incorrect because paying tax is required of certain people by law and so is not a right. Option (5) is incorrect because it is an example of an entitlement.

2. **(3) a government-guaranteed student loan** (Application) This is a benefit provided by the government to people who meet the requirements of a loan, and it can be taken away by the government. Options (1), (4), and (5) involve personal freedom and thus are part of natural rights. Option (2) is a procedural process and is a civil right guaranteed to all Americans in the Constitution.

3. **(5) John Locke was a great political thinker.** (Analysis) This is the only opinion found in the passage or supported by other information in it. Nothing in the passage suggests that the writer holds option (1), (2), or (4) as an opinion. Option (3) is incorrect because it is not an opinion but a statement of fact; in other words, it is true that some people hold the stated belief.

4. **(2) Government can lawfully take away entitlements, but not rights.** (Comprehension) The fact that government can take away entitlements but not rights indicates that rights are more fundamental, or basic. Option (1) is incorrect because many people need the benefits to which they are entitled. Option (3) is incorrect because the passage contradicts it. Nothing in the passage supports option (4) or (5), and neither statement is accurate.

5. **(4) to be limited in where you could travel** (Application) Under a government that controls every aspect of your life, freedom of movement would be restricted. Options (1), (2), and (3) would be unlikely because individual freedoms are extremely limited under this form of government. There is no support in the passage for option (5).

6. **(1) that it has accompanying responsibilities** (Analysis) This opinion is expressed in the last paragraph of the passage. There is no evidence in the passage for option (2), (3), or (4). Because the passage indicates that freedom comes with responsibility, option (5) is incorrect.

7. **(4) It is built on respect for individual differences.** (Comprehension) The chart points out the importance of respect for the individual. Option (1) is wrong because absolute rule by the majority with no attention to other views would lead to tyranny, and the chart points out the importance of compromise. Option (2) is contradicted by the chart. There is no information in the chart or passage to support the opinion expressed in option (3) that any one principle is the most important. The passage expresses the opinion that option (5) is not necessarily true.

8. **(2) that in a democracy no person's rights can be allowed to interfere with the rights of others** (Evaluation) The quote means that each person's rights stop where another person's rights begin. The information in the first row of the chart expresses the principle on which Holmes's statement is based. Option (1) is incorrect because the chart indicates that individual freedom is important in a democracy. Option (3) is a democratic value, but equal opportunity has nothing to do with Holmes's statement. Nothing in the passage supports option (4) as an explanation of Holmes's statement. Option (5) is incorrect because the need for compromise is one of the pillars of democracy, which indicates that differences of opinion are expected and protected in a democracy.

Lesson 12
GED Skill Focus (Page 145)
1. **b.** They provide services to the people of an area.

2. **a.** *S:* who chooses the mayor

   b. *S:* who chooses the council

   c. *D:* who appoints the department heads

   d. *D:* who makes city policy

GED Content Focus (Page 147)
1. **(3) States are represented equally in the Senate and according to their population in the House.** (Analysis) This contrast is stated in the passage. Options (1) and (4) are incorrect because they do not mention any differences between the House of Representatives and the Senate. Option (2) discusses only the House of Representatives and does not contrast it with the Senate. Option (5) is incorrect because it involves similarities rather than differences between the two parts of Congress.

2. **(4) waging war against other nations** (Comprehension) The passage states that the power to declare war rests with Congress but that the president commands the armed forces. Option (1) is a congressional power alone, according to the passage, while the passage and chart indicate that options (2) and (5) are

functions unique to the executive branch. Option (3) is part of the executive branch's treaty-making function.

3. **(3) The Supreme Court can declare laws and executive branch actions to be unconstitutional.** (Analysis) These similar powers are shown in the diagram. Option (1) is contradicted by information in the passage and diagram. Options (2) and (5) are not supported by the information and are, in fact, not true. According to the diagram, option (4) is a function of Congress, not of the Supreme Court.

4. **(2) Congress passes laws, and the executive branch carries them out.** (Analysis) This contrast is indicated in the passage and confirmed by the chart. Option (1) is incorrect because the president makes treaties and the courts decide what they mean if questions or disputes arise over them. Option (3) is a similarity between the two branches, not a contrast. Option (4) is incorrect because the Supreme Court is responsible for interpreting both laws and treaties. Option (5) shows a relationship between the two branches but does not compare or contrast their functions.

5. **(2) The major powers of government have been divided among its three branches.** (Analysis) That the powers have been divided is a fact. Options (1) and (5) are beliefs with which not everyone would agree. Options (3) and (4) are conclusions that are not supported by any facts in the passage, which would also cause them to be disputed by people who disagree with the judgments they contain.

6. **(4) Each of the three branches of government checks the power of the other two branches.** (Evaluation) This is clear from the checks and balances illustrated in the diagram. Options (1), (2), and (3) are incorrect because, in all cases, two branches share the responsibility for checking the power of the third branch. Option (5) is incorrect because the president is part of one of the three branches, so there are only two other branches responsible for checking the president's power.

GED Practice (Pages 148–149)

1. **(3) to compare state and national governments** (Comprehension) The passage compares and contrasts the organization, selection, and powers of offices and officials in the three branches of state government with one another and with the national government. Option (1) is a comparison made in the passage but is not its main focus. Options (2), (4), and (5) are also covered by the passage, but they are details that show the similarities among the states' governments.

2. **(4) how judges are selected** (Analysis) This is a major difference stated in the passage. According to the passage, options (1), (2), (3), and (5) are all ways in which state governments are more similar than different.

3. **(2) the Congress of the United States** (Analysis) The information in the passage about the representation scheme, the two-house structure of most state legislatures, and the differences in the term lengths in each house provides the basis for this comparison. Option (1) is incorrect because Nebraska's legislature is the most different from all the other state legislatures, having one instead of two houses. Option (3) cannot be correct, because it refers to the judicial branch of government, not to the legislative branch. Options (4) and (5) cannot be correct because they refer to the executive branches of government.

4. **(4) a representative democracy** (Application) In a representative democracy, the people elect leaders to represent and govern them. Options (1) and (2) are incorrect because state governments are not headed by powerful executives like dictators or monarchs. Option (3) is incorrect because citizens of the states do not directly vote on laws, but instead elect representatives to make the laws. Option (5) is incorrect because a bicameral legislature is only one part of state government, which also includes executive and judicial branches.

5. **(3) Power in both is divided among branches.** (Analysis) In local governments, the executive power is held by a mayor or city manager and the legislative power by an elected council. Judicial power resides in county courts. This is similar to the governor, legislature, and court system of state government. Option (1) is contradicted by information about state executive officials and city managers and department heads. City councils are not represented as being bicameral, so option (2) is incorrect. The passage points out that some judges at the state level are elected and some are appointed, so option (4) is incorrect. Not enough information exists in the lesson to support option (5).

6. **(3) the amendment changing the selection of senators** (Analysis) By giving the people the power to directly elect senators, who had previously been elected by state legislatures, this amendment increased the people's power. Option (1) is incorrect because it denies the people the opportunity to elect a popular president to a third term. Options (2) and (5) are incorrect because the income tax and limits on pay raises do not increase the people's power. As the passage states, option (4) was proposed as an amendment but never actually became one.

7. (5) adaptability and orderly change
(Evaluation) The fact that they created a device for changing the Constitution shows that they wanted the document to be able to be adapted to changing times and circumstances in an orderly way. Option (1) is incorrect because the people do not directly vote on amendments. Option (2) is incorrect because the Constitution can be and has been amended to increase the power of government as well as to limit that power, and the process itself does not indicate that either increasing or limiting power was valued by the framers. Nothing in the passage supports option (3) or (4) as the answer.

8. (3) They wanted it to be more difficult to add amendments than to propose them.
(Analysis) As the chart shows, it takes only two-thirds support to propose an amendment but three-fourths support to approve it. The framers deliberately made the process difficult so that the Constitution would not be abruptly changed on the basis of some fleeting whim. The passage does not contain any information that would provide a basis for assuming options (1) and (2); in fact, it supplies evidence against these options, since the first ten amendments were added in 1791, less than five years after the Constitution was written. Options (4) and (5) cannot be reasons for the amendment process created by the framers because, as shown by the chart, they inaccurately state those processes.

GED Mini-Test (Pages 150–151)

1. (4) the incumbent, regardless of gender
(Comprehension) The study found that the critical factor in winning an election is incumbency, not the gender of the person running for office. Options (1), (2), and (3) are incorrect because the challenger is likely to lose. Nothing in the passage indicates that previous public service is a factor in winning elections, so option (5) is also incorrect.

2. (3) Women frequently lose against incumbents. (Evaluation) Since most incumbents are males, the fact that incumbents tend to win gives the appearance that women frequently lose elections, although female challengers lose no more often than male challengers. Options (1), (2), and (4), are not supported as conclusions by the information in the passage. Option (5) is a stereotype that also is not supported by the information.

3. (5) a person outside an organization competing for a job with someone inside the organization (Application) The similarity is that the person outside the organization is like the new candidate in a political election, and the person inside the organization is like the incumbent. Option (1) is incorrect because there is not an incumbency system in sports; each year is a new year, with new players who have different talents, so the past champions do not necessarily have an advantage. Option (2) is incorrect because competition with others is not usually the issue in achieving a higher grade. Options (3) and (4) are incorrect because lack of skill or experience may be the deciding factor for the poet and the actor, and there may not be an "incumbent" barring their way.

4. (1) to divide and delegate powers
(Comprehension) The Tenth Amendment ensures that the states and the people will have a share of power and that all power will not be concentrated in the federal government. Option (2) is incorrect because nothing in the amendment suggests expansion of powers for any sector. The Tenth Amendment may be interpreted to limit the powers of the federal government, but it does not limit the powers of the Constitution, so option (3) is incorrect. Neither the Senate nor the House of Representatives is mentioned in the amendment, so options (4) and (5) are incorrect.

5. (5) making decisions in a direct democracy
(Application) The residents are acting directly to handle their affairs themselves rather than through elected representatives. Option (1) is incorrect because no mention of partisanship is mentioned in relation to the neighborhood group, whereas writing a platform for a political party is by nature a partisan activity. Options (2) and (3) are incorrect because they relate to representative democracy and representative government, and the people in a neighborhood association do not elect representatives to vote for them. Option (4) would not be true unless the group formally voted on changing a resolution, proposal, or by-law of the group.

6. (2) a 40-year-old Southern black man in 1860 (Application) African American men did not gain the constitutional right to vote until the Fifteenth Amendment was ratified in 1870. Option (1) is incorrect because a farmer would have met the property qualification in effect for voting at that time. Option (3) is incorrect, because the woman would have gained voting rights from the Fifteenth and Nineteenth Amendments (although the custom of applying poll taxes to African Americans might have prevented her from actually voting). Option (4) is incorrect, because the man would have gained voting rights from the Fifteenth and Twenty-Third Amendments. Option (5) is incorrect because the Twenty-Sixth Amendment lowered the voting age to 18 in 1971, and only persons convicted of serious crimes are denied the right to vote in some states.

7. **(4) They have increased the number of potential voters.** (Analysis) This has been accomplished over the decades by extending the right to vote to people who were previously not allowed to vote because of their place of residence, race, age, or gender. No basis for option (1), (3), or (5) can be found in the passage or chart. Option (2) is contradicted by the information.

8. **(3) an Alabama white woman, age 18** (Application) This is on the basis of the Twenty-Sixth Amendment, which in 1971 lowered the minimum voting age to 18. The Fifteenth Amendment would already have empowered option (1) to vote, and the Fifteenth and Nineteenth Amendments would have empowered options (2) and (4). Option (5) would be unlikely to have voting rights in many, if not most states.

9. **(4) The national government has become more powerful.** (Evaluation) The passage indicates that for a long time, the states made sole determination of who could vote. However, both the chart and the passage indicate that the federal government gradually took over making this determination by amending the Constitution to extend the right to vote to groups that did not have that right under the laws of many states. This illustrates the growth of federal power. Nothing in the passage or chart suggests that option (1) or (2) is true. Options (3) and (5) are contradicted by the passage and the chart.

Lesson 13
GED Skill Focus (Page 153)
1. **a.** Televised candidate debates are uninteresting and lack excitement.

2. **c.** The tendency not to vote is a trait people inherit from their parents.

GED Content Focus (Page 155)
1. **(1) their platforms** (Comprehension) This difference is spelled out in the passage, which summarizes and contrasts each party's platform in recent years. Option (2) is not a difference in substance. There is no evidence in the passage to support option (3) or (4). Option (5) is contradicted by the chart.

2. **(5) If a person is a Republican, he or she is against abortion.** (Evaluation) The Republican Party platforms tend to be against abortion, but this does not mean that all Republicans agree on this issue. To assign this characteristic to the entire group is stereotyping. A person may support a woman's right to choose abortion yet be a Republican because he or she supports the party's stand on other issues. Options (1), (2), (3), and (4) are generalizations that are supported by the information in the passage and the chart.

3. **(3) The election of a Republican shows that voters oppose higher taxes on the wealthy.** (Evaluation) Voters may have other reasons for supporting a Republican candidate. To say that this one reason is the cause of voter behavior is an oversimplification. No cause-and-effect relationship is stated in option (1), so the statement cannot be an oversimplification. Option (2) is a generalization that is supported by information in the passage. Options (4) and (5) are facts that are presented in the chart.

4. **(1) Each ward is made up of a number of precincts.** (Analysis) This can be concluded from the information that ward committeemen appoint all the precinct captains in the ward. Options (2) and (3) are facts that are stated in the chart. There is no basis in the chart for option (4) or (5).

5. **(4) raising money for the party** (Analysis) This is not listed in the chart among the most important functions of a county party, but it is for the state party. Options (1), (3), and (5) are functions of both levels. Option (2) is a function of the ward committeemen, operating on the ward level.

6. **(5) The two parties tend to have opposing views on abortion and tax issues.** (Evaluation) This is evident from the information on party platforms in the passage. Option (1) is an opinion that is not supported by the passage. Option (2) is contradicted by the passage. Options (3) and (4) both demonstrate faulty logic. In addition, option (3) oversimplifies the relationship between higher taxes and the nation's economy. Option (4) stereotypes Republicans.

GED Practice (Pages 156–157)
1. **(3) They have been influential in politics.** (Comprehension) The passage suggests that third-party issues influence the positions of the major parties and that they have cost at least one president reelection. Nothing in the passage suggests that option (1) is true. Option (2) is incorrect because a party cannot exist without support. Information in the passage contradicts options (4) and (5).

2. **(5) Ideological third parties typically live longer than single-issue parties.** (Comprehension) The paragraph indicates that ideological third parties have lasted longer than parties that formed around a single issue and provides examples of such parties. Option (1) is incorrect because it is only a detail provided in the paragraph. Option (2) is an example of the long life of ideological third parties. Option (3) is incorrect because the second paragraph states that single-issue parties arise for this reason.

There is no support in the passage for option (4), and this position is mentioned as being held only by the Libertarian Party.

3. **(4) Voters feel that the major parties are not addressing important problems.** (Analysis) The only way to express dissatisfaction with the positions and policies of both major parties would be to vote for a third party. Options (1) and (5) would more likely result in not voting at all rather than in growing support for third parties. There is no support in the passage for option (2) or (3).

4. **(5) a multiparty system** (Application) A multiparty system has been defined as a political system having three or more major parties. The United States is already a democracy and a republic, so options (1) and (2) are incorrect. Option (3) is wrong because it is the current system. Option (4) is not a recognized party system.

5. **(3) Any elected official holding office for a long time becomes unresponsive to the people.** (Evaluation) This is a gross oversimplification. Elected officials who fail to represent the will of those who elect them are unlikely to serve for a long time because they probably will not be reelected. Options (1), (2), (4), and (5) do not demonstrate faulty logic because they are all statements of fact supported by the passage.

6. **(4) U.S. senator** (Application) The chart establishes that at-large representation on city councils means that all members represent all the people of the city. This is the identical to the way in which a state's U.S. senators represent all the people of the state. Options (1), (2), and (3) are incorrect because the people who hold each of these offices represent specific districts. Option (5) is wrong because Supreme Court justices are appointed, not elected, and as members of the judicial branch represent the rule of law and not the will of the people.

7. **(2) All represent the people of specific geographic areas.** (Analysis) The chart indicates that even U.S. senators and at-large members of municipal councils represent the people of a specific state or city. Option (1) is contradicted by information in the chart, and options (3) and (4) by information in the passage. Option (5) is incorrect because the chart describes the positions and does not discuss individual officeholders or their qualifications to serve.

8. **(3) the will of the people** (Evaluation) This characteristic, as expressed through the election of leaders to represent the people, is the basis of republican government. Option (1) would be true in an authoritarian form of government.

Option (2) is incorrect because term limits are not required for a government to take the republican form and are not in effect for all offices. Option (4) is incorrect because the republican form of government does not require officeholders to be reelected and in fact makes it possible for challengers to be elected. Option (5) is incorrect because although it is a characteristic featured in the chart, it is not presented as being most highly valued.

GED Mini-Test (Pages 158–159)

1. **(3) They distinguish differences in political beliefs.** (Comprehension) This is stated in the first sentence of the paragraph. Options (1) and (2) are incorrect because these labels cannot properly be thought of in terms of "good" or "bad." Option (4) is contradicted by information in the passage. Nothing in the passage suggests that option (5) is true.

2. **(1) Both groups support change.** (Analysis) Even though the changes they want may not be the same, desire for change is what the two groups have in common. Nothing in the passage supports option (2), (3), or (4) as true of either group. Option (5) explains how the groups differ, not how they are the same.

3. **(4) Democrats are always liberals.** (Analysis) This statement assigns the same characteristic to all members of a group, making it a stereotype. In reality, some Democrats are not liberals but tend to be more middle of the road or even conservative. Option (1) is incorrect because liberals favor the development of government programs, which indicates that they favor change. Options (2) and (5) are not stereotypes but are simple statements of fact. Option (3) is incorrect because radicals, by definition, favor change.

4. **(1) radical** (Application) This is the only category of people listed that would favor such extreme changes. Option (2) is incorrect because conservatives would oppose programs that increase government's power and its involvement in people's lives. Option (3) is incorrect because reactionaries support a return to old ways and ideas rather than new ones. Options (4) and (5) apply to members of the two major parties, not to third-party members.

5. **(5) the election of an officeholder who is supported by fewer than half the voters** (Analysis) Without such a system in place for races with three or more candidates, the candidate with the most votes would be the winner even if he or she received fewer than half of all the votes cast. Option (1) is wrong because the system applies to just this situation—when an election includes more than two candidates.

No cause-and-effect relationship exists between the system described and option (2), (3), or (4).

6. **(3) Democrats and Republicans put aside their differences to pass the balanced-budget law.** (Comprehension) This is symbolized by the "marriage" between the two parties to achieve a balanced federal budget. Nothing in the cartoon suggests option (1), (2), or (4). Option (5) is incorrect because of the cartoon's reference to the balanced budget as the "wallet" issue that has joined the parties.

7. **(5) The parties will cooperate in Congress as long as it is in their best interests.** (Comprehension) The "we" in the cartoon relates to the two political parties, as indicated by the word *both* and by the figure of the donkey and elephant. The conditional cooperation of the parties is suggested by "so long as we both shall prosper." Options (1), (3), and (4) are contradicted by this caution. Nothing in the cartoon suggests option (2) as the meaning of the elephant's pledge.

8. **(2) influence** (Evaluation) Making a big contribution to each candidate will gain an interest group access to the officeholder, regardless of an election's outcome. Option (1) is incorrect because if the groups valued money most, they would not give it to candidates. Their practice of contributing to rival candidates and parties suggests that options (3), (4), and (5) are not highly valued either.

9. **(4) Donations to congressional candidates are limited in size.** (Analysis) Candidates for federal office can accept no more than $1,000 from an individual or $5,000 from a PAC. State and local candidates are not subject to these restrictions. Option (1) is incorrect because the passage does not discuss which races are financed by federal funds, and in fact federal funding applies to presidential candidates only. Option (2) is not a difference because it is true for governors too. Options (3) and (5) are incorrect because they are both true, highlighting a similarity, not a difference.

10. **(5) There are no limits on contributions.** (Analysis) The passage states that PACs can give unlimited amounts of money to political parties. The political parties, in turn, use this money to help party candidates in their campaigns. Options (1) and (4) are true, but there is no evidence in the passage that they are responsible for the failure of campaign finance reform. Many individuals contribute to the campaigns of several candidates as well. Options (2) and (3) are unlikely to have an effect, because despite these limits, PACs can contribute unlimited amounts of money to political parties.

Lesson 14
GED Skill Focus (Page 161)
1. **b.** the Department of State
2. **b.** the Department of Justice
3. **a.** the Department of the Treasury

GED Content Focus (Page 163)
1. **(1) unemployment insurance benefits** (Application) Because she did not quit, she is eligible for unemployment benefits. The context does not suggest that she is over age 65 or in need of housing, so options (2) and (4) are not appropriate. There is no information about a history of military service or about her financial need, so options (3) and (5) are also incorrect.

2. **(5) apply to the Department of Veterans Affairs** (Application) Further job training for veterans is offered by the Department of Veterans Affairs. The man is too young for option (1). His wife has a well-paying job, so he would not be eligible for option (2), and he quit his own job, so he is not eligible for option (4). Option (3) provides health insurance and so would not solve the employment and job skills problem.

3. **(3) with the Medicare program** (Application) Because she is an older worker, she might be eligible for some medical benefits. She is not unemployed, so option (1) is not correct. Option (2) is inappropriate because her problem is not poverty or lack of food. There is no evidence that she is a veteran, so option (4) is incorrect. Nothing in the chart or passage discusses option (5), so you cannot assess whether or not the local government would help the woman pay her medical bills.

4. **(2) the Social Security Administration** (Application) As a surviving spouse of a covered worker, the woman is eligible to receive benefits on her husband's social security account. Nothing in the passage indicates that she would be eligible for help from option (1) or (5). Because there is no evidence that she needs help with housing or food, options (3) and (4) are incorrect.

5. **(1) free medical care and hospitalization benefits for veterans** (Application) This is the only give-away listed. Option (2) is a loan. Option (4) is a tax credit, and options (3) and (5) are not a subsidies at all.

6. **(3) It is promoting the general welfare of its citizens.** (Comprehension) The passage implies that the government uses subsidies to help individuals, businesses, and states pay for services or things they might otherwise be unable to afford. This falls under the category of promoting the general welfare, which is one of the goals of government stated in the U.S.

Constitution. Option (1) is incorrect because subsidies are not used to affect the way the government is run. Option (2) is incorrect because even though some subsidies relate to the armed forces, they do not pay for waging war to defend the nation. Options (4) and (5) are incorrect because none of the subsidies mentioned in the passage ensure freedom for this or future generations.

GED Practice (Pages 164–165)

1. **(5) Interest Payments on National Debt** (Comprehension) The passage indicates that the national debt arises from the sale of Treasury notes and bonds. The payment of interest on these obligations would fall into this category. The categories in options (1), (2), (3), and (4) are not appropriate to such payments.

2. **(2) The largest portion of money the government spends is paid directly to the people.** (Comprehension) The graph shows that 47 percent of government spending is for this purpose. Option (1) is not supported by any information in the passage and cannot be determined from the information in the graph. Option (3) is contradicted by the passage, which points out that the government also borrows money to pay for government programs. Option (4) is incorrect because interest on the national debt is an expense of government, not a source of income. Neither the passage nor the graph provides information on the amount the government spends on social welfare, so option (5) is not correct (and is not, in fact, true).

3. **(3) Taxes will increase.** (Analysis) The main source of government income would be the most likely to increase. If the government was spending more money than it was taking in, it would be unable to reduce taxes, so options (1) and (2) are incorrect. Option (4) is incorrect because, with its need for money, the government would be likely to offer more rather than fewer bonds. Option (5) has no support in the passage.

4. **(2) Direct Payments to Americans** (Application) Social security involves monthly benefits paid directly to people who are disabled, who are retired or the spouses of deceased workers, or who are over age 65. The categories in options (1), (3), and (4) do not fit the context of these payments. Option (5) does not relate to money the government spends but rather to money the government takes in.

5. **(5) Part of the Bill of Rights is threatened when citizens do not serve.** (Analysis) If large enough numbers of citizens avoided jury duty, the effect would be to make it more difficult to form juries for trials. If a jury could not be impaneled, the defendant would be deprived of a basic right in the Bill of Rights. The information in the passage implies that option (1) is incorrect. Options (2), (3), and (4) may be true, but they have no relationship to whether a person serves on a jury.

6. **(2) a driver's license** (Application) As a voter registration card authorizes a person to vote, a driver's license authorizes a person to operate a motor vehicle. Both are required documents that the government uses to monitor and control eligibility to perform an activity. The other documents listed do not serve this function. Option (1) represents a line of credit against which the cardholder borrows when using the card to make a purchase; the credit card is not issued by the government. Options (3) and (4) are documents that provide a record of something having happened. Option (5) provides evidence of health, life, or auto insurance coverage.

7. **(1) 220** (Application) This is the number of the precinct in which Michael B. Livens lives, so it is the number the registrar will use to determine where he should vote. None of the other numbers refers to a place to vote. Option (2) identifies the U.S. Post Office that serves Mr. Livens' address; there are likely to be several precincts and polling places within a single zip code. Option (3) identifies the city in which Mr. Livens lives and votes. Option (4) is Mr. Livens' date of birth, and option (5) is the date after which he can vote.

8. **(4) Only the people who meet the eligibility requirements should be allowed to vote.** (Evaluation) Voters must be at least age 18, be citizens, and be residents of the precinct in which they are voting. A registration process is evidence of the intent that would-be voters meet these standards. Nothing in the passage suggests that option (1) or (5) is correct. Option (2) is incorrect because requiring advance registration could reduce the number of people voting. Option (3) is incorrect because the number of people who can legally register to vote is quite large, and all of these people would be eligible to vote if they registered.

GED Mini-Test (Pages 166–167)

1. **(2) It was closer than the black school.** (Comprehension) This intent is stated in the passage. There is no evidence in the passage that suggests that option (1) or (4) was the reason or was even true. The law in Kansas required Brown to enroll his daughter in the black school, not the white school, so option (3) is incorrect. Option (5) is incorrect because if he had supported the doctrine, he would not have wanted his daughter to attend a "whites-only" school.

2. **(4) a feeling of equality and self-worth**
(Evaluation) Justice Warren implied he held these values through his statement in the court opinion in the key document. Although Warren probably believed high-quality education was important, his stand against segregation did not relate specifically to the quality of the education being offered, so option (1) is incorrect. Nothing in his statement supports option (2) or (5). Option (3) is also incorrect, because such teachers would be found in segregated schools as well as integrated ones.

3. **(5) an end to separate seating by race on buses and trains and in movie theaters**
(Analysis) This is the only one of the options that involves segregation. None of the other options offers a context similar to segregation in schools. Options (1) and (2) deal with equal economic opportunities and political power, not the segregation or integration of physical facilities. Options (3) and (4) are the direct and indirect effects, respectively, of option (2), not of the desegregation of public schools.

4. **(4) Their case led to the requirement that public schools be racially integrated.**
(Analysis) This was the effect of the case. There is no support in the passage for option (1) or (3), both of which are untrue. Discrimination continued in society, so option (2) is incorrect. There is no evidence to suggest that option (5) was an effect of this case.

5. **(3) $1,688** (Comprehension) Look at the bar for the year 1950 to find this answer. The other options result from reading the figure for the wrong year.

6. **(4) Between 1980 and 1990, the national debt per person more than tripled.**
(Evaluation) You can see this by comparing the figures given for these two years and/or the length of the bars. Option (1) is incorrect because the per capita debt fell in 1960. To calculate option (2), you would need to know the 1990 U.S. population, which is not given in the graph. You would also need population figures for 1950 and 1960 to know whether option (3) is correct. (It is not an accurate statement.) Although the graph shows that the nation was in debt for the years listed, it does not show every year, so option (5) is not directly supported by the information in the graph.

7. **(1) monthly increases in a credit-card balance** (Application) The continued borrowing that increases national debt is similar to continued charging on a credit card. Although options (2) and (3) involve debt, they have nothing to do with an escalating debt. In fact, they both involve a decrease in the amount of

the debt. Options (4) and (5) have nothing to do with debt.

8. **(5) More interest accumulated on the national debt during 1999 than the government paid off.** (Analysis) The national debt is much like credit card debt. If a credit card is paid down more slowly than interest is accumulating, the total debt will rise despite the payments, even when nothing more is charged on it. Options (1), (2), and (4) cannot be determined from the information provided. Option (3) is contradicted by the paragraph.

9. **(1) They are largely shaped by self-interest.** (Evaluation) Each group is influenced by its own needs. Nothing in the information supports the other options as general factors. Option (2) is incorrect because none of the information is connected to political parties. The information does not mention or imply that the factors listed in options (3) and (4) influence political opinion. Although the information includes occupations as examples, option (5) does not get at the principle behind all of the examples.

Unit 3 Cumulative Review (Pages 168–174)

1. **(1) The World's Charismatic Leaders**
(Comprehension) Most of the passage is devoted to identifying some of the world's greatest charismatic leaders. Options (2) and (4) are not discussed in the passage. Option (3) is incorrect because the topic is barely mentioned and not explained. The passage provides information about where the specific leaders came from, but it does not cover the topic of where charismatic leaders in general come from, so option (5) is also incorrect.

2. **(4) Mohandas Gandhi was a brilliant person.** (Analysis) This is a judgment that cannot be incontestably proven. The other options are all facts that can be proven to be true. Options (1), (3), and (5) are matters of historical record. Option (2) can be demonstrated by the polls conducted while Reagan was president.

3. **(5) The political figures identified will be familiar to readers.** (Analysis) The lack of identifying information about these people indicates that the writer assumes they will be recognized. Nothing in the passage suggests option (1), (2), or (3). Option (4) is incorrect because charisma is explained in the passage.

4. **(3) They all are revolutionaries.** (Evaluation) Because some of the most famous charismatic leaders were leaders of revolutions does not mean that all were, and in fact, some of the leaders mentioned in the passage were elected officials. To characterize all charismatic leaders as

revolutionaries is to stereotype them. The other options are all reasonable statements based on the information in the passage. Option (1) is stated in the passage, and option (2) is implied in it. Options (4) and (5) are a major part of what defines people as charismatic leaders.

5. **(3) federal regulation of the banking industry** (Application) This is a public service of the federal government, which is highly centralized. Regulated banks must meet the same set of standards regardless of their location. Options (1), (2), (4), and (5) are services provided by local or regional governments. The controls and standards established by these governments will vary from place to place.

6. **(2) The Internal Revenue Service collects taxes from individuals and businesses.** (Analysis) You will not be able to understand the cartoon unless you already know this. Option (1) is true but is not prior knowledge that is necessary to understanding this cartoon. Option (3) may or may not actually be true; but the location of the lasso under the welcome mat, indicates the cartoonist considers the Internal Revenue Service (IRS) to be a menace rather than helpful to people. Options (4) and (5) are not related to the content of the cartoon and so are not unstated assumptions; in addition, neither is true.

7. **(5) Federal tax laws make it difficult to successfully run a business in America.** (Comprehension) The free enterprise sign indicates that the cartoon is about businesses and the lasso under the IRS welcome mat is a symbol of tax laws that trap businesses. Option (1) relates to the literal meaning of the cartoon rather than the symbolic meaning. The lasso under the welcome mat serves as a warning against option (2). Nothing in the cartoon indicates that the businessman is corrupt, so option (3) is incorrect. The indications that option (4) is incorrect include the "arm" and "leg" signs on the night depository, showing that the cartoonist believes that the IRS demands unreasonably high tax payments from businesses. (When something is expensive, we say that it "costs an arm and a leg.")

8. **(3) The Internal Revenue Service is fair in its dealings.** (Analysis) The lasso and the deposit box for arms and legs clearly indicate that the cartoonist believes the IRS is trapping taxpayers into paying huge amounts of taxes. Options (1) and (2) are incorrect because they are not opinions, but facts. Option (4) is an opinion with which the cartoonist would agree. Not enough information is present in the cartoon to suggest whether the cartoonist would agree or disagree with the opinion expressed in option (5).

9. **(3) There has been a dramatic increase in the number of elderly people.** (Analysis) This is the only reasonable explanation. In recent decades, a higher standard of living and longer life expectancy have increased the population of older Americans, which has put a strain on the Medicare program by increasing the total amount of benefits it must pay. Options (1) and (5) are opinions that do not explain the causes of the problems with the Medicare program. If option (2) were true, it would have had an effect on Medicare that is the opposite of what has happened. There is no cause-and-effect relationship between option (4) and the financial condition of the Medicare program.

10. **(3) 1976, 1992, and 1996** (Comprehension) The numbers above the bars show that the Democratic candidates got more popular votes than the Republican candidates in this combination of election years. Option (1) is incorrect because the Republican candidate received more votes than the Democratic candidate in 1980 and 1984. Option (2) is incorrect because all three elections were won by the Republican candidates. The Republican candidate won the 1980 election, so option (4) is incorrect, and the Republicans won the election in 1988, making option (5) incorrect.

11. **(5) The Republican candidate had a larger margin of victory in 1984 than in 1988.** (Evaluation) This is the only statement that the graph supports. The Republican candidate received 16 million more votes than the Democratic candidate in 1984, as compared with 6 million more votes in 1988. This indicates a greater margin of Republican victory in 1984 than in 1988. Option (1) is incorrect because the number of third-party voters declined by 10 million between 1992 and 1996. Option (2) is incorrect because the graph shows that the Republicans won three elections during that period (1980, 1984, and 1988). Option (3) is incorrect because the Democrats did not win the 1980 election. Option (4) cannot be determined from the information in the graph. There were more third-party voters in 1996 than in 1980, but the graph does not show whether those voters would have supported the Republican or the Democrat had no third-party candidates been on the ballot.

12. **(4) 1992** (Analysis) In 1992, the total of the Republican and third-party vote was 55 million, while the Democrat received 45 million votes, or less than half the total. The other options are incorrect because the 1976 winner received 40 million votes and the losing candidate received 39 million; the 1980 winner received 44 million votes, compared with 42 million for the two

losing candidates; the 1988 winner received 49 million votes, compared with 43 million for the other candidate; and the 1996 winner received 48 million votes, compared with 45 million for the two losing candidates.

13. **(3) improved safety conditions** (Analysis) Because OSHA was created to oversee safety, the improvements in safety conditions that have occurred can be linked to its activities. Option (1) is the most unlikely result. Options (2), (4), and (5) do not relate to safety in the workplace.

14. **(4) freedom of religion** (Application) Opponents of school prayer would turn to the "establishment clause" of the First Amendment ("Congress shall make no law respecting [requiring] an establishment of religion"), while supporters of school prayer would cite the "free-exercise clause" (that nothing can prohibit "the free exercise [of religion]"). Although proponents of school prayer might turn to option (1), opponents would not. Options (2), (3), and (5) do not relate to the context of this situation.

15. **(3) freedom of association** (Application) The right of people to carry out political party activity is dependent on this freedom, even if that party is opposed to the economic and social order of the nation. Although option (1) is a related right, freedom of association is the principal right in this situation. Options (2), (4), and (5) do not apply in this context.

16. **(5) equal protection of the laws** (Application) This is the only option that directly applies. Discriminating against a person because of race or because the person is female or male deprives the person of equal treatment under the law. Options (1), (2), (3) and (4) do not apply to this situation.

17. **(2) freedom of the press** (Application) Freedom of the press allows newspapers, magazines, and news programs on television and radio to report on the activities of government officials. Freedom of speech issues are not involved because the commentator is reporting news, not expressing an individual opinion, so option (1) is incorrect. Options (3), (4), and (5) do not apply to this context.

18. **(5) education** (Evaluation) Being a well-informed decision-maker requires that people be educated on issues, be able to engage in critical thinking, and have strong decision-making skills, which are also often linked to education. The values listed in options (1), (2), (3), and (4), while they may be important or helpful for other aspects of life, do not necessarily lead people to be well-informed or good decision-makers.

19. **(3) 2,114,000** (Comprehension) This figure appears in the "State" column of the table in the "Education" row. All of the other options involve a misreading of the information in the table.

20. **(1) building public elementary, middle, and high schools and hiring teachers** (Application) The table shows that a total of 9,209,000 people are employed in education at the state and local levels, as compared with 11,000 at the federal level, which indicates that this is primarily a state and local function, rather than a national one. Options (2) and (4) are incorrect because the table shows that all defense and postal service workers are employed at the national level. Option (3) is incorrect because the national government is responsible for paying off its own debt, and there is no information about this function on the table. Option (5) is incorrect because the White House and the monuments in Washington, D.C., are national, not state or local, structures, so the national government is responsible for caring for them; also, the table provides no information on this.

21. **(1) More government workers are involved in education than in any other field.** (Evaluation) The table shows that more education workers are employed by government than any other job category. Options (2) and (3) are incorrect because the table does not contain information on trends. Option (4) is not correct because no pay information is provided. According to the table, option (5) is not true.

22. **(4) to convince government leaders to support certain causes** (Comprehension) This is the job, as specified in the paragraph. Options (1) and (2) relate to politics, as does the job of the lobbyist, but they are not the lobbyist's job. Nothing in the passage supports option (3). Although lobbyists may travel around the country, traveling is not their job, so option (5) is incorrect.

23. **(2) writing a letter to a government official that presents your position on a controversial issue** (Application) In trying to convince the official of your position, you are acting like a lobbyist. Option (1) is not lobbying because it merely reports on government activities and does not try to influence leaders. Options (3) and (4) state a position but do not involve a contact with a government official. Option (5) is incorrect because the mere act of joining an interest group does not constitute lobbying.

24. **(2) The President's Role in Foreign Policy** (Comprehension) This title covers basic topic of the passage. Options (1) and (3) are too general.

Answers and Explanations

Options (4) and (5) reflect issues that are not covered in detail in the passage.

25. **(1) The president has more responsibility for the nation's foreign policy than anyone else.** (Analysis) All the other options are details—examples and explanations of powers and functions that support the conclusion that the president is the nation's single most important foreign policy leader.

26. **(5) power to conduct U.S. affairs with other nations** (Application) By withholding U.S. participation in the Olympics, Carter was showing U.S. displeasure with the Soviet Union because of its invasion of Afghanistan. He did not use the armed forces as an instrument of foreign policy in this situation, so option (1) is incorrect. The U.S. response did not involve recognition or recalling of ambassadors, which eliminates options (2) and (3) as correct answers. Option (4) is incorrect because the president does not hold this position.

27. **(1) Members of Congress present themselves as independent even though they follow the advice of special interest groups.** (Analysis) The cartoon shows that the congressman cannot even declare his independence without the lobbyist telling him what to say. Options (2) and (3) are both facts. Option (4) is not supported by the cartoon. Option (5) may or may not be true, but it is not implied by the statements the figure makes in the cartoon.

28. **(4) $722,000,000** (Comprehension) The table indicates that its figures are in millions of dollars. It shows that California had $722 million left to help fund other operations and programs after the lottery winners' prizes and the lottery's expenses were paid. Options (1), (2), and (3) involve misreading the table. Option (5) is the total amount the lottery took in before prizes and expenses were subtracted. Not all of this money would have been available to fund other state operations.

29. **(2) Lotteries can supply millions of dollars in revenue for some states.** (Evaluation) The data in the third column of the table support this statement. Options (1) and (4) are opinions that are not supported by the information available, which does not define "enough revenue" or explain how to determine which is the "best" lottery. Options (3) and (5) are contradicted by the passage.

30. **(1) Massachusetts** (Analysis) This is demonstrated by the fact that the Massachusetts lottery has the largest disparity (in dollar amount) between its revenues and its proceeds

after expenses. Options (2), (3), (4), and (5) all show slightly smaller profits than Massachusetts, but they also all have much smaller total revenues from ticket sales.

31. **(2) Presidents have sent U.S. forces into combat without a declaration of war.** (Comprehension) This is the only statement that is implied by the information. Option (1) is contradicted by the information. Option (3) is not true, as the names of the conflicts indicate. Nothing in the information implies that either option (4) or (5) is true.

UNIT 4: ECONOMICS
Lesson 15
GED Skill Focus (Page 179)
1. **a.** Trade broccoli to Polly for bread, and trade bread to Maria for ground beef.

   b. Mow Maria's lawn in exchange for ground beef.

2. **a.** *B:* Dan lets Polly use his delivery truck in return for 500 pounds of cabbage.

   b. *M:* Maria sells her store to Polly, and they negotiate the purchase price.

   c. *M:* Polly borrows money from Maria and uses it to buy Dan's delivery truck.

   d. *M:* Dan reduces the price of broccoli in order to entice more customers to buy it.

   e. *B:* Polly repays the loan from Maria by letting Maria use the delivery truck one week each month.

GED Content Focus (Page 181)
1. **(2) how much demand there is for the product compared to the supply available for purchase** (Comprehension) This relationship is summarized in the first paragraph of the passage. Option (1) is incorrect, because it is a definition of *supply*, and does not explain the relationship between supply, demand, and price. Nothing in the passage suggests that option (3), (4), or (5) affects how much a product will cost.

2. **(1) Demand for the product will go up.** (Comprehension) This is discussed in paragraph 2 and established by the demand curve, which illustrates the principle that the lower the price of a product, the greater the demand for that product. So when the price of a product goes down, the demand for the product goes up. Options (2) and (3) are contradicted by information on the demand curve. Options (4) and (5) are contradicted by the information in the supply curve.

3. **(3) at a high price** (Comprehension) This relationship is stated in paragraph 3 and shown on the supply curve. Options (1) and (2) are contradicted by the supply curve. Options (4) and (5) mention factors about which there is no information on the supply curve.

4. **(1) when demand for the product goes down** (Analysis) When demand goes down, this means that fewer purchasers want to buy the product. Therefore, some of the product will remain unsold—in other words, a product surplus will result. Option (2) is incorrect because when demand for a product goes up, a shortage rather than a surplus is likely to result. Option (3) is incorrect because a lower price is likely to stimulate demand, and as with option (2), will result in a shortage rather than a surplus. Option (4) is incorrect; low supply and high prices are most likely to occur when demand is high, again resulting in a shortage rather than a surplus. Option (5) is incorrect because the equilibrium price is when supply and demand meet and in these circumstances it is unlikely that either a surplus or a shortage will result.

5. **(2) $2** (Comprehension) The graph shows that the supply curve and the demand curve meet at this price level. According to the passage, this is the equilibrium point for the candy and the price at which purchasers are willing to buy all the candy that sellers are willing to provide at that price. Options (1), (3), (4), and (5) are incorrect because the supply curve and the demand curve do not meet (supply does not equal demand) at those price levels.

6. **(4) It would lower demand and lower the equilibrium price.** (Application) Such an association between cold sores and eating candy, if shown to be true, would probably lower the demand for the candy, which would result in a lower equilibrium price. Option (1) is the opposite of what would happen. Options (2) and (3) are impossibilities, given the definition of the equilibrium price. Option (5) is incorrect, because in this situation, the demand for the candy and the equilibrium price would go down, as explained above.

GED Practice (Pages 182–183)

1. **(5) teacher and park naturalist** (Analysis) The graph shows that the average starting pay for each of these occupations is $22,000 a year. Option (1) is incorrect because there is a $4,000 difference in the starting pay of teachers ($22,000) and dental hygienists ($18,000). Option (2) is incorrect because there is a $1,000 difference in the starting pay of medical illustrators ($11,000) and sales clerks ($10,000). Option (3) is incorrect because there is a $2,000 difference between messengers ($14,000) and

typists ($16,000). Option (4) cannot be determined because neither the passage nor the graph indicates the earnings of doctors or doctor's office receptionists.

2. **(2) There is less demand for medical illustrators.** (Analysis) The only explanation is that there must be a very low demand for medical illustrators, or a very high demand for messengers, relative to the number of people who are available for such jobs. Applying the same principles of supply and demand to the other options rules them out. Options (1) and (5) are incorrect because they would be reasons for medical illustrators to earn higher pay; both would limit the supply of people to fill illustrator jobs. Option (3) would increase the supply of people wanting to be messengers, which would result in lower pay in that occupation. Option (4) is not an explanation because the demand for people to fill a job compared to the supply of people willing and able to do it, not the number of people in absolute terms, is what sets a job's wages.

3. **(1) The job of police officer is dangerous.** (Application) Supply is the basic principle that applies here. The passage indicates that danger makes certain jobs difficult or undesirable, which limits the supply of available workers, thereby raising pay. When there is a shortage of workers, employers offer higher wages in order to attract more job seekers. Nothing in the passage suggests option (2), which, if true, would cause pay to be lower since the supply of potential officers would be higher than the demand for them. Option (3) is incorrect because some training is required for most jobs, many of which do not pay as well as police officer. Neither the passage nor the graph discusses the effect of gender on salary, so option (4) is incorrect. Option (5) is incorrect because there is no evidence in the passage or chart comparing the salaries and service to society of police officers and doctors.

4. **(4) It was better in the past than it is today.** (Evaluation) The passage indicates that when there was a shortage of lawyers, pay was high; and now that there is a lawyer surplus, wages are subject to the forces of supply and demand. This information supports the idea that starting salaries might have fallen off for lawyers. There is not enough information in the passage and graph to support option (1) or (5). The passage indicates that the trend would be the opposite of option (2). Option (3) is true, but it cannot be concluded from the information provided in the passage and graph.

5. **(3) changing** (Comprehension) The pattern is one of change—from much business activity, to little activity, and back to increased business

activity. Options (1) and (2) are opinions about the cycle that are not supported by the passage. Option (4) is the opposite of what the passage describes. The passage does not discuss the size of the business cycle, so option (5) is incorrect.

6. **(3) trough** (Analysis) The chart suggests that recession and depression are both economic low points that vary in degree of severity. This indicates that they would occur at the bottom of a business cycle. Option (1) is incorrect because neither the chart nor the passage links inflation with depression or recession. Options (2), (4), and (5) relate to prosperous economic periods, the opposite of recession and depression.

7. **(1) inflation** (Application) This is the only option that results in higher prices. Options (2) and (3) are related to economic downturns, in which people have less money, making price increases unlikely. Options (4) and (5) do not correlate definitively to what happens to prices of particular goods.

8. **(5) It is not seriously affected by minor variations in the pattern.** (Analysis) The passage indicates that the business cycle—and with it, the American economy—continues in its overall pattern despite frequent upswings and downswings. There is no discussion in the passage of the current state of the economy or the effect inflation has on it, so options (1) and (2) are incorrect. Option (3) is an opinion that cannot be concluded from any of the information provided. Option (4) is contradicted by information in the passage.

GED Mini-Test (Pages 184–185)

1. **(2) 1933** (Comprehension) The highest figure for unemployment was 24.9 percent in 1933. The figures for options (1), (3), (4), and (5) are all lower.

2. **(4) The 1990s rates are lower than the rates during the 1930s.** (Analysis) The table shows that unemployment rates were greater than 14 percent in the 1930s compared to less than 8 percent in the 1990s. This relationship makes options (3) and (5) incorrect. The rates for 1929 and 1943 make option (1) incorrect. The rates for each year in the 1930s make option (2) untrue.

3. **(3) the year America entered the war** (Evaluation) Knowing that America entered the war in December 1941 would allow a conclusion that the war lowered unemployment. Option (1) does not provide enough information by itself to allow this conclusion. Knowing options (2), (4), and (5) does not provide the kind of information needed to draw this conclusion.

4. **(1) the relationship of supply and demand** (Analysis) The table's unemployment figures indicate that, compared with the number of jobs, the supply of available workers was higher in 1939 than it was in 1929. Options (2), (4), and (5) are economics concepts that have nothing to do with wage levels. Option (3) is contradicted by the information given in the question; if option (3) were true, workers' wages would have been higher in 1939 than in 1929, but instead they were lower.

5. **(5) 6 percent compound interest** (Application) Because the percent of interest in options (4) and (5) is the highest, one of these must be correct. Option (4) is incorrect because Alicia will earn 6 percent only on the original $1,000. With option (5) she will earn interest not only on her $1,000, but also on the interest that has been already paid. Over time, this account will make the most money. Options (1), (2), and (3) will pay less because they offer lower interest rates.

6. **(5) The owners of each get the profits.** (Comprehension) According to the passage, the sole owner gets the profits in a proprietorship, and owners share the profits in a partnership. There is no size comparison given, so options (1) and (2) are incorrect. Option (3) is incorrect because management in a partnership is shared. Option (4) is contradicted by the passage.

7. **(3) responsibility for business debt** (Analysis) According to the passage, partners are liable for the company's debts, but the owners of a corporation have no personal liability. Option (1) is incorrect because the passage does not compare the sizes of partnerships and corporations. Option (2) is incorrect because in both cases profits are divided among the owner-investors according to how much of the company they own. Option (4) cannot be determined from the information in the passage. Option (5) is incorrect because both partnerships and corporations can have more than one owner.

8. **(4) They will agree about business decisions.** (Analysis) Because Ann and Dan's business arrangement is a partnership, neither Ann nor Dan can make decisions alone. If they are unable to agree, nothing can get done. Option (1) is incorrect because, unless Ann and Dan agree to another arrangement, profits in a partnership are split according to percentage of ownership. Option (2) is an opinion and there is no support for it. Option (3) is incorrect because in a partnership all partners are legally liable for the company's debts. Option (5) would be true only if both partners agreed to it.

9. (2) People borrow more money.
(Comprehension) The paragraph states that lower interest rates encourage people to borrow more money and spend it. Options (1) and (3) are incorrect because they state the opposite of what would be true in this situation. Nothing in the paragraph suggests option (4) or (5); in fact, the opposite would likely be true in this situation.

10. (3) He will have fewer customers.
(Analysis) The paragraph establishes that when unemployment rises, people have less money to spend. It also implies that when people feel financially pinched, they tend to buy fewer nonessentials. This would likely mean fewer meals in restaurants. As the paragraph indicates, option (1) is the opposite of what is generally true when unemployment rises. Nothing in the paragraph suggests a relationship between unemployment rates and interest rates or prices, so options (2) and (4) are incorrect. Option (5) is unlikely when unemployment is rising.

Lesson 16
GED Skill Focus (Page 187)
1. **a.** $495 billion

   b. $394 billion

   c. negative $100 billion

2. The nation had a **negative** balance of trade from the year **1990** to the year **1998.**

3. **b.** The balance of trade is a problem area in the American economy.

   c. In general, the value of American exports has been rising.

GED Content Focus (Page 189)
1. **(3) by borrowing money from the Federal Reserve and loaning it to their customers**
(Comprehension) This is stated in the first paragraph of the passage. The opposite of options (1) and (2) is implied by the passage, because either of these would decrease banks' earnings. Options (4) and (5) are incorrect because the passage states that these are set by the Fed, not by the banks themselves.

2. **(5) the Fed raises the discount rate**
(Comprehension) This information is provided in paragraph 3 of the passage. The passage suggests that the opposite of options (1) and (4) would be true. The passage gives no direct information relating interest rates on personal loans and economic depression, so option (2) is incorrect; in fact, the opposite of option (2) is implied. Option (3) is incorrect because the passage states that the prime rate is set by private banks, not by the Fed.

3. **(5) The number of loans decreases.**
(Comprehension) This is implied by the last two sentences of paragraph 3. If high interest rates discourage people from borrowing money, the result will be that less money is borrowed. Options (1), (2), and (4) are contradicted by information in the passage. Option (3) is incorrect because nothing in the passage relates to interest rates on savings accounts, although higher interest rates on loans generally lead to banks paying higher, not lower, interest rates on savings.

4. **(3) Rates on loans stayed about the same.**
(Comprehension) The graph shows that between 1995 and 1998 the prime rate on loans hovered around 8.5 percent. Options (1) and (5) are contradicted by the information in the graph. Options (2) and (4) are incorrect because the prime rate is charged on loans, so the graph doesn't relate directly the interest rate for savings accounts, and in any case, significant changes in savings-account interest rates would not be expected with prime interest rates holding steady.

5. **(1) raised the discount rate** (Analysis)
The graph shows that the prime rate rose sharply from the 1994 figure. The passages states that banks pass increases in the discount rate on to their customers in the form of higher interest rates on loans. So the increase in the prime rate could have been a result of the Fed's raising the discount rate. If option (2) were correct, the prime rate would have dropped rather than risen. Option (3) would probably result in the prime rate's falling, not rising, since the amount of money available for loans would be likely to increase. Options (4) and (5) are incorrect because the Fed does not make requirements about how banks set the prime rate.

6. **(4) The amount of money in the economy increased.** (Analysis) The graph shows that the prime rate dropped sharply from the previous year's figure. This indicates that the Fed lowered the discount rate. According to the passage, the effects of a lower discount rate are a lower prime rate and more lending, which result in an increased money supply. Options (1) and (2) are the opposite of what would happen due to the drop in the prime rate. Option (3) would have led to a higher prime rate in 1986, and the graph shows that this did not happen. Option (5) is incorrect, because the graph doesn't show a steep enough drop in interest rates in 1985 to indicate the onset of a depression.

7. **(3) so money will be readily available to cover a bank's obligations** (Evaluation)
This is the only reason that is supported by evidence from the passage. It is suggested by the

statement that one of the Fed's major functions is to supervise the operations of private banks. There is no evidence in the passage that would lead to option (1), (2), or (5) as a reason. Option (4) is not supported, since the nothing in the passage indicates that the Fed deals directly with consumers.

8. **(1) a bank that is a member of the Fed** (Application) Member banks are closely supervised by the Fed, which suggests that they are more stable and safer than banks that are not members. Option (2) is incorrect because a bank that kept all its money in its vault would not be earning anything on the money, so it would not be the best place to put savings, since the bank would be unable to pay interest on the money. The passage does not tie making loans to bank quality or the lack of it, so options (3) and (4) are incorrect. Option (5) is not correct, since the passage states that Federal Reserve banks are bankers' banks and not for consumers.

GED Practice (Pages 190–191)

1. **(4) the GDP adjusted for price increases that are due to inflation** (Comprehension) This definition is given in the final paragraph of the passage. Option (1) is defined in the passage as the actual GDP. Nothing in the passage states or implies option (2), (3), or (5) as a definition of the real GDP.

2. **(3) an ear of corn grown in Illinois** (Application) The passage defines goods as physical products and states that the GDP is the value of all goods and services produced in the United States during a year. The ear of corn is a physical object that was produced and is thus a good. It is also a food—one of the things cited as types of goods. Option (1) is a good but, as a year-old used car, it would have been counted in the GDP for the year in which it was produced. Options (2) and (4) are services rather than goods because they are not physical objects. Option (5) would not be included because it was produced in Japan rather than in the United States.

3. **(2) The nation's economy grew steadily.** (Comprehension) This can be seen in the steady rise of the lines for both the actual GDP and the real GDP on the graph. None of the other options, even if they are true, can be inferred from the information on the graph.

4. **(1) About a third of the growth in the GDP has been due to inflation.** (Evaluation) The evidence for this statement is in the shaded area on the graph, which represents the part of the GDP that is the result of inflation (the difference between the actual GDP and the real GDP). The graph shows that it amounts to about one-third of GDP growth. Since the graph gives

no data from the 1980s, neither option (2) nor option (3) can be concluded from the graph. Options (4) and (5) are true, but are also not supported by the graph.

5. **(5) Without government protections, companies might knowingly sell products that harm people.** (Comprehension) This is implied by the last statement in the first paragraph of the passage. The passage's focus on government consumer protection agencies suggests that the writer disagrees with options (1) and (4). Option (2) is incorrect because neither the passage nor the chart compares the effectiveness of the FDA to that of the FAA in protecting consumers. Option (3) is incorrect because, although food items are mentioned several times in the passage and chart, nothing in the passage or chart suggests that the writer views food as the most serious product safety issue.

6. **(3) consumers** (Application) This can be determined by applying the information that grocers figure the anticipated cost of their losses from "bad" food when they set their prices, thus passing the cost of these losses on to the consumer. Nothing in the passage or chart suggests options (1), (4), or (5) is the correct answer. Option (2) is incorrect because of the information in the passage about costs being passed to consumers.

7. **(5) to help prevent Americans from buying potentially harmful goods and services** (Analysis) Every agency listed in the chart sets and enforces quality, safety, and labeling regulations and standards that perform this function for some category of goods or services. Option (1) is incorrect because the chart indicates that only the FSIS, the FDA, and the FTC regulate advertising directly or indirectly, (through labeling). Option (2) is incorrect because the chart indicates that only the FTC is involved in preventing price-fixing by competitors. Option (3) is a function of only the FSIS and the FDA. Option (4) is untrue and is neither suggested nor implied by the chart.

GED Mini-Test (Pages 192–193)

1. **(3) Small businesses compete.** (Analysis) This is correct because the passage states that socialism allows some competition. The writer assumes that you know that competition is an aspect of capitalism's "free enterprise." Options (1) and (2) are incorrect because they are features of socialism and communism, not of capitalism. Although providing people with everything they need is part of the theory of communism, the passage does not claim that any system—neither capitalism, nor socialism, nor communism—does

this, so option (4) is incorrect. Option (5) refers only to capitalism.

2. **(4) They are economic systems.** (Analysis) This is the only thing they have in common. In almost every way, communism and capitalism are vastly different systems. Option (1) applies only to capitalism. Option (2) is true, in theory, only of communist systems, not capitalist systems. Option (3) is true of capitalism but not of communism, which, because it depends heavily on central planning, works best in a dictatorship. Option (5) is true in communist systems but not in capitalist ones.

3. **(1) Individual freedom is associated with capitalism.** (Evaluation) According to the passage, private ownership and economic freedom are the main features of capitalism, so individual freedom must be part of it as well. Option (2) is incorrect because the passage has nothing to say about the success or failure of socialism. Option (3) is not supported by the passage, which says only that, in theory, everyone gets what they need under communism. Option (4) is contradicted by information that capitalism is linked with democracy. Option (5) is incorrect because the last paragraph outlines some links between economic and political systems.

4. **(3) what the reality of communism is** (Evaluation) Information about the reality of communism, which is not given in the passage, is needed to draw a conclusion about how it differs from theory as presented in the passage. So option (1) is incorrect. Option (2) is not enough to allow the contrast between reality and theory. Some details of theory are included in the passage, but the passage does not provide any information about reality, so option (4) is incorrect. Option (5) would not lead to a conclusion about communist theory and practice.

5. **(2) consumer protection** (Application) A warranty protects the buyer in case the product does not work right or something else is wrong with it. Warranties are not related to economic systems, so options (1) and (5) are incorrect. Warranties do not relate to national economics or to market forces, so options (3) and (4) are incorrect.

6. **(5) The number of TV stations has risen since 1950.** (Comprehension) The graph shows that the number of stations has increased more than ten-fold since 1950, from about 100 to more than 1,100. Options (1), (2), and (4) are opinions that are not supported or even addressed by the information in the graph. Option (3) is not implied information because it is given directly in the graph.

7. **(1) Some businesses were operating against the public interest.** (Analysis) This is an unstated cause that is implied by the nature of regulatory commissions. There is no support for option (2), (3), (4), or (5) as a reason for the formation of regulatory commissions.

8. **(4) citizens and a radio station** (Comprehension) The passage states that one of the functions of a regulatory commission is to settle disputes and discusses the potential for one station's interfering with another's broadcast and ruining people's entertainment. If people complained about the station, the FCC would become involved. Although the passage names certain industries in which regulatory commissions are most prominent, nothing in the information suggests that the FCC would rule in a dispute involving industries other than the broadcast industry, so options (1) and (3) are incorrect. Options (2) and (5) are incorrect because the FCC is not responsible for resolving political disputes.

9. **(3) Broadcast wavelengths have to be carefully shared.** (Evaluation) This is supported by the information in the passage that states that wavelengths are limited in number and implies that signal interference can occur, and by the graph, which shows the large number of TV stations. No evidence exists in the passage or the graph to support option (1), (4), or (5). The passage establishes that the FCC is powerful, but no information leads to option (2) as a conclusion.

Lesson 17
GED Skill Focus (Page 195)
1. **a.** about 82%

   b. about 25%

2. **a.** Agricultural workers were a much smaller part of the U.S. labor force in 1990 than one hundred years before.

3. **a.** *T:* During the two centuries since the United States was founded, the makeup of the labor force has changed.

   b. *T:* Until the late 1800s, most U.S. workers were agricultural workers.

   c. *F:* After the United States industrialized in the late 1800s, most of the nation's workers were in manufacturing industries.

   d. *X:* By the 1990s, automation had cut deep into the manufacturing sector.

   e. *X:* Now, the fastest-growing occupations are in the service sector of the economy.

GED Content Focus (Page 197)

1. **(2) Labor costs are lower overseas.** (Comprehension) This is stated in paragraph 2 of the passage. The topics of options (1) and (5) are not dealt with in the passage, so these options are incorrect. The passage implies that option (3) is incorrect for U.S. factory workers. Option (4) is incorrect because the passage states that many of the goods made by U.S.-owned companies overseas are sold in the United States.

2. **(4) farm worker** (Comprehension) The graph shows that the lowest projected percentage of workers in 2008 will be in agriculture, forestry, and fishing. So opportunities for farm workers are projected to be very limited. Options (1), (2), (3), and (5) are all jobs that fall into categories that are projected to make up a higher proportion of the U.S. labor force in 2008.

3. **(1) administrative support and clerical** (Analysis) This can be determined by comparing values of each area's bars for 1988 and 2008. By 2008 administrative support and clerical workers are projected to make up 1.9 percent less of the workforce than they did in 1988. This is the largest decline on the graph. Option (2) is projected to rise, while option (3) will decline by 1.4 percent and option (4) by 1.5 percent. Option (5) will decline the least percentage-wise.

4. **(5) The need for operators, fabricators, and laborers is shrinking.** (Analysis) The passage states that the overseas transfer of jobs is shrinking the manufacturing sector, and this trend is reflected in the data for operators, fabricators, and laborers in the graph. Nothing in the information suggests that option (1), (2), or (4) is a consequence of overseas job transfer. The passage states that option (3) has also reduced manufacturing job opportunities; however this option is incorrect because this is not the result of jobs going overseas.

5. **(2) Not enough native-born workers have the needed technical skills.** (Analysis) This is the basic reason for this trend. The passage states that employers must recruit overseas to fill these positions. But option (1) is the *effect* of option (2), not the reason why immigrants fill these jobs. Option (3) is incorrect because the passage states only that people trained overseas are filling these jobs. It does not compare their training with that of native-born workers. Option (4) is true, but it does not apply to this situation because the work is taking place in the United States. Nothing in the information suggests that option (5) is true.

6. **(3) Manufacturing jobs are becoming less important in the U.S. economy**. (Evaluation) The passage states that U.S. manufacturing jobs are going overseas as well as disappearing as a result of the mechanization of U.S. factories. In addition, the graph shows that operators, fabricators, and laborers are becoming a smaller segment of the workforce. All three points provide strong evidence to support this conclusion. There is no evidence in the passage or the graph to support option (1). The graph data contradict options (2) and (5) because they show that the managerial sector's size is increasing as a percentage off the labor market, and that of the four sectors of the economy that are growing, the managerial and marketing and sales sectors are both growing more slowly than the service sector. There is also no evidence in either the passage or the graph to support the cause-and-effect relationship suggested in option (4).

7. **(5) The best job to prepare for is one that requires professional and technical skills**. (Evaluation) The job trends discussed in the passage indicate that there is a shortage of professional and technical workers in the United States and that workers must be recruited from overseas; the graph shows that this is the fastest growing segment of the labor force. These both provide strong evidence to support this opinion. No information in the passage supports option (1), nor does the graph data indicate that people currently working in this sector are threatened with job loss or other economic hard times. The passage suggests that both occupations in option (2) are good fields to pursue because of the shortage of domestic workers in these areas. However, there is no information presented to support the judgment that one of these areas has better employment opportunities than the other. No evidence is presented in either the passage or the graph to support option (3) or (4).

GED Practice (Pages 198–199)

1. **(1) when the company being bought does not wish to be purchased** (Comprehension) This is implied by the last sentence in the first paragraph. Nothing in the passage or table suggests that option (2), (3), or (4) is necessary to a hostile takeover. Option (5) has nothing to do with whether a takeover is hostile or not.

2. **(3) Consumers will have fewer product choices.** (Analysis) This is true because the buyer company will likely eliminate products of its own, or of its former rival company, that are similar and that used to compete against each other. This will result in fewer product choices. No information suggests that option (1), (4), or (5) would occur. The passage suggests that the opposite of option (2) will be more likely to occur.

3. **(5) only the information in the table** (Evaluation) The merger numbers in the table

and the trend they establish are all the evidence needed to support the statement that mergers and takeovers have become facts of American economic life. Options (1) and (2) are incorrect because knowing the names of companies involved in mergers or knowing how many takeovers were hostile isn't necessary to support this conclusion. The conclusion does not mention job loss, so option (3) is incorrect. Option (4) by itself would not provide enough data to support the conclusion. The table is valuable as evidence without it.

4. **(2) the information in paragraph three** (Evaluation) This is the best evidence because it gives statistics of similar past events against which such employees can measure the probability of keeping their jobs. Options (1) and (3) are not as useful because they deal in what might happen and what sometimes happens without hard data to provide a sense of how often these things *do* happen. Options (4) and (5) provide hard data, but not the type that gives information about what happens to employees of the companies involved in mergers.

5. **(3) 1993** (Comprehension) The table shows that 12.3 percent of all families lived in poverty in 1993. Option (1) is the year of the lowest rate. Options (2) and (4) are years cited in the passage for income distribution statistics, but the poverty rates in those years were lower than the rate in 1993. Option (5) is incorrect because, although one of the figures cited in the passage is higher than 12.3 percent, it is the rate for children, not the family rates that are listed in the table.

6. **(1) All people would spend similar proportions of their income on food and housing.** (Application) These two items are necessities of life on which everyone spends money. If everyone had about the same amount of money, the proportion of their income they would devote to these necessities would be similar. This contrasts with the United States, where people with less money spend a higher proportion of their income on necessities than people with more money do. Options (2) and (5) are not necessities, so there would be more difference in people's spending in these areas, depending on their tastes. preferences, and values. Options (3) and (4) are incorrect because neither family size or education level is directly tied to the amount of money that a person has.

7. **(2) Most families in poverty have more than one child.** (Analysis) For the mathematical analysis of the percentage of families living in poverty, the family is considered one unit. For the mathematical analysis of the percentage of children living in poverty, each child is considered a unit. If most

families in poverty have more than one child, this would explain why the percentage of children in poverty is higher than the percentage of families in poverty. Option (1) would not account for this result because it applies to almost all children regardless of economic level. Options (3) and (4) may be true, but neither explains the difference in poverty rates between children and families. Most children do not work at all, so option (5) cannot be the reason.

8. **(4) No, because the table shows that poverty rates have generally been lower in recent years.** (Evaluation) The data in the table show that the percent of families living in poverty is about the same as it was through most of the 1980s and 1990s. In fact, rates have generally been on the decline since 1993. For this reason, option (1) is incorrect. Option (2) is incorrect because the passage does make this connection, although this information is countered by the data in the table which show that poverty is on the decline. Option (3) is incorrect because the writer fails to connect this data in a cause-and-effect relationship to poverty rates. Option (5) is incorrect because this information does not show that poverty rates are rising.

GED Mini-Test (Pages 200–201)

1. **(3) as an issue of fair management versus unfair management** (Comprehension) The passage states that the Labor Department looked for a way to allow fair employers of home workers to continue to operate. Option (1) is incorrect, because only one labor union, the ILGWU is mentioned in the passage. There is no information in the passage to indicate that the Labor Department took the views expressed in option (2). Option (4) is incorrect because it doesn't make any sense and because the passage implies that sweatshops and piecework are similar. Option (5) is incorrect because nothing in the passage suggests that the dispute was based on a discrimination claim.

2. **(4) a salesperson whose income is a percentage of the price of what she sells** (Application) Piecework, like selling on commission, pays based on how much the worker produces. For a salesperson, the "production" is the amount of product that he or she sells. For the Bordeaux pieceworkers, it was how many sweatsuits the worker produced. Option (1) is an example of barter, not piecework. Options (2) and (5) apply the principles of supply and demand. Option (3) is incorrect because the worker is paid by the hour rather than according to the amount of his or her production.

3. **(5) It wanted to end the manufacture of women's wear by home workers.** (Analysis)

The passage states that the basis of the ILGWU's complaint was that the company was violating laws that prohibit the manufacture of women's clothing by home workers, and that the union wanted the Labor Department to uphold these federal restrictions. This suggests that the union was trying to end the practice of using illegal home workers, who were taking jobs that would otherwise be done by union members working legally in factories. Nothing in the passage suggests that option (1) or (2) was behind the union's action, although illegally low wages were one basis for the workers' complaints to the ILGWU. Option (3) is incorrect because the complaint, outlined at the beginning of the passage, specifies a desired end-result, not the means of obtaining such a result, which is what a lawsuit is. Option (4) is incorrect because the union did not complain about home workers' wages, and the passage indicates it was unclear exactly how much the home workers were actually earning.

4. **(5) more about what becomes of teenagers who drop out of school** (Evaluation) The statistic that 15 percent of teenage dropouts are unemployed indicates a problem but does not support the judgment that it is a cause for alarm. Data comparing the current dropout rate to the past rates, tying dropout rates to crime rates, or more nonstatistical information about the dropouts' lifestyles, connection to the cycle of poverty, and so on, are needed to assign the problem the status of "alarming." Option (1) provides information that touches on only one part of the problem—that is, earnings. Option (2) lays out the problem, but does not provide enough specific information to label the problem as alarming. Option (3) also only relates to some teenagers and then to only one aspect of life that could cause financial concern for some teenage dropouts. Option (4) is incorrect since this information touches on only some aspects of possible problems related to the teenage dropout rate.

5. **(3) level of education** (Evaluation) The graph supports this conclusion by showing that income level rises for both men and women as education level rises. This information eliminates option (1) as the correct answer. No evidence is cited in the passage or graph to support option (2) or (4). Option (5) cannot be concluded because the graph shows that although not graduating limits one's earning potential, people who go beyond high school earn much more money than those who stop their education when they earn their high-school diploma.

6. **(2) more children in poverty** (Analysis) The passage suggests that the children of teenagers who drop out of high school are likely to have

inadequate financial support, and thus are more likely to live in poverty. The passage implies that option (1) is a cause of the problem, not an effect of it. The passage does not show any relationship between the wages of high-school dropouts and those of high-school graduates, so option (3) is incorrect. The passage indicates that the opposite of options (4) and (5) is true.

7. **(4) Adult education is popular in America.** (Evaluation) This can be concluded from the high levels of enrollment the data indicate. The information does not include material on motivations or lifestyles, so options (1) and (5) are incorrect. Option (2) cannot be determined without knowing the population figures for each group. There is no data or other information to support option (3).

Unit 4 Cumulative Review (Pages 202–206)

1. **(2) They rose, but more slowly than the increase in the money supply.** (Comprehension) This relationship is shown by the blue solid and dotted lines. The graph shows that prices increased by about 25 percent between years 1 and 10, but the money supply grew by almost 100 percent during that same period. The relationships suggested in options (1), (3), (4), and (5) are all contradicted by the graph.

2. **(1) Inflation causes prices to rise sharply.** (Analysis) The lines on the graph show that between year 10 and year 15, the money supply grew much faster than production—from less than 100 percent to almost 200 percent for the money supply, compared to a growth in production from 125 percent to only 175 percent—this is the condition under which inflation occurs. At the same time, the price line shows prices rising (the definition of inflation) during that 5-year period almost as much as they did during the previous 10 years on the graph. The graph data contradict options (2), (3), and (4). Option (5) is incorrect because there is sufficient information to determine how changes in production, money supply, and prices are related. This is the focus of the graph.

3. **(5) There is not enough information to determine the relationship.** (Evaluation) Although the graph data show how each of these three factors changes as the others do, the data do not provide adequate information to determine which changes are causes and which are effects. Therefore, options (1), (2), (3), and (4) cannot be determined from the data provided. More information is needed.

4. **(3) Households headed by women have a lower standard of living.** (Analysis) The lower earning power of women means that households in which a woman is the chief source

of support generally have a lower standard of living than households with a male earner. Option (1) is contradicted by the information provided. There is no basis for concluding option (2). Option (4) is incorrect because if women earn less, they will also pay less income tax. Option (5) cannot be connected to the difference in pay.

5. **(2) coupons and rebates** (Analysis) Both techniques involve reduction of price to make the consumer feel that he or she has gotten a bargain. None of the other pairings of techniques take a similar approach to marketing.

6. **(5) the costs of finding new markets** (Comprehension) This can be understood from the main idea of the passage: when more goods are produced, more people must be found to buy them. Option (1) would be a cost only when production is restricted. Options (2), (3), and (4) will always be costs of manufacturing; therefore they are not specifically concerns of new markets.

7. **(1) Marketing is an economic fact of doing business.** (Analysis) The writer accepts the marketing of products as an economic fact. No statements in the passage suggest that the writer is making the assumption in option (2) or (3). Option (4) is a fact stated in the passage, so it is not an assumption. The passage implies the opposite of option (5).

8. **(3) advertise office products to home users** (Application) This is an example of trying to sell a product in a new market—the home. Options (1) and (4) are incorrect because they involve existing customers, not new ones. Option (2) is incorrect because you cannot determine that the advertising will reach the new market. Option (5) would not necessarily attract—or be intended to attract—a new market for the product.

9. **(2) It is the stock market.** (Analysis) The term stock market is often shortened to the market. The two men are clearly businesspeople talking in an office, so this choice would make sense. Options (1) and (4) are based on different meanings for the words *market* and *marketing* than are implied by the cartoon. The cartoon gives no support for option (3). Option (5) is based on looking at the word inherit rather than at the cartoon as a whole.

10. **(5) The teachers' union would bargain with the school board.** (Application) By law, the teachers' union would negotiate before it would strike, so option (1) is incorrect. It would also try negotiations before agreeing to option (2) or pursuing option (3). Since a school board would not want to close one of its schools, the school board would be likely try negotiation before turning to option (4).

11. **(1) They are too powerful.** (Analysis) This is a pure judgment with which not everyone will agree. A worker whose union has lost a strike, for example, would not share this view. Option (2) is supported by evidence of higher wages, improved working conditions, and other benefits that unions have won for workers. Options (3), (4), and (5) are facts that are stated in the passage.

12. **(4) compromise** (Evaluation) The passage indicates that collective bargaining is a negotiation in which each side often has to give up something it wants so that the process can continue. This shows a strong commitment to the principle of compromise. The process wouldn't work if option (1), (3), or (5) were most important, for in a union contract each side gives up the ability to act independently on issues related to work and the workplace. Although money issues are always among the most important in a labor-management negotiation, nothing in the process or the passage suggests that option (2) is valued above compromise in successful collective bargaining.

13. **(3) Unions don't truly represent workers' best interests because union leaders are corrupt.** (Evaluation) This statement is the result of both stereotyping and oversimplification. To label all union leaders on the basis of the well-publicized misbehavior of an infamous few is stereotyping. And there is no direct connection between corrupt behavior and misrepresentation of the union's members. Option (1) is a statement of fact. Option (2) is a well-reasoned statement of cause and effect, because wages are a cost of production and companies take their costs into account when they set prices. Option (4) is a reasonable generalization because, as the passage indicates, the threat of a strike can often cause management to agree to union demands. Option (5) is a reasonable generalization given that the passage indicates that once there is a labor union, the employer no longer has absolute authority over its employees, their wages, and their working conditions.

14. **(2) the percentage of workers who are union members now and in previous decades** (Evaluation) Of the choices listed, this would be the best measure of union power. Option (1) would not show whether union power was rising or declining without knowing the results of the strikes. Unions have no direct influence over option (3), so it is not a good measure of their strength. Option (4) is not the best evidence because union strength is only a minor factor that can help increase job safety; more major factors relate to technical advances

and the enactment of safety laws. Option (5) is the poorest evidence, because the speeches will not be objective and unbiased.

15. **(5) Negotiators falsely maintain the image of marathon negotiations.** (Comprehension) What the speaker says (the caption of the cartoon) and what we see in the cartoon don't match, indicating the falseness of the speaker's words. Options (1) and (4) are details only tangentially related to the subject of the cartoon. Options (2) and (3) are not suggested in the cartoon, especially since it is not clear whether the speaker represents labor or management.

16. **(1) are not making progress.** (Evaluation) They have been negotiating a long time without results and are tired. But they don't want to share their lack of progress with the public, which is why they are not telling the press the truth. Option (2) is a misreading of the details in the cartoon showing the negotiators lying down. Option (3) is unlikely because they would be eager to continue and to tell the press if they were about to reach an agreement. Options (4) and (5) are incorrect because it is contradicted by the cartoon's caption.

17. **(3) that the man with the notebook is a reporter** (Analysis) The man outside the room is writing on a notepad and has clearly asked a question, as reporters do. The lack of labels in the cartoon indicates that it refers to general union-management negotiations and not to a specific situation, so options (1), (2), (4), and (5) are incorrect.

18. **(2) saying "The check is in the mail."** (Application) Both messages are intended to reassure the listener while buying a little time for the speaker. Option (1) would cause panic. Option (3) could start an argument. Option (4) would make the listener doubt the speaker's innocence. Option (5) is the opposite of the intended message.

19. **(3) There has been a decline in the number of work stoppages since 1970.** (Comprehension) Since stoppages were at their highest in 1970 and were much lower in 1998, the general trend must have been downward. Option (1) is incorrect because the paragraph states that 1970 was the peak year. Option (2) is contradicted by the data. Options (4) and (5) cannot be concluded from the paragraph.

20. **(1) What is to be produced?** (Application) When deciding between baseballs and footballs, Sam is deciding what to produce. Option (2) is incorrect because Sam is deciding what, not how much. Option (3) is incorrect because Sam is not deciding how he should make his product.

Option (4) is incorrect because Sam is not thinking about who his customers are. Option (5) is incorrect because Sam is not concerned with general economic change.

21. **(4) Who is to receive it?** (Application) Parker's company is considering going after new customers. Option (1) is incorrect because the product is not changing. Option (2) is incorrect because quantities are not being considered. Option (3) is incorrect because they are not considering changing production methods. Option (5) is incorrect because they are not asking a general economic question.

22. **(2) How much should be produced?** (Application) Patricia is considering whether to produce more of her product. Options (1) and (3) are incorrect because there is no change in the product or how it is produced. Option (4) is incorrect because the same people will buy the chips, just more of them. Option (5) is incorrect because Patricia is not concerned with general economic change.

23. **(3) A minimum wage law has applied to most U.S. workers for more than 60 years.** (Comprehension) The focus of the paragraph is on the fact that a minimum wage law passed in 1938 still covers most U.S. workers. Option (1) is incorrect because it focuses on the exceptions to the law. Options (2) and (4) deal only with the law's history, which is not the major point of the paragraph. There is no information in the paragraph about option (5).

24. **(5) The minimum wage law guarantees that the standard of living of American workers will not fall below a certain level.** (Analysis) Many of the details in the paragraph lead up to and support this statement. Options (1), (2), (3), and (4) provide some of those details.

UNIT 5: GEOGRAPHY
Lesson 18
GED Skill Focus (Page 211)

1. **b.** The map shows major cities and interstate highways in Texas and Oklahoma.

2. **a.** *F:* San Antonio is located at the junction of Interstate Highway 20 and Interstate Highway 35.

   b. *T:* Austin is the capital of Texas and is located west of Houston and south of Dallas.

   c. *T:* Lubbock is a city in Texas that is located about halfway between Oklahoma City and El Paso.

   d. *F:* Forth Worth, Texas, is closer to El Paso, Texas, than it is to Ponca City, Oklahoma.

e. *F:* San Antonio, Texas, is located about 200 miles southwest of Houston.

f. *T:* The state of Texas is more than twice the size of the state of Oklahoma.

g. *T:* Dallas is on Interstate Highway 35 about midway between Austin and Oklahoma City.

3. Drive south on I-35 from Oklahoma City to the junction with I-20 at Fort Worth, Texas. Take I-20 west for more than 400 miles until it ends at I-10. Continue west on I-10 for about 150 more miles until you reach El Paso.

GED Content Focus (Page 213)

1. **(4) Its places must have some characteristic or feature in common.** (Comprehension) The passage states that a region is an area whose places share characteristics or features that make them different from surrounding areas. Those common characteristics are not limited to language, religion, or physical features, so options (1) and (2) are not correct. Option (3) is incorrect because the common characteristics that identify regions do not have to involve people—as exemplified by physical regions and climate regions. The information on the map showing only one climate region across most of northern Africa makes it clear that option (5) is not true.

2. **(4) a common language or religion** (Comprehension) The passage states that cultural regions can be defined by a language, by racial or ethnic groupings, or by another characteristic of human culture. Religion would qualify as an aspect of human culture. Option (1) defines a political region, not a cultural region. Regions of all types have boundaries, so option (2) is incorrect. Option (3) defines a physical region, not a cultural region. Option (5) defines a climate region, not a cultural region.

3. **(1) Russia** (Application) Russia is a country, and so it is a political region. Options (2) and (5) are physical, not political, features. Options (3) and (4) describe larger geographic units, which are not political regions.

4. **(5) a warm, humid climate** (Comprehension) This can be determined from the information on the map. Option (1) does not apply to Australia's east coast, but rather to the interior of the country. Options (2) and (4) are not found in Australia. According to the map, option (3) applies to only a small part of Australia's east coast.

5. **(4) Central India has a dry climate while the coasts get a lot of rain.** (Comprehension) The map shows most of India, including the coasts having a tropical rainy climate with the

central section having a dry climate. The map shows that most of Africa has a dry climate and shows nothing about forests, so option (1) is incorrect. The map shows that Great Britain and New Zealand both have a warm, humid climate, so option (2) is incorrect. Since the Plateau of Tibet has a mountain climate and the North China Plain has a warm, humid climate, option (3) is incorrect. Option (5) is incorrect because northern Asia has a polar climate and northern Africa has a predominantly dry climate with some warm, humid regions.

6. **(2) Northeastern Europe has a cool climate, while the rest of Europe has a warm climate.** (Analysis) The map key designates a cool humid climate and a warm humid climate. Options (1) and (3) are incorrect because they are based on misreadings of the map. Options (4) and (5) cannot be determined from the map and so are incorrect.

7. **(2) physical and political maps** (Application) A physical map would show each continent's landforms and other natural features, while a political map would locate the countries and cities on each continent. The maps could then be compared with the climate map on page 212 to determine how climate and physical features affect the location of major cities in Africa and Asia. Options (1), (3), (4), and (5) are incorrect because cultural maps and road maps do not consistently show physical features and major cities, which is the information needed to make the determination asked for in the question.

GED Practice (Pages 214–215)

1. **(2) Illinois** (Comprehension) The map shows that the population in Illinois averages more than 25 persons per square mile. Options (1), (3), and (4) have much smaller regions with this population density, and most areas in these states contain less than 25 people per square mile. Option (5) has no areas where the population density is as high as it is in Illinois.

2. **(1) The eastern United States is more densely populated than the western United States.** (Comprehension) The map shows that the largest areas of low population density are in the West and that the population density of the East is generally higher overall. Option (2) is contradicted by the map because the largest area of high population density is not on the West Coast, but in the New Jersey-New York area, on the East Coast. Options (3) and (4) cannot be determined from the map. Option (5) is an opinion and not a restatement of information provided on the map.

3. **(5) Major cities are located in these areas.** (Analysis) Cities are places where large numbers

of people live close together, thereby creating areas of high population density. Option (1) is incorrect because tourists are temporary visitors, so tourism doesn't affect population density. Option (2) cannot be determined from the map and, in any case, a mountainous area is an unlikely place for great numbers of people to live. Option (3) is untrue because some of the highest-density areas are not in warm-weather areas. Option (4) is unlikely because rural areas are regions where people are spread out, not packed closely together.

4. **(3) Ohio** (Application) The map shows that Ohio has higher population densities across the state than any of the other choices. Having a lot of people living in the area would be important because customers would be needed to make each restaurant successful. Option (1) is not the best choice because most of this state's people live in one small area, and the rest of the state is sparsely settled. Options (2) and (5) have higher population densities than option (1), but still lower than Ohio. Like option (1), option (4) is very sparsely settled except for one region.

5. **(4) It varies from north to south.** (Comprehension) The passage states that the northern island of Hokkaido gets cold, while the southern island of Kyushu has subtropical weather. Option (1) is incorrect because nothing in the passage suggests that Japan's volcanic eruptions influence its climate. Option (2) is contradicted by the passage. The passage indicates that Japan's mountainous terrain, not its climate, is the reason why the country has little farmland, so option (3) is incorrect. Option (5) is incorrect, because the passage gives no information about the distribution of Japan's cities.

6. **(2) Tokyo is a more important city than Kobe.** (Analysis) That Tokyo is a more important city is a statement of opinion with which not everyone would agree. The map and passage establish option (1) as a fact. Options (3), (4), and (5) are also facts that are set forth in the passage.

7. **(3) Japan's main islands are formed of mountain ridges ringed by coastal plains where most of the people live.** (Comprehension) The map shows that the main islands are formed of a ridge of mountains ringed by coastal plains, where the nation's major cities are located. Options (1) and (2) are contradicted by information on the map. Option (4) is not related to the subject of the map. The maps shows no information about volcanoes, so option (5) is also incorrect.

8. **(5) More Japanese live on Honshu than on any of the other islands.** (Evaluation) The map shows that Honshu is the largest island and that it contains most of the nation's major cities,

so this is a reasonable conclusion from the evidence provided. The map does not label Japan's highest mountains, so option (1) cannot be concluded from the map. Option (2) is contradicted by the evidence on the map; the island of Shikoku is clearly smaller than the island of Kyushu. Major cities are found on both the eastern and western coasts of Japan's major islands and farm regions are not shown, so option (3) cannot be concluded from the information on the map. Option (4) is incorrect because the map provides no information about Japan's economy.

GED Mini-Test (Pages 216–217)

1. **(3) The Transantarctic Mountains divide it into eastern and western regions.** (Comprehension) The map shows that these mountains form the border between the two regions, which are identified on the map. Nothing on the map suggests option (1), which is, in fact, incorrect. Options (2) and (4) are contradicted by the map. Option (5) is incorrect because the map shows that the South Pole is not located in one of Antarctica's mountainous areas.

2. **(5) Places with little precipitation are deserts.** (Comprehension) The passage implies that Antarctica is desert because very little precipitation falls there each year. This suggests that a low level of precipitation is the defining characteristic of a desert. Nothing in the passage suggests that option (1), (3), or (4) is true (they aren't). Option (2) is incorrect, because it is contradicted by the passage; precipitation level, not temperature, defines a desert.

3. **(4) The interior has no good food source.** (Analysis) The passage states that only a few plants exist in Antarctica and only a few insects live beyond the edges of the continent, so large animals would not have a source of food. Large animals are able to survive in other cold polar regions and in rugged mountains, so options (1) and (2) are incorrect. Option (3) does not explain why large animals don't live inland, since the passage states and the map shows that most of the continent is covered with a thick layer of ice. There is no information to support option (5). (It is not true.)

4. **(1) curiosity—to learn more about the continent** (Evaluation) The map provides the information that the settlements in Antarctica are research stations. This indicates that the nations that sponsor them want to learn more about the continent. Option (2) might be a motive for individuals to live in Antarctica but not for a nation to set up research stations there. Option (3) is incorrect because, as the passage indicates, there never were permanent settlers in Antarctica. Option (4) is incorrect because

Antarctica's animals are not endangered and nothing in the passage or map indicates that they are. Option (5) is incorrect because the settlements are research stations, not industrial sites, which would be difficult to operate in the extremely cold environment.

5. **(2) Climate varies because of land features.** (Comprehension) This is the main point of the information contained in the passage. The passage does not compare weather and climate, so option (1) is incorrect. Option (3) is a detail that helps explain U.S. climate; it is not a summary of the passage. Option (4) applies only to the discussion of coastal areas. Option (5) is generally true in the United States, but it is not a summary of the passage.

6. **(5) Much of the climate is either humid subtropical or humid continental.** (Comprehension) The map shows that these two climate regions together cover more than half of the United States. Options (1) and (4) are contradicted by information on the map. The map does not provide enough information to support option (2) or (3).

7. **(3) The oceans would have a greater effect.** (Application) The passage states that the mountains block ocean air moving inland, which is what gives the West Coast its unique climates. If these mountains ran east and west, they would not have such a strong blocking effect, which would allow the oceans to be more influential on the nation's climate. There is no support for option (1), (2), or (4). Option (5) is incorrect because the passage implies that there would be a change.

8. **(4) roads** (Application) Physical maps are maps that show landforms and other features of physical geography. This is the only option that is human made. Options (1) and (2) are landforms. Option (3) is a type of physical region. Option (5) is a climate.

Lesson 19
GED Skill Focus (Page 219)
1. **b.** Trade flourishes when good transportation is available.

   c. Thriving trade draws more people to the area, where they can find jobs or open new businesses.

2. **b.** The major cities of the United States exist because traders, merchants, and workers could get to them easily.

3. **c.** Jamestown

GED Content Focus (Page 221)
1. **(2) Resources help determine where people live, but technology has made them less important as a factor.** (Comprehension) This

is the main focus of the passage. Most of the details and examples in the passage support this concept. Options (1) and (4) are discussed, but they are not the central point of the passage. Options (3) and (5) are not discussed or implied by the passage.

2. **(5) gold** (Application) The chart suggests that nonrenewable resources tend to be mineral resources, of which gold is an example. Option (1) comes from a plant, which the chart indicates are renewable resources. Options (2) and (3) are an animal and an animal product, so they are renewable resources. Option (4) comes from trees, and the chart lists forests as a renewable resource.

3. **(1) The availability of resources has affected where people live.** (Analysis) The other information in the paragraph leads to this conclusion. Options (2), (3), (4), and (5) are supporting details that help explain how and why the conclusion is true.

4. **(3) Fish are a major source of food for many of the world's people.** (Analysis) Without already knowing this, you will not be able to comprehend why the heavily populated coastal regions support the conclusion that "the number of people who live in an area is often directly related to its resources." Option (1) is incorrect because there is no information in the passage implying how many coastal dwellers earn their living by fishing; and it is untrue. Option (2) is true of only some coastal regions and also does not aid comprehension of the conclusion. Option (4) is incorrect because it is stated in the passage. Option (5) is true, but knowing this information does not help you to understand the paragraph's conclusion. In fact, it tends to weaken the conclusion because the passage establishes that polar regions are sparsely settled.

5. **(4) Few people will live in a place if an important resource cannot be provided.** (Analysis) Paragraphs two, three, and four all provide information that supports this conclusion. Option (1) is contradicted by information in the passage. Options (2) and (3) are judgments (opinions) that are not supported by information in the passage or the chart. Option (5) is contradicted by the information in the passage. Even though most renewable resources are exhaustible, not all are. For example, energy from the sun cannot be depleted by overuse.

6. **(2) People in desert and polar regions live in primitive and isolated conditions.** (Evaluation) This conclusion is the result of both oversimplification and stereotyping. Today, it is possible to live comfortably in such regions

because technology makes it possible to bring in food, to heat or air-condition dwellings, and the like. Similarly, people in such regions are not isolated because they can use technology to travel and to communicate with others worldwide. Option (1) is not an example of faulty logic because it is a demonstrable fact. Options (3) and (4) are not examples of faulty logic because they are reasonable conclusions based on the examples and other evidence presented. Option (5) is not an example of faulty logic because it is supported by the information in the fifth paragraph of the passage.

GED Practice (Pages 222–223)

1. **(2) How Resource Depletion Affects Settlement** (Comprehension) The story told in each paragraph centers around this idea. Nelsonville's story makes option (1) incorrect. Option (3) is wrong because this passage is about more than just events in these two towns. Option (4) is discussed but is not the main focus of the passage. Option (5) is too broad and not the main focus of the passage.

2. **(1) The landscape of America is littered with towns that failed to achieve their dreams.** (Analysis) This opinion is a broad generalization that requires support to make it believable. Options (2), (3), (4), and (5) are all details that comprise one example of how the first statement is true.

3. **(2) Mining was the basis of each economy.** (Analysis) This is the only similarity that is presented in the passage. Option (1) is incorrect because the passage contains no information about the origins of Nelsonville. Option (3) is not correct because although Nelsonville declined, it is not described as a ghost town. Option (4) is contradicted by the passage. Option (5) is incorrect; although the passage describes similarities between the two towns, it does not indicate that the same people lived in both towns.

4. **(3) Many fancy restaurants were built there.** (Evaluation) This is the only option that provides direct evidence of wealth. It suggests that the townspeople must have had a lot of money to spend in order to patronize such places. Option (1) is incorrect because the passage gives no evidence that the miners who founded the town were wealthy. Option (2) is incorrect because a place's population is not evidence of how wealthy its people are. Option (4) is not good evidence because it does not indicate whether wealth obtained from gold- and silver-mining stayed in Virginia City or whether it went to mine owners in some distant location, making *them* the wealthy ones. Option (5) is incorrect because it is related to the town's decline and

does not support the conclusion that the town was a center of wealth.

5. **(5) A factory lays off workers because people no longer use the only product it makes.** (Application) The decline that occurred in all three situations is similar, as is the idea of depending on only one resource or product. Option (1) is incorrect because what happened to the towns was not the result of an action by the workers. Option (2) is incorrect because it describes a successful event, which is the opposite of what occurred in the towns. Option (3) is incorrect because neither city declined when one company gained a monopoly over production of a particular good. Option (4) is incorrect because neither city's decline was the result of high taxes or of an action by city government.

6. **(2) Most cities are found miles inland, on a fall line separating the highlands of the interior from the plains of the East Coast.** (Comprehension) This is the only statement to describe the map's information about where eastern cities are located. Options (1) and (5) have nothing to do with the information shown on the map. Option (3) explains why these cities are where they are, but it does not summarize any information that is shown on the map. Option (4) is incorrect because, while the map shows the rivers and the fall line, it does not provide the other information contained in the statement.

7. **(3) Travel by land from the coast into the interior was difficult in early times.** (Comprehension) The information that settlers traveled inland by river and stopped when they could go no further by water implies that overland travel was difficult. Nothing in the passage suggests option (1). Options (2) and (5) are contradicted by facts stated in the passage. Option (4) is incorrect because the passage provides no information about areas outside the region.

8. **(5) Water resources created most of the cities that exist along the eastern seaboard today.** (Analysis) Most of the other sentences in the paragraph lead to this conclusion. Option (1) provides information that explains the role that water played in the founding of these cities. Options (2), (3), and (4) establish a cause-and-effect relationship that explains how water helped these places grow into cities, while most of the towns on the coast did not.

GED Mini-Test (Pages 224–225)

1. **(4) The flooding allowed farmers to produce more crops.** (Analysis) This effect is suggested by the last sentence in the second

paragraph. Nothing in the passage suggests that option (1) or (3) resulted from the flooding. Options (2) and (5) are contradicted by the passage.

2. **(5) Farmers along the Nile have had to enrich their soil with expensive chemical fertilizers.** (Evaluation) This detail provides an example of how changing the Nile by damming it has affected some people. Options (1) and (2) state ways a river can change but they provide no information about how such changes affect people. Option (3) is an example of how a river changed, but it does not illustrate or explain how people's lives were affected. Option (4) describes the river and the way people lived before the change. It does not support the conclusion that changes in the river changed people's lives.

3. **(2) Rivers are economically important.** (Evaluation) Farmers, fishers, and other Egyptians depend on the Nile for electricity and their livelihoods. There is no evidence in the passage that supports options (1) and (3). Option (4) cannot be determined from the passage. Option (5) is contradicted by the passage.

4. **(3) Changes in Earth are caused by nature and by people.** (Comprehension) This is the general idea of the paragraph. Options (1), (2) and (5) are details that support the main idea. Option (4) is incorrect because it is not stated in the paragraph and because it is not true.

5. **(4) the West Coast of the United States** (Comprehension) This is the only other area indicated by the map legend as a winter home for the butterflies. The map shows that option (1) is part of their warm-weather range. The map does not indicate that option (2) or (3) has anything to do with the monarchs. Option (5) is the first land reached by monarchs crossing the Gulf of Mexico, but the map does not indicate that they stay there.

6. **(5) A monarch has orange-and-black wings.** (Analysis) This knowledge is necessary to understand the writer's reference to an orange-and-black sky. The butterflies' relation to birds provides no useful information, so options (1) and (4) are incorrect. Option (2) is directly stated in the passage. Nothing in the passage suggests that option (3) is true.

7. **(2) a wildlife refuge** (Application) This is land set aside by government to protect plants and animals, as Mexico's preserve is intended to do. Option (1) is incorrect because the monarchs would not be held in captivity. Nothing in the passage suggests any farming on the Mexican preserve, so option (3) is not correct. Although there are tourists in the preserve, nothing in

the passage indicates that the preserve was set up to be a resort or that it provides recreational facilities or activities, which eliminates options (4) and (5) as answers.

8. **(1) Logging the forest threatens the well-being of the monarchs.** (Analysis) The passage indicates that the monarchs stay on the trunks and branches of trees. Cutting down trees in their forest would harm them by destroying their habitat. Option (2) is incorrect because the passage gives no evidence the Mexican government created the monarch preserve at the request of the tourists. The passage implies that the government created the preserve to stop the logging, so option (3) is incorrect. Nothing in the passage implies that option (4) is true. Option (5) is contradicted by the information the passage presents about the continued logging of the preserve.

Lesson 20
GED Skill Focus (Page 227)
1. **b.** People who recycle are concerned about conserving the nation's resources.

2. **a.** In our throw-away society, the average person produces 1,500 pounds of garbage per year.

   c. Some enlightened states require deposits on metal and glass beverage containers.

   d. This encourages the thoughtless public to return these items rather than throw them away.

3. **a.** apple juice in a bottle made of glass capped with a metal lid

4. **a.** People who waste resources are behaving badly; those who do not are behaving well.

GED Content Focus (Page 229)
1. **(1) the Northeast** (Comprehension) The map shows above-average or worse acid rain damage in most states in the northeast quadrant of the United States. Options (2), (3), (4), and (5) are incorrect because the damage in these areas is generally not as bad as in the Northeast.

2. **(5) Some chemical wastes harm people.** (Comprehension) The information implies that chemicals in the fish of some polluted lakes are so harmful to humans that the fish should not be eaten. Options (1) and (3) are directly stated in the passage. Option (2) is incorrect because this overgeneralization is not supported by the passage. The passage does not compare pollution levels of air and water, so option (4) is incorrect.

3. **(3) coal-burning power plants** (Comprehension) The passage states that one cause of acid rain is the burning of coal. The map shows that most states with heavy acid

rain damage either have large numbers of coal-burning power plants or are located near such states. There is nothing from the passage or map to support option (1), (2), (4), or (5) as a source of acid rain.

4. **(2) Pollution can spread long distances.** (Evaluation) Both the map and the passage support this conclusion. Option (1) is not supported by the information in the passage, which establishes that water pollution is a serious problem. The conclusion in option (3) cannot be legitimately drawn from the information provided. Nothing in the passage or on the map supports option (4) or (5) as a conclusion.

5. **(3) Public health is important.** (Evaluation) Posting signs that warn against eating the fish shows that protecting human health is of major concern to government authorities. Options (1) and (2) are incorrect because the signs have nothing to do with conserving resources and were not motivated by a desire to protect the fish. Posting the signs also does not indicate agreement with the judgments expressed in options (4) and (5).

6. **(4) use chemicals on their lawns** (Evaluation) The passage states that chemical runoff is a source of water pollution. Option (1) is incorrect because this activity shows concern for the environment. Options (2), (3), and (5) are incorrect because these activities are not in themselves damaging to the environment.

7. **(2) Yes, because states east of those with large numbers of coal-burning power plants tend to have above-average acid rain damage.** (Evaluation) This is the general pattern indicated on the map. Options (1) and (5) are both incorrect because the reason each gives for stating that the map does not support the passage is insufficient to disprove the passage's claim, given the other evidence on the map. Option (3) is wrong because its information is contradicted by the map. Since the map does not show where the coal-mining regions are, there is not enough information to evaluate the accuracy of option (4).

GED Practice (Pages 230–231)

1. **(3) Water pollution is a widespread problem.** (Comprehension) This expresses the main idea of the passage. Options (1) and (2) are details, not the main idea. Option (4) is not suggested in the passage. Option (5) is an opinion related to a specific circumstance and not the main idea of the passage.

2. **(4) People who get their drinking water from wells should have it periodically tested.** (Evaluation) The passage states that harmful chemicals can get into groundwater and then into well water, which can be hazardous

to human health if the water is consumed. Option (1) is contradicted by information in the first paragraph of the passage. Options (2) and (3) are incorrect because the passage makes no judgment about which water source is more polluted. Option (5) cannot be concluded because the passage states that the effects of lead poisoning occur over time and that only some older homes present potential lead-poisoning problems.

3. **(1) their health** (Evaluation) The passage indicates that the motive behind drinking bottled water is to avoid polluted drinking water, which may contain substances harmful to human health. Nothing in the passage suggests that option (2) is correct. Although lead pipes in old houses are mentioned as a source of pollution of household drinking water, option (3) is incorrect because the passage indicates that many people decide to drink bottled water because of concerns about the groundwater; so concern about lead from pipes in old homes is not the only reason to drink bottled water. Options (4) and (5) are incorrect because drinking bottled water does not conserve water resources or help to clean up the environment.

4. **(5) Yes, because seepage from rainwater could carry these chemicals into the groundwater.** (Analysis) This cause-and-effect relationship can be inferred from the discussion of groundwater and its sources. The information given in options (1), (3), and (4) may be true, but this information has nothing to do with whether or not buried chemicals are a source of water pollution. Option (2) contradicts the passage.

5. **(3) trap the sand** (Comprehension) The diagram shows that jetties trap sand that waves that form the longshore current would otherwise carry away. Option (1) is incorrect because it describes the effect of a breakwater, as shown by the waves being turned back from the shore. Option (2) is incorrect because the diagram shows that the jetties affect the waves that reflect off the shore, not the incoming waves. Option (4) is incorrect because, as the passage indicates, longshore currents are caused by the waves that hit the shore at an angle, not by jetties. Option (5) is incorrect because, according to the passage, sand bars are created by waves that strike land directly, which is unrelated to the action of a jetty.

6. **(1) Protecting property is important.** (Evaluation) The passage makes it clear that the primary reason for preventing beach erosion is to protect homes, businesses, and other development along coastlines. This development and the efforts to protect it makes option (2) incorrect. The construction of the devices contradicts option (3). Option (4) is incorrect

Answers and Explanations

because the devices change the coastline and can, in themselves, be considered eyesores. Nothing in the passage suggests that option (5) is a value related to the construction of these devices.

7. **(4) a guardrail along a highway** (Application) Both are protective devices that redirect the energy of incoming substances or objects. The diagram shows that a breakwater stops the waves that are coming toward the beach and redirects them back out to sea. A highway guardrail prevents vehicles from going off the road by changing their direction when they hit it. Options (1) and (2) are incorrect because they are not protective devices but transportation devices solely intended to move something from one place to another. Option (3) is not a protective device. Option (5) is a protective device but it does not accomplish its mission by redirecting energy as do a breakwater and a highway guardrail.

8. **(5) Breakwaters and jetties accelerate erosion.** (Analysis) The phrase "some experts believe" in the passage indicates that this information is someone's opinion. In addition, the other information suggests that breakwaters and jetties have the opposite effect. The passage and diagrams establish that options (1), (2), (3), and (4) are facts rather than opinions.

GED Mini-Test (Pages 232–233)

1. **(4) A fisherman has caught a fish that has eaten people's trash.** (Comprehension) This description covers the important point of the cartoon. Options (1) and (2) are not supported by the cartoon. Option (3) does not describe the main action shown in the cartoon. Option (5) is incorrect because fish are not used to clean up the oceans.

2. **(2) The world's oceans are polluted.** (Analysis) The cartoonist portrays the fish spitting out a big pile of trash, which the fish presumably ate while in the ocean. There is no evidence in the cartoon to support the opinions expressed in option (1), (3), (4), or (5).

3. **(3) It is all right to litter if people cannot see it.** (Evaluation) This is a common attitude among people who toss empty bottles, cans, and other trash into the water, and trash in the water is the subject of this cartoon. Options (1), (4), and (5) are also values that some people hold, but none of them is suggested by the cartoon. There is also nothing in the cartoon to suggest option (2).

4. **(5) Pollution affects the ocean's animals.** (Evaluation) The cartoon shows that fish are affected by people dumping garbage in the ocean. Nothing in the cartoon suggests option (1) or (2). The cartoon is not critical of fishing methods or of fishing itself, so options (3) and (4) are incorrect.

5. **(3) a window** (Application) Like windows, communications satellites allow things going on in one place to be seen and/or heard in another. Option (1) is incorrect because it is a barrier like an ocean or desert that blocks communication and movement from one place to another. Options (2), (4), and (5) are incorrect because these structures generally block rather than facilitate communication and movement between people in different parts of a building.

6. **(5) Most Americans live in urban areas, which are part of the environment.** (Comprehension) The paragraph discusses cities as being part of the environment and indicates that most Americans live in urban areas. Option (1) is incorrect because it is a detail that supports the main idea of the paragraph. Option (2) is incorrect because the passage does not compare the number of people who live in suburbs with the number who live in cities. Option (3) is incorrect because the paragraph does not compare the amount of space taken up by cities and by farms; it compares only the relative populations of urban and rural areas. Option (4) is incorrect because the passage indicates that all land is part of the environment, not only urban and suburban land.

7. **(3) The problems that cities face result from many people being concentrated in a small area.** (Analysis) This conclusion is given in paragraph 2. Options (1), (2), (4), and (5) are details that support this conclusion.

8. **(2) too many people** (Analysis) If a city has too many people for the amount of water that is available, a water supply problem results. Options (1) and (3) could result in water supply problems, but they do not occur in all cities and thus are not the general cause of such problems. Options (4) and (5) could be problems in some cities and at certain times, but they would not have a negative effect on the supply of water.

9. **(3) Urban growth has not been well planned.** (Analysis) Despite the urban problems cited in the passage, the quality of the nation's preparations for urban growth is the author's opinion, with which some experts might disagree. Options (1) and (2) are established facts stated in the passage. Option (4) is a fact that can be confirmed by noting legislation and urban programs some politicians have worked to put in place. Option (5) is a fact that can be demonstrated by confirming the existence of such laws.

10. **(3) As Americans have become more aware of urban problems, government has come under more pressure to improve cities.** (Analysis) The passage suggests that as more voters have come to live in cities and have become aware of urban problems, elected officials have grown more sensitive to those concerns and more willing to do something about them. Although the passage states that the amount of land occupied by cities is small, nothing suggests that option (1) is correct. No information supports option (2) or (5). Nothing in the passage suggests that city dwellers are unhappy, so option (4) is also incorrect.

11. **(1) The oil spill was an environmental disaster.** (Evaluation) The information that it was the worst oil spill in North America and the statistics indicating its size and consequences support this conclusion. Option (2) cannot be supported on the basis of this single incident alone. Not enough details are provided to prove that option (3) or (4) is true. Nothing in the paragraph supports option (5) as a conclusion.

Unit 5 Cumulative Review (Pages 234–237)

1. **(5) Immigrants are people who were not born in the country where they currently live.** (Comprehension) This is suggested by the way the writer uses the term in the passage. Options (1), (2), and (4) are incorrect because nothing in the passage gives information about how immigrants enter the United States, where most settle, or what their economic status is when they come. The passage focuses on immigrants coming to the United States and gives no information on immigrants to other regions, so option (3) is also incorrect.

2. **(1) All Americans have ancestors who came from somewhere else.** (Analysis) Most of the other information in the passage in one way or another provides evidence to support this statement. Options (2), (3), and (4) are details that lead to this conclusion. Option (5) is additional information that is not directly tied to the conclusion.

3. **(4) France** (Application) The passage suggests that in recent years, most immigrants have come from places other than Europe and Africa. Options (1) and (5) cannot be ruled out because the information states that Asia is a major source of recent immigrants and that many settle in California. Option (2) is not correct because the passage identifies Mexico as a recent major source of immigration. The passage provides no information by which to judge the likelihood of option (3).

4. **(3) Americans buy a lot of disposable plastic items.** (Comprehension) The graph shows that millions of tons of plastic is thrown out annually. This suggests that Americans buy and use a lot of such items. The graph gives figures for diapers only, not for babies, so option (1) is incorrect. Option (2) cannot be inferred from the graph. The graph implies the opposite of options (4) and (5).

5. **(4) Gasoline, which powers automobiles, is a fossil fuel.** (Analysis) Unless you know this, you cannot appreciate the meaning of the cartoon's caption. The cartoon's focus is not on water resources, so options (1) and (2) are incorrect. (In addition, option (1) is untrue because water is not a fossil fuel.) Options (3) and (5) may or may not be true but they do not aid understanding of the cartoon.

6. **(1) We are too dependent on fossil fuels.** (Evaluation) This is supported by the information that so little energy comes from other sources, even though some experts believe that fossil fuels may fairly soon be exhausted, and by the scene and caption of the cartoon. Even though option (2) may be a good idea, no facts provided in the paragraph or opinions expressed in the cartoon lead to this conclusion. Option (3) contradicts the paragraph. No information is provided that would lead to the conclusions stated in option (4) or (5).

7. **(4) far from the equator with a high elevation** (Application) According to the paragraph, the higher a place is, the colder it is, and the closer a place is to the equator, the hotter it is. Therefore, moving away from the equator would make a place colder. The combination of distance from the equator and a high elevation would produce the coldest place. Options (1), (2), (3), and (5) do not provide the right combination for the coldest temperature.

8. **(1) The varied landscapes of the United States provide vacations for everyone.** (Comprehension) This idea is expressed in the first sentence, which is the topic sentence of the paragraph. Option (2) is an opinion that relates to only two specific geographic areas. Options (3) and (4) are details about specific landscapes. Option (5) is not discussed.

9. **(3) Vermont and the Arizona's White Mountains** (Analysis) The passage implies that both are mountainous areas. The places listed in options (1), (2), (4), and (5) are not similar because they have contrasting geographic features.

10. **(5) Camping generally costs less than staying in a hotel.** (Analysis) This is the only statement that can be proven true. The other options are all opinions. Option (1) is an opinion (key = *exciting*) because some people find the

activity boring or terrifying. Option (2) is a viewpoint (key = *enjoyable*) that would be held only by those who like to vacation outdoors. Some people might think the beaches of Virginia, North Carolina, or some other place are better, so option (3) is not a fact (key = *best*). Not everyone would agree with option (4) (key = *dangerous and expensive*); for example, people who are wealthy might not consider skiing as costing a lot of money.

11. **(4) wealth** (Evaluation) The passage states that they went there to find their fortunes, which indicates that they valued the region's minerals over the area's natural appeal or the challenge of exploring the region. This makes options (1) and (2) incorrect. Nothing in the paragraph suggests that option (3) or (5) would have been true.

12. **(2) People vacation outdoors because they love adventure.** (Evaluation) To assign this one reason to all people is an oversimplification of why people vacation outdoors. People take outdoor vacations for other reasons—for the adventure of whitewater rafting, for example, or to relax on the beach. Option (1) is a statement of fact. Options (3) and (4) are not oversimplifications because they only apply to some people. Option (5) is an opinion based on the fact that backpacking is a strenuous physical activity.

13. **(3) Women tend to live longer than men.** (Evaluation) The information in the table supports this generalization because, in every country cited, women's life expectancy is longer then men's. Options (1) and (2) are not true according to the table. Option (4) cannot be determined because the table does not relate its data to climate. Option (5) cannot be concluded because the table does not provide the life expectancy figures for other South American countries.

14. **(1) The Worldwide Movement of People** (Comprehension) The map shows people moving all over the world. Options (2) and (4) are incorrect because the map does not indicate the past or the future. Options (3) and (5) are incorrect because the map shows more than U.S. immigration or patterns of European settlement.

15. **(5) North America and Australia** (Comprehension) The arrows on the map show people coming to these continents and no one moving away from them. In none of the other options do both continents show this characteristic; people are shown leaving Europe, making option (1) incorrect, and Africa and Asia, making options (2), (3), and (4) incorrect.

16. **(3) Immigration affects all continents.** (Comprehension) All continents have arrows, which indicates that people have moved to or from them. Options (1) and (2) are incorrect because the map does not show patterns over time. Option (4) is incorrect because the map shows that African immigrants also go to North and South America, and it does not indicate relative numbers of immigrants. Option (5) is incorrect because the map does not suggest why people move.

17. **(2) Much environmental damage has resulted from people's pursuit of more comfortable lives.** (Analysis) The basic idea of the paragraph is that by pursuing a lifestyle made possible by industrialization people have damaged Earth and depleted its resources. Nothing in the paragraph suggests option (1). The cause-and-effect relationships put forth in options (3), (4), and (5) are all stated explicitly in the paragraph.

Posttest (Pages 240–255)

1. **(1) the potential power of the united colonies** (Comprehension) Divided into separate "pieces," the colonies had little power. Formed into a single snake, they became much more powerful. Option (2) is incorrect because the colonies are shown as parts of a single thing. Option (3) is incorrect because the snake is divided in pieces, rather than being a unified single piece. Nothing in the cartoon supports option (4) or (5).

2. **(4) The colonies should unite against Britain.** (Analysis) The publisher's use of the cartoon shows his opinion that the colonies should join together. Options (1), (2), and (3) are facts and are not relevant to the cartoon's point that the colonies need to unite. Option (5) is an opinion but it has nothing to do with the cartoon or the publisher's use of it on the newspaper's masthead.

3. **(2) Workers at a company form a labor union and demand changes from their employer.** (Application) Like the colonies, the workers will be more powerful if they are united against the employer than they would be if each made his or her demands alone. None of the other options express the idea of uniting to increase one's strength and power to achieve a goal. Options (4) and (5) are also incorrect because the cartoon is not about snakes. The snake is just a symbol that the cartoonist has used to express an idea.

4. **(2) about 15 percent of all children** (Comprehension) This can be determined from the value of the color line of the graph for 1971. Option (1) is the rate among Americans age 18 to 64. Option (3) is the poverty rate in 1971 for people age 65 and over. Option (4) is the poverty

rate for the age 65 and over group in 1969. Option (5) is the upper range of values shown on the graph.

5. **(3) The poverty rate for elderly Americans has shown the most improvement over time.** (Evaluation) This is supported by the line on the graph for people aged 65 and over, which shows the poverty rate falling from about 28 percent of all elderly people in 1966 to less than 10 percent in 1999. Option (1) is incorrect because the graph shows that children's 1999 poverty rate of about 17 percent was the highest of the three groups shown on the graph. Option (2) is incorrect because the graph shows that the poverty rate among this group has consistently been lower than that of children and lower or about the same rate as that of the elderly Americans. Option (4) cannot be determined from the graph because the graph deals in percentages of a group, without regard to the actual size of the group. Option (5) is contradicted by the graph, since the poverty rate for children rose in the 1980s and the early 1990s and only fell lower than the 1966 level in 1999.

6. **(2) President Johnson launched a series of antipoverty programs in 1964.** (Analysis) After the government launched a war on poverty in 1964, the poverty rates in all three categories shown on the graph generally fell for the next several years. This suggests that the government's antipoverty programs had their intended effect. Option (1) would have no direct effect on poverty. The data from the graph do not suggests any cause-and-effect relationship exists between changes in poverty rates among three age groups and option (3) or (5). If option (4) were related to poverty rates, one would expect the rates among working-age Americans and their children to decline, since college graduates typically earn more than people without a college education.

7. **(5) Europe** (Comprehension) The map legend shows the key to population growth rates for each continent. It shows that Europe's population has a negative annual growth rate and therefore is actually declining. While the growth rate of option (1) is low, it is not as low as that of Europe. The growth rates for options (2) and (4) are in an even higher range. Option (3) is incorrect because it has the highest growth rate, not the lowest.

8. **(1) a director of a United Nations social services agency** (Application) Such a person would be interested in international population projections for planning purposes. Options (2), (3), (4), and (5) are incorrect because a historian, earthquake scientist, psychologist, and specialist in ocean resources would not necessarily be interested in a region's current and future population figures.

9. **(2) The populations of Central America and Africa are rising faster than those of other world regions.** (Evaluation) These two regions are the only ones to have a growth rate of 2.1 to 3 percent, as shown by the map. Option (1) is incorrect because Australia also falls within the same range of relatively slow growth as North America, but the population of both continents is growing less slowly than Europe's population. Both Asia and South America are shown as growing between 1.1 and 2 percent, so it is not possible to determine whether option (3) is true. Options (4) and (5) are incorrect, although they are both true, because total population figures are not given for the continents.

10. **(1) The U.S. government tries hard to protect Americans against consumer fraud and dangerous products or practices.** (Analysis) The other information in the paragraph supports the conclusion that the government is trying to protect consumers. Options (2), (3), and (4) are supporting details because they show how the government is trying to protect consumers. Option (5) is also a detail because it provides an example of what the FTC does.

11. **(5) TV commercials claiming that a breakfast cereal prevents heart disease** (Application) The paragraph states that the FTC's job is to protect consumers from false or misleading advertising. Since this is a matter that involves product advertising, it would fall to the FTC to investigate this claim. Options (1) and (3) are matters that would concern the FDA. Option (2) would not fall within the jurisdiction of any of these agencies, but would instead interest some other government consumer-protection agency. Since option (4) affects airline passenger safety, it would be a matter for the FAA.

12. **(3) citizens' safety** (Evaluation) This is indicated by these government agencies' efforts to protect the American people from potentially harmful goods and services. There is no information in the paragraph to indicate that option (1), (2), or (5) is addressed by the agencies mentioned. Option (4) might be of concern to the FDA and the FTC, but they are less important to these regulatory agencies than is consumer safety.

13. **(2) After the Communist occupation of South Korea, UN forces pushed the invaders back to the Chinese border.** (Analysis) The first map shows the invasion of South Korea by Communist troops from the north, and the second map shows the retaking of territory by UN forces, who pushed through North Korea, reaching the Chinese border in the western part of the country. Options (1), (3), (4), and (5) are all details that support this

conclusion, and each is shown on only one of the two maps.

14. **(2) slavery extension** (Application) By banning slavery in states yet to be formed, the Missouri Compromise was dealing with the issue of slavery's extension into new territory. Option (1) is incorrect because the compromise did not end slavery where it currently existed. Option (3) is not correct because the compromise had nothing to do with taxes on imported goods. Options (4) is incorrect because there is no suggestion that the legitimacy of an existing federal law was being questioned in this case. Option (5) is incorrect because the compromise was about the admission of new states to the Union, not about a state leaving it.

15. **(1) abolitionism and slavery extension** (Analysis) Both dealt with taking some action related to slavery. Options (2), (3), (4), and (5) are not at all topically related as issues.

16. **(2) White southerners generally favored the extension of slavery into western territories.** (Evaluation) The passage states that the cotton gin expanded the growing of cotton and the plantation system. This would cause white southerners, who depended on slave labor on the plantations, to favor the spread of slavery as new lands were planted in cotton. All the other conclusions are incorrect because they are based on faulty logic. Options (1) and (3) are incorrect generalizations based on stereotypes. Many northerners were not opposed to slavery and most slaves worked at least as hard as northern factory workers, if not harder. Options (4) and (5) are oversimplifications. In addition to issues and events related to slavery, other issues and events not related to slavery also led to the secession of the southern states and to the Civil War.

17. **(2) having enough money** (Comprehension) In the cartoon, money is represented by the first hurdle and the big pit behind it, into which a racer who cannot leap extraordinarily far will fall. The racer must be able to overcome this hurdle in order to continue the race on to Iowa and New Hampshire. The cartoon does not refer to either option (1) or (3) as a difficulty or obstacle. Options (4) and (5) are presented as obstacles, but not as difficult as the "money" obstacle.

18. **(5) It is about gaining a political party's nomination for president of the United States.** (Analysis) The clues include the election year on the official's card and the hurdles labeled Iowa and New Hampshire, which are the first two states that choose Republican and Democratic candidates for the nomination. Without this knowledge the cartoon makes no

sense. There is no support in the cartoon for option (1), (2), (3), or (4).

19. **(3) higher prices for consumers** (Analysis) One way that sellers get consumers to buy its product instead of its competitors' is to lower its price. But there is no competition in a price-fixing situation, so the price is likely to stay high. This rules out option (1). Because prices are directly related to profits, option (2) is unlikely in a situation where there is no competition. Option (4) is unlikely because without competition, sellers would have no incentive to improve their product. Option (5) is incorrect because one would not expect sellers who fix prices to produce more than they could sell.

20. **(4) By mid-1975, North Vietnamese troops had overrun South Vietnam.** (Evaluation) The map shows many South Vietnamese cities, including the capital, Saigon, falling to the Communists in the spring of 1975. It also shows most of South Vietnam under Communist control by this time. Options (1), (2), (3), and (5), are true, but they are not supported by the map.

21. **(1) a stronger and more stable nation** (Comprehension) One clue is in the phrase "to form a more perfect Union." This implies that the nation already existed, and the other goals stated in the Preamble suggest that the nation was plagued by discontent and unrest. Therefore options (2) and (4) are incorrect. Although the Preamble mentions "common defense," there is no indication that option (3) was a goal. Nothing in the Preamble suggests option (5).

22. **(3) Through most of its history, the United States has had a two-party political system.** (Comprehension) Only this statement reveals the main point of the information. Option (1) is untrue, according to the information. Option (2) is not mentioned in the paragraph. Option (4) is generally true today, but it is a detail and not the main point of the paragraph. Option (5) is a restatement of John Quincy Adams's opinion.

23. **(3) the House debate on the bill** (Application) Of the options listed, this is the first time Representative B can influence the bill. At this stage, the representative can attempt to convince other House members of his or her position on the bill during the debate and/or by offering amendments from the House floor. Options (1) and (2) are incorrect because they refer to the process in the Senate, of which the representative is not a member. Options (4) and (5) describe House processes that take place after the debate on the bill.

24. **(2) the spirit of compromise** (Evaluation) The chart shows that step 12 is the step in which a conference committee resolves the differences in the versions of the bill that the House and Senate have passed. A willingness to compromise on these differences will be needed to create a revised version of the bill that will be acceptable to both the House and the Senate. Respect for option (1) or (5) has little to do with the success of reconciling House and Senate differences over the bill. Attaching too much importance to options (3) or (4) could cause the conference committee version of the bill to fail to pass in the Senate if committee members paid too much attention to the will of the House on the bill, or vice versa.

25. **(5) the president** (Analysis) The chart shows that if the president vetoes the bill, it can still become law if both the House and the Senate pass it again by a two-thirds majority. According to the chart, the actions expressed in options (1), (2), (3), or (4) effectively keep the bill from becoming law. If a bill is not approved by a committee of the House or the Senate or passed by the full House and the full Senate, it would not move forward to the next step on the chart.

26. **(3) the Essequibo River** (Comprehension) This marks the eastern-most extent of the territory that both nations claimed. Options (1), (4), and (5) are incorrect because they are not in the disputed territory. Option (2) is near the edge of the disputed territory, but it makes no sense that Venezuela would claim this border because it would mean giving up all the disputed territory.

27. **(1) The United States had little influence in the settlement of the dispute.** (Evaluation) The passage states that the United States sided with Venezuela, but the map shows that most of the disputed territory was awarded to Great Britain. This suggests that the dispute was not settled in the way the United States wanted. There is no evidence in the passage and map to support options (2) and (5), and both options are untrue. Option (3) is true, but it also cannot be determined from the information provided. The presence of Dutch Guiana on the map indicates that option (4) is untrue.

28. **(4) two neighbors arguing over where to erect a fence to separate their backyards** (Application) This is the only one of the options that involves a boundary dispute. Options (1) and (5) share almost nothing in common with the British-Venezuelan dispute. Option (2) is a conflict over use of a common resource rather than its ownership or division. Option (3) is a dispute that is related to South America, but it is not an argument that involves boundaries between territories.

29. **(5) The South American nation of Guyana used to be a British colony.** (Analysis) The final two sentences in the passage, when combined with the information on the map, leads to the assumption that Guyana used to be British Guiana, and was thus once a British colony. Nothing in the map or passage suggests that option (1), (2), (3), or (4) is true.

30. **(4) decreases, the advertising budget will increase.** (Evaluation) Advertising is a fixed cost, because it costs the same to advertise a product whether you produce 100 or 100,000. Furthermore, since you as owner can control this cost, it is illogical to assume that you would increase your advertising budget if you have less product to sell. Options (1) and (5) are logical assumptions because they are variable costs that will rise and fall with production. The assumptions in options (2) and (3) are also logical because, as fixed costs, these will not change, no matter what happens to production.

31. **(3) that members represent geographical areas** (Analysis) The chart indicates that senators are elected by the people of a state and House members by the people of a district within a state, so each represents a specific constituency. This is the only similarity between the two bodies that is stated in the options. Option (1) is incorrect because senators serve six-year terms and House members just two. Option (2) is also a way in which the two bodies are different, not similar. Option (4) is incorrect because the leader of the Senate is the Vice President of the United States, while the House Speaker is elected by the membership. Option (5) is incorrect because the chart shows a new House is elected every two years, compared to only a third of the Senate.

32. **(3) a region with heavy industry and average rainfall, like Germany and central Europe** (Application) The description in the paragraph includes the two factors of industry and rainfall. Only this option includes both factors. None of the other options present this combination of geographic factors. Option (1) is incorrect because there is no industry in the region from which the wind originates. Option (2) would lack the rainfall needed to carry the pollutants back to Earth. Option (4) lacks industry. Option (5) is incorrect because it is likely that such a small landform surrounded by large bodies of water would have the concentration of industry discharge that would make pollution a problem. The large bodies of water would serve to dissipate or carry away, not contribute more or concentrate, any pollution that was generated.

33. **(4) Los Angeles and Atlanta** (Analysis) The map shows that both cities will be partly cloudy and dry, with highs in the 60s. Option (1) is incorrect because the map shows clouds, rain, and cool temperatures in Seattle and partly cloudy, dry, and warmer in San Francisco. Option (2) is incorrect because New York will be sunnier and colder than San Francisco. Option (3) is incorrect because Richmond will be sunny and it is raining in Chicago. Option (5) is incorrect because Dallas will be cloudier and warmer than Denver.

34. **(1) Snow delays flights at Minneapolis airport.** (Analysis) The map shows snow and below-freezing temperatures in Minneapolis, making accumulations and flight delays possible. Options (2) and (4) are incorrect because the map shows Denver and New York to be mild and sunny. Option (3) cannot be determined from the map information. There is no information on the map about hurricanes, so option (5) is not supported.

35. **(3) Precipitation often occurs when cold air and warm air meet along cold fronts.** (Evaluation) This conclusion is supported by the information in the map, which shows two fronts. Along both there is precipitation in the form of either rain or snow. Option (1) is contradicted by information in the passage. No information is presented that would support option (2). Option (4) cannot be concluded because one day's weather on the map is no indication of a region's overall climate. Option (5) is contradicted by the map.

36. **(2) World War I resulted in the break-up of Austria-Hungary.** (Analysis) The left-hand map shows Austria-Hungary before World War I and the right-hand map shows several small nations occupying the same territory after the war. This leads to the conclusion that the war resulted in the breakup of Austria-Hungary. Option (1) is a map detail that supports the status of Austria-Hungary before the war, while options (3), (4), and (5) are map details about Europe after the war. These details all support the conclusion that Austria-Hungary was broken up as a result of the war.

37. **(4) better advertising and marketing** (Application) Iacocca says that Americans do not know how good American cars are and that they must be told. He suggests that if U.S. automakers could get this message across to consumers, Americans would buy more U.S. cars instead of those made by Japanese companies. Options (1) and (2) are incorrect because Iacocca believes that U.S. car makers are already producing high-quality cars. Options (3) and (5) are incorrect because he does not indicate that wages or prices are part of the problem.

38. **(5) Most southern workers were required to work as long as their employer demanded.** (Analysis) The map shows that most southern states had no laws in the 1920s to limit the length of the workday. This information establishes that the statement in option (5) is a fact. Option (1) is an opinion that cannot be proven from the map information, and it is a matter of judgment regarding what makes someone "better off." Working fewer hours might be better for one's health, but for most hourly employees it would result in a smaller paycheck. Options (2) and (4) are also judgments with no factual support on the map. Just because an employer's business is in a state with no workday limit does not mean that the employer is unconcerned about employees; nor does working long hours necessarily make someone a better worker than someone who works less. The word "probably" identifies option (3) as an opinion that also cannot be proven from the map information.

39. **(2) the growth of industry in the Midwest** (Analysis) The paragraph cites industrialization as the prime reason for urban growth, even though that growth did not occur evenly in all three regions. So the logical conclusion is that the growth of Midwestern towns and cities resulted from industrialization in the region. There is no basis in the information to suggest that option (1), (3), (4), or (5) caused this growth.

40. **(3) Gore overwhelmingly won three of the states, Bush overwhelmingly won one of the states, and the fifth was closely contested.** (Comprehension) The chart shows that Gore overwhelmingly won California, Illinois, and New York and Bush overwhelmingly won Texas; Florida was closely contested. Options (1), (2), and (4) are contradicted by the chart. Option (5) is true but is not a summary of the information in the chart.

41. **(5) Per person energy use varies widely among the nations of the world.** (Analysis) Energy use among the countries shown on the graph varies widely, which leads to this conclusion. Options (1), (2), (3), and (4) are all details from the graph that support the conclusion.

42. **(1) the growth of democratic institutions in ancient Athens** (Comprehension) Each event recorded in the chart shows movement toward democracy in ancient Athens. Options (2) and (5) are incorrect because the chart deals only with ancient Athens and not with all of Greece or all time periods in its history. Option (3) is incorrect because there is no information about modern Greek government in the chart. Option (4) is covered in the chart, but its main

focus is on ways in which government became more democratic.

43. **(5) Americans spend most of what they earn on the basic necessities of life.** (Analysis) The graph indicates that nearly 60 percent of the typical family's annual income is spent for food, housing, clothing, and transportation—all of which generally are necessary to survive and function. Options (1), (2), (3), and (4) are all details that support the conclusion in option (5). Option (1) establishes that most Americans spend very little of their incomes on a luxury like entertainment. Options (2), (3), and (4) establish how much of their incomes Americans spend on each separate necessity—food, shelter, and transportation.

44. **(4) The government should own and operate basic productive resources.** (Comprehension) This is a restatement of the information about socialism that is given in the chart. Option (1) is incorrect because it is the definition of economic planning and applies to the theory of communism as well as to socialism. Option (2) is incorrect because it describes what happens in nations that follow the capitalistic economic theory rather than socialism. Option (3) is incorrect because it is a restatement of the communist economic theory. Option (5) is incorrect because it is a restatement of the capitalist economic theory.

45. **(2) socialism and capitalism** (Application) In both systems, at least some of the productive resources are privately controlled. This means that, to some extent, laissez faire operates in both systems. Options (1), (3), and (4) are incorrect because the government controls all economic planning and operations in a communist system. Option (5) is incorrect because laissez faire is important in a capitalist system, too.

46. **(1) It is the freedom of private businesses to operate competitively for a profit with little government regulation.** (Analysis) The paragraph implies that free enterprise is the opposite of economic planning and assumes the reader realizes that free enterprise relates to a relative lack of government control over the economy. Option (2) is incorrect because the sentence that discusses free enterprise implies the opposite. Options (3), (4), and (5) are incorrect because they make no sense in the context of the sentence discussing free enterprise and the final sentence of the paragraph.

47. **(4) the Civil Rights Act of 1964** (Application) The subject of Kennedy's speech was race. This law is the only option that dealt directly with race, protecting civil rights by outlawing racial discrimination. Therefore options (1), (2), (3), and (5) are incorrect.

48. **(3) to move the products of U.S. companies there for export and sale to the United States** (Analysis) The graph shows that American companies had heavy investments in mining, petroleum, and agriculture. In a country with a developing economy, roads and railroads would need to be built to transport the oil, ore, and agricultural goods produced by these investments so that the products could be sold. Options (1) and (4) are not likely because the graph shows that the U.S. was heavily invested in transportation. Nothing in the paragraph or graph indicates a U.S. interest in increasing the income of Latin American countries, so option (2) is incorrect. Option (5) is unlikely since the paragraph suggests that the companies had little regard for the well-being of the people in the countries where they invested.

49. **(2) Since 1910, population in the South and West has grown faster than in the North and East.** (Evaluation) This would account for the fact that the map shows the nation's population center steadily shifting southward and westward since 1910. Option (1) is contradicted by the paragraph and map. Options (3) and (5) are incorrect because these places are the center of the nation's population, not the place where most people live. While option (4) is true, it cannot be concluded based on the information provided.

50. **(1) bypass their elected representatives.** (Analysis) In initiatives and referenda, people have a direct voice in what happens. Only a referendum allows voters to repeal laws, ruling out option (2). Only an initiative allows voters to propose laws, which rules out option (3). Neither initiatives nor referenda are related to options (4) and (5).

Simulated Test (Pages 258–273)

1. **(2) Latin America** (Comprehension) The graph for 1998 shows that 43 percent of immigrants are from Latin America. This is the largest percentage of the groups shown in the modern graph. Options (1) and (3) represent smaller percentages of immigrants. Option (4) is not shown on the graph. Option (5) is not true.

2. **(1) The percentage of immigrants coming from Asia greatly increased during the 1900s.** (Analysis) This is a fact that can be proven by comparing the pie graphs. Options (2), (3), (4), and (5) are opinions that have no basis in the factual information presented, and with which not everyone would agree.

3. **(3) The United States has become a more ethnically and culturally diverse nation.** (Analysis) Coming from all parts of the world, immigrants bring elements of their own culture

with them and thereby diversify the culture of the United States. Nothing in the passage or graphs suggests that option (1) or (2) is an effect of immigration, or even that either is true. (Neither is true.) Option (4) cannot be determined because the graphs do not provide information on when Angel Island closed or what has happened to the number or percentage of Asian immigrants since it closed. Nothing in the paragraph or graph supports the cause-and-effect relationship stated in option (5).

4. **(2) Europe is no longer the most important source of immigrants to the United States.** (Evaluation) This is supported by the graph's evidence that while Europe provided about 85 percent of immigrants in 1900, it accounts for only about 14 percent today. Option (1) is not supported because no information is provided about where Asian immigrants settle in the United States. Option (3) is incorrect because the graphs compare the composition of immigration but provide no total numbers of immigrants for either year shown. There is no information in the paragraph to indicate whether option (4) or (5) is true.

5. **(4) organization** (Evaluation) All the activities and accomplishments described involve a high degree of organization. Option (1) is incorrect because, although armies are mentioned, there is no suggestion that a high value was placed on waging wars. The paragraph gives no evidence that option (2), (3), or (5) was especially valued.

6. **(3) The Second Amendment gives people the right to bear arms.** (Analysis) The cartoon expresses the opinion that gun ownership in the United States is not working the way the Second Amendment intended. Readers will not grasp this message unless they know that the Second Amendment involves the right to bear arms. Options (1), (2), and (4) are all true, but knowing these things does not help in understanding the meaning of the cartoon. Option (5) is incorrect because it is untrue and is unrelated to subject of the cartoon.

7. **(5) The present-day coastal cities of the eastern United States will be flooded.** (Analysis) The map shows the United States' eastern and southern shorelines. According to the map, the shoreline has moved inland over the past 15,000 years and will continue to do so. The effect will be to put today's East Coast cities under water. Nothing in the map suggests that temperature changes or earthquakes will result, ruling out options (1) and (2). A changing shoreline would not necessarily be a cause of population changes in the country as a whole, so options (3) and (4) are incorrect.

8. **(1) the president** (Application) Like the governor of a state, the president is the chief officer of the executive branch of government. Option (2) is incorrect because the vice president is second in command. Option (3) is incorrect because the secretary of state is not the chief executive officer of the national government and because the U.S. secretary of state is responsible for foreign affairs. Options (4) and (5) are incorrect because these are legislative rather than executive offices.

9. **(5) comptroller and treasurer** (Analysis) Both offices have many similar functions, most of which revolve around the receipt and spending of money by the state. No similarities are noted in the chart for the offices in options (1) and (2). The offices in option (3) are similar only to the extent that they both keep records. In option (4), the comptroller's job is to uncover the wrongdoing, while the attorney general's job is to represent the state in court.

10. **(2) to make sure that the governor does not have too much power** (Analysis) The passage states that these officials are either elected by the people or appointed by the governor. A governor appointing these key officials might choose only people who support his or her actions and positions. The effect would be that governor would have much more power than if these officials were elected. So having these officials elected acts as a check on the governor's power. Option (1) would not be an effect of choosing state officials by election rather than appointing them because it costs more to run an election than to appoint an officeholder. No direct cause-and-effect relationship exists between electing state officials and option (3) or (5). Option (4) might be true, but it would result from an abuse of the power mentioned in option (2).

11. **(5) black female workers** (Comprehension) This can be determined by a correct reading of the graph, which shows that black women on average earn just over $20,000 a year. This is less than the average annual earnings shown on the graph for options (1), (2), (3), and (4).

12. **(2) the practice of not promoting women or minority employees beyond a certain level** (Comprehension) This connection is implied by the writer's reference to "an invisible barrier" that blocked the career progress of women and minorities beyond a certain point in management. The passage states that prejudice and fear is a cause of the glass ceiling not its definition, so option (1) is incorrect. Nothing in the passage suggests option (3), which merely took its name from the term. Option (4) is one result of the glass ceiling, not the meaning of the term. Option (5) is incorrect because the passage

states that women comprise 40 percent of the workforce and that minorities had gotten middle management jobs.

13. **(4) Both groups earn less on average than male workers of the same race.** (Analysis) The graph shows that the average annual earnings of white female workers is less than that of white male workers, and that the average annual earnings of black female workers is less than that of black male workers. Option (1) is not a similarity because the passage states that white females hold 5 percent of the top executive jobs, while minorities hold just 3 percent, and most of these top minority executives are men. Nothing in the passage or graph supports option (2). The passage indicates that women and minority executives are generally middle-managers, not that most women workers are employed at this level, so option (3) is incorrect. Option (5) is contradicted by the information in the passage.

14. **(5) The pay difference for male and female executives was greater than for the other groups on the graph.** (Evaluation) The glass ceiling refers to the inability of people in certain race and gender groups to reach top jobs in management. The much greater difference in earnings between male and female executives, compared to the difference in earnings for male and female workers in general, suggests that not many women executives were in the high-paying top jobs. This suggests that a glass ceiling still existed for women in 2000. Options (1), (2), (3), and (4) all involve correct readings of the graph but the relationships they note do not provide evidence of whether or not the glass ceiling still existed for women.

15. **(2) the west coast of South America** (Comprehension) The map shows that the west coast of South America lies in an earthquake and volcanic activity zone. No such zone exists on South America's east coast, so option (1) is incorrect. According to the map, options (3) and (5) are near regions where the earthquake rate is high, but neither is in such a zone. Option (4) is also outside the zones of high earthquake and volcanic activity.

16. **(1) A large earthquake will soon occur along the West Coast of the United States.** (Analysis) This is an area of many earthquakes and volcanoes, according to the map, so it seems possible that an earthquake will occur in that areas, but we cannot be certain when or if it might. Therefore, this statement is an opinion. The map confirms that options (2), (3), (4), and (5) are all statements of fact.

17. **(5) More earthquakes and volcanic eruptions occur in the oceans than on dry land.** (Evaluation) This conclusion is supported by the fact that the map shows most of the high-activity zones as being in the oceans rather than on dry land. The map suggests nothing about "unnoticed" earthquakes, which rules out option (1). It also gives no information about predicting volcanic eruptions, so option (2) is incorrect. One cannot tell from the map how many active volcanoes there are or the relative thickness of Earth's crust on the ocean floor and on dry land, so options (3) and (4) are also not supported by the map.

18. **(5) Voters will not vote for someone they see as having little chance of victory.** (Analysis) The writer explains that even former presidents cannot get elected later as candidates of a third party and that no third-party candidate has ever become president, so voters will not support someone they think has little chance of winning. Option (1) is a detail that introduces the discussion of third parties. Options (2), (3), and (4) are all details providing evidence that helps support the writer's conclusion.

19. **(4) Slavery existed in states that remained in the Union.** (Evaluation) This is direct evidence that there were considerations other than slavery in a state's decision whether to support the Union or the Confederacy. Options (1), (2), (3), and (5) are all true, but they do not support the statement that slavery was not the only issue of the Civil War.

20. **(2) the western United States** (Application) Drought-resistant wheat would most likely be grown in areas with little rainfall. As the map shows, there is less rainfall in the western United States than in any of the region given in options (1), (3), (4), and (5).

21. **(3) to create a water distribution system** (Comprehension) This is established in the first paragraph, which states that the first laws dealt with irrigation and that laws were required to ensure the fair use of water. The passage does not state or imply that option (1), (2), (4), or (5) was the object of lawmaking, although ancient Egypt later did develop laws related to trade and the construction of buildings for government and for religious purposes.

22. **(2) The fertile soil produced abundant harvests.** (Analysis) This is the basic cause for the food surpluses, which in turn allowed arts and crafts to develop and led to trade and the exchange of ideas and inventions. Options (1), (3), and (4) are the effects of this basic cause. There is no evidence in the passage to support option (5).

23. **(1) cooperation** (Evaluation) The passage points out that the irrigation systems that were

Answers and Explanations

key to Egypt's prosperity were the result of people working together. There is nothing in the information to suggest that option (2), (3), (4), or (5) was especially important.

24. **(3) A person is innocent until proven guilty in a court of law.** (Comprehension) The amendment requires "due process of law." In other words, before a person can be found guilty of a crime and deprived of "life, liberty, or property," he or she must be given a fair trial that follows a set procedure. Option (1) is not implied as long as due process of law occurs. Options (2), (4), and (5) are ideas that are not addressed in this amendment.

25. **(4) Maria has worked as a carpenter for three years and has her own tools and a car.** (Application) Maria has one year less experience than is required for an apprentice, but she meets more of the job requirements (experience, tools, car) than the applicants in options (1), (2), (3), and (5).

26. **(5) Dallas** (Application) The graph lists the pH levels of several cities and indicates that the closer the pH of rain is to 5.6, the less acidic and so the less potentially harmful it is to plant and animal life. Of the cities listed, Dallas has rain with a pH closest in value to 5.6, so vegetables there would be the least damaged. Options (1), (2), (3), and (4) all have lower pH values, so their rain is more acidic and potentially more damaging to the plants in a garden.

27. **(5) The population of Norway is more educated than the population of the United States.** (Evaluation) This conclusion is supported by graph data showing that higher percentages of Norway's people have completed grammar school and secondary school than have the people in the United States. Option (1) cannot be concluded because not every country in the world is shown on the graph. Option (2) is incorrect because the percent of people educated at each level is not an indicator of how much money a nation is spending on education. Options (3) and (4) are not supported because no graph data establish any relationship between the percent of people who attend a nation's schools and the quality of those schools, or between education level and income level in a nation.

28. **(2) The amendment sets forth the rights of people being tried for crimes.** (Comprehension) This is the only statement that covers the entire contents of the amendment. Options (1) and (5) state only part of the guarantees that the amendment contains. Options (3) and (4) state protections found in other amendments in the Bill of Rights. They are not covered by the Sixth Amendment.

29. **(3) If a person accused of a crime cannot afford a lawyer, the court will appoint one at no cost to the accused person.** (Application) The Sixth Amendment states that a person accused of a crime has a right "to have the Assistance of Counsel for his defense." In 1963, the Supreme Court ruled in the Florida case of *Gideon* v. *Wainwright* that, if a defendant could not afford a lawyer, the state had to provide one at no cost. Options (1), (2), (4), and (5) involve legal principles established by Supreme Court decisions resulting from its interpretation of other parts of the Constitution, specifically, the First, Fifth, Fourth, and Fourteenth amendments, respectively.

30. **(1) the fair application of the law** (Evaluation) The Sixth Amendment outlines the things that must be done when someone is accused of and tried for a crime in order to assure that the law is applied to each person in the same way. Options (2), (3), (4), and (5) are not addressed by the Sixth Amendment, but rather by other amendments, other parts of the U.S. Constitution, and by specific Supreme Court decisions related to these values.

31. **(3) Buffalo and Chicago** (Analysis) These two cities have the closest average daytime highs and lows in each of the four seasons represented in the table. Option (1) is incorrect because Bismarck has much colder January temperatures than Indianapolis and is somewhat cooler in October. Option (2) is incorrect because Las Vegas is much cooler than Brownsville in January and hotter in July. Option (4) is incorrect because Cheyenne temperatures are cooler than El Paso's year-round. Option (5) is incorrect because Los Angeles temperatures are also cooler than Miami's in each month shown on the table.

32. **(4) for geographical characteristics** (Comprehension) Nearly all the culture regions are named for such geographical characteristics as topographical features (for example, plateau and plains), location (for example, northeast and southwest), or climate (for example, arctic and subarctic). The map shows no culture areas named for option (1), (2), (3), or (5).

33. **(2) Many Europeans felt they were culturally superior to Native Americans.** (Analysis) The passage states that the Europeans thought "native peoples were uncivilized savages." It is therefore a fact that they held this opinion. Option (1) is an opinion, not a fact. Options (3) and (4) are opinions whose accuracy cannot be determined from the information provided. Option (5) is the unsubstantiated opinion that was held by the Europeans.

34. (4) excise tax (Application) This tax is paid by the manufacturer and included in the price of the product, so the consumer has no way of knowing the exact amount of the tax. In options (1), (2), (3), and (5), the person who pays the tax knows the exact amount, so these are direct taxes.

35. (2) Taxes place an unfair burden on all Americans. (Evaluation) This is a hasty generalization. Many Americans, such as children, for example, pay almost nothing in taxes and wealthy Americans can easily afford to pay taxes. Option (1) is a reasonable conclusion because, unlike income taxes, a sales tax remains the same regardless of the income of the purchaser. So a poor person who buys a washing machine, for example, pays the same tax as a wealthy person who buys the appliance. With income taxes, poorer people pay less tax than wealthy people do. Options (3), (4), and (5) are also reasonable conclusions, based on the information.

36. (5) the West Indies (Comprehension) The map shows that some of the slave ships that traveled northwest from Africa across the Atlantic had the West Indies as their destination. The paragraph indicates that options (1) and (2) were countries that profited from the slave trade as opposed to being destinations for slaves. The map shows that only raw materials, not slaves, flowed from North America to Great Britain, so option (3) is incorrect. Nothing in the paragraph or map supports France as a destination for enslaved Africans, so option (4) is incorrect.

37. (3) Slaves taken to South America were from a different part of Africa than those taken to North America. (Analysis) The map shows that slaves arriving in South America came from Angola, while those transported to North America were from Senegambia and Guinea-Bissau. Options (1) and (4) are incorrect because neither the number of slaves taken to each continent nor their selling price once there can be determined from the map. Neither the passage nor the map information provides any information concerning nationality of slave ships to support option (2) as a difference. The map shows that option (5) is not true.

38. (1) Many women are single parents and are struggling to raise families. (Analysis) The graph shows that nearly half the women with two jobs are working at the second job in order to meet household expenses or to pay off accumulated debts. Since single parents overwhelmingly tend to be women, this is the most logical cause-and-effect relationship of the options stated. No information in the graph suggests a cause-and-effect relationship exists between either option (2) or (3) and multiple

job-holding or even that either option is true. Options (4) and (5) are stated reasons, according to the graph, but they are not nearly as common an explanation for multiple job-holding as is the attempt by women to meet current household expenses and pay their debts.

39. (4) the flowering of the early civilization of ancient Egypt (Application) Like the Indus civilization, which the map shows developed around the Indus River, the early Egyptians also developed their civilization in a river valley. In Egypt's case it was the Nile River. Options (2) and (3) are incorrect because the map does not show the conquest of one people by another and the creation of an empire. Option (1) is incorrect because Native American cultures were scattered across the continent in all geographic regions, with very few centered in river valleys. Option (5) is incorrect because the most of the early British colonists in New England settled along the coast, not in a river valley.

40. (4) the rights of individual citizens (Evaluation) By guaranteeing a number of important personal freedoms (for every individual), this amendment shows that the members of Congress placed a high value on rights of each person. The other options have nothing to do with the content of the amendment.

41. (3) an increase in U.S. fuel oil production (Analysis) The graph shows that the price of fuel oil dropped 25 percent in 1986. The most likely cause of this change would have been a major increase in the available supply of fuel oil. Option (1) is incorrect because the drop in oil prices is much greater than the overall drop in prices. If there is any cause-and-effect relationship between these two changes, it is likely that the sharp drop in oil prices caused a small drop in the overall Consumer Price Index. Options (2) and (4) are incorrect because the oil shortages that would have resulted from each would have raised prices, not lowered them. Option (5) is not related to fuel oil prices.

42. (5) the Truman Doctrine (Application) The chart indicates that the Truman Doctrine offered U.S. aid to countries trying to prevent a communist takeover. Since the threat of U.S. force was not involved, option (1) does not apply. Option (2) is incorrect because Reagan did not use investment or trade to influence events in El Salvador. U.S. intervention in another nation's affairs eliminates option (3) as the basis for Reagan's action. Option (4) is incorrect because the action had nothing to do with World War II.

43. (3) the Good Neighbor Policy (Application) By withdrawing U.S. troops, the president was proving that he respected the independence and rights of Nicaragua and Haiti. Options (1) and (5) are incorrect because the U.S. was not using or threatening force, but was instead withdrawing it. Option (2) is incorrect because the action did not include trading with or investing in the nations. Option (4) is incorrect because the action did not involve economic aid or World War II.

44. **(5) the Truman Doctrine** (Application) Both these policies are linked by their mutual goal of preventing communist takeovers in countries where the communists did not yet have control. Options (1), (2), and (3) were not driven by this goal. Option (4) was indirectly related to preventing communism from taking hold in countries devastated by World War II, but its main purpose was to rebuild these countries and their economies.

45. **(2) a terrorist** (Comprehension) It is clear from the label on the truck and the ticking bomb in the back of the truck that a terrorist is driving the truck. The label and the lack of any other identifying features on the truck indicate that options (1) and (5) are incorrect. Options (3) and (4) are unlikely because the truck is moving toward the hikers, not putting them out of danger by taking the bomb away.

46. **(5) The people hiked to this isolated place to get away from terrorism and crime.** (Analysis) Despite the hikers' belief that they are in a safe place, a truck carrying a ticking bomb is speeding up the mountain toward them. Without the assumption stated in option (5), the cartoon makes no sense. This understanding is central to the cartoonist's message that there is no place safe from terrorism. Options (1), (2), and (4) are not suggested by the cartoonist. Assuming option (3) does not aid in understanding the cartoon.

47. **(1) The first high-rise buildings were built in U.S. cities.** (Analysis) The graph shows U.S. steel production increasing. This made more steel available for construction, especially for the steel beams and girders that are required in the production of skyscrapers. No direct cause-and-effect relationship exists between the growth of steel production and option (2), (4), or (5). Option (3) is the opposite of the effect that increases in steel production had on industry.

48. **(3) The photo showed an important and strategic victory for the Allies** (Analysis) Capturing an island in the Pacific was critical in 1945 for the American forces because of its proximity to Japan. Neither the photo nor the passage supports any of the other options.

49. **(3) Unemployment is much lower among whites than among blacks.** (Analysis) The graph shows that unemployment rates for black men and women are about double those of their white counterparts. Options (1), (2), (4), and (5) are factual details from the graph that support this conclusion.

50. **(5) The Cherokee of the Midwest today are descended from the Cherokee of the South.** (Analysis) This can be concluded from the map, which shows the Cherokee moving from northeast Georgia and vicinity to what is today Oklahoma. Options (1), (2), (3), and (4) are details from the map about where the Cherokee originated, the fact that they moved, and where they relocated. They are details that support the conclusion in option (5).

Glossary

abolitionist a person who wanted to do away with slavery

absolute monarchy authoritarian government in which all authority is held by a king or queen

acid rain type of precipitation made acidic by air pollutants as a result of burning fossil fuels

Age of Exploration the period during which European nations sponsored expeditions by sea to unknown parts of the world (1400s to 1600s)

amendment addition or change to a constitution

appropriate information information that supports an idea, generalization, or conclusion

aristocracy the highest social class, usually of noble birth; means "rule by the best"

arms race the competition (1950s through the 1980s) between the United States and the Soviet Union to develop nuclear weapons

Articles of Confederation the first U.S. constitution (1781–1789), which established a confederation of sovereign states

assumption an idea, theory, or principle that a person believes to be true; something taken for granted and not explained

authoritarian advocating obedience; not allowing personal liberty

authority power to give orders, take action, and command obedience; party having this power

balance of trade the difference between the total value of goods and services exported and the total value of goods and services imported

barter system economic system in which goods and services are exchanged between two parties, rather than being paid for with money

bias a strong opinion held by a person about a topic, often unfairly or without good reason

bicameral consisting of two legislative bodies

Bill of Rights first ten amendments to the U.S. Constitution, listing the rights of individuals

boycott a form of protest in which a group refuses to buy the products of a country or company until it makes some demanded change

breakwater a wall built in a lake or sea to protect a shoreline from the force of waves

business cycle the increasing and decreasing of business activity through four phases: expansion, peak, contraction, and trough

cabinet a group of advisors to a chief executive

cause what makes something happen or produces a result or consequence

centralized government a type of government in which political power is held at one point

charter a document that establishes an organization, such as a city or a corporation, and defines organization type and purpose

city-state an early form of organization and government; town or city and land it controls

civil rights the rights and freedoms democratic governments guarantee to all citizens

Civil War a sectional conflict between the Northern and Southern states (1861 to 1865)

civilization an advanced and highly organized society; the culture, society, and way of life in a particular place during a particular time

clan group of people with a common ancestor

climate the general weather conditions of an area over a long period of time

Cold War struggle for world power between the United States and the Soviet Union (1945 until the Soviet Union's collapse in 1989)

collective bargaining a negotiation between employers and labor union leaders regarding working conditions, pay, and other issues

colonial relating to a colony or area controlled and settled by people from another country

colonists persons who leave their native country to settle in a colony

colonization sending people to establish political, cultural, and economic control over another area

communism an economic system in which the government owns the means of production and plans the economy of the nation

Communist Bloc a group of nations allied with the Soviet Union during the Cold War

compare to look for similarities in things

compass rose map tool indicating the four principal directions—North, South, East, West

concept an idea or principle that applies to a variety of separate situations or circumstances

conclusion a judgment or decision based on facts and details

conservation the careful use and protection of natural resources

constitution a plan that provides the basic organization and rules for a government

context the circumstances or setting in which an event occurs

continents seven large landmasses on Earth

contraction a reduction in business activity

contrast to look for differences in things

cost-push inflation higher prices caused by a push for higher wages (wage-price spiral)

Crusades expeditions from Europe to the Middle East (11th and 14th centuries) to impose Christian rule on Muslim areas

culture the knowledge, beliefs, arts, morals, laws, and customs of a society

currency a country's system of money

daimyo a feudal lord in Japan from the 9th to 16th centuries whose power came from the samurai warriors loyal to him

data facts, measurements, or statistics used as a basis for reasoning, discussion, or calculation

demand the amount of a good or service consumers are willing to buy at a certain price

demand-pull inflation a condition of higher prices due to demand for goods in short supply

democracy rule by the people

democratic government system of government in which the people rule, either directly or through elected representatives

depression the condition that results from a severe reduction of business activity

desert a large area of land that receives little yearly precipitation

developing nation country with few manufacturing industries in which most people make a living mainly through agriculture

dictatorship system of government in which one person (not a king or queen) or a small group rules, usually through fear and force; usually not responsive to the will of the people

discount rate the rate of interest a Federal Reserve Bank charges other banks

discrimination the unequal treatment of individuals based on race, gender, ethnicity, age, religion, disability, or sexual orientation

dynasty ruling family whose members govern one after another over a long period of time

effect something brought about by a cause; a result or consequence

empire a group of countries or territories that are united under one ruler or government

environment all the things that make up our existence on Earth, including land, air, water, plants, animals, cities, and towns

equilibrium condition existing when supply of a product or service and demand for it are equal

erosion the wearing away of land, usually by the action of water, wind, or ice

ethnic relating to a nation or race that has a common cultural tradition

excise tax tax on production, transportation, sale, or consumption of a certain good or service

executive administering and enforcing laws and putting other government or organization plans and decisions into effect; the person in charge

expansion the phase of the business cycle characterized by an increase in business activity

exports goods produced in one country and sent to another country for sale

fact a real occurrence or event

fall line border between upland region and lowland region marked by waterfalls and rapids resulting from the elevation change

federal system of government in which several states unite but keep vast control over their own affairs; the national government of the U.S.

Federal Reserve System (the Fed) the central banking authority in the United States, which supervises commercial banks by monitoring accounts and controlling interest rates

feudalism system of government based on the granting of land in return for military assistance

force the means by which a ruler, government, or other party uses power, often through fear, to shape the behavior of others against their will

fossil fuel class of combustible materials (coal, natural gas, and petroleum) formed from the remains of prehistoric plants and animals

generalization a broad statement applied to an entire class of things or people

global economy the increased economic interdependence of the world's nations

goods physical things people produce and use

Gross Domestic Product (GDP) the total monetary value of goods and services produced in a nation during a year

groundwater water coming from underground sources such as a well, spring, or aquifer

hostile takeover a process in which one company purchases or otherwise gains control of another against the wishes of those who operate it

House of Representatives the U.S. Congress chamber or house in which each state is assigned seats according to its population

humanism a movement that began in Italy in the 1100s focused on the study of ancient Greek and Roman literature and emphasizing the dignity of human values

ideology a set of basic beliefs about life, culture, government, and society

immigration the process by which people leave one country to settle in another country

imperialism practice in which a nation uses power to control the territory, politics, or economic or cultural affairs of another nation

implication something that is not openly stated but is hinted at or suggested

implied cause a reason for something that is not directly stated, but is only suggested or hinted at

imports goods brought into a country that are produced in another country

incorporate to form a city government, legal community, or company that has the legal organization and protections of a corporation

Industrial Revolution the period when machines replaced most production by hand

inflation a general increase in the prices due largely to a decline in the value of money

influence the power to affect actions or beliefs without the use or threat of force

inorganic waste discarded items made from materials that were never alive

jetty a structure extending from land into a body of water that influences the water's flow in order to protect the land

Jim Crow laws laws in many Southern states enforcing the segregation of the African-American and white populations

judicial review power of courts to declare legislative and executive actions to be in violation of the Constitution

kingdom area ruled by a king or queen

knights under feudalism, mounted warriors in Europe who were the lowest level of persons who held land in return for military service

labor union a group of workers organized to improve the working conditions of its members

landmass the part of Earth above water

legal authority authority based on and permitted by law

legend the map tool that explains the meaning of the map's symbols

legislature a group of persons that makes the laws of a nation or state

legitimate power the power exercised by a leader who has the authority to make decisions that the people will follow

levy to place and collect a legal assessment; tax

literacy test a test limiting voting to those who could read; used mainly to deny voting rights to Southern African Americans after the Civil War

lobbyist a person who tries to influence the voting of those in government

longshore current a current that flows parallel to the coastline of a large body of water

lord a person of noble birth

main idea what a paragraph or article is about; the broadest, most important idea

manifest destiny the 19th-century belief that the United States would be expanded from the Atlantic to the Pacific coasts

mass participation political or social activism by a large diverse group rather than a small or elite group

merger the uniting of two or more companies to form a single business, usually accomplished when one company takes over another

Middle Ages period in European history that began with the collapse of the Roman Empire and ended with the Renaissance in the 1300s

minimum wage the lowest legal wage that may be paid to a worker

missionary a person sent to teach the Christian religion to people who are not Christians

money economy a system by which goods and services are paid for with money

monopoly a condition in which one company has sole control over a good or service

multiparty system a political system in which three or more major political parties exercise power in government

nation large community of people with a common culture, language, and history, living in a particular area under the same government

national debt the total amount of money that a nation's government owes

natural resources the materials people use that are supplied by nature

noble a person who has a high social rank, usually because of his or her birth

nominate to choose a political party's candidate to run for elective office

nonaligned nations the nations that did not side with either the United States or the Soviet Union during the Cold War

nonrenewable resources natural resources that cannot be replaced by natural processes, or that are replaced very slowly

opinion beliefs or feelings about something

oversimplification a description that makes a concept seem less complex than it really is

parliamentary system a form of government in which the lawmaking and executive functions are held by an elected legislature, or parliament

pharaoh title given the ruler of ancient Egypt

piecework a wage system in which a worker is paid for each unit that he or she produces

place a specific location on Earth described by its position in degrees of longitude and latitude

plantation a large farm on which the work is performed by laborers who live on the property

platform a statement of a political party's basic beliefs and positions

political party a group organized to nominate candidates for elective office, win elections, and conduct government

poll tax a tax people had to pay in order to vote, banned by the 24th Amendment in 1964

pollute to make something less pure by adding harmful substances to it

power ability to take action or exercise control; possession of authority, influence, or control over others; a legal or official authority or right

precinct the smallest voting district

precipitation droplets of water that fall as rain, snow, sleet, or hail

presidential system form of government in which executive and legislative functions are separate and held by independent and equal branches of government, with the chief executive chosen by the people, not the legislature

prime minister the leader of the executive branch in a parliamentary system of government

prime rate the lowest interest rate that banks charge their best customers

public land land owned directly by a government and therefore belonging to the entire nation, state, or community

radical a person who supports extreme changes in traditional policies and practices

ratify to formally approve something, such as a constitutional amendment or a treaty

real GDP the value of a nation's production of goods and services during a year, corrected for the effects of inflation

recession a period when production declines and people have less money

Reconstruction period of rebuilding the society and economy of the South after the Civil War

recycle to reuse solid and non-solid waste for the same or a new purpose

referendum an election that allows citizens to accept or reject a law that has been proposed or passed by state or local government

region an area with common characteristics making it different from other areas

Renaissance a revival of interest in art and learning in Europe that began in Italy in the 1300s and lasted until the 1500s

renewable resource something that can be replenished by Earth's natural processes

repeal to revoke or do away with a law

republic a government in which citizens hold the power and exercise it through elected representatives

reservation tract of federal land set aside for use by a specific group or for a specific purpose; federal land set aside for Native Americans

reserve requirement the percentage of their deposits that member banks must keep available in a Federal Reserve Bank

resources something available for use, may be natural or financial

restate present information in another way

samurai a warrior in feudal Japan, similar to a knight in feudal Europe

sandbar a ridge of sand built above water level by currents in a river or near a coastline

satellite nation a communist nation of Eastern Europe whose government was controlled by the Soviet Union during the Cold War

seawall a wall or embankment built on land to protect a shoreline from being eroded by waves

secede to withdraw from an organization or a federation

segregation separation of a group from the rest of society due to religious, cultural, or racial differences

self-government political system in which a society conducts functions of government itself or elects leaders to carry out those functions

Senate "upper" chamber or house; in the U.S. Congress each state is represented equally and has two seats

serf a person in feudal society who was bound to the land and who served whomever owned it

service sector the part of the economy that does not produce physical goods but instead performs functions that meet human needs

services nonmaterial or nonphysical things that are produced and used by people

sharecropping a system in which a landowner provides farmers with land, housing, tools, seed, and supplies in return for a share of the crop

shogun the chief military and governmental officer in feudal Japan

shortage a situation in which the demand for a service or good exceeds the available supply

slavery a practice in which a person is owned by and forced to work for another person

social welfare organized public or private services to assist disadvantaged persons or groups

special interest group an organization that carries out programs to influence government policies in order to benefit its members

sphere of influence area over which a nation exerts political or economic control

standard of living quality of life, determined by necessities and luxuries possessed

state territory with defined borders within which a government functions

stereotype a fixed idea or image of a particular type of person or thing that is often not true

strike a withholding of labor services to pressure employer to agree to workers' demands

subsidy governmental financial incentive granted to encourage activity benefiting the public

summary a brief account of the main idea of a piece of writing or a graphic

supply amount of a good or service sellers are willing to offer for sale at a certain price

supporting details the evidence or facts that lead to a conclusion

surface water water present on Earth's surface— rivers, streams, oceans, seas, lakes and ponds

surplus an excess in supply of a good or service

sweatshop a factory or company in which workers are employed for long hours at low wages and under unhealthy conditions

takeover act of assuming control or possession, such as a military seizure of a government or the acquisition of one company by another

tariff tax on imported goods as a source of income and a means by which a government regulates trade and reduces foreign competition

tenement overcrowded city apartment building with minimum standards of sanitation and safety

term limits provisions in a constitution or charters limiting elected officials to a specific number of terms in office

third party any political party in the United States other than the two major parties

topic sentence a sentence that tells the reader what the paragraph is about

totalitarian of a centralized government that does not tolerate opposing political opinions

transcontinental crossing an entire continent, such as a transportation system

tribe a group of numerous families and clans with common ethnic or cultural bonds

two-party system a political system dominated by two major parties, such as the Republican and Democratic parties in the United States

unemployment rate the percentage of people in the labor force who are not working but who are looking for work

unicameral consisting of a single legislative chamber or house

urban relating to a city or cities

values goals and ideals; what people consider important, good, beautiful, worthwhile, sacred

vassal a person in a feudal society who is granted land from a lord in return for services

Acknowledgments

This page constitutes an extension of the copyright page.

Grateful acknowledgment is made to the following authors, agents, and publishers for permission to use copyrighted materials. Every effort has been made to trace ownership of all copyrighted material and to secure the necessary permissions to reprint. We express regret in advance for any error or omission. Any oversight will be acknowledged in future printings.

"Conference of Non-Aligned Nations" by Jerry Barnett, as submitted. Jerry Barnett, *The Indianapolis News,* 1987. Reprinted by permission. (p. 122)

"As a member of Congress I'm deeply offended . . ." by Clay Bennett, as submitted. Clay Bennett, North America Syndicate. Reprinted by permission. (p. 173)

"This innocent man is not really dead. He is only sleeping." by Linda Boileau, from *Frankfort State Journal.* Linda Boileau, *Frankfort State Journal,* Rothco Cartoon Syndicate. Reprinted by permission. (p. 126)

"We plan to bargain all night until an agreement is reached" from *Can Board Chairmen Get the Measles?* edited by Charles Preston, as submitted. From *The Wall Street Journal*—Permission, Cartoon Features Syndicate. (p. 205)

"South African Vote" by Jack Higgins, © 1994 *Chicago Sun-Times.* Jack Higgins, courtesy of the *Chicago Sun-Times.* (p. 132)

"Second Amendment Backfiring" by Ed Stein, 1993, as submitted. Ed Stein. Reprinted with permission of the *Denver Rocky Mountain News.* (p. 259)

"By the powers vested, we declare ourselves joined at the wallet . . ." by Draper Hill © 1997. Reprinted with permission from *The Detroit News.* (p. 159)

"Oil! . . ." by Bob Gorrell, 8/3/90, *The Richmond News Leader/* Copley News Service. Reprinted by permission of Bob Gorrell and Creators Syndicate, Inc. (p. 121)

The Granger Collection, New York for "American Commissioners of the Preliminary Peace Negotiations with Great Britain" by Benjamin West. (p. 45) Bostonians Paying the Excise Man. (p. 86)

"Do you suppose there's any significance in the fact that we got tranquilizers just before they got sputniks?" by Phil Interlandi. Reprinted by permission of Phil Interlandi. (p. 123)

"Now shake hands . . . gently." by Jim Borgman. Reprinted with special permission of King Features Syndicate. (p. 124)

"Berlin Wall" by Jeff Koterba, © 1989. Jeff Koterba/*Omaha World-Herald.* Reprinted by permission. (p. 127)

"We'll Be Safe Here." © 1995 by Mike Luckovich, as submitted. Reprinted by permission of Mike Luckovich and Creators Syndicate, Inc. (p. 272)

"Attention, Bosnian Serbs! . . . This is your last chance to throw down your weapons!" by Malcolm Mayes from *Edmonton Journal.* Malcolm Mayes/artizans.com. (p. 125)

"IRS" by Wiley 2/17/95. NON SEQUITUR © Wiley Miller. Dist. by UNIVERSAL PRESS SYNDICATE. Reprinted with permission. All rights reserved. (p. 169)

"Have you given any thought to. . ." by Koren © 1973, as submitted. © The New Yorker Collection 1973 Edward Koren from cartoonbank.com. All Rights Reserved. (p. 235)

Print Collection, Miriam and Ira D. Wallach Division of, Art, Prints and Photographs, The New York Public Library, Astor, Lenox and Tilden Foundations. (p. 73)

"As the presidential candidates finally meet face-to-face, a hush falls over the nation" by Scott Nickel, 1996. Scott Nickel. Reprinted by permission. (p. 153)

Cartoon by Peter Porges, © 1975, as submitted. Reprinted by permission. (p. 232)

Steel Strike. STOCK MONTAGE. (p. 82)

"Start . . . Money" © 1995 by Jeff MacNelly, as submitted. © Tribune Media Services, Inc. All Rights Reserved. Reprinted with permission. (p. 245)

Austin American-Statesman by Ben Sargent, 10/6/93. SARGENT © *Austin American-Statesman.* Reprinted with permission of UNIVERSAL PRESS SYNDICATE. All rights reserved. (p. 120)

"Soviet Union" © 1986 by Joseph Szabo, as submitted. "Soviet Union" © 1986 Joe Szabo. Reprinted by permission. (p. 25)

"The meek will inherit the earth, but NEVER the market." September 14, 1989, by Dean Vietor, as submitted. Copyright 1989, *USA TODAY.* Reprinted with permission. (p. 203)

Page numbers in parentheses indicate pages in the *Steck-Vaughn GED Social Studies* book.

Index

Answer Sheet

GED Social Studies Test

Name: _____   Class: _____   Date: _____

○ Pretest   ○ Posttest   ○ Simulated Test

1 ①②③④⑤	11 ①②③④⑤	21 ①②③④⑤	31 ①②③④⑤	41 ①②③④⑤
2 ①②③④⑤	12 ①②③④⑤	22 ①②③④⑤	32 ①②③④⑤	42 ①②③④⑤
3 ①②③④⑤	13 ①②③④⑤	23 ①②③④⑤	33 ①②③④⑤	43 ①②③④⑤
4 ①②③④⑤	14 ①②③④⑤	24 ①②③④⑤	34 ①②③④⑤	44 ①②③④⑤
5 ①②③④⑤	15 ①②③④⑤	25 ①②③④⑤	35 ①②③④⑤	45 ①②③④⑤
6 ①②③④⑤	16 ①②③④⑤	26 ①②③④⑤	36 ①②③④⑤	46 ①②③④⑤
7 ①②③④⑤	17 ①②③④⑤	27 ①②③④⑤	37 ①②③④⑤	47 ①②③④⑤
8 ①②③④⑤	18 ①②③④⑤	28 ①②③④⑤	38 ①②③④⑤	48 ①②③④⑤
9 ①②③④⑤	19 ①②③④⑤	29 ①②③④⑤	39 ①②③④⑤	49 ①②③④⑤
10 ①②③④⑤	20 ①②③④⑤	30 ①②③④⑤	40 ①②③④⑤	50 ①②③④⑤